CRITICAL APPROACHES TO LITERATURE
Psychological

CRITICAL APPROACHES TO LITERATURE

Psychological

Editor
Robert C. Evans
Auburn University at Montgomery

SALEM PRESS
A Division of EBSCO Information Services, Inc.
Ipswich, Massachusetts

GREY HOUSE PUBLISHING

Cover of George Orwell's *1984* (9780451524935, Signet 1950) used by permission of Penguin Random House.

Copyright © 2017 by Grey House Publishing, Inc.

All rights reserved. No part of this work may be used or reproduced in any manner whatsoever or transmitted in any form or by any means, electronic or mechanical, including photocopy, recording, or any information storage and retrieval system, without written permission from the copyright owner. For information, contact Grey House Publishing/Salem Press, 4919 Route 22, PO Box 56, Amenia, NY 12501.

∞ The paper used in these volumes conforms to the American National Standard for Permanence of Paper for Printed Library Materials, Z39.48-1992 (R2009).

Library of Congress Cataloging-in-Publication Data
(Prepared by The Donohue Group, Inc.)

Names: Evans, Robert C., 1955- editor.
Title: Critical approaches to literature. Psychological / editor, Robert C. Evans.
Description: [First edition]. | Ipswich, Massachusetts : Salem Press, a division of EBSCO Information Services, Inc. ; Amenia, NY : Grey House Publishing, [2017] | Includes bibliographical references and index.
Identifiers: ISBN 978-1-68217-272-8 (hardcover)
Subjects: LCSH: Psychology in literature. | Literature--History and criticism--Psychological aspects.
Classification: LCC PN56.P93 C75 2017 | DDC 809.93353--dc23

PRINTED IN THE UNITED STATES OF AMERICA

Contents

Dedication	vii
About this Volume, Robert C. Evans	ix
On Psychological Approaches to Literature: Looking at Books with the Mind's Eye, David Willbern	xiv

Critical Contexts

Crews Missiles: Attacks and Counterattacks Concerning Freudian Literary Criticism, Robert C. Evans	3
Psychological Approaches to Literature: A Review of Select Scholarship, Robert C. Evans	20
A Family Systems Theory Reading of Saul Bellow's *Humboldt's Gift,* Allan Chavkin & Nancy Feyl Chavkin	37
Freud and Poe: A Dialogue, James S. Baumlin and Tita French Baumlin	52

Critical Readings

Literary Prehistory: The Origins and Psychology of Storytelling, Michelle Scalise Sugiyama	67
"Is This Her Fault or Mine?": Hysteria, Misogyny, and Voice in Shakespeare's *Measure for Measure*, Laura B. Vogel	84
Trauma in Shakespeare's *Macbeth,* Robert C. Evans	101
John Donne, Neuroscience, and the Experience of Empathy, David Strong	119
Poe's Ideal of Love and the Broken World: Crowd Psychology in Some Tales and Poems, Jeffrey Folks	135
Death and Freud in the Poetry of Edna St. Vincent Millay, Jenna Lewis	152
Grasping *The Great Gatsby*: A Cognitive Approach, Nicolas Tredell	171

Hemingway's Suicides: A Psychobiographical Approach
to Literature, Jeffrey Berman ... 187

"Written in his face": Ambivalence and Mirroring in *Nineteen
Eighty-Four*, David Willbern ... 207

"One Destroyed Being": A Post-Jungian Appraisal of
Darth Vader, Steve Gronert Ellerhoff ... 221

The Hero's Quest in the *Harry Potter* Books and Films,
Christine Gerhold Zahorchak ... 238

Driving Each Other Crazy: Existential Psychology in Hanif
Kureishi's *The Buddha of Suburbia*, Susie Thomas ... 257

Resources

Psychological Pluralism: A Variety of Possible Psychological
Approaches to Literature and Film ... 275

Chronology ... 291

Additional Works on Psychological Approaches to Literature ... 295

Bibliography ... 299

About the Editor ... 301

Contributors ... 303

Glossary ... 307

Index ... 313

Dedication

To Ruth, Taylor, Martha, and Rafe (who have brought me so much joy) and in loving memory of Taylor (whom we dearly miss)

and

To Betsy Maury (editor extraordinaire!)

About This Volume

Robert C. Evans

This volume is deliberately diverse. It offers essays on novels, short stories, dramas, poems, and films. It presents commentary on works from numerous places and periods of time, as well as numerous kinds of creative minds. And, unlike other essay collections dealing with psychological approaches to literature and cinema, this one stresses a wide range of psychological approaches rather than any single perspective in particular. Although it presents a number of essays that employ Freudian ideas, every effort has been made to include non-Freudian (and even anti-Freudian) voices as well. Finally, the present volume also tries to suggest, especially in its final pages, the sheer variety of potential ways of thinking about literature and film from numerous *different* psychological perspectives, including many whose possible bearings on the arts remain largely unexplored.

The volume opens with a splendid introductory essay by David Willbern. Willbern begins by discussing, in general terms, just what it can mean to focus on "psychology" when thinking about authors, texts, and readers. He then moves to explaining the basic concepts of Sigmund Freud, surely the most famous of all psychologists, although he also touches on the concepts of Erik Erikson, Carl Jung, and Jacques Lacan as well as on the recent rise of cognitive psychology. Taking Herman Melville's *Moby-Dick* as his touchstone, Willbern comments on the "doubloon" scene in that book as an example of the ways different people, through a process resembling Freudian "free association," can perceive the same object in different ways. Later, Willbern focuses on Captain Ahab himself as a figure who generates diverse reactions from readers and also as a figure who may be one of American literature's most famous trauma survivors.

Following Willbern's introductory essay is a section of "Critical Contexts" essays. Each of these is designed to offer a different basic perspective on psychological criticism. The first such essay, by Robert C. Evans, offers an overview of the history of debates about Freudianism generated by Frederick Crews. Crews began as one of the most important of all Freudian literary critics, but he soon decided that both Freud and his ideas were often vulnerable to severe criticism. Crews spent the rest of his career offering serious challenges to Freud and his many followers (including Jacques Lacan). Since Freudian and especially Lacanian ideas are still so influential among students of culture today, there seems some value in reviewing Crews' attacks on Freud and Freudianism as well as the responses his attacks have provoked. Crews was always willing to debate anyone who disagreed with him, and so this chapter offers a sense of the kinds of arguments (both pro and con) that Freudianism can generate.

In another essay, Evans offers an overview of some basic scholarship dealing with psychological approaches to literature. He notes that many introductory textbooks to literary criticism confine their discussions of psychology and literature to discussions of *Freudian* (and occasionally Jungian) psychology. Evans also notes the widespread interest in Lacanian thinking among current cultural critics. But Lacan, as this chapter demonstrates, is rarely, if ever, discussed in most standard introductions to psychology, nor is Lacan taken very seriously in most academic departments of psychology. In those departments, even Freud is regarded mainly as an important *historical* figure, not as the focus of much contemporary research. Evans then reviews a number of basic books that explore the sheer variety of possible psychological approaches, beginning with the ancient Greeks and moving down to the present day. He stresses the importance of Norman Holland's contributions to the study of literature and psychology, and he notes further skepticism (by Holland and others) regarding the work of Jacques Lacan.

In the third of the "Critical Contexts" chapters, Allan Chavkin and Nancy Feyl Chavkin show how one psychological approach in particular (family systems theory) can be used to comprehend a particular text (in this case, Saul Bellow's novel *Humboldt's Gift*). Emphasizing the work of psychologist Murray Bowen, the

Chavkins suggests all the various ways in which the personality of the novel's central character is influenced by his interactions with members of his family. Finally, in the last of the "Critical Contexts" chapters, James S. Baumlin and Tita French Baumlin show how works by the same writer can be discussed in two contrasting ways. James S. Baumlin suggests the relevance of Freudian approaches to writings (especially short stories) by Edgar Allan Poe, while Tita French Baumlin suggests that Poe's works may be more deliberately playful and ironic than many Freudians have thought. Whereas psychoanalytic critics have often taken Poe very seriously indeed (as James S. Baumlin shows), Tita French Baumlin suggests that Poe himself, in his short fiction, may often have been having fun with his readers.

The next major section of the book—"Critical Readings"—offers a wide variety of distinct psychological approaches to different kinds of works. Organized in basic chronological order, this section begins with a cutting-edge essay by Michelle Scalise Sugiyama on the origins of storytelling in the prehistory of the human race. As an example of the intense recent interest in "evolutionary psychology," this essay suggests some of the reasons that early humans, given their particular genetic history and makeup, may have found it useful to tell stories. These have included not only what we might call "short stories" but even much longer works. Scalise Sugiyama explores the relevance of storytelling to such basic human interests as the desire to inform and delight, the promotion of social norms, the regulation of sex and marriage, preparation for warfare, the need to subsist and survive, and various other basic challenges of human existence.

In an essay on Shakespeare's *Measure for Measure*, Laura B. Vogel—a practicing psychologist—adopts a Freudian approach to overt and implied sexual attitudes in this play. Vogel suggests that the chaste and virtuous Isabella is in fact a highly seductive character whose language is shot through with sexual innuendo. Vogel explores Shakespeare's treatment of misogyny in this work as well as the importance of erotic fantasies to a proper understanding of Isabella's character. In another essay on a Shakespeare play (*Macbeth*),

Robert C. Evans discusses the surprisingly underexplored issue of trauma in that work. He shows how this theme pervades the drama, which depicts Macbeth and his wife as characters who initially cause trauma and then suffer from it themselves. Evans shows just how many standard symptoms of trauma are exhibited by these characters and others, and he also reviews basic concepts of "trauma theory," which has been so influential in the study of works by authors other than Shakespeare. Finally, in another essay on an important writer from the English Renaissance, David Strong studies the secular love poetry of John Donne by employing some of the concepts of contemporary neuroscience, particularly in attempting to understand the ways Donne's poems both depict and generate empathy. Concentrating especially on two of Donne's most famous lyrics ("A Valediction Forbidding Mourning" and "The Ecstasy"), Strong suggests the relevance of studies of the human brain both to the writing and reading of any kind of literature and to the creation and perception of any kind of art.

As the book turns from British to American literature, Jeffrey Folks uses an emphasis on "crowd psychology" (formulated by Elias Canetti) to "understand the role that fantasies of ideal love, male gallantry, and withdrawal from the world" play in the imagination of Edgar Allan Poe. Folks begins by examining Poe's personal psychology and then focuses on the stories "Ligeia" and "Eleanora" to argue that such writings "should be considered an artistic rendering of a universal condition of victimization that Poe was among the first to diagnose." According to Folks, "Poe's marriage tales, dominated by the author's intense desire for idealized love, are allegories as well of the cycle of aggression and flight that he observed in society." Later, an essay by Jenna Lewis examines various poems about death written by Edna St. Vincent Millay. Lewis studies these poems in terms of their relevance to Freud's thinking about death, especially his controversial ideas about a possible "death instinct." The essay first compares and contrasts Millay's "death poems" to previous American poems on that topic before then examining the relatively unexplored topic of Freud's possible influence on Millay.

In an essay on F. Scott Fitzgerald's *The Great Gatsby*, Nicolas Tredell uses "cognitive psychology"—one of the most important of current approaches to the human mind—to study one of the most important of twentieth-century American novels. Tredell uses three key cognitive ideas ("figure and ground," "mental spaces," and "the embodied reader") to discuss how the novel tries to influence readers' perceptions of its structure, details, and meanings. Tredell cautions that his cognitive approach is not intended to exclude other possibilities but that it does explore "processes of cognition, involving mind, body and senses, which operate in all human beings, in reading literature and living life." Meanwhile, in an essay on Ernest Hemingway, Jeffrey Berman examines not only this author's works but especially his own life and death, particularly his life-long thoughts and feelings about suicide. Berman adopts a "psychobiographical" approach, and in the process, he discusses the history of psychobiographical scholarship, including its strengths, its weaknesses, and its continuing potential. Highlighting especially Hemingway's novel *For Whom the Bell Tolls*, Berman examines the relevance of suicide to the plot and meaning of that book before then discussing Hemingway's own eventual decision to kill himself.

David Willbern's essay on George Orwell's novel *Nineteen Eighty-Four* makes extensive use of the ideas of Jacques Lacan (but is by no means confined to a Lacanian perspective). Discussing the importance of faces in Orwell's book, Willbern explores concepts of "mirroring," not only in that text but in human relations generally, especially the relations between mothers and children. Willbern also comments on such other key issues in Orwell's book as paranoia, ambivalence, writing, representation, and trust. Meanwhile, in an essay on the *Star Wars* films, Steve Gronert Ellerhoff uses ideas associated with Carl Jung (the father of "archetypal" or "myth" criticism) to discuss the mythic aspects of Darth Vader in particular. Ellerhoff draws especially on comments by Joseph Campbell, one of Jung's great explicators, to show how the *Star Wars* films draw on archetypes deeply embedded in the human psyche.

A Jungian approach is also employed by Christine Gerhold Zahorchak in her essay on the Harry Potter books and films.

Zahorchak (a practicing psychologist) especially emphasizes the fundamental idea (associated with both Jung and Campbell) of "the hero's journey," but she also discusses such other emphases as "the shadow," the journey through adolescence, the importance of parental figures, the symbolism of "The Wise Old Man," the significance of Harry's peers, and the role of "the trickster." Her essay nicely complements the one by Ellerhoff. The final essay, however, uses an entirely different approach—a perspective associated with the "existential" psychologist R. D. Laing and the postcolonialist thinker Frantz Fanon. Discussing Hanif Kureishi's novel *The Buddha of Suburbia*, Susie Thomas examines the importance of family relations in the book and suggests that the novel illustrates "not only the crippling dualities of what [Laing] called 'the false-self system' but the possibility of a breakdown leading to a breakthrough into a more fulfilled life." She also discusses the book in light of Fanon's concept of the "colonial Oedipal complex," in which the role of the child is played by non-white colonials and the role of the father is played by white colonialists.

The book concludes with a lengthy section that surveys key concepts associated with many of the psychological theories already mentioned above, in addition to many other theories as well, including theories that are taken quite seriously by many collegiate departments of psychology. In these closing pages, then, the book tries to suggest the sheer variety of possible psychological approaches that can be taken to any film or literary text. By applying many different theories to one particular text (Ben Jonson's poem "On My First Son"), this section tries to suggest the practical interpretive implications of numerous psychological theories.

On Psychological Approaches to Literature: Looking at Books with the Mind's Eye

David Willbern

Introduction: "I look, you look"

As a reward for the first crewman to espy the white whale, the mad captain Ahab orders a gold coin nailed to the ship's mainmast. It's an Ecuadoran doubloon, adorned with various symbols: political, geographical, zodiacal.[1] Although now fixed fast to the mast, it was first currency, passing through the global marketplace just as Moby Dick swam through the ocean currents to intersect once again with Ahab. As the focal point of a quest—for the men, it's the coin; for Ahab, the whale—the doubloon absorbs the attention of all. The captain first stops to examine it, noting how "it was set apart and sanctified" and is now "the white whale's talisman" (Melville 441). Studying the images, he sees "something ever egotistical" (441), towers and volcanoes that represent his own grandiose images of himself. Then Starbuck, the first mate, examines the coin and finds symbols of God and the Trinity, anchors of his traditional faith (442). Stubb, second mate, improvises a comical reading of zodiacal signs that satirizes astrological interpretations of that day and ours. Finally he sees only its market value: "I'd not look at it very long before spending it. Humph! . . . I see nothing here but a round thing made of gold" (444). Queequeg, the Polynesian harpooner, is illiterate, but he can compare etchings on the coin to those on his own tattooed body. Finally Pip, the black cabin boy whose small madness mirrors Ahab's grand monomania, offers a simple conjugation, or meta-observation: "I look, you look, he looks; we look, ye look, they look" (445).

As it reflects the sun's light, the doubloon reflects the personalities of those who view it (its name echoes "double"). Through the crew's associations, the coin becomes an emblem of "the round world." Its circle signifies fullness, but also emptiness, a sign of zero. Melville likens it to a round mirror "which, like a magician's glass, to each and every man in turn but mirrors back

> *There's another rendering now; but still one text. All sorts of men in one kind of world, you see.*
> Herman Melville, Moby-Dick [1851] 433

his own mysterious self" (442). Characteristically, Stubb makes a joke: "Here's the ship's navel, this doubloon here, and they are all on fire to unscrew it. But, unscrew your navel, and what's the consequence?" (445). The answer (using a nineteenth-century term), is that your bum falls off. Stubb's humorous association joins all the others in a matrix of metaphors around the coin. As the ship's navel and the whale's talisman, it represents a primary, umbilical connection between the *Pequod* and Moby Dick. (Perhaps its bright point of reflected light shining in the distance helps the whale identify the particular ship. After all, Moby Dick is after the prize as well.) Besides navel and talisman, the coin evokes numerous comparisons: circle, sun, zodiac, world, cipher, mirror, deity. As well, it is a symbol of the novel it inhabits: an object to be read.

What Melville may have been doing in writing his chapter on the doubloon—what I imagine as his method of composition—was to enter the projected minds of his characters and then associate to the emblematic object, in a process analogous to "free association" as recommended by Freud in the practice of psychoanalysis.[2] It's a core component of therapy (even called a rule), and of writing and reading, as well. I don't propose that Melville was writing automatically, putting down the first things that came to his mind. But Melville's mind was a capacious storehouse of resources from the Bible, Western and Eastern mythology, English and American literature, history, philosophy (such as American Transcendentalism), technology (especially the practice of whale-hunting), and natural science (especially cetology), plus the profuse inventions of his own genius. By analogy, to begin a practice of reading psychoanalytically, readers might allow themselves the freedom to associate—along with close attention to the text. There *is* a coin nailed to the mast (or so we read).[3]

As Stubb overhears each person's address to the doubloon, he is unimpressed by their efforts to read the "signs and wonders," markings to him superficially recognizable but ultimately indecipherable. "Book!" he exclaims. "You lie there; the fact is, you books must know your places. You'll do to give us the bare words and facts, but we come in to supply the thoughts" (Melville 443). As usual, Stubb is about half right. By themselves, the bare words of a book are inadequate. To be effectual, they require the supplement of a human mind, animating them through reading—but not by thoughts alone and not by mastery. The interaction of written word and human cognition—a blend of thought and emotion—produces the complex process of reading, or of imagining a character or event through what Hamlet called "the mind's eye" (Shakespeare 159). Although a book is a real object, it does not become a literary text until it is engaged by a reader. Until removed from the shelf, books are merely interior decoration. Once entered into, a literary work invites (I might say demands) a relationship, empathic or otherwise, with the reader. By analogy with the patient's free association, the analyst listens in a similar state. The American psychoanalyst, Thomas Ogden, who considers his practice as much art as science, speaks of the therapist listening in a state of "reverie."[4]

Reading as a Psychological Event

Analogies between writing, reading, daydreaming, and analytic listening characterize reading as an internal psychological event, in which a literary text is transformed in a reader's mind into imagined experience. Literature is a special category of art, distinguishable from painting, sculpture, and music—objects or phenomena that impinge directly on the physical senses (eyes, ears).[5] When read, a poem becomes a mental object (exceptions are the poem as heard, or a poem whose form involves visual patterning, such as George Herbert's lines shaped like an altar, or modern "concrete poetry.") Literature happens in a virtual world, an arena of illusion, a type of play-space. Reading is a process of pretend cognition, a thought experiment, a subjective experience. Subjective experience is precisely the province of psychoanalysis. Elisa Galgut describes the process of "mentalization" as a means to connect with a literary character, or an imagined subjectivity in a text. This process of "engaging with the mind of another" is similar to child's play, whereby children recognize that others have mental states and that those states represent their identities. Thus we learn to recognize the subjectivity of the other.[6]

The British psychoanalyst D. W. Winnicott has described an intermediate zone between infant and mother where an infant experiences first a union, then a gradual separation of self and other, that he called "potential space." This is for Winnicott the original field of creative play, and ultimately the ground of all cultural experience. Using this concept, Murray Schwartz suggests that literary experience lies in this area "between objectivity and subjectivity . . . in which we are free to engage in active interplay between ourselves and the external world of persons and objects" (763). This idea essentially solves what Norman Holland, a pioneer in the theory and practice of psychoanalytic criticism, called "the task of establishing a conceptual bridge between objective and subjective views of literature" (*Dynamics* xiii). The object is "the words on the page," produced by creative interactions among an author's intentions and memory (conscious and unconscious), knowledge, research, and artistic skills. The subject is the reader, with his or her memory, knowledge, research, imaginative skills, and personal identity.[7]

Reading, then, is a dialectical interaction between a text and a self. When we settle in to read a literary text, we ideally prepare to enter into an imaginative play-space where we can relax our normal expectations of reality and immerse ourselves in a virtual world. Samuel Taylor Coleridge famously termed this process the "willing suspension of disbelief for the moment" (6). In psychoanalytic terms, the process involves a relaxation of ego boundaries, opening our minds to alien experiences without the risk of having to react as in reality. It describes a special receptiveness to imaginative experience, a potential opening of a reader's full psychic processes, conscious and unconscious, to the full psychic processes of the author.

The Freudian Unconscious

What then is "the unconscious"? According to Freud, it is a set of dynamically repressed mental activities, operating alongside and without awareness of the conscious mind. Thus our minds are not unified but divided and function under active resistance to full awareness of our wishes and fears. The unconscious is not a repository of hidden energies, like Pandora's box, but a different process or style of thinking. Our verbal and written expressions, whether mundane or sublime, are mediated by unconscious processes that simultaneously enable and disguise original motives.[8] For Freud, the most significant such expressions were dreams, whose interpretation he called "the royal road to the knowledge of the unconscious activities of the mind." (*Interpretation* 5: 608). He defined the dream as a (disguised) fulfillment of a (repressed) wish. A process of "dream-work" configures present elements, unconscious memory, and censorship through various styles of representation that both express and disguise unconscious material, shaping it into a relatively coherent narrative. By analogy, a literary work is a defensive transformation of unconscious thoughts and emotions into consciously manageable form.

As an aspect of his idea of the unconscious, Freud theorized two different styles of thinking—or more properly, mentation: "primary process" and "secondary process." The former ignores conventional notions of temporality, causality, and logic, and is governed by the pleasure principle. The latter respects ideas of time, sequence, and rationality, and is governed by the reality principle. Both composition (an author writing) and reception (a reader reading) involve a blend of these two modes of mentation (*Interpretation* 4: 262). A goal of the psychoanalytic reader is to get in touch with these different styles, through her or his own associations (aided by some knowledge of psychoanalytic theory).

A central organizing principle of the Freudian unconscious is the triangulation of desire denoted by the Oedipus complex. The idea proceeds from the theory of infantile sexuality, wherein pleasure is felt at developing biological and psychological stages: oral, anal, and genital erotogenic zones. Because our primitive sexual desires emerge in the prolonged context of family, they are incestuous. (The power of incestuous desire is marked by rigorous extra-familial, cultural taboos against it.) The child experiences a combination of desire and hostility toward both parents (or parental surrogates). Initially the mother, as provider of nurturance and love, is the desired object; father, as a rival in the mother's love, is an agent of interference. The classic Greek myth of Oedipus dramatizes this two-fold wish to eliminate the father and possess the mother. Beyond its content, the legend also dramatizes the process by which the hero discovers, resists, and then rediscovers core elements of his own life history. As Freud noted, "the story can be likened to the work of a psychoanalysis" (*Interpretation* 4: 262). Oedipus's fame was his ability to solve riddles, yet he was ignorant of the riddle of himself. The Sphinx asked, "What goes on four legs in the morning, two in the afternoon, and three in the evening?" Oedipus correctly answered, "Man," but that obscured the better answer: himself. His conscious (secondary process) reasoning revealed yet concealed his unconscious (primary process) wish.

Of course Freudian theory is not the only set of psychological concepts. A contemporary, Carl Jung, devised what he called "analytical psychology," which posits pre-existing super-personal agencies, such as the "shadow," or the "anima," and a pantheon of "archetypes" that populate a "collective unconscious" in the human race. Jungian theory credits an explanatory mythology that Freudian theory would prefer to interpret as itself an imaginative production. For instance, archetypes are projected versions of parental imagoes, like divine figures in religions ("God the Father"). For me, Freudian theory is more congenial to the study of literature because it proceeds from individuals and their personal contexts, in family and culture. There is no "collective unconscious," only personal psyches developed from a person's relations to body, family, and society.[9]

Beyond Freud

Since Freud, there have been many modifications to psychoanalytic theory. For Freud, the ego was "first and foremost a bodily ego" that encompassed unconscious as well as conscious processes, as our defensive strategies transformed representations of bodily impulses and archaic styles of thinking into adaptive relations to others and the world. By mid-century, the psychoanalyst Erik Erikson had mapped developmental stages of the human life cycle in the formations of individual identity, while retaining Freud's view of gendered Oedipal destiny (see *Childhood and Society*). The patriarchal bias of Freud's theories evoked opposition in his own time. Several women analysts of the early twentieth century developed their own ideas about human development and sexuality. Broadly envisioned, their project was to shift the primary theoretical model from patriarchal phallocentrism to maternal mirroring—a shift further explored by object-relations analysts who described our gradual development from symbiotic maternal dependence to inter-relation, separation, and autonomy (see Sayers). In the mid-1960s, intellectual and political ferment in France provoked a school of feminist thought that reacted against Freud and his even more strictly patriarchal disciple, Jacques Lacan (see Marks). Female analysts and cultural critics advanced radical revisions of psychoanalytic theory, championing a style of thinking and writing termed *"l'écriture féminine"* (see Jones).

Lacan's theories resituated Freud's ideas in a strict linguistic context, claiming that "the unconscious is structured like a language" and that the human "subject" is not a stable agent (or ego) but a provisional, illusory identification within a system of signifiers (like the subject in a sentence). Lacan rejected the corporeal basis of object-relations and posited instead an illusory subject defined by "the desire of the other." His ideas, many of them abstruse and arcane, were especially popular in the 1970s and 80s, as their challenge to psychological assumptions about natural, intrinsic meaning correlated to styles of "deconstructive" reading also prevalent at the time.[10]

Another kind of psychology focuses on mental activity, especially that of reading. Cognitive psychology emerged in the mid-twentieth century as a study of the mind based on "information processing"—analogous to the development of computers and algorithmic programs. Experiments and research showed how children learn rules of language from the culture they inhabit, rooted in an innate human linguistic capacity (as theorized by Noam Chomsky). In studying reading, cognitive psychologists watch eye movements and speak of "inner voices," by which they mean a "phonological coding" of words (sub-vocalization).[11] Neuroimaging, or brain scans, can show specific locations of mental activity while reading. But these ideas do not involve subjective states. A CAT scan can indicate *that* a person is having a subjective experience and even *where* it is located in the brain, but it reveals nothing about *what* the experience may be.

Symbolism

Because it proceeds from actual human experience and deals with subjective states, psychoanalytic theory is for me the best basis for psychological literary interpretation. A further value of a psychoanalytic perspective is its focus on the exact language of the author: the specific rhetorical and symbolic forms of representation. Some general qualities of literary language, as compared to nonfiction, are a density of metaphor and allusion, and an openness to ambiguity—as in Melville's various depictions of the gold doubloon. These qualities are especially appealing to literary critics. (I should add a caveat: Any description of "literature" that neglects its reader is already limited.)[12] In the last part of this essay, I will return to literature (and to *Moby-Dick*), but first, I want to discuss the idea of symbolism by means of a famous Freudian moment.

In *Beyond the Pleasure Principle* (1920), Freud described a game his grandson invented at the age of one and a half, before he could speak many words (18: 14-15). He used to throw small objects away from him, then happily say, "o-o-o-o." Later, he took a wooden spool attached to a piece of string, and threw it over the edge of his cot so that it disappeared. After saying "o-o-o-o," he would pull it back to himself and say "da," again with pleasure. He repeated this game over and over. Freud and the boy's mother understood him to be saying "*Fort*" and "*Da*" (German for "gone" and "there"). Freud theorized that this game of disappearance and return allowed the child to manage his anxiety about the disappearance of his mother, to whom he was very attached. By controlling the *actual* presence and absence of an object, he was able to manage the *symbolic* presence and absence of his mother. This game (known in the psychoanalytic literature as the "*Fort / Da*" game) was the child's invention of symbolism: the use of one object (wooden spool) to represent an absent object (mother). His acts were accompanied by rudimentary speech. The development of symbolism occurs alongside the emergence of language, or the child's entry into the field of culturally significant sounds and words. Freud's grandson was not merely representing his mother as a symbolic object. More importantly, he was representing a *relationship* (with mother) and coming to terms with a *concept* (mother can be gone yet still there, in memory and play). Language is the means by which we give presence to people, ideas, events, and feelings. It's how we recover the past, or make what is gone, there.

Symbols are typically considered a core element of psychoanalytic literary criticism. Freud's grandson invented a game that provided a satisfactory subjective experience in the face of disappointment (his mother's absence). His act and affect satisfied a wish, by means of a symbol. Does this mean that wooden spools symbolize mother? (How about yo-yos?) No. For this boy at that time, yes. One way to think about symbolism is not in terms of essence but in terms of function: not a symbolic equation, but a symbolic relationship. What matters is context. A snake, for example, may function as a penetrating phallic symbol, an oral devouring symbol, a mythic symbol of evil, or eternity (the Ouroboros), depending on the literary or cultural context (see Slater 80-91).

How then might the white whale function symbolically in Melville's novel and in our readings of it? Our narrator, Ishmael, actually refers to the whale, or remembers it, long before it appears in his story. At the very end of chapter 1, he alludes to "one grand hooded phantom, like a snow hill in the air" (Melville 7). At the beginning of his land-locked retrospective narrative, the sea creature suddenly appears—an uncanny premonition, wish, or fear—as mysterious to him now as it was then. (Indeed, the concepts of "now" and "then" become obscure at this moment.) When we as readers finally reach the chapters about the whale, the mystery only deepens. At times, the whale clearly represents hyper-masculinity, a phallic power to be feared and admired. At other times, it corresponds to a mysterious Nature, with maternal resonances (see chapter 87, "The Grand Armada"). Or it figures the implacable wildness and Otherness of the external world, closed off from human ken. Or it's a "monumental white shroud," death and oblivion. (Melville 198). In his chapter on "The Whiteness of the Whale," Melville gestures toward some "vague nameless horror" that he will try to explain in "some dim, random way" (189). He evokes instances in nature of fearful whiteness: the polar bear, the great white shark, the albatross, the Albino human. He then abstracts the figure into the concept of absence: white is "the visible absence of color," yet "the great principle of light" reveals all natural objects (198). The whale is "a dumb blankness, full of meaning" (198). Perhaps, like the gold doubloon, it's a blank screen for the projections of characters and readers.[13] D. H. Lawrence, a provocative reader of American literature, wrote of Moby Dick: "Of course he is a symbol. Of what? I doubt if even Melville knew exactly" (157). Lawrence eventually offered his own interpretation:

> What then is Moby Dick? He is the deepest blood-being of the white race; he is our deepest blood-nature.
>
> And he is hunted, hunted, hunted by the maniacal fanaticism of our white mental consciousness. . . .
>
> The last phallic being of the white man. Hunted into the death of upper consciousness and the ideal will: Our blood-self subjected to our will. (173)

Characteristically, Lawrence finds a division between "blood-being" and consciousness in a reading that expresses his own personal mythology. His interpretation is as much about himself as about Melville—but it is also about Melville. Perhaps the deepest analogy in *Moby-Dick* is the relation between "the universal cannibalism of the sea" and the "green, gentle, and most docile earth." "Consider them both, the sea and the land," Ishmael asks,

> and do you not find a strange analogy to something in yourself? For as this appalling ocean surrounds the verdant land, so in the soul of man there lies one insular Tahiti, full of peace and joy, but encompassed by all the horrors of the half-known life. God keep thee! Push not off from that isle, thou canst never return. (Melville 281)

Here the intrapsychic division is between a private, pacific identity and the frightful "horrors of the half-known life" that involve brutal appetite and aggression. Both Melville and Lawrence develop literary versions of the traditional split between mind and body, but do so in their own unique styles.

Character

Psychoanalytic criticism can attend to various subjects: the author, the reader, literary characters, or specific language. In *Moby-Dick*, the most prominent character for most readers is Ahab, whose defiant grandiloquence promotes him as a tragic hero on the scale of Shakespeare's Lear or Milton's Satan (both of which lie behind Melville's captain). In a soliloquy prior to his final assault on Moby Dick, Ahab interrogates his own obsession, wondering, "Is Ahab, Ahab? Is it I, God, or who, that lifts this arm?" (Melville 546). Is he his own man, or an agent of Fate, subject to forces beyond his control? In Melville's era the question of determinism versus free will was a philosophical and religious issue. Today the question may be framed in a neurological register. Are our decisions products of our wills, or involuntary consequences of our brain chemistry?[14]

Ahab's desperate self-division and self-interrogation ("Is Ahab, Ahab?") may have more than traditional philosophical resonance. For Melville describes his character as a trauma survivor, in terms that are fully consistent with current psychological theories of trauma. In his first encounter with Moby Dick, the whale ripped off Ahab's leg. He endured weeks of agony, during which his unswerving quest for revenge took root. Later we learn that he suffers nightmares, sleeps with clenched hands, "and wakes with his own bloody nails in his palms" (Melville 204). In his anguish, Melville writes, "a chasm seemed opening in him." He would cry out and "burst from his state room as though escaping from a bed that was on fire" (204).

> For, at such times, crazy Ahab, the scheming, unappeasedly steadfast hunter of the white whale; this Ahab that had gone to his hammock, was not the agent that so caused him to burst from it in horror again. The latter was the eternal, living principle or soul in him; and in sleep, being for the time dissociated from the characterizing mind, which at other times employed it for its outer vehicle or agent, it spontaneously sought escape from the scorching contiguity of the frantic thing, of which, for the time, it was no longer an integral. (Melville 204)

What Melville so dramatically describes is a victim of physical and psychological trauma, subject to nightmares and flashbacks, as though a separate identity were again enduring the catastrophic event, and like a "frantic thing" feeling intense and inescapable pain. Melville even uses the current clinical term, "dissociated," indicating a split between the traumatized psyche and the "characterizing" or rational mind. (On trauma and dissociation see, for instance, Caruth.) Ahab's psyche is literally dis-integrated ("no longer an integral"). The figurative burning bed he flees is actually the "scorching contiguity" of his conscious mind's contact with his split, unconscious, traumatized self.

At this moment, Melville's description of Ahab is a vivid demonstration of the literature *of* psychology. As Freud acknowledged, the poets were there before he was. The author creates a fictional character, then imagines his mind, then enters it and portrays what he finds. In *Moby-Dick*, Melville created dozens of characters, and two mighty antagonists, Ahab and the whale. As readers, we might try to immerse ourselves in all these fictional agents, being aware that the minds we engage are a creative amalgam of the author's, the characters', and our own.

Notes

1. A one-ounce, solid gold coin, the Ecuadoran eight escudos doubloon was minted in Quito between 1838 and 1843. It was then worth about sixteen American dollars. It is now known in the numismatic world as "the Moby Dick coin." Images are available online.
2. Freud also found a reciprocal analogy; see his essay on "Creative Writers and Day-dreaming" (147-48).
3. There is a pedagogical technique based on this idea; see Holland and Schwartz.
4. The idea of reverie derives from the British psychoanalyst Wilfred Bion.
5. For an astute consideration of the ontological status of literature, see Wellek.
6. According to cognitive psychologist Steven Pinker and philosopher Rebecca Goldstein, the development of empathy through reading stories about others qualifies fiction as "a kind of moral technology," or "the shadow life of ethics" (48-49). The question receives detailed attention in Koopman and Hakemulder.
7. Holland's theories are congenial to those of reading theorists Louise Rosenblatt and Wolfgang Iser; see Works Cited.
8. A special issue of the journal *Cognition*, "The Cognitive Neuroscience of Consciousness" (vol. 79, April 2001) reviews the newest models of unconscious processes and mental representations of reality.
9. Paul Kugler, a Jungian analyst, provides (in *Raids*) a review of analytical psychology while offering a dialogue between Jung's ideas and Freud's.
10. A history of psychoanalytic theory—or better, the emergence of psychoanalytic theories—is beyond the scope of this essay. For the interested student, a good introduction to these ideas is via *The Johns Hopkins Guide to Literary Theory and Criticism*; see Groden et al.). The volume has been recently reprinted as *Contemporary Literary and Cultural Theory: The Johns Hopkins Guide* (2012). Relevant sections are Linda Hutcheon, "Sigmund Freud" (214-220); David Willbern, "Psychoanalytic Theory and Criticism: 1. Traditional Freudian Criticism" (401-04); Christopher Morris, "Psychoanalytic Theory and Criticism 2: Reconceptualizing Freud" (404-07); Michael Clark and James Penney, "Jacques Lacan" (281-87); and Sharla Hutchison, Chiara Briganti, and Robert Con Davis-Undiano, "Psychoanalytic Theory and Criticism: 3. The Post-Lacanians" (407-11). For a one-volume map of the territory, I recommend Holland, *Holland's Guide*.
11. See Rayner et al.

12. In a recent consideration of the issue, Marjorie Garber avers, "*Literature is a status rather than a quality*" (her italics); see *The Use and Abuse of Literature* (116). Chapter 3, "What Isn't Literature," offers a sensible overview; see pp. 77-116.
13. Bertram Lewin imagines a "hypnagogic" experience of the infant's memory of nursing; the dream screen represents the maternal breast.
14. For a review of the historical concept of free will and the psychology of consciousness as framed within today's neurosciences, see Baumeister et al.

Works Cited

Baumeister, Roy, Cory Clarke, and Jamie Luguri. "Free Will: Belief and Reality." *Surrounding Free Will: Philosophy, Psychology, Neuroscience*, edited by Alfred Mele. Oxford UP, 2015, pp. 49-71.

Caruth, Cathy, editor. *Trauma: Explorations in Memory*. Johns Hopkins UP, 1985.

Coleridge, Samuel Taylor. *Biographia Literaria*. 1817. Clarendon Press, 1967.

Erikson, Erik. *Childhood and Society*. W. W. Norton, 1950.

Freud, Sigmund. *Beyond the Pleasure Principle*. 1920. *The Standard Edition of the Complete Psychological Works of Sigmund Freud*, edited by James Strachey et al., vol. 18, Hogarth, 1974, pp. 3-23.

———. "Creative Writers and Day-dreaming." 1908. *The Standard Edition of the Complete Psychological Works of Sigmund Freud*, edited by James Strachey et al., vol. 9, Hogarth, 1974, pp. 143-53.

———. *The Interpretation of Dreams*. 1900. *The Standard Edition of the Complete Psychological Works of Sigmund Freud*, edited by James Strachey et al. vols. 4 and 5, Hogarth, 1974.

Galgut, Elisa. "Reading Minds: Mentalization, Irony, and Literary Engagement." *International Journal of Psycho-Analysis*, vol. 91, 2010, pp. 915-935.

Garber, Marjorie. *The Use and Abuse of Literature*. Random House, 2011.

Groden, Michael, Martin Kreiswirth, and Imre Szeman, editors. *The Johns Hopkins Guide to Literary Theory and Criticism*. Johns Hopkins UP, 2005.

Holland, Norman. *The Dynamics of Literary Response*. Oxford UP, 1968.

———. *Holland's Guide to Psychoanalytic Psychology and Literature-and-Psychology*. Oxford, UP, 1990.

——— and Murray Schwartz. "The Delphi Seminar." *College English*, vol. 36, no. 7, 1975, pp. 789-800.

Iser, Wolfgang. "The Reading Process." *The Implied Reader: Patterns of Communication in Prose Fiction from Bunyan to Beckett*. Johns Hopkins UP, 1974, pp. 274-294.

Jones, Ann Rosalind. "Writing the Body: Toward an Understanding of 'L'Ecriture Feminine.'" *Feminist Studies*, vol. 7, 1981, pp. 247-263.

Koopman, Eva Marie, and Frank Hakemulder. "Effects of Literature on Empathy and Self-Reflection: A Theoretical-Empirical Framework." *Journal of Literary Theory*, vol. 9, 2015, pp. 79–11.

Kugler, Paul. *Raids on the Unthinkable: Freudian and Jungian Psychoanalyses*. Spring Journal Books, 2005.

Lawrence, D. H. *Studies in Classic American Literature*. Heinemann, 1924.

Lewin, Bertram. "Sleep, the Mouth, and the Dream Screen." *The Psychoanalytic Quarterly*, vol. 15, 1946, pp. 419-434.

Marks, Elaine, editor. *New French Feminisms: An Anthology*. Schocken, 1981.

Melville, Herman. *Moby-Dick*. U of California P, 1979.

Ogden, Thomas. *Reverie and Interpretation: Sensing Something Human*. Rowman & Littlefield, 2004.

Pinker, Steven and Rebecca Goldstein. "The Seed Salon." *Seed* (May 2004): 47-52.

Rayner, Keith, Alexander Pollatsek, Jane Ashby, and Charles Clifton, editors. *Psychology of Reading*. 2nd ed., Psychology Press, 2012.

Rosenblatt, Louise. *The Reader, the Text, the Poem: the Transactional Theory of the Literary Work*. Southern Illinois UP, 1978.

Sayers, Janet. *Mothers of Psychoanalysis: Helene Deutsch, Karen Horney, Anna Freud, Melanie Klein*. Norton, 1991.

Schwartz, Murray. "Where is Literature?" *College English*, vol. 36, 1975, pp. 756-765.

Shakespeare, William. *Hamlet*, edited by Ann Thompson and Neill Taylor, Thomson Learning, 2007. Arden Shakespeare.

Slater, Philip. "Symbols, the Serpent, and the Oral-Narcissistic Dilemma." *The Glory of Hera: Greek Mythology and the Greek Family*. Princeton UP, 1968, pp. 75-124.

Wellek, René. "The Mode of Existence of a Literary Work of Art." *Southern Review*, vol. 7, 1941, reprinted in Wellek and Austin Warren, *Theory of Literature*. 1949. Harcourt Brace, 1956, pp. 142-57.

Winnicott, D. W. "The Location of Cultural Experience." *Playing and Reality*. Tavistock, 1971, pp. 95-103.

CRITICAL CONTEXTS

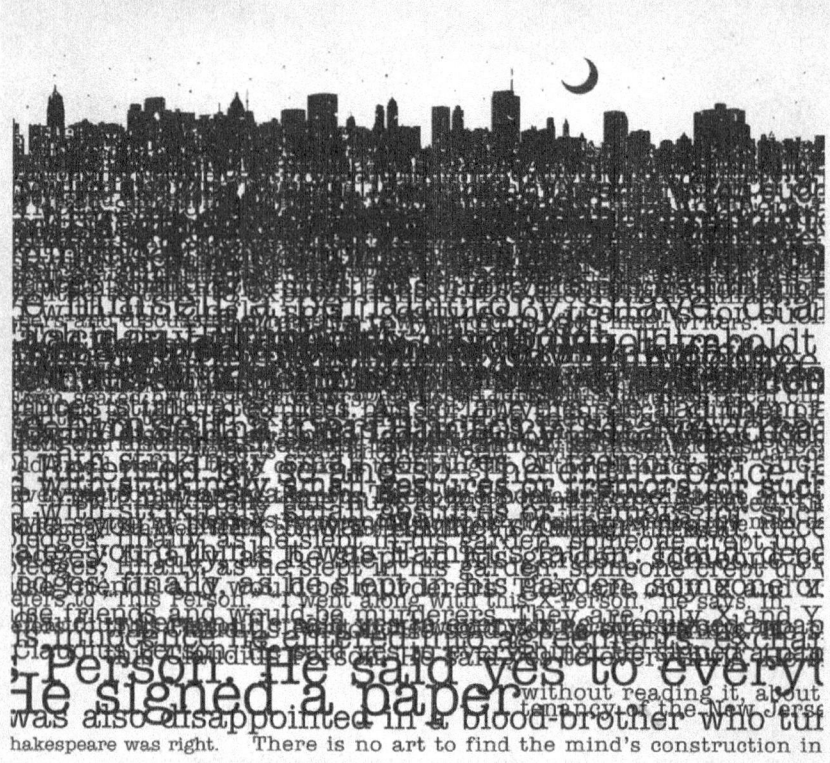

PENGUIN CLASSICS

SAUL BELLOW

Humboldt's Gift

Introduction by JEFFREY EUGENIDES

Crews Missiles: Attacks and Counterattacks Concerning Freudian Literary Criticism

Robert C. Evans

When students and their teachers think about the topic of "psychological approaches to literature," they often think about approaches rooted in the psychological ideas of Sigmund Freud or, more recently, of Freud's most famous follower, Jacques Lacan. Certainly Freud and Lacan are the two psychological theorists (other than Carl Gustav Jung) most frequently represented in standard textbooks about critical approaches to literature. Recently, "evolutionary psychology" (rooted in the ideas of Charles Darwin) has begun to have a serious impact on literary study, but numerous critics and theorists still look to Freud for inspiration and guidance. The fact that Freud is very rarely taken very seriously (except as an historical figure) in most American psychology programs and textbooks does not seem to trouble many recent literary theorists. English departments, rather than departments of psychology, are still the hotbeds of Freudian thinking on most US college campuses. Freud and Lacan are far more likely to be studied seriously by humanities majors than by majors in the "hard" or social sciences. Just the reverse is true of "evolutionary psychology," which "real" psychologists often take quite seriously indeed.

Precisely because Freud and Lacan *are* still so highly respected in humanities departments, it seems valuable to review the critiques of Freud (some would call them nuclear attacks) issued over many decades by Frederick Crews. Crews, a long-time professor at the University of California at Berkeley, began his career as an ardent Freudian. His early book titled *The Sins of the Fathers: Hawthorne's Psychological Themes* (1966) offered a dogmatically Freudian approach not only to Hawthorne but to literature in general. Indeed, the book was *so* dogmatic that Crew later repudiated its inflexibility when the volume was reissued in 1989. In the intervening two decades, Crews had gone from being one of the most prominent and committed Freudian literary analysts in America to being one of the very harshest critics anywhere in the world of Freud and Freud's ideas. For this reason, reviewing the career of Frederick Crews and his numerous debates with Freud's defenders involves reviewing some of the most important ideas in modern approaches to the psychological interpretation of literature.

Crews as Defender of Freud

During the mid-1960s, Crews was often the "go-to guy" for anyone who wanted to see how Freud's ideas could be used to interpret literature. His 1966 book on Hawthorne has already been mentioned, and in 1967, he authored the chapter on "Literature and Psychology" issued as part of an essay collection about literary studies published by the Modern Language Association for use by teachers and their students. In that chapter, Crews called Freudian psychoanalysis "the only psychology to have seriously altered our way of reading literature" (*Out* 4). Only the psychoanalyst, Crews argued, "undertakes to find motives for every rendered detail" in a literary work (*Out* 5). Crews challenged claims that "psychoanalysis remains wholly unverified" (*Out* 7). Conceding that not all psychoanalytic claims had yet been corroborated scientifically, Crews nevertheless maintained that "the confirmation and refinement of Freud's discoveries have been proceeding in a fairly orderly way for many years; the essential concepts of psychoanalysis have been adequate to characterize the findings of innumerable independent workers" (*Out* 8). Crews challenged approaches to Freud that de-emphasized "sexual nastiness," but he did praise "present-day psychoanalysis" for having "passed beyond Freud's almost exclusive emphasis on instinctual demands and infantile traumas" (*Out* 9). Crews dissented from the common Freudian idea that art and artists were necessarily neurotic (*Out* 10-11), emphasizing instead the artist's creativity and imagination (*Out* 11). He conceded that Freudian critics often neglected literary form (*Out* 12-13), and he often praised "ego psychology" as one answer to this problem (*Out* 13). All in all, Crews acknowledged the shortcomings of much psychoanalytic criticism, suggested solutions to those shortcomings, and praised various critics who used Freud's ideas responsibly.

In 1970, Crews edited a book titled *Psychoanalysis and Literary Process*. This volume contained an essay of his own ("Anaesthetic Criticism") that made a vigorous case for intelligent Freudian literary analysis. Freud (according to Crews in 1970), "discovered that human beings can neither freely accept nor freely deny the parental demand that sexual and aggressive urges be tamed. All men, he saw, struggle not only against unregenerate impulses but also against their guilt for continuing to harbor those impulses" (Crews, *Psychoanalysis* 12). Psychoanalytic criticism, he argued, was quite well prepared to deal with many of the psychological complexities inherent in readers, writers, and texts (*Psychoanalysis* 15-16). Admittedly, Crews conceded, "Freud's achievement" had become "entangled in an embarrassingly careless scientific tradition" (17). Freud's followers had often failed to use his ideas carefully and reasonably, so that "Freudian criticism is always problematic and often inept" (*Psychoanalysis* 18). But in 1970, Crews still seemed willing to defend Freud and Freudian criticism.

Soon, however, Crews would become relentlessly critical of Freud and Freudian literary theory. One of the most impressive aspects of his career, in fact, is that he has long since freely admitted that his trust in psychoanalysis was (in his view) a massive mistake. If intellectual honesty is a virtue, Crews certainly has displayed it in this respect. Moreover, Crews never tries to disguise or deny his early commitment to Freud. In his 1975 book titled *Out of My System: Psychoanalysis, Ideology, and Critical Method*, he willingly reprints his 1967 MLA chapter, retrospectively calling it "too charitable toward the scientific claims of psychoanalysis" (Crews, *Out* 3).

In an essay later in the same book, he still argues that "principles of Freudian criticism can be usefully applied to literary criticism" but admits that he now finds himself "repeatedly assailed by doubts" about "the theory itself, about methodological pitfalls, [and] above all about the weak and sometimes comical record of the Freudian critical tradition" (Crews, *Out* 166). He now expresses real concerns that Freudianism may be "inherently reductionistic," liable to "dogmatism" and "clinical presumption," and guilty of "monomania" (*Out* 166). In a sentence that must have been difficult to write, Crews worries that the Freudian critic risks becoming "the purveyor of a particularly silly kind of allegory" (*Out* 166). He states that Freudian criticism is not only bound to be reductive but is bound to be reductive "to a degree unmatched by any other school" (*Out* 169), for reasons his essay then goes on to explain. Crews, if not yet a complete apostate, was certainly close.

Crews as Opponent of Freud
Crews' full break with Freudianism became especially evident in a series of essays reprinted in a 1986 book titled *Skeptical Engagements*. In the introduction to that volume, Crews announced that he had slowly and reluctantly come to see Freudian thinking not as a science but as "a faith like any other" (*Skeptical* xi). He now considered it "a doctrine that compels irrational loyalty" (xii). He argued that "psychoanalysis is not appreciably different in epistemic rigor from the reading of tea leaves" and compared the occasional cogency of Freudian ideas to "the fortune teller's lucky guess" (xvi). These assertions might have seemed merely idiosyncratic if Crews had not, by this time, become one of the grand synthesizers of anti-Freudian findings. He would eventually draw on scores of other scholars who challenged not only Freud himself but the whole Freudian legacy. The essays reprinted in *Skeptical Engagements* not only chart Crews' own loss of faith in Freudian ideas but also point to a rising tide of academic doubt about the persuasiveness and truthfulness of Freud's ideas as well as to real challenges to Freud's reputation for personal and scientific honesty. Before long, Crews would be marshalling plenty of evidence suggesting that Freud was not simply mistaken but was, in fact, an unethical fraud.

    Crews' claims about Freud the man are often very troubling, but I want to keep my focus here on Freud's ideas and their continuing influence. By the mid-1970s, Crews could claim that there was now "wide agreement that the logic of Freudian reasoning is suspiciously loose; that its data are too private and inferential to be scientifically trustworthy; [and] that many of its particular assertions, especially regarding women, have owed more to ideology and superstition than to 'clinical fact'" (*Skeptical* 5). In 1980, in an essay titled "Analysis Terminable," Crews challenged not only the scientific plausibility of Freudian thought but also its clinical usefulness and effectiveness. Here he asserted that Freud's authority had become "eroded by a flood of books detailing his logical and empirical mistakes, his frailties of temperament, and his deafness to reasonable objections" (*Skeptical* 19). But Crews also offered reasons to think that "if all psychotherapies were to be judged about equally effective, psychoanalysis"—which often took years to complete—would rank as the least efficient of therapies, bar none" (*Skeptical* 21). Freud himself, Crews showed, often failed as a therapist, and so did many of his followers. At the very least, they succeeded no better than non-Freudians, and their methods took much longer and were far more expensive than other treatments.

Crews was now highly suspicious of Freudianism both as a theory and as therapy (*Skeptical* 24), and he even quoted P. B. Medawar, a Nobel prizewinner in medicine, as saying that "'doctrinaire psychoanalytic theory is the most stupendous intellectual confidence trick of the twentieth century'" (*Skeptical* 25)—an implausible faith perpetuated both by Freud and by his followers. Freudians constituted (in Crews' view) a self-selecting priesthood spreading a highly doubt-worthy gospel (*Skeptical* 34). In a 1984 essay titled "The Freudian Way of Knowledge," Crews broadly challenged these true believers, not only ones living in Freud's day but especially ones living in the late twentieth century. Drawing on new biographical evidence, Crews here painted a very disturbing picture of Freud himself, calling into question both his scientific and his personal ethics, not to mention his untrustworthy methods. Crews now felt that "Freud's legacy . . . consists chiefly of pseudoscience that cannot be defended on any grounds" (*Skeptical* 70).

A 1985 essay—"The Future of an Illusion"—was even more important. In this piece, Crews reviewed a massive 1984 book by the highly respected philosopher of science, Adolf Grünbaum, titled

The Foundations of Psychoanalysis. Crews argued that Grünbaum had attempted to be fair to Freud, both in defending him against certain previous attacks and in leaving open the possibility that Freud *might* be proved right some day on some questions (*Skeptical* 82). Nevertheless, Crews found Grünbaum's critique of Freud "shattering" (*Skeptical* 82), both to Freud's ideas and to the recent innovations of his followers (*Skeptical* 85). In a 1985 essay titled "Beyond Sulloway's *Freud*: Psychoanalysis Minus the Myth of the Hero," Crews drew on the recent work of a major scholar (Frank Sulloway) to conclude that "psychoanalysis was founded not on observation but on deductions from erroneous dogma, and as a result the entire system can make no claim on our credence" (*Skeptical* 97). Once again, Crews called Freud's own honesty into question, even terming him a "congenital liar" (*Skeptical* 101-02). Most importantly, however, he continued to draw on a wide range of sources to make his case against psychoanalysis as a system, not just against its founder.

In the 1989 "Afterword" to the reprint of *The Sins of the Fathers*, Crews presented one of the clearest, most succinct statements he ever offered of his doubts about psychoanalytic explanations:

> Psychoanalysis amounts to a classic pseudoscience—that is, an allegedly scientific doctrine that fends off counterexamples, and thus shields its postulates from falsification, in indefensible ways. In its normal practice, psychoanalysis gratuitously proliferates constructs and hypotheses; it seizes upon "deep" causal factors without first weighing simpler ones; it turns its back on the scientific requirement that a given explanatory framework be tested against others instead of just being employed and elaborated; it relies on anecdotal and self-servingly edited instantiations; it uses tainted data (anything-but-"free" associations) as supporting evidence; it encourages extraordinary hermeneutic liberties that allow the interpreter to see confirmations of his hunches everywhere; it wildly overstates its therapeutic successes and then cites them as demonstrations of the theory; and it declares that the only people qualified to criticize that theory are those who have been indoctrinated in the lengthy regimen of thought reform accompanying it. These are telltale signs of a cultlike

indifference the risks of error. (*Sins* 278-79)

These were points Crews would make repeatedly throughout the next two decades. Crews, however, unlike many academics, was willing not only to make his points and walk away but to provoke and participate in extended debate. Inevitably, his charges against Freudianism provoked vigorous counterattacks, but Crews was more than willing to respond to his critics.

Freud's Legacy in Dispute

Nowhere is Crews' willingness to debate Freudianism more evident than in a 1995 book titled *The Memory Wars: Freud's Legacy in Dispute* (hereafter abbreviated as *MW*). Crews is listed as the primary author of this volume, but the title page also lists eighteen other contributors, most of them highly critical of Crews. The book resulted from the publication of several essays by Crews that in turn prompted numerous responses. Crews, in typical Crewsian fashion, gathered together his essays, the responses, and his responses to the responses, so that *The Memory Wars* amounts to that rare thing in academic publishing: an actual extended debate. It gives readers the chance to see how and why Crews attacked Freudians; how Freudians responded to those attacks; and how Crews replied to their replies. For anyone interested in assessing the intellectual merits of psychoanalysis, *The Memory Wars* is not merely a feast but a genuine smorgasbord of conflicting perspectives.

A key focus of *The Memory Wars* is the "Recovered Memory Therapy" (RMT) movement of the early 1990s. This movement involved heated charges (and denials) that numerous children had been sexually abused by parents and caregivers—abuse that resulted in severe psychological disturbances. I will, for the most part, ignore the merits or flaws of RMT here; instead I will focus on Crews' attacks on Freudianism in general, on others' responses to those attacks, and on his responses to those responses. I will also, again, steer clear, for the most part, from Crews' numerous indictments of Freud the man. Those indictments, if persuasive, are certainly disturbing, but it is always possible that Freud could have been an unethical, unscrupulous person and an unreliable scientist without his theories themselves being flawed.

In his "Introduction" to *The Memory Wars*, Crews repeats many of the charges against psychoanalysis he had already leveled previously. He also cites scores of other critics of Freud's methods and ideas. If for no other reason, *The Memory Wars* is valuable as a compendium of anti-Freudian scholarship and claims. In one efficient footnote, Crews lays out many crucial charges against psychoanalysis, including:

> its cult of the founder's personality; its casually anecdotal approach to corroboration; its cavalier dismissal of its most besetting epistemic problem, that of suggestion; its habitual confusion of speculation with fact; its penchant for generalizing from a small number of imperfectly examined instances; its proliferation of theoretical entities bearing no testable referents; its lack of vigilance against self-contradiction; its selective reporting of raw data to fit the latest theoretical enthusiasm; its ambiguities and exit clauses, allowing negative results to be counted as positive ones; its indifference to rival explanations and to mainstream science; its absence of any specified means for preferring one interpretation to another; its insistence that only the initiated are entitled to criticize; its stigmatizing of disagreement as "resistance," along with the corollary that, as Freud put it, all such resistance constitutes "actual evidence in favour of the correctness of the theory" ([Freud,] S[tandard] E[dition] 13:180); and its narcissistic faith that, again in Freud's words, "applications of analysis are always confirmations of it as well" (SE, 22:146). (*MW* 61-62; see also 108-110 for fuller versions of these charges)

How did Crews' critics respond to his charges? Many of them responded mainly to his attacks on Freud, the allegedly deceitful founder of a credulous cult. Crews, in turn, offered massive counter-responses, not only in this book but in later writings as well. More relevant here are the efforts of Crews' critics to defend Freudianism rather than Freud himself. Among those efforts are the following:

(1) Herbert S. Peyser, MD, a New York psychoanalyst, argued that:

Adolf Grünbaum, while demonstrating that Freud's methods of proof are not adequate for a truly scientific discipline, does not give up the idea of such proof being possible. He even points out ways to do it. He believes it can be done and should be done, as he has stated in his books. You would not know that from Professor Crews's article. (*MW* 86)

Crews responded only briefly and dismissively to this charge, making clear that he now considered Grünbaum not only a friend but also an ally (*MW* 118). Indeed, he had earlier cited a recent essay by Grünbaum titled "Does Psychoanalysis Have a Future? Doubtful" (*MW* 10). Throughout his writings, Crews always makes clear that Grünbaum is willing to entertain the theoretical possibility that some points of Freudian thinking could, conceivably, someday be scientifically confirmed; but Crews also makes clear his and Grünbaum's views that this has not yet happened.

(2) David D. Olds, MD, a psychiatrist and professor of psychiatry at Columbia, argued that Crews had confused admittedly unscientific (as well as "wild, capricious, and self-serving") practices by Freud and some of his early followers with the current practice of responsible psychoanalysis. Olds conceded the "extremely shaky practices of early pioneers" but considered them irrelevant to the latest methods and procedures (*MW* 90). Olds felt that psychoanalysis had "moved forward over the graves of bad ideas" (*MW* 93). Crews, in contrast, was unwilling to cede any territory. Responding to Olds and others, he later claimed that "[a]ll of the defining traits of pseudoscience that I listed in note 24 of my essay [the note quoted above] apply equally to Freud's work and to that of his improvers." He argued that "although each of Freud's ideas has been challenged from within his own tradition, that tradition itself remains one of deplorable conceptual sloppiness and circularity" (*MW* 125)—claims he discussed in further detail on pages 118-19.

(3) Marian Tolpin, MD, a psychiatrist and professor of psychiatry at Chicago Medical School, argued that Crews had neglected to mention severe criticism of Freud by latter-day Freudians, such as Erik Erikson (*MW* 93-96). Tolpin maintained that latter-day psychoanalysts had gone "on ahead of" Freud,

although she conceded that Freud's "tendentious arguments to prove his point were extremely harmful to some of his patients and to the field he tried so hard to establish" (*MW* 96). As already noted, Crews replied that even latter-day Freudians were guilty of flawed ideas and sloppy methods that were still often harmful to patients and to legitimate attempts to understand human psychology (*MW* 125). Crews argued that Erikson's own ideas and methods were open to challenge because they were built on infirm Freudian foundations (*MW* 124-26). According to Crews, "because the liberalized versions of psychoanalysis continue to use amorphous uncharacterized terms and to make untested claims, the relationship between psychoanalytic dogma and therapeutic effects remains as imprecise and prayerful as ever" (*MW* 127).

(4) Mortimer Ostow, MD, a noted "psychiatrist and psychoanalyst," argued that Freudian psychoanalysis was still widely practiced, especially outside the United States (*MW* 98-99). Ostow also reported that after reviewing the cases of thirty-seven of his former patients (all of whom "had had at least a minimum amount of psychoanalytic treatment"), he had concluded that five had improved dramatically, nine had improved impressively, sixteen had shown limited improvement, and seven had shown no improvement at all (*MW* 100). Ostow reported that the "distribution and degrees of improvement among patients who had no medication did not differ from those who had medication" (*MW* 101). Crews responded by criticizing Ostow and others for their failure to control for "factors shared by all [kinds of] treatment" or for "factors originating outside of treatment" as possible explanations for various results (*MW* 128). "It is sad enough," he wrote, "that, even though Ostow had employed 'medication along with analysis,' a full 62 percent of those patients had improved very little or not at all." Even more "pathetic," Crews wrote, was "Ostow's total unawareness that, thanks to his failure to control for nonpsychoanalytic effects, his survey lacks any validity" (*MW* 129).

(5) Lester Luborsky, professor of psychology at the University of Pennsylvania, argued that there were "no adequate studies comparing psychoanalysis with other forms of therapy so there is

no proof that it is better or it is worse" (*MW* 103). Luborsky thought that psychoanalysis was "probably at least as good as other forms of psychotherapy" (*MW* 103). He concluded that the "evidence is overwhelming that these different forms of psychotherapy produce very meaningful benefits for the majority of patients" (*MW* 103). Crews responded that he was quite familiar with Luborsky's scholarship (*MW* 129). He contended that Luborsky himself had elsewhere admitted that "psychotherapies succeed (when they do) thanks to factors that they all share—that is, placebo factors" (*MW* 131). Freudian treatment, as Luborsky himself had conceded, was no more effective than other forms of treatment, but it was (Crews noted, here and elsewhere), the longest lasting, the most expensive, and the most remunerative to therapists, which was why increasing numbers of insurance companies were failing to pay for it. Patients benefitted, when they benefitted at all, not from psychoanalysis *per se* but from "the more mundane and mildly effective process of renting a solicitous helper" (*MW* 131).

(6) Finally, Harold P. Blum and Bernard L. Pacella, both medical doctors and prominent Freudians, readily conceded many of Crews' charges against Freud himself. (So, in fact, did most of the critics of Crews represented in *The Memory Wars*.) But Blum and Pacella, like other defenders of psychoanalysis, argued that Freud's basic method had subsequently "developed independent of the person, personality, and personal life of its creator" (*MW* 106). Since Crews had already answered this objection when responding to the previous critics cited above, he spent most of his response to Blum and Pacella indicting them for failing to protest restrictions placed on open access to Freud's archives.

(7) Robert R. Holt, "Professor Emeritus of Psychology at New York University" (*MW* 140), defended the potential of psychoanalytic methods to be scientifically validated. "All that Grünbaum has done," Holt contended, "is to make a strong a priori case that psychoanalytic data" derived from free association and other techniques are "contaminated; he has not proved that any particular set of free associations are useless" (*MW* 143). Holt conceded that "the future of psychoanalysis as a science is hardly rosy," but he

maintained that "neither is it merely a dream of self-deluded people" (*MW* 144). Scientific validation was at least conceivably possible. Crews responded at length to Holt's contentions (*MW* 150-53). He argued (a) that the "free associations" of patients actually "aren't free at all," since they are almost inevitably tainted by the analyst's suggestions (*MW* 151); (b) that to his knowledge no psychoanalytic study had ever demonstrated that "a mere *theme* in a patient's contemporary mind" could be "certified as an early *determinant* of that patient's neurotic disposition" (*MW* 152); and (c) "even if associations did point to potential causal factors, psychoanalysts would still face the obstacle of trying to decide which ones actually governed a particular dream or symptom" (*MW* 152). Quoting the eminent philosopher Karl Popper, Crews ended his reply to Holt by comparing the self-confirming methods of psychoanalysts to the self-confirming methods of astrologers (*MW* 153).

(8) Morris Eagle, a prominent psychoanalyst, accused Crews of assuming that "psychoanalysis is a monolithic entity" (*MW* 145). While admitting that some aspects of Freudian theory had been "misleading and harmful," Eagle contended that other aspects of Freud's thinking could still be suggestive and fruitful in developing new theories (*MW* 146). Responding to Eagle, Crews quoted "a paper of 1983 where he denounces certain post-Freudian claims that 'are either incoherent or without any evidential support'" (*MW* 154), and he also insisted that "repression—Eagle's one example of a heuristically fruitful psychoanalytic idea—has been involved in every pernicious instance that could be named, from the supposed causes of homosexuality and female irrationality through false memory syndrome" (*MW* 154). Crews also disputed Eagle's claim that Crews had overlooked "the heterogeneity of psychoanalytic propositions. They are so heterogeneous, I have argued, as to constitute a self-condemning jumble of dubious and incompatible claims" (*MW* 155).

Not all the letter-writers who responded to Crews were critical. One of them, Allen Esterson (author of *Seductive Mirage: An Exploration of the Work of Sigmund Freud*), wrote that "the evidence for the dubious nature of almost all of Freud's supposed sexual findings can be found throughout his work" (*MW* 148). He further concluded that "Freud's reporting of his clinical experiences is not to be trusted" (*MW* 150). This is one letter to which Crews, understandably, did not reply. He did, however, respond at length to many other correspondents who challenged his comments about RMT or who objected to his attempts to show that the failings of RMT were directly related to the failings of psychoanalysis in general. However, since the present essay is not concerned with RMT, and since Crews' objections to psychoanalysis have by now been made exceedingly clear, readers interested in this later debate are invited to read it for themselves.

Crews Contra Holland

Crews' own attacks on Freud and Freudianism in *The Memory Wars* are hard to ignore, but even more devastating are the attacks he amasses in *Unauthorized Freud: Doubters Confront a Legend*. This book, a collection of twenty essays or excerpts by prominent critics of Freud, covers practically every aspect of Freud's career, influence, ideas, and methods. The critics' conclusions, along with Crews' introductory commentaries, make *Unauthorized Freud* perhaps the key text for anyone interested in seeing precisely how and why Freud and his ideas are open to challenge. It is, by turns, a disturbing, shocking, and sometimes even hilarious book.

More pertinent to our present concerns, however, is an exchange Crews conducted in 2006 with Norman Holland, surely the dean of American Freudian literary theorists, in a relatively obscure journal called *The Scientific Review of Alternative Medicine*. Holland's contribution to the dialogue was a summary of an even longer paper he had published online (see Works Cited), but even the summary is very valuable. In it, Holland began by claiming that "experimenters have in fact generated much empirical evidence for the validity of at least some of psychoanalysis's theory of mind" (21). According to Holland, experimenters had confirmed "the clusters of traits associated with orality and anality" and had also found support for the "oedipal stage," although researchers had found that "a good superego is likely to come from a loving rather than fearful relationship with the father" (21). Importantly, Holland conceded that there "is no support for any of Freud's ideas on female development" (21). Holland summarized findings by Drew Westen, who had cited 350 scholarly references finding support for such basic modern psychoanalytic assumptions as: (a) the existence of "unconscious motivations and defenses"; (b) "conflict and compromise" between various mental functions; (c) the assumption that "personality patterns form in childhood and continue through life"; (d) the assumption that "early patterns of attachment guide later relationships and symptoms"; and (e) the assumption that "personality development involves changing dependency but also pre-oedipal stages (oral, anal, etc.)" (22).

Holland argued that both attackers and defenders of psychoanalysis tended to ignore this kind of experimental confirmation. He asserted that most non-Freudian psychologists were prejudiced against Freudian ideas, and he pointed to "geology, astronomy, oceanology" and other disciplines that, like psychoanalysis, "do not lend themselves to repeatable experiments" but that are still considered "genuine sciences" (22). Holland challenged the common "stimulus-response view of humans" taken for granted by many psychologists (22). Holland reported that during "years of asking students and colleagues for a large generalization about human nature given us by experimental psychology, I have come up blank" (22). He concluded his summary of his larger article by making two assertions: "1) there is considerable evidence from experimental psychology that psychoanalytic theory is, in part, valid; 2) within psychoanalysis, the therapist uses an accepted scientific method appropriate to a human subject to arrive at generalizations" (23).

Crews, responding to Holland, made various points. First, he argued that most respected psychology departments treated psychoanalysis as "a prescientific, historical curiosity, not as a viable body of theory" ("Response to Holland" 24). Secondly, he quoted a survey of scholarship indicating that "'psychoanalytic research has been virtually ignored by mainstream scientific psychology over the past several decades'" ("Response to Holland" 24). Thirdly,

Crews alleged that Holland had cited no one who disagreed with him ("Response to Holland" 24). Fourthly, Crews repeated his earlier charges that psychoanalysis was a "pseudoscience" that had actually caused real harm to real people ("Response to Holland" 25). Fifthly, he repeated one of his lengthy list of objections to psychoanalysis ("Response to Holland" 25). Sixthly, he noted that one scholar, Robert F. Bornstein, whom Holland had cited as supporting Freudian ideas, had recently published an article titled "'The Impending Death of Psychoanalysis,' in which he charged analysts with 'the seven deadly sins' of 'insularity, inaccuracy, indifference, irrelevance, inefficiency, indeterminacy [that is, conceptual vagueness], and insolence'" ("Response to Holland" 25).

But Crews (in typical Crewsian fashion) was not finished yet—not by any means. He chastised Holland for allegedly failing to deal with various prominent challenges to scholarship supporting psychoanalysis (Crews, "Response to Holland" 26). He cited five specific problems with supposed confirmations of psychoanalytic approaches, arguing that many of the studies had "been conducted by people holding a prior affinity for psychoanalysis," making them "riddled with confirmation bias and demand characteristics" ("Response to Holland" 26). He argued that ideas that had been confirmed were not distinctively Freudian; that many of those ideas were commonplace well before Freud adopted some of them; and that insofar as "vapid truisms constitute the ground to which psychoanalysis has now fled in its retreat from Freud's heedless guesswork, they illustrate the bankruptcy, not the scientific validation, of his movement" ("Response to Holland" 26). Even now, Crews was not done, but most of the points he made on the final page of his rejoinder were ones he had made in previous attacks on psychoanalysis ("Response to Holland" 27).

Responding to Crews' response, Holland found Crews' reliance on "philosophers and historians" less persuasive than Holland's own citations of "experimentalists" ("Response to Crews" 29). He conceded the shortcomings of some psychoanalytic practitioners, again pointed to Drew Westen's scholarship, and suggested that Crews and his supporters were themselves often biased

("Response to Crews" 29). Most importantly, Holland insisted that "psychoanalysis does not equal psychoanalysts," nor is it equal to Freud ("Response to Crews" 30). Freud and some of his followers may have erred, but psychoanalysis still, in Holland's opinion, had been partly confirmed by experimentation and was still worthy of study. Holland found it difficult to take seriously Crews' use or citation of sources; objected to the allegedly ad hominem tone of Crews' rhetoric; and pointed to newer reasons for thinking that psychoanalysis was in many respects scientifically respectable ("Response to Crews" 29-30).

Even more interesting, in some ways, than the exchange between Holland and Crews was the ensuing assessment of that exchange by the psychiatrist Peter Barglow. Barglow's lengthy response expressed real skepticism about much twentieth-century psychoanalysis (31); noted that psychoanalysts had often "bitterly resisted" attempts to confirm their views scientifically (31); reported that some recent psychoanalysts had shown a willingness to consider biological explanations of psychological conditions (31); found these developments encouraging (31); and conceded that in reviewing his own use of psychoanalysis with patients, he had become more skeptical of certain psychoanalytic assumptions (32). Barglow also compared the training of psychoanalysts to the indoctrination of seminarians (32); expressed real doubts about the integrity of various psychoanalysts and their studies (32); but suggested that although "many of the claims of psychoanalysis have been disproven by now," it might "be premature to discount the contribution of psychoanalysis for all future time" (32). Nevertheless, Barglow admitted that "psychoanalysis was completely useless to treat schizophrenia, childhood autism, and addiction pathology" (33), and he conceded that many of Freud's "concepts have not held up to systematic scrutiny" (34). In conclusion, Barglow agreed "with most of Crews' negative opinion of the 20th-century accomplishments of psychoanalysis" but continued, like Holland, "to treasure a few of Freud's contributions," such as his non-technical language, his emphasis on the unconscious, his belief in listening carefully to patients (a belief Crews has often claimed that

Freud did not really practice himself), and his idea that childhood experiences could affect an adult's thoughts and feelings (34).

Crews, surely, would have responded even to the genuinely sympathetic Barglow if he had had the chance. Crews has always been more than willing and eager to engage in debate. And that, in fact, is precisely why he will likely remain an important figure in the history of thinking about psychoanalysis. His path—from early advocate to wholesale apostate—is one of the most interesting intellectual trajectories of recent decades. The challenges he raised to psychoanalysis, and the responses those challenges provoked, will always be interesting to anyone concerned with discovering psychological truths and applying psychological insights to literary texts.

Works Cited

Barglow, Peter. "Response to Holland and Crews." *The Scientific Review of Alternative Medicine*, vol. 20, 2006, pp. 31-35.

Crews, Frederick C. *Out of My System: Psychoanalysis, Ideology, and Literary Method*. Oxford UP, 1975.

———, ed. *Psychoanalysis and Literary Process*. Winthrop, 1970.

———. "Response to Holland." *The Scientific Review of Alternative Medicine*, vol. 20, 2006, pp. 24-28.

———. *Sins of the Fathers: Hawthorne's Psychological Themes*. 1966. U of California P, 1989.

———. *Skeptical Engagements*. Oxford UP, 1986.

———, ed. *Unauthorized Freud: Doubters Confront a Legend*. Viking, 1998.

——— et al. *The Memory Wars: Freud's Legacy in Dispute*. New York Review of Books, 1995.

Holland, Norman. "Psychoanalysis as Science." *PsyArt: An Online Journal for the Psychological Study of the Arts*, 22 May 2004. psyartjournal.com/article/show/ n_holland-psychoanalysis_as_science/. Accessed 22 Oct. 2016.

———. "Psychoanalysis as Science." *The Scientific Review of Alternative Medicine*, vol. 20, 2006, pp. 21-23.

———. "Response to Crews." *The Scientific Review of Alternative Medicine*, 10, 2006, pp. 29-30.

Psychological Approaches to Literature: A Review of Select Scholarship

Robert C. Evans

Anyone surveying textbooks designed to introduce students to the psychological study of literature will be surprised by the narrow range of psychological approaches typically discussed. One of the best of such books—by Ann B. Dobie—concentrates (on the one hand) on Sigmund Freud and his follower Jacques Lacan and then (on the other hand) on Carl Jung and a related critic, Northrop Frye. Freud was the founder of psychoanalytic theory, while Jung was the founder of archetypal (or "myth") theory. Both kinds of theory have significantly affected the study of literature, and so it makes sense that most surveys of literary theory focus on Freud and on Jung. It is Freud, though, and more recently Lacan, who tends to receive the lion's share of attention. In fact, in some books (such as the superb survey by Lois Tyson), Freud and Lacan are discussed at length, while Jung is barely mentioned. Likewise, Terry Eagleton's landmark study of literary theory mentions Freud repeatedly but Jung not at all, and much the same is true of such fine other representative books as those by Barry, Castle, Fry, Klages, Parker, Ryan, and Anne H. Stevens. These texts—chosen more or less at random—are typical of many others: Freud and Lacan are clearly in the spotlight, while Jung is deep in the shadows (if he appears at all). This emphasis on Freud and Lacan in introductory texts to literary theory reflects a similar emphasis on Freud and Lacan in numerous critical books and articles by practicing literary critics. Freud and Lacan are generally the major figures of interest in psychological approaches to literature. Other perspectives—such as cognitive and Darwinian psychology—have, admittedly, begun to attract some recent attention, but in advanced classes and in graduate schools, Freud and Lacan still prevail.

What is surprising about this fact is that Freud and Lacan—the two psychological theorists apparently taken most seriously by contemporary students of literature—receive almost no current attention from actual psychologists or in actual departments of psychology. Typing the words "Introduction to Psychology" into Google Books will immediately generate a long list of basic texts in which Freud is mentioned mainly as a historical figure and in which Lacan is not mentioned at all. Jung, on the other hand, is mentioned often, even though literary theorists seem to be paying less and less attention to him. Using Google's "search inside the book" feature reveals some interesting statistics. Thus, in the introductory textbook by Kalat, Freud's name appears on forty pages, Jung's on seventeen, and Lacan's on none. In the similar book by Coon and Mitterer, the score is Freud, forty-one; Jung, seventeen; Lacan, zero. In the book by Plotnik and Kouyoumdjian, it's Freud, thirty-eight; Jung, three; Lacan, zero. In Koffman and Walters: Freud, forty-eight; Jung, nineteen; Lacan, zero. In Nicholas: Freud, twenty-six; Jung, seven; Lacan, zero. These statistics suggest a clear trend: Freud is taken seriously enough as a pioneering psychologist that he is mentioned often for his historical contributions (along with numerous other pioneers, such as Jung), whereas Lacan is apparently not taken very seriously—by actual psychologists—at all. But perhaps the texts just cited are too broad in focus. Perhaps it would be better to examine introductory books dealing with various theories of personality. Here again, though, the results are similar. In the book on personality theories by Schultz and Schultz, Freud merits fifty references, Jung forty-nine, and Lacan zero. In the book by Ryckman, the tally is Freud, forty-nine; Jung, forty-nine; Lacan, zero. In the book by Feist, Feist, and Roberts, the score is Freud, fifteen; Jung, six; Lacan, zero. In the text by Engler, it's Freud, forty-nine; Jung, thirty; Lacan, zero.

These findings suggest several conclusions. First, students of literature may be devoting far too much thought and time to Lacan than Lacan's reputation among "real" psychologists seems to justify. Second, the relative lack of recent attention to Jung among literary critics seems unmerited. And, third and most important by far: there are numerous psychologists and theories of psychology and personality whose work receives almost no attention in standard textbooks of literary theory. The study of literary theory and of psychological approaches to literature can seem woefully inadequate and out of date if one compares such scholarship with the actual study, by psychologists, of psychology itself. Opportunities for real original research seem to abound if only students of literature would occasionally turn their attention away from Freud (and especially Lacan) and direct it toward the numerous other psychologists and psychological theories taken seriously by actual experts in the field.

Getting Started

Anyone interested in "psychological approaches" to literature would benefit from surveying not only the history of psychology but also the extremely wide variety of approaches to psychology that presently exist. One good, brief survey (among many other candidates) is an essay by Jennifer A. Vadeboncoeur. It takes up eighteen large pages and is valuable for being comprehensive without being overwhelming. Vadeboncoeur discusses such important figures in the history of psychological thought as Plato, Aristotle, Descartes, Locke, Rousseau, Kant, and J. S. Mill. She then presents the thinking of more recent figures such as Wundt, Tichener, James, Hall, and Dewey, who participated in debates about "structures" vs. "functions" in the mind. Next, she discusses the "gestalt" psychologists Mach, Wertheimer, Koffka, and Lewin. Then, she reviews the kind of psychoanalysis associated with the Freuds (Sigmund and Anna) and with Adler, Jung, Horney, Erickson, and Marcia. Next, she covers such behaviorists and students of mental measurement as Thorndike, Pavlov, Watson, Skinner, Bandura, Binet, and Goddard. "Humanist psychology" is represented by Maslow and Rogers; "Developmental" and "Cognitive" psychology by Piaget, Vygotsky, Bruner, Atkinson and Shiffrin, Craik and Lockhart, Gardner, Gazzaniga, von Glasserfield, and Wertsch; and "Social Psychology" is represented in Vadeboncoeur's survey by Allport, Kenneth and Mamie Clark, Gilligan, and Walkerdine (1328).

This is a lengthy list of names, but even this list only scratches the surface of important psychologists and kinds of psychology worth exploring by students of literature. Most of these names go unmentioned in most standard introductions to literary theory. Better to be flooded with names than to assume that Freud and Lacan are the only names worth mentioning. Better to be reminded that psychology is an immensely rich and complicated field than to think that the serious study of psychology and literature should be limited to studying a Viennese pioneer and his Parisian disciple. After reading surveys like Vadeboncoeur's, one might next want to read longer introductions to psychology (such as the textbooks mentioned above and listed below). One such book worth consulting is the standard and highly representative textbook by Daniel Cervone and Lawrence A. Pervin titled *Personality: Theory and Research*. Since most literary texts raise questions about the personalities of characters, narrators, or authors, focusing on the study of personality theories seems a useful, concentrated way "into" the study of literature and psychology.

Cervone and Pervin offer detailed discussions of the theories associated with such names as Freud, Adler, Jung, Horney, Sullivan, Rogers, Maslow, Allport, Eysenck, Cattell, Watson, Pavlov, Skinner, Kelly, Bandura, Mischel, Ellis, Beck, and many others. They devote extended attention to theories they label "psychodynamic," "psychoanalytic," "phenomenological," "trait theory," "factor analysis," "the biological foundations of personality" (including evolution, genes, and neurology), "behaviorism," "learning approaches," "cognitive theory," "social cognitive theory," and so on. Freud and Jung are well represented (Lacan is not mentioned), but so are many theorists and theories that tend to go mostly unnoticed in textbooks dealing with approaches to the study of literature. Moreover, Cervone and Pervin discuss the alleged strengths and weaknesses of each theory they survey, and they also list numerous studies that either support or undermine the conclusions of each theory. Finally, they discuss how to evaluate theories (asking, for instance, if a theory is systematic, testable, comprehensive, logically self-consistent, and so on). Anyone who reads books such as theirs will come away with a far more comprehensive, complex sense of the existence and nature of psychological concepts than one typically receives from texts in literary theory.

Basic Guides to the Psychological Study of Literature

The best place to begin any study of any literary topic is, of course, the International Bibliography compiled and constantly updated by the Modern Language Association. This has long since been available online, making subject searches exceedingly quick and easy. Also worth consulting, however, are various bibliographies or bibliographical guides that are now dated but still useful. One of these is the massive two-volume (but unannotated) bibliography compiled by Norman Kiell, which runs to 1269 closely printed pages. The index surveys references to primary authors, primary texts, and various subjects (including particular psychologists). Predictably, Freud is mentioned far more often than any other theorist, but this fact merely illustrates another one: Freudian approaches dominated the study of literature and psychology in the twentieth century (and often still do).

Helpful, for precisely this reason, is Jos van Meurs' survey of over nine hundred applications of Jungian approaches to literary criticism, a survey that is fully (sometimes very fully) annotated. Much briefer annotations appear in the book-length bibliography compiled by Joseph Natoli and Frederik L. Rusch. The largely chronological organization of this volume is useful, however, and both Freudian and Jungian approaches receive roughly equal emphasis. A thorough (if now somewhat dated) fifty-page bibliography appears at the end of Martin S. Lindauer's 1974 study titled *The Psychological Study of Literature: Limitations, Possibilities, and Accomplishments*, and Lindauer's book also includes a thorough index of topics. Indeed, Lindauer's volume is worth reading for numerous reasons: it is lucidly written, clearly organized, balanced in tone, and fair to all sides. Because of all these traits, it is worth reviewing in some detail.

Chapter 1 of Lindauer's study is titled "Psychology's Neglect of Aesthetics and Literature." Here he discusses how and why standard academic (scientific) psychologists had (at least before 1974) paid relatively little attention to art and creative writing. Unlike so many other introductions to the field, Lindauer does not overemphasize Freud; numerous names unfamiliar to most people interested in the psychological study of literature appear in his book. These helpfully remind readers that Freud was just one of many voices in twentieth-century psychology. Lindauer concludes that many psychologists neglected the study of literature because such study often seemed subjective and hard to verify empirically (14), and surely this is true. Psychological discussions of literature have often been wildly speculative and have proved embarrassing even to many scholars who favor the psychological study of art.

The title of Lindauer's next chapter—"The Dominance of Psychoanalysis in the Psychology of Literature"—speaks for itself. Lindauer estimates that 90 percent of twentieth-century scholarship on literature came from followers of Freud (18). He surveys Freudian ideas and scholarship but retains an objective attitude, neither embracing nor rejecting psychoanalytic views in any wholesale fashion. He does note that most academic psychologists "have generally viewed psychoanalytic efforts disdainfully or dismissed them altogether. Their essential criticism has been that psychoanalytic concepts are used too facilely, proving anything—and therefore nothing" (Lindauer 24). Lindauer suggests that a scientific psychological approach to literature *is* possible. He responds to claims that it is not, reviews various studies, but concedes that "many of the problems encountered by a scientific study of literature cannot be overcome or satisfactorily resolved" (40). Literature, he concludes, is so complex that many then-current scientific approaches to psychology cannot do it adequate justice. Here, as throughout his book, Lindauer seems reassuringly objective; he seems beholden to no particular assumptions or methods. He surveys a wide variety of previous studies; acknowledges both their strengths and limitations; and ends by holding out the prospect of greater success in the future.

Even more impressive than Lindauer's book is Robert N. Mollinger's 1981 study titled *Psychoanalysis and Literature: An Introduction*. Mollinger's chapters offer "A Review of Psychoanalytic Literary Criticism," "An Introduction to Psychoanalysis," and discussions of such topics as authors, characters, works, symbols, form, and levels of meaning from psychoanalytic points of view.

Authors examined include Wallace Stevens, Edgar Allan Poe, Herman Melville, Sylvia Plath, and Dom Moraes. Mollinger begins by asserting that he considers psychoanalysis "a developing discipline—one in which some hypotheses are certain, some are yet to be ascertained, and some are questionable" (ix). He summarizes the arguments of Freud and various Freudians in an extremely lucid fashion, giving extended attention to the little-known (at least to literary scholars) Ernst Kris and paying proper respect to Norman Holland, perhaps the most important of all English-language Freudian literary theorists. He fairly reviews objections to psychoanalysis, indicates why he still finds psychoanalytical approaches worth pursuing, and shows (much more than is common in such books) the sheer diversity of kinds of psychoanalysis. He also offers a valuable sense of the ways psychoanalytic ideas have developed over the decades. Freud is an important figure in Mollinger's book, but he is not a god. Typical of Mollinger's comprehensiveness is his statement that there has been:

> a progressive movement in emphasis on the key factor in creativity—from unconscious conflict (Freud), to controlled regression to unconscious conflict (Kris), to defensive mechanisms and their relation to unconscious conflict (Holland), to the preconscious (Kubie), to the secondary processes (Rothenberg), and finally to the integration of all factors (Aretti, Roland). (18)

Anyone who reads Mollinger will get a strong sense of the sheer diversity of psychoanalytic approaches and of which figures seemed (at least to Mollinger) to have made the most significant contributions to the field by the early 1980s. Thus, Lacan is mentioned on two pages, whereas Erik Erikson is discussed on ten, Norman Holland on sixteen, Carl Jung on thirteen, and D. W. Winnicott on ten. Freud, of course, as the founder of psychoanalysis, receives the most extended discussion (twenty-seven pages in all). If there were just one early introduction to psychoanalytic approaches that one might want to recommend to readers (aside from the various important works by Norman Holland, which really deserve a chapter of their own), Mollinger's survey might easily qualify. It, along with Lindauer's volume, gives a solid sense of the "state of play" in the psychological study of literature before the last two decades of the twentieth century.

In a series of important books over a long (and still on-going) career, Holland (now in his 90s!), has distinguished himself as perhaps the most thoughtful, thorough, wide-ranging, and influential of all psychoanalytic literary theorists of modern times (at least before the arrival of Lacan). Holland is the author of more than ten important books of psychological approaches to literature, not to mention scores of essays. Moreover, Holland has shown an admirable willingness to face objections, explore new territory, and modify and develop his thinking. Perhaps the most immediately helpful of his books for readers of the present essay is titled *Holland's Guide to Psychoanalytic Psychology and Literature-and-Psychology*. This idiosyncratic text is essentially a fully annotated bibliography with a long list of relevant additional readings. It offers Holland's opinions about which ideas are most worth considering, which books are most worth reading, and why. It is deliberately designed to be user-friendly, particularly to newcomers to the field. Although Holland definitely has his own opinions, he tries to be (and succeeds in being) fair in his summaries of others' views.

Holland begins by tracing the historical evolution of psychoanalytic ideas and their relevance to literature, commenting on developments (after Freud's death) in such nations as Great Britain, France, the United States, West Germany, and Israel. He concedes some problems with psychoanalytic methods (as when he mentions that "clinical data are notoriously subject to the theoretical and other preconceptions of the clinician" [Holland 12]), but one wishes that he had given more attention to the by-then voluminous and ever-developing scholarship devoted to challenging Freud and Freud's intellectual legacy. Frederick Crews, for instance (a one-time champion of Freud who quickly became Freud's most vocal critic), is represented in the bibliography only by a reference to one of his early, pro-Freudian texts. Numerous other important critics of Freud (such as the twenty contributors to *Unauthorized Freud: Doubters Confront a Legend*, edited by Crews) are also not cited. The challengers to Freud whom Holland does cite tend to be thinkers writing within the Freudian tradition.

Especially valuable sections of Holland's book include chapter 4 ("Literature-and-Psychology"), the "Epilogue," and the section on "Research Aids." In these sections, Holland offers his most detailed commentaries and recommendations. He wisely notes, for instance, that in "the largest sense, all criticism is psychological criticism, since all criticism and theory proceed from assumptions about the psychology of the humans who make or experience or are portrayed in literature" (Holland 29). He comments on the beginnings and subsequent phases of psychoanalytic thinking, notes the importance of Freud's 1908 essay on "Creative Writers and Day-Dreaming" (34), and summarizes the ways various early Freudians adopted and adapted Freud's ideas (35). Particularly helpful in a book so much concerned with Freud is Holland's outline of the distinctive views of Jung (36-37). Here, as so often elsewhere in his book, Holland cites both primary and secondary texts (both works by Jung and works by Jungians [42-44]). Holland also covers such important topics as "Object-relations theory" (41-42), "Identity theory" (44), "Third force psychology" (44-45), and "'French Freud'... primarily Lacan" (45- 49).

Because Lacan is, today, by far the most influential of Freudians in the study of literature and culture (far more influential, oddly, than the always-lucid Holland himself), it seems worth pausing to listen to one eminent Freudian's assessment of another. Holland begins by offering an objective overview of Lacan's ideas. He notes, for example, that for "Lacan, . . . the ego is the carrier of neurosis and self-deception. Therapy should aim, not to strengthen the ego (as in American ego-psychology) but to recognize the split, de-centered self, which is 'the truth of the subject'" (Holland 47). Holland opines that Lacan's:

> kind of thinking appeals strongly to intellectuals because culture and language (at which intellectuals are adept) replace the biological models of classical and second-phase psychoanalysis. The mind [for Lacanians] is determined by language, not by organs of the body or brain and not by the object-relations

> of British theory.... Lacan... proclaims that psychoanalysis must subvert every kind of intellectual establishment. All this, of course, has made Lacan a favorite of the intellectual establishment. (46-47)

"Lacan," continues Holland in a generous understatement, "wrote in an avowedly obscure style." Therefore "much Lacanian theory simply tries to explicate Lacan" (47). Discussing the implications of Lacan's ideas for the interpretation of literature, Holland notes that Lacanian thinking (like many "postmodern" approaches) "leads to the impossibility of arriving at textual meaning" (48). Lacan fundamentally assumes, in Holland's paraphrase, that the "conscious and unconscious are *opposed*." Holland responds that there is "no evidence" for this assumption, "neither experimental evidence nor clinical evidence from first- or second-phase psychoanalysts" (48). Lacan, Holland concludes, "characteristically renders as either-or or as an opposition what had previously made good sense as 'both-and or' an interaction: conscious vs. unconscious, self vs. not-self, unity vs. conflict, science vs. unconscious truth, and so on" (49). Here, as always, Holland is clear in thought and style (which may be one reason that Lacan still appeals to a certain mindset: it is easy to understand precisely what Holland thinks and says; this is much, much, much less true of Lacan).

After finishing his extended discussion of Lacan, Holland turns to a variety of other approaches, such as "Narcissism theory" (49-50), "Feminist psychoanalysis" (50-53), "Cognitive psychology" (53-54), "Reader-Response Criticism" (54-58). In discussing this last topic, Holland mentions in passing how he himself changed some of his own earlier thinking in response to newer developments in the field (56). This willingness to consider and reconsider ideas is one trait that makes Holland such an admirable thinker and valuable guide. But even the open-minded Holland has trouble taking Lacan seriously, and so he returns to that topic in one paragraph of his "Epilogue." Lacanians," he says, "render psychoanalysis merely language. [Everything becomes] merely words. This mental tactic seems to me a classic example of what psychoanalysts term *the omnipotence of thoughts* or *magical thinking*" (60). Holland does not reject Lacan entirely, but he says that he distrusts "any version of psychoanalysis that gets too far away from the actual experience of couch, clinic, and laboratory" (61).

In one of the most interesting sections of the book, Holland defends standard psychoanalysis from many of the criticisms leveled against it by such skeptics as Frederick Crews (although Holland does not mention Crews by name, nor does he mention by name many of the other scholars whom Crews cites for support). Holland twice rejects the charge that "psychoanalysis is untested and untestable" (62). He cites six kinds of evidence that he thinks lend support to psychoanalytic theories: "free association" by patients; "unconscious dimensions to our language"; "the image-clusters of childhood stages"; "a theme-and-variations [concept of human] identity"; "feedback" from the physical world about human assumptions; and Winnicott's concept of "potential space" (72-73). Both of the latter ideas imply that humans are "constantly testing and trying" (72). This is not the place to judge whether Holland's defense of psychoanalysis against the critics he mostly doesn't name or cite is persuasive (for more on this topic, see the essay on Frederick Crews in the present volume). But it is very much to Holland's credit that he does at least *try* to offer a defense rather than ignoring criticism altogether.

Another standard, more detailed (but sometimes less lucid) guide to Freudian and related theories is Elizabeth Wright's *Psychoanalytic Criticism: A Reappraisal*. Originally published in 1984 as *Psychoanalytic Criticism: Theory in Practice*, Wright's book in its renamed second edition appeared in 1998. It offers substantial chapters on Freud, id-psychology, ego-psychology, Jungian theories, object-relations theory, Lacanian ideas, and a variety of other approaches, including emphases on feminism, subversion, dialectic, and the psyche as text. Wright's book has been highly praised and is certainly one of the best places to turn for a one-volume survey of the Freudian field.

Broadening, altering, and exploring that field in intriguing new ways are the purposes of a fascinating book from 2000 by Leonard

Jackson and titled *Literature, Psychoanalysis, and the New Sciences of Mind*. As this title suggests, Jackson explains the important rise, in the second half of the twentieth century, of cognitive psychology, a significantly different (more scientifically testable) way of thinking about the mind than the kind outlined by Freud and pursued by Freud's followers. Jackson argues, however, that some aspects of Freudian thinking can be rescued if they can be grounded in what Jackson calls the "bio-cognitive sciences" (vii). Jackson begins by asserting that:

> almost no cognitive scientist . . . finds Freud empirically satisfactory; and the Freudian variants—Jung, say, or Lacan—are very much worse; speculative religious nonsense, or empty rhetorical extravagance studded with pseudoscientific claims. Modern scientific theories of mind and sexuality generally have no place for psychoanalysis. (1)

Jackson does his best (and his best is very good) to make cogent arguments for a new, scientific grounding of some features of Freudian thought. He claims, for instance, that Freud's emphasis on the importance of unconscious fantasies "is one of the most powerful explanatory theories of the twentieth century" and "has not been superseded by cognitive science. On the contrary, it fits easily alongside plausible cognitive models" (Jackson 3). Jackson, then, tries to find some support for some Freudian ideas in the new sciences of the human brain.

Jackson's book is never less than lucid, and it is also very clearly organized, with an exceptionally detailed table of contents. Jackson also tends to explain others' ideas fully and objectively before then issuing his own (sometimes skeptical or caustic) evaluations of them. Key terms are highlighted in bold print; numerous secondary sources are cited; detailed suggestions for "further reading" appear near the conclusion; and the book is in general a splendid introduction to cognitive science as well as a spirited attempt to ground some parts of Freudian thinking in cognitive scientific approaches. Part of the real value of Jackson's volume is that he writes as someone who appreciates Freud but who is more than willing to criticize the shortcomings of some aspects of Freudian thinking and some kinds of Freudian theory.

Because Lacan is (at least in the humanities) still perhaps the most influential of all recent Freudians, it is worth hearing what Jackson has to say on this subject. Essentially, Jackson argues

"that at the heart of Lacan's work is a defensible cognitive theory: that the ego is only an imaginary representation of the self and that at least part of the unconscious is structured like a language. But in general Lacan . . . is not a scientist as Freud was, nor a credible philosopher" (132). As is typical with Jackson, he gives Lacan credit for any plausible ideas he may have explored, but Jackson never fails to find fault when a thinker verges toward what Jackson considers nonsense. Thus he suggests that some of Lacan's writings make him sound like "the leader of a cult, not a scientist" (133). He finds in much of Lacan's rhetoric a "colossal apparatus of bluff and double-bluff, near-simultaneous assertion and denial, obscure technicality and scalding emotion, [and] paranoid bullying and pathos of the lonely misunderstood excommunicate" who was attacked by many of Freud's other followers (142). Jackson claims that "far from adopting a complex and inclusive account of language, [Lacan] adopts an astonishingly crude and simple one" (146). Jackson also critiques the ideas of other thinkers either resembling Lacan or influenced by him. He thinks that Lacan is, "by the standards of cognitive science, guilty of grossly oversimplifying" key psychological issues (156). "The worst thing one can say about Lacan," Jackson continues, is that when facing difficult problems "he had no real solution for, and no real interest in solving, he hid the fact from himself and his followers by covering it up with philosophical rhetoric" (157).

Interestingly, although Jackson criticizes various theories by Jung (and especially by undisciplined Jungians), he does maintain that Jung's position "is in some ways an easier position to align with biological realities than Freud's" (195). This is an argument developed at great and intriguing length by Anthony Stevens (a prominent Jungian), first in a book titled *Archetypes: A Natural History of the Self* (1983) and then in a revised version of that book titled *Archetype Revisited: An Updated Natural History of the Self* (2000). These texts are just two among many works in which Stevens tried to show that many of Jung's ideas could be grounded in the developing field of evolutionary psychology. The first version of the book lays out Stevens' basic arguments; the second version adds supplements to each chapter. These provide more recent evidence to support the book's various claims. Essentially, Stevens ties Jung's key belief—that human thoughts and feelings are rooted in very basic and widely shared "archetypes" of the "collective unconscious"—to modern findings about genetic evolution. Human beings (and human cultures) resemble one another, Steven claims, because most humans share the same fundamental genetic inheritance. Like Jackson, Stevens provides very valuable overviews of recent thinking about the biological, evolutionary bases of psychology, and he rightly lists several of his own books as major contributions to the field: "*The Two Million-Year-Old Self* (1993), *Private Myths: Dreams and Dreaming* (1995), *Ariadne's Clue: A Guide to the Symbols of Humankind* (1998a) and *An Intelligent Person's Guide to Psychotherapy* (1998b)" (31).

In a passage typical of Stevens' claims and wide reading, he cites a variety of recent evolutionary psychologists who use terms and ideas very similar to Jung's concept of the archetype:

> Different workers have called them by different names but all are referring to similar structures with parallel functions. While Paul Gilbert (1997) refers to them as 'mentalities', Russell Gardner (1988) of Galveston, Texas, calls them 'master programmes' or 'propensity states' and Brant Wenegrat (1984) of Stanford University calls them 'genetically transmitted response strategies'. David Buss (1999) of Austin, Texas, who has done most to elucidate the archetypes underlying characteristic features of masculine and feminine psychology, refers to them as 'evolved psychological mechanisms', Randolph Nesse (1987) of the University of Michigan School of Medicine to 'prepared tendencies', Sally Walters (1994) of Simon Fraser University, British Columbia, to 'algorithms' and Leda Cosmides and John Tooby (1992) of the University of California at Santa Barbara to 'multiple mental modules'. (53-54)

Stevens also cites a number of researchers who, like himself, have begun to explore possible relevant connections between evolutionary thinkers and Jungian theory:

> These include Charles Card (2000), Richard Gray (1996), George Hogenson (1999), Alan Maloney (1999), Maxim J. McDowell (1999), Robin Robertson (1995), Virginia Routh (1981), Meredith Sabini (2000) and Sally Walters (1994), only two of whom (Hogenson and McDowell) are Jungian analysts. (54-55)

The point of reporting all these names here is simply to indicate that Stevens is not alone in seeking to link Jung's ideas to those of modern science. And he is certainly not alone in emphasizing the strides that evolutionary psychologists and cognitive scientists have recently made toward a fuller, more empirically grounded understanding of the human mind.

The implications of cognitive science and evolutionary psychology for the study of literature are so vast—and the relevant scholarship is now so extensive—that there is no space left to do justice to it here. Interested readers should definitely consult the work of the various scholars included or cited in such works as those edited by Boyd et al., Cave, Jaén and Simon, and Zunshine. My fundamental purpose in the present chapter has simply been to review some of the main claims of made by people working in the broad Freudian tradition (after all, even Jung began as a Freudian). I have also wanted to shed a somewhat skeptical light on the importance of Lacan, if only because he is still the writer about psychology whom most professional students of literature seem to take most seriously. The fact that he is not taken very seriously at all by most actual psychologists is reason enough for encouraging literary critics and literary theorists to cautiously rethink their often wholesale embrace of Lacanian ideas and consider some of the many other options open to them.

Works Cited

Barry, Jonathan. *Beginning Theory: An Introduction to Literary and Cultural Theory*. 2nd ed., Manchester UP, 2002.

Boyd, Brian, et al., editors. *Evolution, Literature, and Film: A Reader*. Columbia UP, 2010.

Castle, Gregory. *The Literary Theory Handbook*. Wiley Blackwell, 2013.

Cave, Terence. *Thinking with Literature: Towards a Cognitive Criticism*. Oxford UP, 2016.

Cervone, Daniel, and Lawrence A. Pervin. *Personality: Theory and Research*. 10th ed., Wiley, 2008.

Coon, Dennis, and John O. Mitterer. *Introduction to Psychology: Gateways to Mind and Behavior*. 14th ed., Cengage, 2015.

Crews, Frederick, editor. *Unauthorized Freud: Doubters Confront a Legend*. Viking, 1998.

Dobie, Ann B. *Theory into Practice: An Introduction to Literary Criticism*. 3rd ed., Wadsworth, 2012.

Eagleton, Terry. *Literary Theory: An Introduction: Anniversary Edition*. Blackwell, 2008.

Engler, Barbara. *Personality Theories*. 9th ed., Cengage, 2013.

Feist, Jess, Gregory Feist, and Tomi-Ann Roberts. *Theories of Personality*. 8th ed., McGraw-Hill, 2013.

Fry, Paul H. *Theory of Literature*. Yale UP, 2012.

Holland, Norman. *Holland's Guide to Psychoanalytic Psychology and Literature-and-Psychology*. Oxford UP, 1990.

Jackson, Leonard. *Literature, Psychoanalysis and the New Sciences of Mind*. Longman, 2000.

Jaén, Isabel, and Julien Jacques Simon. *Cognitive Literary Studies: Current Themes and New Directions*. U of Texas P, 2013.

Kalat, James W. *Introduction to Psychology*. 11th ed., Cengage, 2017.

Kiell, Norman. *Psychoanalysis, Psychology, and Literature: A Bibliography*. 2 vols, 2nd ed., Scarecrow, 1982.

Klages, Mary. *Literary Theory: A Guide for the Perplexed*. London: Continuum, 2006.

Koffmann, Andrew, and M. Grace Walters. *Introduction to Psychological Theories and Psychotherapy*. Oxford UP, 2014.

Lindauer, Martin S. *The Psychological Study of Literature: Limitations, Possibilities, and Accomplishments*. Nelson-Hall, 1974.

Mollinger, Robert N. *Psychoanalysis and Literature: An Introduction*. Nelson-Hall, 1981.

Natoli, Joseph, and Frederik L. Rusch. *Psychocriticism: An Annotated Bibliography*. Greenwood, 1984.

Nicholas, Lionel. *Introduction to Psychology*. 2nd ed., UCT P, 2008.

Parker, Robert Dale. *How to Interpret Literature: Critical Theory for Literary and Cultural Studies*. 3rd ed., Oxford UP, 2015.

Plotnik, Rod, and Haig Kouyoumdjian. *Introduction to Psychology*. 10th ed., Cengage, 2014.

Ryan, Michael. *Literary Theory: A Practical Introduction*. 2nd ed., Blackwell, 2007.

Ryckman, Richard M. *Theories of Personality*. 10th ed., Cengage, 2013.

Schultz, Duane P., and Sydney Ellen Schultz. *Theories of Personality*. 11th ed., Cengage, 2017.

Stevens, Anne H. *Literary Theory and Criticism: An Introduction*. Broadview, 2015.

Stevens, Anthony. *Archetype: A Natural History of the Self*. Routledge & K. Paul, 1982.

———. *Archetype Revisited: An Updated Natural History of the Self*. Inner City, 2003.

Tyson, Lois. *Critical Theory Today: A User-Friendly Guide*. 3rd ed., Routledge, 2015.

Vadeboncoeur, Jennifer A. "Psychology Survey." *Reader's Guide to the Social Sciences*, edited by Jonathan Michie, vol. 2, Fitzroy Dearborn, 2001, pp. 1326-44.

Van Meurs, Jos. *Jungian Literary Criticism 1920–1980: An Annotated Bibliography of Works in English (with a Selection of Titles after 1980)*. Boston: Sigo, 1991.

Wright, Elizabeth. *Psychoanalytic Criticism: A Reappraisal*. Taylor & Francis, 1998.

———. *Psychoanalytic Criticism: Theory in Practice*. Methuen, 1984.

Zunshine, Lisa, editor. *The Oxford Handbook of Cognitive Literary Studies*. Oxford UP, 2015.

A Family Systems Theory Reading of Saul Bellow's *Humboldt's Gift*

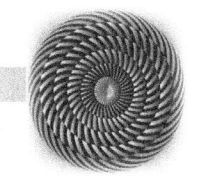

Allan Chavkin & Nancy Feyl Chavkin

Bellow's Familiarity with Psychology

While Saul Bellow's *Humboldt's Gift* has attracted much attention, critics have not discussed the issue of family dysfunction in the novel. This is not surprising because, unlike some of Bellow's other novels, such as *Seize the Day*, family is not this book's central focus. Yet the dysfunctional family and absent, deceased, and abusive parents do play a crucial role in the formation of the major characters' lives. One puzzling aspect of the novel is the perplexing character of the narrator and protagonist, Charlie Citrine. Charlie is a successful, Pulitzer-Prize-winning author with a younger, voluptuous girlfriend, but he does not behave as one might expect a successful person to behave. He is so passive that he allows a comic gangster, Rinaldo Cantabile, to bully him repeatedly, even at one point acceding to his outrageous demand that Charlie remain in a bathroom stall with Cantabile while the gangster defecates. Other characters also intimidate and manipulate him, including his ex-wife Denise, his girlfriend Renata, and his older brother Julius. Charlie's passivity and impracticality can finally be considered self-destructive. He is so preoccupied with pondering the mystical anthroposophy of Rudolf Steiner and the possibility of life after death that at times he is unable to deal effectively with problems in the everyday world.[1]

How can one make sense of Charlie's otherworldly inclinations and his self-destructive passivity? The most profitable answer is to employ psychology. As Daniel Fuchs and Andrew M. Gordon have shown, Bellow knew psychology well and was sometimes treated by psychotherapists, including Chester Raphael, a follower of Wilhelm Reich; Paul Meehl, a clinical psychologist; Albert Ellis, a sexologist and a pioneer in cognitive behavior therapy; and Heinz Kohut, founder of "self-psychology" (Atlas 162-166; 263- 265; 295-296; 384-386). Early unpublished drafts of his novel *Herzog* mention Freud's "Mourning and Melancholia," and the eponymous hero writes an imaginary letter to Dr. Freud disputing that essay's argument (Fuchs 45). Wilhelm Reich's ideas about masochistic personalities influenced Bellow's portrayal of the protagonist of *Seize the Day*, an early draft of which specifically mentioned Reich's concept of character-armoring (Chavkin, "Suffering"133-137).

Throughout Bellow's canon, one finds not only psychological terms and language but also contemptuous remarks about psychoanalysis, which some might regard as defensive. In any case, his many years of reading Freud, Jung, Reich, and other psychological theorists and his personal involvement with various psychotherapists affected his thinking. His characters are often very neurotic and occasionally psychotic. Various Bellow characters, such as Tommy Wilhelm, Moses Herzog, Charlie Citrine, Demmie Vonghel, Von Humboldt Fleisher, Clara Velde, Ithiel "Teddy" Regler, and Bummidge, are treated by psychotherapists, who are sometimes portrayed comically. Bellow eventually rejected some aspects of psychoanalytic thought while accepting others. While he was ambivalent about psychoanalysis and disavowed aspects of it on occasion (Boyers 19; Brans 142-143), it unquestionably influenced his outlook and novels. The particular psychological approach that we will use to demystify Charlie Citrine's character is one that many family therapists would use with their clients today—family systems theory in conjunction with some psychoanalytic concepts that are relevant to the particular case.

> "*I believe you got stuck in your childhood.*"
> (Rinaldo Cantabile speaking to Charlie Citrine, Humboldt's Gift 185)

Family Systems Theory

Although therapists frequently use family systems theory in real-life situations, literary critics rarely employ it.[2] This fact is unfortunate, for the theory is a helpful tool in understanding seemingly mysterious behavior. Various thinkers have contributed to family systems theory, but the American psychiatrist Murray

Bowen (1913–1990) is considered the pioneer of this approach.[3] He assumed that individuals cannot be properly understood in isolation but must be seen within the contexts of family and society. He argued that interactions of family members are not accidental but controlled by hidden structural patterns. The family, as an "emotional unit" or "emotional field," has a huge impact on individual family members. Michael Kerr and Bowen describe how this "emotional field" influences behavior:

> The emotionally determined functioning of the family members generates a family emotional "atmosphere" or "field" that, in turn, influences the emotional functioning of each person. It is analogous to the gravitational field of the solar system, where each planet and the sun, by virtue of their mass, contribute gravity to the field and are, in turn, regulated by the field they each help create. One cannot "see" gravity, nor can one "see" the emotional field. The presence of gravity and the emotional field can be inferred, however, by the predictable ways planets and people behave in reaction to one another. (55)

Interactions of family members produce predictable behavior patterns that underpin the family system. The behavior of one family member reverberates throughout the family and causes a range of responses. Repeated interactions result in "patterns of how, when, and to whom to relate" (Sauber, L'Abate, Weeks, and Buchanan 65). As Peter Titleman explains, "the *family system* includes *the interlocking, reciprocal functioning in the relationship system*: change in one person . . . or one segment . . . brings about compensatory change in other(s) or other parts" (Titelman, "Concept of Differentiation" 22).

Bowen describes eight essential concepts of his theory, but the ones most relevant for understanding Charlie Citrine are differentiation of self, sibling position, emotional cutoff, and triangles. Differentiation of self, the cornerstone of Bowen's theory, is particularly useful in this case. "Differentiation of self" involves a person's ability "to distinguish between the subjective feeling process and the more objective intellectual (thinking) process" (Gibson and Donigian 28). It also involves the individual's ability to avoid emotional fusion with the family and instead "differentiate" himself from his family even while remaining in the family's emotional field. Those with low levels of differentiation are unable to separate from the family, and, particularly at times of tension, they often emotionally fuse with the family or behave in other dysfunctional ways in order to try to cope with anxiety. When individuals fail to differentiate from their families, "people are dominated by their automatic emotional system" (Sauber, L'Abate, Weeks, and Buchanan 101). When emotional fusion occurs, family members have "less flexibility, less adaptability, and are more emotionally dependent on those around them" (Sauber, L'Abate, Weeks, and Buchanan 101). Other dysfunctions include employing emotional cutoff and becoming part of a triangle.

When Bowen mentions "fusion," he means feeling completely engulfing thinking. Individuals become so emotionally reactive that boundaries between people collapse, as in symbiotic relationships (Prochaska and Norcross 374). Fusion often occurs when individuals depend excessively on approval from other family members. Such families involve a huge pressure toward groupthink or "emotional oneness" (Titelman, "Emotional Cutoff" 21). Lacking independent thought and desiring to conform, individuals with low levels of differentiation fuse with the family and accept dysfunctional activities as normal and appropriate.

Family Systems Theory and *Humboldt's Gift*

The family system enormously affects each member of Charlie's family, which resembles Bellow's own family (Atlas 12, 15-16, 427-437; Leader 72-77, 109-11, 597-598). While Charlie does not extensively recount his childhood and adolescence, he does say enough to allow us to reveal how his family system helped shape his personality. Charlie's family consists of his parents and an older brother Julius (the favorite of his mother, who doted on him, according to Julius). This Jewish family emigrated from Kiev, eventually residing in Polish Chicago. The father, a gentleman in the Old Country, had to take menial jobs in the US. Having become a low-status "immigrant desperate battler" (Bellow, *Humboldt's* 65), he is often angered by trivial matters. For example, once he rages at Julius for dunking his bread in cocoa. This example might suggest defensive displacement: the father's anger at his own demeaning situation is displaced onto an innocent but convenient target.

Like his father, Julius is also angry. Growing up in their dysfunctional household, he bullied young Charlie, who nevertheless adored him. Young Julius's irate temperament led to constant fistfights. His adult personality did not change. Once, he shot at a car turning around in his driveway and was subsequently sued (Bellow, *Humboldt's* 355). Julius's domineering and hostile character can partly be attributed to what Anna Freud called identification with the aggressor, in which a victim eventually resembles his abuser (109-121). Julius's harsh father emotionally abused him, and Julius acts toward others as his father treated him. Bowen uses the term "multigenerational transmission process" to describe the reoccurrence in successive generations of the same family relationship patterns associated with emotional dysfunction. In this case, older, powerful family members emotionally abuse younger, vulnerable family members (O'Toole 1172).

Unlike her first-born son Julius, the mother was kind and doting; she died when Charlie was young, and he regards her as "a sacred person" (Bellow, *Humboldt's* 348). Her death was one of two traumas from his youth that transformed his character. The other was an illness that caused a lengthy separation from his family. He spent his eighth year in a TB sanitorium, where he became keenly aware of his mortality. "Kids hemorrhaged in the night and choked on blood and were dead. In the morning the white geometry of made-up beds had to be coped with" (65). In the sanatorium, "my disease of the lungs passed over into an emotional disorder," says the adult Charlie to his daughter (65). He thus became a Hallelujah and Glory type and came to adore his family. "Oh, I loved them all terribly, abnormally. I was all torn up with love. Deep in the heart. I used to cry in the sanatorium because I might never make it home and see them" (74). Charlie's literal fever thus metamorphoses into a love fever, and he becomes "a passionate, morbid little boy" (74). In family systems terminology, he emotionally fused with his family: he was able to perceive them only through the distorted lens of abnormal emotion. Later, when his mother died, he began his search for a woman to replace this "sacred" woman, though he was not conscious of the reasons for his behavior (348). This quest became a perpetual activity, for attaining this goal was impossible; no woman could replace his mother.

Charlie, without knowing so, suffers from a low level of differentiation and has fused with his family. He romanticizes all aspects of his growing up. He views anything connected with those years through a sentimental lens. Unlike Julius, who says that he has "no memory except for business transactions" and insists that he cannot remember his mother at all, Charlie can recall the most minute details of anything associated with his family, relishing them, though at one point he does acknowledge that such a preoccupation might be abnormal: some "clinical experts . . . think that such completeness of memory is a hysterical symptom" (Bellow, *Humboldt's* 386). When Charlie accidentally encounters his old high school girlfriend Naomi Lutz, his reaction is typical: excessively emotional, sentimental, and inappropriate. He proclaims: "If I had been able to hold you in my arms nightly since the age of fifteen I would never have feared the grave" (213). Naomi flatly rejects this hyperbolic assertion—"Oh Charlie, tell it to the Marines" (213).

The disconnect between Charlie's sentimental recollections and reality becomes even clearer when one compares his assertions of his love for Julius with some disturbing details that call the assertions into question. Some family system theorists, including Bowen, argue that birth order helps explain relationships among siblings. In this case, Julius does possess many of the reputed traits of the domineering older brother, while Charlie possesses many standard negative traits of a younger brother. When Charlie asserts that he adores Julius, he seems blind to any negative aspects of his family and sees only his brother's positive aspects. To do otherwise would subvert his idealized view of his family and his youth. During the course of the novel, however, the wealthy Julius clearly seems a narcissistic bully who badly mistreats his brother and others. Autocratic and rapacious, he is grandiose and lacks empathy. His narcissism disguises a profound emptiness (Holmes 136). Julius'ss essential hollowness is suggested when he asks Charlie to buy him a seascape painting devoid of any life. Unlike Charlie, Julius rejects family bonds. He apparently thinks brotherly love would make him vulnerable to exploitation. Julius copes with his excessively emotional brother, who is a source of anxiety for him, by engaging in what Bowen calls "emotional cutoff." This is a way of coping with unresolved fusion with one's family by distancing or cutting oneself off emotionally from the source of anxiety (Titelman, "Emotional Cutoff" 19-23). While Charlie's feelings for Julius are "vivid, almost hysterically intense" (Bellow, *Humboldt's* 244), the hardboiled Julius condescendingly regards Charlie as "some sort of idiot" (245).

When Charlie hears that Julius faces risky heart surgery, he postpones a European trip, and Renata leaves without him. This decision has fatal consequences for his relationship with Renata: once in Europe, she dumps Charlie for his romantic rival, Flonzaley. The self-centered Julius would not care about this turn of events if he knew about them. Julius is the kind of person who "needed to be wronged," and he puts his younger brother in what family systems theorists call a double bind: any decision Charlie makes will fail to satisfy his difficult brother (Shahrokh, Hales, Phillips, and Yudofsky 87). On one hand, Julius implies that he might resent his brother coming to see him before his open-heart surgery because Charlie will be a "death-pest" fluttering about him with his disturbing excessive affection just when Julius needs calm and level-headedness (Bellow, *Humboldt's* 389). On the other hand, at the same time, Julius also suggests that he will resent Charlie if Charlie does not abide by his brotherly obligation and visit him before his surgery.

Faced with this no-win situation, Charlie visits his unappreciative brother, who relates to him as he always has: by excessively criticizing him. Julius calls Charlie "dumb," an "overeducated boob," and a "poor nut" (Bellow, *Humboldt's* 384). He ridicules Charlie's accomplishments ("I can't read the crap you write. Two sentences and I'm yawning" [384]), and his wife ("then you up and marry this fierce broad. She'd fit in with the

Symbionese or the Palestine Liberation terrorists" [384]). He also mocks the spiritual preoccupations so important to Charlie: "You were born trying to prove that life on this earth was not feasible. Okay, your case is practically complete" (384). Julius'ss overbearing personality and need to control his younger brother are epitomized by a command he gives when they see each other for the last time before the surgery. If he should die, says Julius, Charlie must marry his widow, Hortense. Charlie does not really dispute this astonishing order but only asks, "Have you discussed this with Hortense?" Julius explains that he has written this command, which he says Hortense will follow, in a letter to be read if he should "die on the table" (398). Charlie does not reply.

Charlie reveals that his decision to postpone his European trip results not only from brotherly love and a sense of family obligation, for he "had come to get something from Ulick [Julius]—I was revisiting the conditions of childhood under which my heart had been inspired" (Bellow, *Humboldt's* 396). Fixated on his family, Charlie regards his youth as a golden age. He fetishizes his brother, who represents for Charlie "the sustaining time" of their childhood. Julius is linked in Charlie's eyes with the "sweet dream-time of goodness" that he associates with his family (396). Renata does not understand this sentimental emotion; she is puzzled by Charlie's attitude toward his brother. "The more he puts you down," she says, "the more you worship the ground" he walks on (355).

Julius's behavior toward Charlie is motivated not only by a desire to dominate and manipulate but also by jealousy prompted by the fame Charlie has won from his Pulitzer-Prize-winning book. Julius is closely modeled on Bellow's older brother Maurice, who envied his younger brother's success. In a letter to Susan Glassman Bellow, the author describes a meeting with Maurice, who said that except for a few chapters of *The Adventures of Augie March* he could not read the "nonsense" Bellow had written and could not understand how he could be "published profitably" (Bellow, *Letters*, 230). Bellow responded mildly, saying that since Maurice had devoted his efforts "to business and love," he was not a "trained reader." Maurice was deeply offended by this reply and claimed that Saul was terrible and lacked respect for his older brother. To defuse the tense situation, Bellow embraced Maurice and said he was Maurice's "loving brother" (230). In this situation and in the novel, the older brother's behavior can be explained by the unconscious process of "projective identification" (Kellerman 191-192; Blackman 20-21). The older brother disavows aspects of his own self and then projects them onto the younger brother, whose defensive response after being attacked is interpreted as hostile and confirms the older brother's assumption that he is a victim of his younger brother's hostility.

At one point, Charlie mentions his "lifelong trouble—the longing, the swelling heart, the tearing eagerness of the deserted, the painful keenness or infinitizing of an unidentified need," which provides an important clue to understanding his character (Bellow, *Humboldt's* 414). Charlie realizes that he does suffer from this "lifelong trouble" but does not recognize its origin. The death of Charlie's mother was one of the two traumatic childhood events that profoundly shaped his personality. While Julius insists that he cannot remember their mother at all, Charlie confesses that "she had come," to him, "to be a sacred person" (348). Naomi Lutz expresses surprise at "a big important clever man going around so eager from woman to woman," and she asks Charlie, "Haven't you got anything more important to do?" (303). What both Naomi and Charlie do not understand is that Charlie's going from woman to woman results from his unconscious desire to find the ideal woman to replace his mother. Charlie felt deserted when she died, and it is significant that the normally nonviolent Charlie becomes violent when a girlfriend either deserts him or he feels threatened by that possibility. In high school, when Naomi Lutz attends a dance with a basketball player, the excessively emotional Charlie physically abuses her. The middle-aged Naomi reminds him how he acted: "you almost choked me to death" (298). When another woman, Renata, actually does desert Charlie to marry Flonzaley, the normally mild-mannered Charlie responds with imagined violence. He fantasizes her brutal death by picturing her being hit by a truck: "her chest was crushed, her face was destroyed, her lungs were punctured. She died in agony" (426). He adds that leukemia would be too good for her, instead preferring the gory violence involving the truck.

Charlie's passivity, his humor, his cheerfulness, his sentimentality, and his otherworldliness mask his real character: he is a "depressive" full of anxiety and guilt and is searching for the woman who will rescue him from his profound sense of loss (Bellow, *Humboldt's* 164).[4] Because Charlie's mother died when he was growing up, as Bellow's mother also did, the excessive overvaluation of a mother that a child loses as he gains a more realistic perception as he matures did not occur. Instead, Charlie's mother remains for Charlie an ideal woman. His psychological development has been stunted, and unconsciously, he seeks a woman who can replace his sacred mother. Because of the incest taboo, however, he also unconsciously seeks a woman who does not too closely resemble his mother. That is, he seeks a highly sexualized woman. He regards women as either idealized maternal figures or sluts. Invariably, when Charlie describes women, he focuses on their sexuality. At one point he explicitly describes the responses of Renata, Doris Scheldt, and Demmie Vonghel at the moment of orgasm. His relationship with Demmie Vonghel seemed much more than merely sexual, so it is odd that he should remember the deceased woman this way:

> As soon as I began to think of Demmie Vonghel . . . . I received violent impressions. I always saw her handsome and naked as she had been and looking as she had looked during her climaxes. They had always been convulsive, a series of them, and she used to go violently red in the face. There always was a trace of crime in the way that Demmie did the thing and there had always been a trace of the accessory in me, wickedly collaborating. (Bellow, *Humboldt's* 440)

At one point, his remarks about his own young daughter suggest that he sees females primarily in sexual terms: "Mary is sure to be an intelligent woman. . . . My heart is often troubled for Mary . . . . She will be a straight-nosed thin broad . . . . And personally I prefer plump women with fine breasts. So I felt sorry for her already" (Bellow, *Humboldt's* 73).

Charlie's preoccupation with voluptuous women results from his mother fixation. Because of the incest taboo, he cannot express sexual feelings for a woman who resembles his mother too closely, and therefore, he is only attracted to women who least resemble her. Thus he feels an unconscious compulsion to degrade women sexually, making them more profane so that they resemble his sacred mother even less. In her letter defending her decision to desert Charlie and marry Flonzaley, Renata remarks that Charlie did not consider her suitable for marriage but thought of her only as his whore, whom he needed to degrade: "The role you got me into was the palooka role. I was your marvelous sex-clown. You had me cooking dinner in a top hat and my behind bare" (Bellow, *Humboldt's* 429). She goes on to say, "You wouldn't remember that I was the mother of a boy. You showed me off in London as your spectacular lay from Chicago" (429). She reveals that she felt degraded, and she complains that others (because of how Charlie has treated her) saw her as a slut—even the Chancellor of the Exchequer gave her a "private feel" (429).

Charlie's unconscious search for a woman who can replace his lost, sacred mother is a lifelong quest for an unattainable goal. His various relationships with women are fraught with anxiety and conflict. Charlie's search "for salvation in female form" invariably ends in failure (Bellow, *Humboldt's* 203). The pattern of this failure can be understood with the help of Bowen's theory of triangles. Although triangles operate in diverse and complicated ways, some of which are positive, triangles can create problems and undermine relationships, especially with people with low levels of differentiation. Bowen argues that when there is tension between two people in a relationship, it is common for a third person to be triangled in to relieve the tension (Titelman, "Concept of the Triangle" 19-20). Prochaska and Norcross explain that when a triangle arises, one person is on the outside and two people are on the inside of the triangle, and there is intense maneuvering for the favored inside positions (374). Such maneuvering increases conflict and anxiety and undermines relationships. When anxiety in a triangle cannot be adequately contained, a fourth person is brought in, creating what Bowen calls an interlocking triangle, which can further complicate the situation and destabilize relationships. The emotion-driven relationship dynamics of triangles and interlocking triangles "occur automatically, and for the most part, outside of the awareness of the members of the relationship system" (Moran 509).

Tension develops between Charlie and Renata because Charlie resists Renata's pressure to marry her. This resistance results in an interlocking triangle that began a year before the novel's present action. To increase pressure on Charlie, Renata abandoned him for an affair with the wealthy Flonzaley. Charlie was devastated by this affair and began his own affair with Doris Scheldt. Eventually, Charlie and Renata left these two lovers and became a couple again, though the original problem causing the tension between them is still present. So is the possibility that one or both of them will return to other lovers. To ease the tension between himself and Renata, Charlie unconsciously triangles in others, such as Cantabile, who otherwise would seem an unlikely character for Charlie to be involved with for almost any reason. Ultimately, Charlie's "triangling in" of others does not save his relationship with Renata: at the end of the novel, he has resigned himself that he has lost her to Flonzaley.

Humboldt's Gift is a long, complex novel with many dimensions. Our essay is not meant to be comprehensive but only to explore a neglected aspect of this book. To properly understand Charlie's behavior, one should see him as a person who has been shaped by a family system that includes a kind mother, an angry father, and a domineering older brother. Raised in this dysfunctional family, he becomes a perplexing, contradictory person with a low level of differentiation. He is outwardly cheerful but inwardly depressive, a Pulitzer-Prize-winning author whose passivity and otherworldliness seem out of character for a celebrity. Separation from his family because of an extended hospitalization in a TB sanatorium at age eight and the death of his beloved mother when he was an adolescent are the two most important factors that help explain his emotional fusion with his family and his getting "stuck" psychologically in childhood. Relying on various defense mechanisms, especially splitting and idealization, he views his childhood and his family through rose-tinted lenses. He searches for an ideal woman to replace his sacred mother and to recapture the fantasized paradise of his childhood. His hopeless quest for salvation in female form follows predictable patterns that involve triangles and interlocking triangles. Although he ultimately asserts that he will live differently and focus on spiritual matters, he never indicates that he understands the family dynamics that have shaped his character. One suspects that his interpersonal relationships, especially with women, will continue to follow past dysfunctional patterns of which he is unaware.

Notes

1. Smith and McSweeney see *Humboldt's Gift* as a radical departure from Bellow's previous fiction because of the protagonist's fascination with the transcendentalism of Rudolf Steiner, which they see as the key to the novel. Cohen and Siegel see an ambivalence toward Steiner's mysticism in the novel, while other critics note a skepticism, comic self-ridicule, and English romantic sensibility not only in *Humboldt's Gift* but also throughout Bellow's work (see Chavkin, Sandy, and Yetman). In an interview with Joseph Epstein, Bellow observed that he was "intrigued with Steiner's ideas" but was not "a Steinerian." He also observed: "I think people were confused by seeing Rudolf Steiner's work pop up in a novel a good part of which was comic in intent" (93).
2. For examples of literary critics who use family systems theory, see Chavkin and Chavkin and Knapp and Womack.
3. This section is a condensed version of an overview of family systems theory that is the first section of the chapter in Chavkin and Chavkin, pp. 19-25.
4. In an interview with Steers, Bellow remarks: "Well, I am a melancholic . . . a depressive temperament" (37).

Works Cited

Atlas, James. *Bellow: A Biography*. Random House, 2000.

Bellow, Saul. *Humboldt's Gift*. Viking, 1975.

———. *Letters*, edited by Benjamin Taylor, Viking, 2010.

Blackman, Jerome S. *101 Defenses: How the Mind Shields Itself*. Brunner-Routledge, 2004.

Boyers, Robert T. "Literature and Culture: An Interview with Saul Bellow." *Salmagundi*, vol. 30, 1975, pp. 6-23.

Brans, Jo. "Common Needs, Common Preoccupations: An Interview with Saul Bellow." *Conversations with Saul Bellow*, edited by Gloria L. Cronin and Ben Siegel, UP of Mississippi, 1994, pp. 140-160.

Chavkin, Allan. "*Humboldt's Gift* and the Romantic Imagination." *Philological Quarterly*, vol. 62, no. 1, 1983, pp. 1-19.

———. "Suffering and Wilhelm Reich's Theory of Character-Armoring in Saul Bellow's *Seize the Day*." *Essays in Literature*, vol. 9, no. 1, 1982, pp. 133-137.

Chavkin, Allan, and Nancy Feyl Chavkin. "A Bowen Family Systems Reading of *Tracks*." *Louise Erdrich: Tracks, The Last Report on the Miracles at Little No Horse, The Plague of Doves*, edited by Debra L. Madsen, Continuum, 2011, pp. 19-33.

Cohen, Sarah Blacher. "Comedy and Guilt in *Humboldt's Gift*." *Modern Fiction Studies*, vol. 25, no. 1, 1979, pp. 47-58.

Epstein, Joseph. "A Talk with Saul Bellow." *New York Times Book Review*, 5 Dec. 1976, pp. 92-93. Rpt. in *Conversations with Saul Bellow*, edited by Gloria L. Cronin and Ben Siegel, UP of Mississippi, 1994, pp. 132-139.

Freud, Anna. *The Ego and the Mechanisms of Defense. The Writings of Anna Freud*. Rev. ed., vol. 2, International UP, 1974, pp. 109-121.

Fuchs, Daniel. "Bellow and Freud." *Saul Bellow in the 1980s*, edited by Gloria L. Cronin and L. H. Goldman, Michigan State UP, 1989, pp. 27-50.

Gibson, Joan M., and Jeremiah Donigian. "Use of Bowen Theory." *Journal of Addictions & Offender Counseling*, vol. 14, no. 1, Oct. 1993, pp. 25-35.

Gordon, Andrew M. "Psychology and the Fiction of Saul Bellow." *Critical Insights: Saul Bellow*, edited by Allan Chavkin, Salem P, 2012, pp. 33-52.

Holmes, Jeremy. *The Therapeutic Imagination: Using Literature to Deepen Psychodynamic Understanding and Enhance Empathy*. Routledge, 2014.

Kellerman, Henry. *Dictionary of Psychopathology*. Columbia UP, 2009.

Kerr, Michael E., and Murray Bowen. *Family Evaluation: An Approach Based on Bowen Theory*. Norton, 1988.

Knapp, John V., and Kenneth Womack. *Reading the Family Dance: Family Systems Therapy and Literary Study*. U of Delaware P, 2003.

Leader, Zachary. *The Life of Saul Bellow: To Fame and Fortune, 1915–1964*. Knopf, 2015.

McSweeney, Kerry. "Saul Bellow and the Life to Come." *Critical Quarterly*, vol. 18, no. 1, 1976, pp. 67-72.

Moran, Carol. "Societal Emotional Process and Interlocking Triangles." *Triangles: Bowen Family Systems Theory Perspectives*, edited by Peter Titelman, Haworth, 2008, pp. 503-521.

O'Toole, Marie T. *Mosby's Medical Dictionary*. 9th ed., Mosby/Elsevier, 2013.

Prochaska, James O., and John C. Norcross. *Systems of Psychotherapy: A Transtheoretical Analysis*. 6th ed., Thomson Brooks/Cole, 2007.

Sandy, Mark. "Webbed with Golden Lines: Saul Bellow's Romanticism." *Romanticism: The Journal of Romantic Culture and Criticism*, vol. 14, no. 1, 2008, pp. 57-67.

Sauber, S. Richard, Luciano L'Abate, Gerald R. Weeks, and William L. Buchanan. *The Dictionary of Family Psychology and Family Therapy*. 2nd ed., Sage Publications, 1993.

Shahrokh, Narriman C., Robert E. Hales, Katherine A. Phillips, and Stuart C. Yudofsky. *The Language of Mental Health: A Glossary of Psychiatric Terms*. American Psychiatric Publishing, 2011.

Siegel, Ben. "Artists and Opportunists in Saul Bellow's *Humboldt's Gift*." *Contemporary Literature*, vol. 19, no. 2, 1978, pp.143-164.

Smith, Herbert J. "*Humboldt's Gift* and Rudolf Steiner." *Centennial Review*, vol. 22, no. 4, 1978, pp. 479-489.

Steers, Nina. "'Successor' to Faulkner?" *Show*, vol. 4, Sept. 1964, pp. 36-38. Rpt. in *Conversations with Saul Bellow*, edited by Gloria L. Cronin and Ben Siegel, UP of Mississippi, 1994, pp. 28-36.

Titelman, Peter. "The Concept of Differentiation of Self in Bowen Theory." *Differentiation of Self: Bowen Family Systems Theory Perspectives*, edited by Peter Titelman, Routledge, 2014, pp. 3-64.

———. "The Concept of the Triangle in Bowen Theory: An Overview." *Triangles: Bowen Family Systems Theory Perspectives*, edited by Peter Titelman, Haworth, 2008, pp. 3-61.

———. "Emotional Cutoff in Bowen Family Systems Theory: An Overview." *Emotional Cutoff: Bowen Family Systems Theory Perspectives*, edited by Peter Titelman, Haworth, 2003, pp. 9-66.

Yetman, Michael G. "Who Would Not Sing for Humboldt?" *ELH*, vol. 48, no. 4, 1981, pp. 935-951.

Freud and Poe: A Dialogue

James S. Baumlin and Tita French Baumlin

[**Editor's Note:** In the following unconventional "dialogue," James S. Baumlin and Tita French Baumlin adopt two contrasting views of Freudian approaches to the short fiction of Edgar Allan Poe. In the first half of the piece, James S. Baumlin examines both Poe's works and life from explicitly psychoanalytic points of view. He surveys various ways in which psychologists have interpreted Freud's works and also the ways psychological critics have related the works to the author's biography. In the course of his survey, he suggests that Freudian critics can tell us a good deal about both the mind of the writer and the kinds of writing he produced. Tita French Baumlin, on the other hand, raises skeptical questions about the value of Freudian approaches to Poe. After providing an overview of the ways Freudians have diagnosed Poe as suffering from any number of possible mental illnesses, she raises the interesting possibility that many of his odd, strange, seemingly perverse stories may have been elaborate jokes—clever parodies that reveal both a fundamentally sane intelligence and a real sense of humor. The Baumlins wish to thank a number of students who contributed to the research underlying this exchange, including Erin Boschen, Alex Conner, Jessie Curtis, Abigale Fridley, Adam Suraud, and Joe Welch. —R.C.E.]

Reading Poe: Psychological Perspectives

Edgar Allan Poe's essay "The Philosophy of Composition" tells us as much about Poe's psychology as it does his method of composing. The essay shows that he was committed to art-for-art's-sake, an aesthetic that clashed with the moralizing tendencies of his age. For Poe, "beauty is the sole legitimate province of poetry" ("Philosophy" 678). Fair enough. But his definition of beauty turns maudlin, since the "tone" of "beauty's manifestation . . . is one of sadness . . . which excites the sensitive soul to tears" (678). And Poe goes further, hinting at the macabre: since the "most melancholy of topics" is also the "most poetical," then *"the death . . . of a beautiful woman is, unquestionably, the most poetical topic in the world"* ("Philosophy"

680; emphasis added). Needless to say, Sigmund Freud (1856–1939) would have a field day with this assertion. It's hard not to read this claim against the backdrop of Poe's own life, which was marked by the loss (by abandonment) of his father, the early loss (through death) of his mother, and the losses (through death) of his foster mother; the love of his youth; and of his beautiful, young, sickly wife.

That death, in January 1847, sent Poe into a paralyzing depression that stifled his creativity. In a letter dated January 4, 1848, Poe admitted the maddening effects of living in constant fear (and expectation) of his wife's passing. Surely her impending death hung like a pallor over his writings. And if the fear led to an "insanity" (which he sought to medicate with alcohol), the inevitable reality of her passing led to an unbroken "melancholy" or depression.

In "Mourning and Melancholia" (1917), Freud himself observes that "the obsessional character of melancholia . . . caus[es] the mourner *to assume blame for the loss of the loved one*, as if he or she 'desired it'" (132; emphasis added). J. Gerald Kennedy elaborates:

> Melancholia exaggerates the ambivalence inherent in love relationships, evoking a hatred or hostility toward the lost loved one that is invariably projected upon the self through its "narcissistic identification" with the love object. In this way, Freud observes, "the sufferers [of melancholia] usually succeed in the end in taking revenge, by the circuitous path of self-punishment . . . having developed the latter so as to avoid the necessity of openly expressing their hostility against the loved ones" [Freud, "Mourning" 132-33]. . . . Clearly, Poe's recurrent experience of orphanhood—of losing, again and again, his maternal nurturers and paternal protectors—deepened his melancholia, shattered his sense of self-worth, and intensified his need to inflict self-torment. (Kennedy, "Violence" 543-44)

If Kennedy is right, then Poe's later years seem to alternate between narcissism and a masochistic "self-torment." Freudian psychology treats madness as a self-inflicted punishment over the violation of some taboo. (If we approach Poe's dreamscapes through Freudian terms, we can say that "evil punished" is their *manifest content*, while "evil or taboo unleashed" describes their *latent content.*) For Freud, the wounded psyche is a *guilty* psyche above all, one that cannot accept or admit its own fears and desires; at the same time, the wounded psyche cannot will its desires away or banish its fears entirely to the unconscious.

The relatively healthy psyche, in contrast, is capable of repression: one might hold murder in one's heart, but the forbidden desire is *hidden*, nonetheless, within deep recesses of the unconscious. Not so for Poe's literary psychopaths, whose obsessions overwhelm the ego-consciousness; and, in the dire moment when the individual bites the apple, giving in to sin, the psyche plays its own judge and jury, punishing itself for the very acts which it feels compelled to perform.

From a Freudian perspective, the madness of Freud's psychopaths *is their punishment*. In "The Tell-Tale Heart," the murderous narrator does not need policemen to bring him to justice: the deafening heartbeat—product of his own guilty imaginings—becomes itself an agent of justice. As Freud writes in *The Ego and the Id* (1923), "Criminals do not feel guilt because they are already criminals, *but they become criminals because they already feel guilt*" (393-94; emphasis added): such is the strange logic of criminal pathology (Yang 597), which Poe's murderers put to the test.

In a work like "The Tell-Tale Heart," there's also a "psychic merging of killer and killed" (Robinson 97), as E. Arthur Robinson observes:

> The loud yell of the murderer is echoed in the old man's shriek, which the narrator, as though with increasing clairvoyance, later tells the police was his own. Most of all the identity is implied in the key psychological occurrence in the story—the madman's mistaking his own heartbeat for that of his victim, both before and after the murder. (97)

And what about the title character of "William Wilson"? Does he kill his doppelgänger or himself? In a more than symbolic sense, Poe's murderers *murder themselves*—psychologically at first, and then physically through the death sentence that typically follows.

The above ideas describe one half of Poe's dark romanticism, wherein a man falls prey to madness, becoming maniacally murderous. The other half of Poe's romanticism depicts a man lost in dreamscapes of sorrow, incapable of moving past the memory of lost love. The interpretation is again Freudian in that the psyche is wounded here, too, though not by taboo; instead, its wounding comes from the force of *unfulfilled desire*. Poe's psychopathic murderers *take* what cannot be theirs—typically, another man's life—and fall ever deeper into madness. Poe's melancholy dreamers *lose* what cannot be theirs—in each case, a woman's love—and they, too, fall ever deeper into despair and madness. When Poe's plot lines vary from these two basic scripts, the wounded psyche remains engaged: the narrator of "The Pit and the Pendulum" (1842), for example, suffers innocently at the hands of tyrannical authority. It's as if the narrator acts *as victim* of a Poe-esque psychopath. For love *must* be lost, guilt *must* be punished, and the lone individual *will suffer* in his isolation from humanity: such is the triple equation of the wounded psyche, as recorded in Poe's art.

Freudian approaches to Poe can perhaps raise as many questions as they answer. There's no doubt that Poe, in the words of Joseph J. Moldenhauer, "anticipat[es] . . . modern psychology in his dramatization of irrational drives" (831). Still, Moldenhauer puts the issue succinctly: shall we read "The Tell-Tale Heart" (among other gothic tales) "as a study of the deranged mind," or "as a controlled exercise in madness" (Moldenhauer 839)? Which is it, indeed? For Richard Wilbur, "Poe's esthetic, Poe's theory of the nature of art, seems . . . insane" (823). It's one thing to say that "Poe's tales are always concrete representations of states of mind" (Wilbur 811); it's another thing altogether to declare that the mind thus represented is Poe's—and that the pathologies of his characters are symptomatic of Poe's own wounded psyche. But that's precisely what Wilbur declares: "The typical Poe story occurs *within* the mind of the poet; and its characters are not independent personalities, but . . . figures representing the warring principles of the poet's divided nature" (821).

Within the Freudian vocabulary, Poe's art reflects the psychic processes of *sublimation*: rather than act out his neuroses in the "real world," the artist transforms (that is, sublimates) forbidden id-urges into the "dream worlds" of fiction—thus *allowing his protagonists* to act out what the ego-consciousness rejects as taboo. Freud himself had read and appreciated Poe. In his preface to Marie Bonaparte's *Life and Works of Edgar Allan Poe* (1933), the founder of psychoanalysis names Poe a "great writer of a pathological type," someone who studied "the laws of the human mind as exemplified in outstanding individuals" (qtd. in Yang 598). Clearly, Freud pays Poe a compliment in declaring him a fellow student "of the human mind" and its "laws." Had Poe in fact "influenced the way in which Freud depicted the id" (598), as Amy Yang suggests?

What strikes us is that Freud's description of the id invokes qualities of the Byronic hero. In his *New Introductory Lectures on Psychoanalysis* (1933), Freud describes the id as that "dark, inaccessible part of our personality" (91); being inaccessible to ego-consciousness, "what little we know of it we have learned from our study of . . . dreamwork and of the construction of neurotic symptoms" (91). It is "a chaos, a cauldron full of seething excitations" (91) that "knows no judgments of value: no good and evil, no morality" (Freud 93; Yang 598). Are these not themes of dark romanticism? In his gothic fiction, was Poe not a precursor to Freud? And don't we know the psyche—particularly in its penchant for good and evil—a little better now, because of Poe?

Poe's Last Laugh

The many and varied ways that psychoanalytic critics throughout the twentieth century tended to read Poe's tales as "coded autobiography" yielded a lengthy rap sheet, and the proposed mental disorders ranged from the neurotic to the full-blown psychotic in as colorful an array as perhaps only a madman, with his eye in a fine frenzied rolling, could imagine. There's Poe the manic-depressive (Moldenhauer 830) and Poe the sado-masochist (Pruette 382; Praz 380). There's the "sexually inhibited" Poe (Praz 377) and the necrophiliac Poe (Bonaparte 1.691; qtd. in Praz 377). And, of course, caught up in rivalries with his adoptive father (Kennedy) and fixated upon his foster mother (Krutch), there's the Oedipal Poe. As Mario Praz points out,

> One does not need to be a follower of psychoanalysis to admit that the sight of his consumptive mother dying through the bursting of a blood vessel when Poe was hardly three years old must have left an indelible trace in the child, which he was later to transpose to the figures of Berenice, Morella, Eleonora and Ligeia. (377)

Some critics have viewed Poe as a narcissist:

> His nature demanded the adoration and approval of "woman," . . . and he worshiped in his poems a feminine idealization to which he ascribed various names. These women are never human; . . . they are simply beautiful lay figures around which to hang wreaths of poetical sentiments. His emotional interest lay in himself, rather than in outer objects; he wished to be loved, rather than to love. (Pruette 379-80)

And then there's the Adlerian Poe (Pruette 379-80), whose "inferiority complex" led him to pick fights with pretty much every (male) literary rival. Poor man.

There seems something unsettled about this mental portrait that so many critics and biographers try to build with the puzzle-pieces of Poe's horrific stories. It's not *simply* that we can't know from our current vantage point what was going on inside Mr. Poe's ample cranium. There are other problems with what I'll call the "madman Poe" approach to his writings.

Consider, if you will, a short story called "Metzengerstein" (1832), Poe's first published piece of fiction. It begins with a narrator's discussion of metempsychosis (that's when a human soul transmigrates into animal bodies), though he refuses to give his own opinion on this ancient belief; instead, he offers a tale about two feuding families, both of the old Hungarian aristocracy, who loathe each other with a near-maniacal hatred. The Berlifitzing family and estate are destroyed in a fire rumored to have been started by the young and degenerate Count Metzengerstein, who then, inexplicably, finds an enormous and unruly stallion in his stable. (The ostlers say the horse appears to be the only survivor of the fire: it was the favorite of the elder Berlifitzing, who burned to death trying to save it.) The young count becomes obsessed with riding the vicious horse, and the tale ends with the monstrous steed breaking its reins, leaping the moat, and carrying its rider, the powerless count—from whom "a solitary shriek [had escaped] his lacerated lips, which were bitten through and through in the intensity of terror" (Poe, "Metzengerstein" 89)—up the stairs and into his own abode. As he disappears into the roaring flames of his now-burning castle, a white cloud of smoke forms overhead, in the shape of a horse's head.

Is this scary? Actually, the jury is still out on that. While some readers consider this story a straightforward tale of revenge (a theme to which Poe will return, time and again, throughout his career), others find it to be a perfect *parody* of the gothic tale, containing all the right elements—haunted castles, a terrible prophecy, madness, dark and mazelike corridors, unnatural and inexplicable events, gruesome sights, and so on: this story has them all, to the nth degree. It is by no means the best parody that Poe will ever write, but it is so thoroughly *over the top* that we cannot dismiss the possibility that it is, indeed, burlesque.

Thus the question: could the mad, the necrophiliac, the sadomasochistic, the Oedipal, the narcissistic, the maniacally jealous, the obsessively revengeful, the *psychotic* Mr. Poe have written such a finely-etched parody of the most popular form of literature at the time? If this story were the anomaly, of course the answer could be no, but actually it is not. Poe did, in fact, write more parodies and straightforwardly comic short stories, as well, some of them macabre in nature and some of them downright silly—and some, like "Metzengerstein," difficult to determine yet clearly intelligent enough, clever enough, to have come from an intellect fully in possession of its faculties.

A quick perusal of a few is convincing, I should think, though many of them, such as "Loss of Breath" (1832) and "The Man Who Was Used Up" (1839), are such intricate political satires that analyzing them fully would require a book in itself; instead, I'll skip to my favorite among his undeniably comic and parodic tales, "A Predicament" (1838), which is appended to another story, titled "How to Write a Blackwood Article" (1838). The introductory story rambles through all manner of subjects but, in effect, sets up "A Predicament" as the example of "a Blackwood Article" that has just been discussed in the "How to" section. Both parts are narrated by one "Signora Psyche Zenobia," who seems to be something of a socialite as well as an intellectual snob, racist, and "corresponding secretary to the *Philadelphia . . . Association, To, Civilise, Humanity*" (Poe, "How to" 321).

It's worth noting that Poe often lampooned *Blackwood's Edinburgh Magazine* for publishing the wildly popular and formulaic "sensation" tales that its readers loved despite their lack of literary merit—and the more lurid and gruesome these tales were, the better. In "How to Write a Blackwood Article," Mr. Blackwood himself describes to Signora Zenobia some of the magazine's most successful stories, like *The Involuntary Experimentalist*, "all about a gentleman who gets baked in an oven and comes out alive and well, although certainly done to a turn" (Poe, "How to" 323) and *The Man in the Bell*, about a fellow who falls asleep "under the clapper of a church bell, and is awakened by its tolling for a funeral. The sound drives him mad, and, accordingly, pulling out his tablets, he gives a record of his sensations" (323). He advises Signora Zenobia that if she ever finds herself drowning or being hanged, that would be a good time to write down her sensations, particularly since every page of that kind of stuff can bring her tons of money (323).

In "A Predicament," that's exactly what Signora Zenobia does: caught in a pickle, she puts that advice to work. Having climbed a tall cathedral steeple to get a better view of the bustling city of Edina, Signora Zenobia discovers only one tiny window through which to thrust her head to look out, though she later finds that this aperture is in the face of the clock in the tower. Engrossed in the scene below, she soon comes to a realization:

> I perceived, to my extreme horror, that the huge, glittering, scimitarlike minute-hand of the clock had, in the course of its hourly revolution, descended upon my neck. . . . There was no chance of forcing my head through the mouth of that terrible trap in which it was so fairly caught, and which grew narrower and narrower with a rapidity too horrible to be conceived. The agony of that moment is not to be imagined. . . . Down, down, down it came, closer, and yet closer. . . . Down and still down, it came. It had already buried its sharp edge a full inch in my flesh, and my sensations grew indistinct and confused. (Poe, "A Predicament" 332)

As the minute-hand of the clock continues to cut deeper into her neck, she describes the "exquisite pain," though she adds that she "could not help repeating those exquisite verses of the poet Miguel De Cervantes"—in her own mangled Spanish, of course (Poe, "A Predicament" 332-33). And then "a new horror presented itself, and one indeed sufficient to startle the strongest nerves":

> My eyes, from the cruel pressure of the machine, were absolutely starting from their sockets. While I was thinking how I should possibly manage without them, one actually tumbled out of my head, and, rolling down the steep side of the steeple, lodged in the rain gutter which ran along the eaves of the main building. The loss of the eye was not so much as the insolent air of independence and contempt with which it regarded me after it was out. There it lay in the gutter just under my nose, and the airs it gave itself would have been ridiculous had they not been disgusting. Such a winking and blinking were never before seen. This behaviour on the part of my eye in the gutter was not only irritating on account of its manifest insolence and shameful ingratitude, but was also exceedingly inconvenient on account of the sympathy which always exists between two eyes of the same head, however far apart. I was forced, in a manner, to wink and to blink, whether I would or not, in exact concert with the scoundrelly thing that lay just under my nose. I was presently relieved, however, by the dropping out of the other eye. In falling it took the same direction (possibly a concerted plot) as its fellow. Both rolled out of the gutter together, and in truth I was very glad to get rid of them. (Poe, "A Predicament" 333)

Of course, the huge minute-hand is still progressing in its sweep, and, "at twenty-five minutes past five in the afternoon precisely," it severs her head—a loss which, she says, she is not sorry about, since it "had occasioned me so much embarrassment" (Poe, "A Predicament" 333). First, it "rolled down the side of the steeple, then lodged, for a few seconds, in the gutter, and then made its way, with a plunge, into the middle of the street" (333). With great detail, she describes the sensations derived from being unable to decide whether her "self" resides in her body still standing in the steeple or in her head down in the street below (where the head presently makes a speech, though she hears it only "indistinctly" since, naturally, she has no ears). There follows a sequence during which she tries to take a pinch of snuff (thinking it will help to "clear [her] ideas" [333]) and eventually resorts to tossing the snuff-box down to the head to let it take its own snuff, for which it "smiled me an acknowledgment in return" (333). After many erudite quotations from antiquity, she realizes that nothing prevents her now from leaving the little window. She is perplexed at the reactions of her servant on the street and grieved at the fact that her beloved dog has died in the interim. Yet another wonder is in store, as she beholds the "departed spirit, the shade, the ghost of [her] beloved puppy" sitting in the corner, reciting poetry: "Harken! for she speaks, and, heavens! It is in the German of Schiller!" (334).

Is this not an especially clever piece of writing? Granted, it's all a lampoon of the kind of stories that *Blackwood's* frequently published; but it's also as much a send-up of Poe's own style of horror as it is of the usual *Blackwood's* fare. And yet, it's amazing how many critics miss the point. Thomas Disch calls it a "moronic," "truly god-awful tale" (49). (And whoever wrote the *Wikipedia* entry actually states, "It is unclear how much of this essay is meant to be sarcastic." Unclear? *Unclear!?*) The illustrious Joseph Wood Krutch writes that Poe's comic stories fail because Poe had no sense of humor (203); but arguably it's the *critics* who don't have a sense of humor. How can anyone read "A Predicament" without laughing out loud?

Daniel Hoffman—a rare, astute critic among the barbarous crowd—actually values "A Predicament" for showing us, in an unrefined way, how Poe's finest horror stories are built (qtd. in Disch 49). But what if "A Predicament" shows us only a more *straightforward* satire than is subtly crafted into Poe's more famous stories? I think it's only a short hop from an eyeball that pops out of the narrator's head and rolls down a gutter to look back at her to a cat that a man simply can't get rid of ("The Black Cat") or to a man who, shortly after the burial of his beloved, finds himself covered in mud and possessing a box filled with her teeth! ("Berenice"). How much more outrageous can a horror story get? And, more to the point, how much more deftly and subtly will Poe test his readers' sense of irony—and of credulity?

Marshall Trieber seems to agree: "Humor was . . . an integral part of Poe's makeup" (32). Trieber goes on to discuss the work that I have long thought to be at the center of Poe's literary artistry—the essay entitled "Diddling" (1843). At the time, "to diddle" meant "to dawdle" or waste time; it also meant to swindle someone or pull off a hoax. Poe, however, adds his own slant: "diddling" is not just the *act* of carrying off a hoax but the *attitude* with which one does it and the satisfaction one receives in the privacy of one's own heart of hearts. "Minuteness, interest, perseverance, ingenuity, audacity, *nonchalance*, originality, impertinence, and *grin*" (Poe, "Diddling" 351) he calls it, with all due emphasis on that last quality, as follows:

> Your *true* diddler winds up all with a grin. But this nobody sees but himself. He grins when his daily work is done—when his allotted labors are accomplished—at night in his own closet, and altogether for his own private entertainment. . . . He divests himself of his clothes. He puts out his candle. He gets into bed. He places his head upon the pillow. All this done, and your diddler *grins*. (Poe, "Diddling" 359)

Poe's essay goes on to give various examples of "diddlers" and tricksters, but perhaps the most subtle and ingenious diddler of all is none other than Mr. Edgar Allan Poe himself. It's not just that he turns out to have been so much more brilliant an author than anybody guessed (though perhaps that would be enough); it's that all those psychoanalyzing critics and biographers who saw in his stories such a "mad" author—a deeply neurotic, or even psychotic, manic-depressive, sadomasochistic, narcissistic, revenge-haunted, broken man—have fallen into the perfectly wrought trap laid for them. Mr. Poe gets the last laugh after all.

Works Cited

Bonaparte, Marie. *The Life and Works of Edgar Allan Poe: A Psycho-Analytic Interpretation*. Translated by John Rodker, 2 vols., Hogarth, 1949.

Disch, Thomas. *The Dreams Our Stuff Is Made Of: How Science Fiction Conquered the World*. Simon, 1998.

Freud, Sigmund. *The Ego and the Id*. 1923. Edited by James Strachey, Norton, 1962.

———. "Mourning and Melancholia." *A General Selection from the Works of Sigmund Freud*, edited by John Rickman. Anchor, 1957, pp. 124-40.

———. *New Introductory Lectures on Psychoanalysis*. 1933. Edited by James Strachey, Norton, 1965.

Griswold, Rufus Wilmot, editor. *The Works of Edgar Allan Poe*. 4 vols. W. J. Widdleton, 1865. *Google E-book*, books.google.com/.

Kennedy, J. Gerald. *Poe, Death, and the Life of Writing*. Yale UP, 1987.

———. "The Violence of Melancholy: Poe against Himself." *American Literary History*, vol. 8, no. 3, 1996, pp. 533-551. *JSTOR*, www.jstor.org/.

Krutch, Joseph Wood. *Edgar Allan Poe: A Study in Genius*. Knopf, 1926.

Moldenhauer, Joseph J. "Murder as Fine Art: Basic Connections between Poe's Aesthetics, Psychology, and Moral Vision." *PMLA*, vol. 83, 1968, pp. 284-97. Rpt. Thompson, pp. 829-44.

Poe, Edgar Allan. *Complete Stories and Poems of Edgar Allan Poe*. Doubleday, 1984.

———. "Diddling." *Complete Stories and Poems of Edgar Allan Poe*, pp. 358-65.

———. "How to Write a Blackwood Article." *Complete Stories and Poems of Edgar Allan Poe*, pp. 320-27.

———. "Metzengerstein." *Complete Stories and Poems of Edgar Allan Poe*, pp. 250-55.

———. "The Philosophy of Composition." Thompson, pp. 675-684.

———. "A Predicament." *Complete Stories and Poems of Edgar Allan Poe*, pp. 328-34.

———. "William Wilson." Thompson, pp. 216-32.

Praz, Mario. "Poe and Psychoanalysis." *The Sewanee Review*, vol. 68, no. 3, 1960, pp. 375-389. *JSTOR*, www.jstor.org/.

Pruette, Lorine. "A Psycho-Analytical Study of Edgar Allan Poe." *The American Journal of Psychology* 31.4 (1920): 370-402. *JSTOR*, www.jstor.org/.

Robinson, E. Arthur. "The Tell-Tale Heart." *Twentieth Century Interpretations of Poe's Tales*, edited by William Howarth, Prentice-Hall, 1971, pp. 94-102.

Thompson, G. R. "Introduction: Romanticism and the Gothic Tradition." *The Gothic Imagination: Essays in Dark Romanticism*, edited by G. R. Thompson, Washington State UP, 1974.

———, editor. *The Selected Writings of Edgar Allan Poe. A Norton Critical Edition*. Norton, 2004.

Trieber, J. Marshall. "The Scornful Grin: A Study of Poesque Humor." *Poe Studies*, vol. 4, 1971, pp. 32-34.

Wilbur, Richard. "The House of Poe." Anniversary Lectures, 1959. Library of Congress, 1959. Rpt. Thompson, pp. 807-23.

Yang, Amy. "Psychoanalysis and Detective Fiction: A Tale of Freud and Criminal Storytelling." *Perspectives in Biology and Medicine*, vol. 53, no. 4, 2010, pp. 596-604.

CRITICAL READINGS

Signet Classic

GEORGE ORWELL 1984

Literary Prehistory: The Origins and Psychology of Storytelling

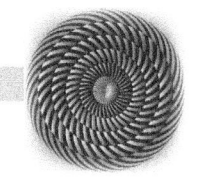

Michelle Scalise Sugiyama

Origins

The origins of literature are an academic no-man's-land. Literary study sidesteps the question by equating the emergence of literature with the emergence of the earliest written texts (e.g., *The Epic of Gilgamesh*). Psychology explores the cognitive foundations of literature (e.g., Schank) but does not concern itself with the socioecological context in which it emerged. Cultural anthropology is chiefly interested in storytelling vis-à-vis ritual, worldview, and belief systems, and has thus tended to focus on myth. Classic and linguistic approaches focus on the metrics and other performative aspects of oral tradition (e.g., Lord, Hymes), while folklore tends to focus on comparatively recent oral storytelling traditions that managed to survive the transition to industrialized life (e.g., fairy tales, tall tales). Because of their tightly circumscribed foci, none of these disciplines is charged with addressing the origins of the behavior they study.

In contrast, the study of art customarily begins with an examination of its prehistory—the forms that it took and the contexts in which it was produced prior to recorded history. There is good reason for this: examining a behavior in its context of origin illuminates continuities of form and use between the past and the present, which is critical to understanding motivation and function. Literary theory derived solely from written texts proceeds from an incomplete and possibly inaccurate set of assumptions about the nature of storytelling. Accordingly, this essay reviews the origins of storytelling to lay the groundwork for a more comprehensive theoretical approach. Although literature typically embraces poetry as well as narrative, this essay emphasizes the latter because oral storytelling has affinities with verse—such as the use of rhythm, repetition, alliteration, and line breaks (Tedlock, "On the Translation"; "Toward")—which suggest that, in early human societies, the line between prose and verse was more blurred than it is today. Moreover, among hunter-gatherers, poetry (which is largely confined to song) tends to reference or relate a story. Thus, the term *storytelling* effectively captures both of these art forms.

What we know today as literature began as oral tales told in small hunter-gatherer bands. Several lines of evidence indicate that storytelling has long been an integral part of human experience (Scalise Sugiyama, "Reverse-engineering"). Our species, *Homo sapiens*, emerged around 200,000 years ago, at which point language was firmly in place (Pinker). The recent finding that 85 percent of nighttime conversation among San foragers is dedicated to the recounting of stories and myths (Wiessner) attests to the prominence of this activity in modern and—by implication—ancestral hunter-gatherer life. Unfortunately, behavior doesn't fossilize, so we don't have access to the stories told by our ancestors. However, thanks to texts collected by early anthropologists and extant oral traditions kept alive by dedicated tribal elders, we have a good sense of what storytelling was like in recent foraging groups. Due to contact with industrialized state societies and access to Western goods (Lee and DeVore), recent forager life differs somewhat from that of our ancestors; however, their story traditions date to a time when they lived in small, nomadic or semi-nomadic bands and made their living by hunting and gathering. Thus, these traditions are the product of an existence that was very similar to that of early humans—a life without agriculture, social stratification, economic specialization, motorized transport, telecommunication, or modern medicine (Marlowe). For this reason, research on modern foraging peoples is seen as a valuable tool for reconstructing the hominid past (Tooby and Cosmides, "Past"). Similarly, the oral traditions of ethnographically documented foragers provide a model of storytelling in ancient environments.

Environment played an important role in the emergence of storytelling. Like all species, humans are adapted to a specific ecological niche. An ecological niche is not where a species lives, but how it makes its living. The human ecological niche is known as the *foraging niche*, and is characterized by a pronounced dependence on knowledge (Tooby and DeVore). Humans lack the keen senses that other animals have, as well as anatomical advantages such as camouflage, speed, strength, and sharp claws and teeth. Instead, humans depend on their ability to extract and apply information using *improvisational intelligence* (Barrett et al.)—the ability to invent new ways of doing things and improvise solutions to problems as they arise. This ability enables humans to bypass their anatomical limitations by inventing complex tools and strategies that, in turn, enable them to access resources that would otherwise be unattainable (Kaplan et al.). For example, hunter-gatherers use traps, snares, nets, poisons, and projectile weapons to hunt animals that are too fast for them to catch otherwise. The use of these complex techniques requires extensive knowledge: what raw materials to use, how to locate and process those materials, and how to use tools and tactics effectively—the latter of which requires considerable botanical, zoological, and geographical knowledge (Boyd et al.). For humans, then, information is a vital resource: it is the resource that is used to acquire all other resources (Tooby and Cosmides, "Past"). Even though humans no longer live by hunting and gathering, their ecological niche remains the same: modern agriculture, industry, and technology depend on a body of knowledge that has accumulated over scores of centuries and is so vast it can't possibly be stored in a single human mind. Arguably, humans are even more dependent on information in modern environments than they were in the past.

This information-dependent niche is the context in which storytelling emerged. To determine what role it plays in this context, we need to establish what storytelling is and—importantly—what it is not. The terms *narrative*, *fiction*, and *storytelling* are often used interchangeably, but they refer to discrete phenomena. Story structure elucidates these differences by highlighting the essential ingredients of narrative: you can't make a cake without eggs, flour, and butter, and you can't make a story without characters, actions, events, setting, sequence, and conflict and resolution (Scalise Sugiyama, "Reverse-engineering"). Collectively, these ingredients illuminate the type of information that narrative treats: information about the experiences of human or anthropomorphized beings. What we perceive as "narrative" is the workings of a representational format that organizes information about what happened to whom; where, when, and why it happened; the problems that resulted from this happening; and whether and how they were resolved (Scalise Sugiyama, "Narrative"). Narrative thus comprises any representation of a set of temporally and causally related events—not only stories, but gossip, memories, plans, dreams, and even fantasies. As this list indicates, narrative also lends itself to the representation of imaginary events. Pretense, or the ability to reason counterfactually (Leslie), enables us to visualize things that don't exist. Combined with narrative, pretense enables us to represent hypothetical events—events that might have happened in the past, might be happening now, or might happen in the future. Fictional stories can thus be thought of as counterfactual narratives. Storytelling occurs when we share true or fictional narratives with others. Thus, while narrative and pretense are cognitive processes, storytelling is a behavior—a communicative act deliberately performed to transmit experiential information.

The emergence of storytelling was a milestone in human evolution. As Biesele notes, it marked the point at which humans acquired the ability to "recreate situations for others and to convey to them what has been found to be of interest and of value" (42). Prior to the evolution of language, the rich store of knowledge accumulated over a lifetime's worth of experience died with the individual. Thus, the opportunity to share verbal recreations of experience greatly increased the amount of knowledge a person could acquire in a lifetime, while greatly reducing the costs of acquiring it. With the advent of storytelling, it became unnecessary for individuals to invest large amounts of time and energy or risk their lives seeking out first-hand educational opportunities. Simply by listening to the utterances of another human being, an individual could learn how leopards stalk and attack their prey or what the terrain was like on the other side of a mountain range. Storytelling also facilitated planning: knowing what happened in the past enabled individuals to better prepare for the future.

For instance, stories about famine reminded people that resource shortages periodically occur and described coping strategies used to survive them (Minc; Sobel and Bettles). Similarly, stories about warfare noted where attacks had occurred and who perpetrated them, described offensive and defensive tactics, and reminded people to be vigilant (Burch). The ability to reason counterfactually also enabled humans to share hypothetical experiences—to share and discuss speculations about events that might occur, problems that might ensue, and solutions that might be mounted.

In short, storytelling enabled humans to acquire knowledge of an experience without actually having to undergo that experience. The result was an explosion in the rate of knowledge acquisition: individuals no longer had to wait around for educational opportunities to arise and could access the wisdom of everyone in their social network. Moreover, because stories were passed on from generation to generation, humans could also access the knowledge of individuals who were no longer living. The process of oral transmission enabled early human societies to accumulate and store the collective knowledge of thousands of individuals (Tomasello).

Broadly speaking, then, storytelling originally served as an educational system (Scalise Sugiyama, "Storytelling as Evidence"). As de Laguna notes, "Without writing, the only method of preserving and communicating the wisdom of the elders was through oral discourse" (75). She notes that Dena stories "instruct, not only describing the characteristics of animals and birds of which the Dena should take note, but teaching the difference between right and wrong conduct" (de Laguna 290). Similar observations pervade hunter-gatherer ethnography. Among the Ojibwa, for example, "storytelling was an important part of teaching children. . . . Some legends were just for fun, while others taught children about nature or proper behavior" (Devens 190). Likewise, among the Ju/'hoansi, "much verbal sharing of information, about animal behavior for instance . . . is indirectly rather than directly accomplished. In fact, many sorts of knowledge are acquired (by young and old Ju/'hoansi alike) through hearing the dramatized story of a day's events"

(Biesele, *Women* 43). Similarly, Iñupiaq history was transmitted through both formal and informal storytelling: "The formal context was the storytelling session, during which experts recounted legends and tales before assemblages made up of people of all ages. . . . Informal contexts included conversations and narratives delivered as people traveled about the country, crossing or passing localities of historical interest as they did so" (Burch 48). The claim that forager storytelling is largely pedagogical is substantiated by the testimony of indigenous informants, who explicitly characterize storytelling as a form of instruction (see, for instance, Gwich'in Elders 17 and Opler ix, xii).

In short, Horace's claim that the aim of the poet is to "utter words at once both pleasing and helpful to life" (Fairclough 479 [l. 333]) is an apt description of storytelling in recent—and presumably ancient—forager populations. As Wiessner observes in her discussion of Ju/'hoan storytelling, "Those who listened were entertained while collecting the experiences of others with no direct cost" (14029). In psychology, "helpful to life" is captured by the concept of *generalizable knowledge*: information that is applicable beyond the original learning context to other places, times, and situations (Csibra and Gergely). The remainder of this essay reviews a representative sample of cross-cultural themes to show that forager storytelling consists largely of generalizable knowledge.

To Inform and Delight

Many themes recur predictably across forager oral tradition. Biesele characterizes this subject matter as a "hunting-gathering imaginative substrate" (*Women* 13), noting that the tales of Ju/'hoansi foragers "deal with problem points in living which must always have characterized the hunting-gathering adaptation, such as uncontrollable weather, difficulty in procuring game, danger from carnivore attacks, and correct relations with in-laws" (Biesele, *Women* 13). Other common themes are antisocial behavior, marriage, warfare, game animals, famine, topography, and natural disasters. These themes point to topics of universal and perennial concern for hunting-and-gathering peoples, supporting the claim that storytelling is used to transmit information that is generalizable to recurrent problems of forager life. This information can be divided into knowledge concerning the physical environment (e.g., animals, plants, natural disasters) and knowledge concerning the social environment (e.g., social norms, marriage practices, warfare). This section reviews a selection of common themes and genres to illustrate the nature and range of the generalizable information transmitted in forager oral tradition. Because I have discussed ecological knowledge elsewhere (Scalise Sugiyama, "Food"; "Forager"; "From Theory"; "Narrative"; Scalise Sugiyama and Sugiyama, "Once"), the present discussion will be confined to social information.

Social Norms

Hunter-gatherers do not have savings accounts, insurance policies, or social services they can turn to in an emergency. Instead, they depend on cooperation with others. To buffer privation resulting from bad hunting luck, incapacity, or other misfortune, foragers share their food, labor, and other resources with kin, fellow band members, and trading partners (Lee; Sugiyama and Chacon; Gurven et al.). This practice is contingent on maintaining civil relations among group members. Conflict jeopardizes group cohesiveness and, consequently, individual well-being: if a band dissolves, its members lose their support network. In the absence of police, courts of law, and prisons, group harmony is maintained chiefly by encouraging pro-social behavior and discouraging antisocial behavior. This is accomplished largely through public opinion, which is expressed by means of gossip, criticism, and verbal art forms such as singing (Biesele, "Aspects"; Oswalt) and storytelling. Public opinion can be a very effective check on anti-social behavior because, in small-scale societies, people are highly sensitive to the disapproval of others. The Dena, for example, "are very sensitive to what others may say. . . . [and] the unwritten laws of the people are enforced through the strength of public opinion" (de Laguna 76). Similarly, among the indigenous peoples of Oregon, order was maintained "through a tradition of community approval and disapproval. . . .

Instead of fearing a guilty conscience, a potential wrong-doer in an Indian community feared public exposure and shame above all" (Ramsey xxxi). Because stories are representations of experience, they are particularly well-suited to illustrating antisocial behavior and the consequences of engaging in it, the latter of which serves as a veiled threat: stories show what happens to people who break the rules. In so doing, they both model and enforce social norms. For example, an Iglulik story tells of a family who are abandoned by the rest of their group on account of their stinginess and end up starving to death (Rasmussen, *Intellectual* 259-260). The Serrano trickster, Coyote, is killed by the people because he lazes around all day and steals their food (Benedict 14). A Wasco boy is abandoned by his people for bullying and killing some of his playmates (Sapir and Curtin 260-261). And a Netsilik man who murders all of the women in his village while the men are away hunting is executed by the men when they return (Rasmussen, *Netsilik* 434).

A powerful testimony to both the problem of social control and the use of storytelling to deal with it is the trickster genre, which is dedicated to identifying and condemning proscribed behaviors (Scalise Sugiyama, "Narrative"). Across forager societies, the trickster is widely regarded as a model of bad behavior—as "the incarnation of greediness, lust, cruelty, and stupidity" (Thompson xviii; Chapman 5; Nelson 19; de Laguna 75; and Opler 263). The traits of the trickster read like a laundry list of antisocial behaviors. He is a liar, a thief, and a cheat, using deception rather than cooperation to get what he wants. Lazy, greedy, and gluttonous, he is always trying to get something for nothing, always wants more than he needs, and always tries to take more than his fair share. He is also arrogant and incorrigible, never learning from his mistakes, and habitually ignoring the advice and warnings of others. Impulsive, short-sighted, and irresponsible, he doesn't think through the possible consequences of his actions, which often end up hurting him and others. When others suffer as a result of his rash behavior, he doesn't care and sometimes doesn't even notice. Consummately self-absorbed and self-indulgent, he always puts himself first and holds himself above the rules. He is unscrupulous and exploitative to the point of being a sociopath. As Boas puts it, "no trick is too low to be resorted to, if it helps him to reach his end" (4).

In short, trickster tales "can be seen as moral examples reaffirming the rules of society . . . [and] demonstrating what happens if the prescriptions laid down by society are not observed" (Street 85). Punishment often takes the form of ridicule, which is the source of the humor in these often hilarious tales. We laugh *at* trickster, not with him: he is an object of scorn and derision. Among the Koyukon, for example, he "is treated with scant respect" (Chapman 5), and White Mountain Apache elders often concluded a trickster tale by warning, "'Don't do like Coyote did in the story. He did a lot of bad things for us long ago such as marrying his daughter and stealing!'" (Goodwin ix).

Sex and Marriage

Stories also transmit information about gender norms and sexual practices. As Wiessner explains, "because marriages were quiet affairs within small camps, the experience of any one individual was limited," so stories offered a means of acquiring "a broader picture of rites and procedures of marriage" (14030). In hunter-gatherer societies, marriages are typically arranged (Apostolou) and entail numerous obligations between in-laws. Oral tradition is an effective means of broadcasting these behavioral prescriptions. For example, two of the stories Wiessner collected "give the basic rules, practices, and values around arranging marriages, ceremonies, and bride service, as well as the grammar of etiquette between in-laws" (14030). Not surprisingly, arranged marriage is a common source of conflict between parents and offspring, and offspring resistance is another pervasive theme in forager literature. The story of the dog husband is a case in point. Variants of this tale are found in Siberia and throughout western North America. In the story, a young girl being pressured by her father to marry rejects all of her suitors for no apparent reason. She is punished by falling in love with her father's dog, which has been transformed into a man. When she gives birth to puppies, her family and fellow villagers abandon her. In some variants, she manages to transform the puppies into children and is invited to rejoin the band, but in others she kills her father (see, for instance, Teit 62; Rasmussen, *Netsilik* 227-228; and Menovshchikov). By exploring the possible negative outcomes of behavioral choices, stories may prompt the audience to consider alternative means of resolving marital conflicts. As Wiessner observes of Ju/'hoan storytelling, "situational variations in marriage gave a range of strategies tried: for example, one story told of two assertive sisters who rejected their prospective spouses for personal reasons and later chose their own spouses" (14030).

Warfare

Another problem presented by the social world is warfare. Both true and fictional narratives can provide generalizable information about combat: even if the events described are hypothetical, exaggerated, or an amalgam of several battles, the story may nevertheless contain practical, reliable information. As Burch explains:

> One major element in the preparation for armed conflict was education. Stories of armed confrontations, both successful and otherwise, played a central role in Iñupiaq narrative history. By the time a person reached adulthood, he or she had heard countless stories of raids and battles as well as analyses of the strategy and tactics involved in each one. . . . The one or two survivors from a defeated force who were allowed to return home surely reported not only on the general outcome of the conflict but also on which tactics succeeded and which failed. Detailed information on warfare was part of the common fund of Iñupiaq knowledge, shared by men and women, adults and children. (72)

Stories can provide information about offensive and defensive tactics, preventative and evasive measures, and escape strategies (see, for instance, Bogoras 28-29, 90-92; Rasmussen, *Intellectual* 298; Jacobs and Jacobs; Ellis 177). Because war narratives often mention where and when a battle occurred, they point to terrain or sites that are vulnerable to attack, and times of the day or year when attacks are likely to occur (Rink 132-34; Ellis 177). Stories also provide information about the location of hostile groups, such as what direction they live in and, thus, from what direction an attack is likely to come (Wilbert and Simoneau 109; Opler 383). Significantly, these stories often contain information about the military strength and practices of neighboring groups, such as armaments, the number and condition of fighting-age men, and the number of casualties they inflicted in a given battle (Rink 132-134; Bogoras 28-29). Collectively, these stories may help people weigh the potential costs and benefits of attacking other groups.

Subsistence Stress

Even in the richest habitats, foragers face periodic food shortages, which may lead to malnutrition, hunger, and even starvation. Some shortages (e.g., winter scarcity of game and plant foods in temperate zones) are predictable, but some are not, especially those that occur at intervals longer than a human lifespan. Although subsistence stress is an ecological problem, many of the strategies used to cope with it involve cooperation, making it a social problem as well. The simple act of telling stories about famine is strategic because it serves to warn or remind others that food shortages can occur. In societies that store food for predictable periods of scarcity, famine stories may encourage people to work hard and not waste food. The Koyukon people are a case in point: "From childhood they have heard stories about families who perished from hunger in the cold winter. . . . Persistent reminders of extreme want, even of famine, keep vividly before their consciousness the necessity of expending their full energies during the fishing season, and impel them to concentrate both their thoughts and their activities on the food quest" (Sullivan 29). Another strategy, as discussed above, is to discourage stinginess or hoarding or, conversely, encourage sharing (Rand 351). Stories about famine often emphasize reciprocity: one should help others when one is able so that the favor will be returned when needed. This point is often quite explicit, as when a Siberian tale warns a stingy family to "'remember the ancient custom of the Lamut. When you have food, give the best morsel to your poor neighbor'" (Bogoras 31). Stories are also used to criticize those who do not help others in time of need (Sapir and Curtin 227) and to show that stinginess will be punished (Bogoras 30-32; Rasmussen, *Intellectual* 259-260).

Conclusion

In modern environments, the most popular storytelling media are visual: film, television, and the internet. Yet even a casual survey indicates that humans still gravitate toward stories about social norms and rules (e.g., *Breaking Bad, Law and Order*); sexual and familial relations (e.g., *Modern Family, Sex in the City*); warfare (e.g., *Independence Day, Game of Thrones*); predators (e.g., *The Walking Dead, Jurassic Park*); and other challenges presented by the physical environment (*The Revenant, Life of Pi*). It would appear, then, that storytelling is still being used to explore possible contingencies, courses of action, and quandaries encountered in the human ecological niche. The pronounced correlation between cross-cultural themes and recurrent problems of forager life suggests that genre might be productively understood in terms of pan-human ecological constraints and challenges.

Another underexamined continuity between ancient and modern storytelling is reperformance: humans often derive enjoyment from a story even if they've heard it before. This suggests that there is something to be gained from revisiting a story. Collins suggests that this benefit is contemplation: "Suspense and surprise have no place in reperformed songs and narratives. . . . Once one fully learns a certain sequence of events, one need not concern oneself with following the plot's twists and turns or anticipating the range of possible outcomes; one can now afford to meditate on the explicit meanings of the story" (73). This hypothesis is supported by de Laguna's observation that, among the Dena, "repetition of the tale helps the listener to ponder the lesson therein" (75) and by the Blackfoot practice of telling "moral dilemma" stories aimed at provoking group discussion about the characters' decisions and actions (Wissler and Duvall 160-162).

Literary prehistory exposes other, less obvious continuities between ancient and modern storytelling. For example, as Lord,

Hymes, Niles, and others have shown, the poetics of oral and written narrative evince distinctive differences. Story length is a case in point: if time allows, an oral tale can be told over several nights, but if not, it can be told in abbreviated form. Oral storytellers are sensitive to audience attention and might wrap up a story if interest flags: Kroeber, for example, reports that a Mohave storyteller narrates "until his audience drops off or falls asleep" (2). Adding to this flexibility is the episodic nature of much forager narrative. Many tales comprise a series of incidents in the life of a focal character, such as a trickster or transformer. Each incident is a story unto itself but, collectively, these small stories form a larger tale. This structure allows a narrator to relate only that part of the story that is pertinent to the situation at hand (Tedlock, "Translation Style"; "Oral Poetics"; Biesele, *Women*). For example, although most Mohave tales "take a night to tell, or a night and part of the morning, or up to two nights, according to the narrators," in his conversations with Mohave storytellers, Kroeber got "the impression that many of them had never told their whole myth continuously through from beginning to end" (2). As a result of these practices, many oral stories do not have a predetermined length. Thus, forms such as the "novel" and "short story" are constructs of literate culture: because most modern storytelling is recorded rather than live, story length is necessarily fixed.

However, this perception is belied by the phenomenon of serialization. For example, many early novels were initially published in installments and were thus experienced as self-contained episodes that formed part of a larger story. This practice continues today in the form of book series, such as superhero comics and the Harry Potter novels. Similarly, television series, movie sequels, and even fan fiction are essentially story cycles that trace the collected adventures of a focal character or characters. From a psychological perspective, the pervasiveness of this phenomenon is striking and points to an overlooked and potentially rich mine of information on the motivational aspects of storytelling. In this and other ways, the study of literary prehistory may help us better understand why we tell stories and why we listen.

Works Cited

Apostolou, M. "Sexual Selection under Parental Choice: The Role of Parents in the Evolution of Human Mating." *Evolution and Human Behavior*, vol. 28, 2007, pp. 403-409.

Barrett, H. C., L. Cosmides, and J. Tooby. "The Hominid Entry into the Cognitive Niche." *Evolution of mind: Fundamental questions and controversies*, edited by S. W. Gangestad and J. A. Simpson, Guilford, 2007, pp. 241-248.

Benedict, R. *Zuni Mythology*. Vol. 1, AMS Press, 1926.

Biesele, M. "Aspects of !Kung Folklore." *Kalahari Hunter-Gatherers*, edited by Richard B. Lee and Irven DeVore, Harvard UP, 1976, pp. 302-324.

———. *Women Like Meat: The Folklore and Foraging Ideology of the Kalahari ju/'hoan*. Indiana UP, 1993.

Boas, F. Introduction. *Traditions of the Thompson River Indians of British Columbia*, edited by J. Teit, Houghton Mifflin, 1898, pp. 1-18.

Bogoras, W. *Tales of the Yukaghir, Lamut, and Russianized Natives of Eastern Siberia*. Anthropological Papers of the American Museum of Natural History, Vol. XX, American Museum Press, 1918, pp. 1-148.

Boyd, R., P. J. Richerson, and J. Henrich. "The Cultural Niche: Why Social Learning is Essential for Human Adaptation." *Proceedings of the National Academy of Sciences*, vol. 108, supplement 2, 2011, pp. 10918-10925.

Burch, E. *Alliance and Conflict: The World System of the Iñupiaq Eskimos*. U of Nebraska P, 2005.

Chapman, John W. *Ten'a Texts and Tales from Anvik, Alaska*. With Vocabulary by Pliny Earle Goddard. Publication of the American Ethnological Society, no. 6, E. S. Brill, 1914.

Collins C. *Neopoetics: The Evolution of the Literate Imagination*. Columbia UP, 2016.

Csibra, G., and Gergely, G. "Natural Pedagogy." *Trends in Cognitive Sciences*, vol. 13, no.4, 2009, pp. 148-153.

de Laguna, F. *Tales from the Dena*. U of Washington P, 1995.

Devens, Carol Green. "Anishnabek Childhood: Nineteenth and Early Twentieth Centuries." *Michigan Historical Review*, vol. 20, no. 2, 1994, pp. 184-197.

Ellis, C. Douglas, ed. *Cree Legends and Narratives*. U of Manitoba P, 1995.

Fairclough, H. Rushton. "Ars Poetica." *Horace: Satires, Epistles and Ars Poetica*. Translated by H. Rushton Fairclough, Harvard UP, 1942, pp. 442-489.

Goodwin, G. *Memoirs of the American Folklore Society: Myths and Tales of the White Mountain Apache*. Vol. 33, J. J. Augustin, 1939.

Gurven, M., W. Allen-Arave, K. Hill, and M. Hurtado. "'It's a wonderful life': Signaling Generosity among the Ache of Paraguay." *Evolution and Human Behavior*, vol. 21, no. 4, 2000, pp. 263-282.

Gwich'in Elders. *Gwich'in Words About the Land*. Gwich'in Renewable Resource Board, 1997.

Hymes, D. *"In vain I tried to tell you": Essays in Native American Ethnopoetics*. U of Pennsylvania P, 1981.

Jacobs, E., and M. Jacobs. "Those People." *Nehalem Tillamook Tales*. U of Oregon Books, 1959.

Kaplan, H., K. Hill, J. Lancaster, and A. Hurtado. "A Theory of Human Life History Evolution: Diet, Intelligence, and Longevity." *Evolutionary Anthropology*, vol. 9, 2000, pp. 156-185.

Kroeber, A. L. "Seven Mohave myths." *Anthropological Records*, vol. 11, no.1, 1948, pp. 1-70.

Lee, R. B. *The Dobe !Kung*. Holt, Rinehart and Winston, 1984.

———, and I. DeVore, editors. *Man the Hunter*. Aldine, 1968.

Leslie, A. "Pretense and Representation: The Origins of 'Theory of Mind.'" *Psychological Review*, vol. 94, 1987, pp. 412-426.

Lord, A. *The Singer of Tales*. Harvard UP, 1960.

Marlowe, F. "Hunter-gatherers and Human Evolution." *Evolutionary Anthropology*, vol. 14, 2005, pp. 54-67.

Menovshchikov, Georgii Alekseevich. *Let Me Tell a Story: Legends of the Siberian Eskimos*. Alaska Native Language Center, 2003.

Minc, L. "Scarcity and Survival: The Role of Oral Tradition in Mediating Subsistence Crises." *Journal of Anthropological Archaeology*, vol. 5, 1986, pp. 39-113.

Nelson, Richard K. *Make Prayers to the Raven*. U of Chicago P, 1983.

Niles, J. D. *Homo Narrans: The Poetics and Anthropology of Oral Literature*. U of Pennsylvania P, 1999.

Opler, M. *Myths and Tales of the Jicarilla Apache Indians*. American Folklore Society, 1938.

Oswalt, W. *Eskimos and Explorers*. Chandler and Sharp, 1999.

Pinker, S. *The Language Instinct*. Harper Perennial, 1994.

Ramsey, J. *Coyote Was Going There: Indian Literature of the Oregon Country*. U of Washington P, 1977.

Rand, S. "The Beaver Magicians and the Big Fish." *Legends of the Micmacs*. Longmans, Green, and Company, 1894.

Rasmussen, K. *Intellectual Culture of the Iglulik Eskimos.* Report of the 5th Thule Expedition 1921–24, Vol. VII (1), Gyldendalske Boghandel, Nordisk Forlag, 1929, pp. 1-304.

———. *The Netsilik Eskimos: Social life and spiritual culture.* Report of the 5th Thule Expedition 1921–24, Vol. VIII (1-2), Gyldendalske Boghandel, Nordisk Forlag, 1931, pp. 1-542.

Rink, H. *Tales and Traditions of the Eskimo.* 1875. Dover, 1997.

Sapir, E., and J. Curtin. "A Famine at the Cascades." *Wishram Texts.* E. J. Brill, 1909.

Scalise Sugiyama, M. "Fitness Costs of Warfare for Women." *Human Nature*, vol. 25, no. 4, 2014, pp. 476-495.

———. "Food, Foragers, and Folklore: The Role of Narrative in Human Subsistence." *Evolution and Human Behavior*, vol. 22, 2001, pp. 221-240.

———. "The Forager Oral Tradition and the Evolution of Prolonged Juvenility." *Frontiers in Evolutionary Pyschology*, vol. 2, 2011, pp. 1-19. DOI 10.3389/fpsyg.2011.00133/.

———. "From Theory to Practice: Foundations of an Evolutionary Literary Curriculum." *Style*, vol. 46, 2012, pp. 317-337.

———. "Narrative as Social Mapping—Case Study: The Trickster Genre and the Free Rider Problem." *Ometeca*, vol. 12, 2008, pp. 24-42.

Scalise Sugiyama, M. "Reverse-engineering Narrative: Evidence of Special Design." *The Literary Animal*, edited by J. Gottschall and D. S. Wilson, Northwestern UP, 2005, pp. 177-196.

———. "Teaching Consilience: A Course Design Template." *Interdisciplinary Literary Studies*, vol. 16, 2014, pp. 30-56.

———. "Narrative." *Encyclopedia of Evolutionary Psychological Science*, edited by T. Shackelford and V. Weekes-Shackelford, Springer, forthcoming.

———. "The Relevance of Popularity: Ecological Factors at Play in Story Pervasiveness." *Popular Literature and Culture Under an Evolutionary Lens* (working title), edited by L. B. Cooke and D. Vanderbeke, under review.

———. "Oral Storytelling as Evidence of Pedagogy in Forager Societies." Under revision for *Frontiers in Psychology.*

——— and L. Sugiyama. "'Once the child is lost, he dies': Monster Stories vis-a-vis the Problem of Errant Children." *Creating Consilience*, edited by Edward Slingerland and Mark Collard, Oxford UP, 2012, pp. 351-371.

Schank, Roger C. *Tell Me a Story: Narrative and intelligence.* Northwestern UP, 1990.

Sobel, E., and G. Bettles. "Winter Hunger, Winter Myths: Subsistence Risk and Mythology among the Klamath and Modoc." *Journal of Anthropological Archaeology*, vol. 19, 2000, pp. 276-316.

Street, B. "The Trickster Theme: Winnebago and Azande." *Zande Themes: Essays Presented to Sir Edward Evans Pritchard*, edited by A. Singer and B. Street, Rowman and Littlefield, 1972, pp. 82-104.

Sugiyama, L., and R. Chacon. "Effects of Illness and Injury among the Yora and Shiwiar: Pathology Risk as Adaptive Problem." *Human behavior and adaptation: An anthropological perspective*, edited by L. Cronk, N. Chagnon, and W. Irons, Aldine, 2000, pp. 371-95.

Sullivan, Robert J. *The Ten'a Food Quest*. Catholic U of America P, 1942.

Tedlock, Dennis. "On the Translation of Style in Oral Narrative." *Journal of American Folklore*, vol. 84, no. 331, 1971, pp. 114-133.

———. "Toward an Oral Poetics." *New Literary History*, vol. 8, no. 3, 1977, pp. 507-519.

Teit, J. *Traditions of the Thompson River Indians of British Columbia*. Houghton Mifflin, 1898.

Thompson, Stith. *Tales of the North American Indians*. 1929. Indiana UP, 1966.

Tomasello, M. *Cultural Origins of Human Cognition*. Harvard UP, 1999.

Tooby, J., and L. Cosmides. "The Past Explains the Present: Emotional Adaptations and the Structure of Ancestral Environments." *Ethology and Sociobiology*, vol. 11, 1990, pp. 375-424.

Tooby, John, and I. DeVore. "The Reconstruction of Hominid Behavioral Evolution through Strategic Modeling." *The Evolution of Human Behavior: Primate Models*, edited by W. Kinzey, SUNY P, 1987, pp. 183-237.

Wiessner, P. W. "Embers of Society: Firelight Talk among the Ju/'hoansi Bushmen." *Proceedings of the National Academy of Sciences*, vol. 111, no. 39, 2014, pp. 14027-14035.

Wilbert, J., and K. Simoneau. *Folk Literature of the Yanomami Indians*. UCLA Latin American Center Publications, University of California, 1990.

Wissler, C., and D. C. Duvall. "Mythology of the Blackfoot Indians." *Anthropological Papers of the American Museum of Natural History*, vol. 2, 1908, pp. 1-163.

"Is This Her Fault or Mine?": Hysteria, Misogyny, and Voice in Shakespeare's *Measure for Measure*

Laura B. Vogel

Male bewilderment and consternation about female desire are timeless. Shakespeare's understanding that women may also harbor repressive and punitive attitudes towards their own desire, rendering female desire both unacknowledged and unspoken, predated psychoanalytic description of this phenomenon by three centuries. Isabella, the would-be nun in *Measure for Measure*, exhibits classic symptoms of female "hysteria."

In 1895, Freud and Breuer postulated that intrapsychic trauma and conflict experienced and repressed in their hysterical patients produced psychological consequences; these patients were prone to sensory and motor disturbances in which conflicts were "converted" into physical symptoms. Subsequent generations of psychoanalysts have found that hysterics demonstrate repressed sexual desire for forbidden objects, often in conjunction with Oedipal dynamics (McWilliams 314). Hysterics unconsciously wish to have sexual relations with their parent of the opposite sex and feel anger towards their same-sex parent. In response to their forbidden erotic longings, they experience unconscious shame and guilt and seek atonement and punishment. Even as they repress and deny sexual desire, hysterics simultaneously behave seductively.

As the play opens, the Duke of Vienna empowers Angelo, his protégé and puritanical deputy, to deal with the moral laxity and sexual licentiousness that he perceives is destroying his realm. The Duke then absents himself, disguised as a friar, to better spy on his wayward subjects. Angelo closes the brothels and resurrects a long neglected law that punishes fornicators with execution. The immediate consequence is the arrest of Isabella's brother, Claudio, for having impregnated his fiancée, Juliet. (Juliet's life will be spared because she is carrying a child.) Claudio's friend Lucio persuades Isabella, who is on the verge of entering a convent, to meet with

Angelo and plead for her brother's life. The articulate, chaste, and attractive Isabella engages in a passionate and well-matched debate with Angelo, who experiences sudden desire. Aware of his unwelcome arousal, Angelo exclaims "What's this? What's this? Is this her fault or mine?" (2.2.163).[1]

This question—whether women are responsible for male desire—speaks to the perception that to maintain social order, female sexuality must be controlled so that it will not provoke male lust. However, Isabella's repression and denial of her sexual responses, far from protecting her, actually endanger her. These defenses render her more vulnerable to the misogyny directed towards her first by Angelo and then by the Duke.

Facing imminent execution, Claudio enlists his friend Lucio to persuade Isabella to intervene on his behalf with Angelo, remarking that:

> . . . in her youth
>
> There is a prone and speechless dialect
>
> Such as move men; beside, she hath prosperous art
>
> When she will play with reason and discourse,
>
> And well she can persuade. (1.2.172-176)

Claudio exploits multiple meanings of "prone" as "natural," "lying down," and perhaps "in a posture of submission." "Move" evokes sexual arousal. "Play" suggests that Claudio values his sister's capacity to arouse men, as well as to persuade them, with her voice.

Having heard Claudio's sly assessment of Isabella, the audience then encounters her just before Lucio arrives at the convent. Isabella wishes to withdraw from contact with men in order to secure her chastity and contain her sexuality. She wears the garments of a novice and speaks with a nun:

> Isabella: And have you nuns no farther privileges?
>
> Nun: Are not these large enough?

> Isabella: Yes, truly; I speak not as desiring more,
>
> But rather wishing a more strict restraint
>
> Upon the sisters stood, the votarists of Saint Clare. (1.4.1-5)

The nun reminds her of the convent's rules:

> When you have vow'd, you must not speak with men
>
> But in the presence of the prioress;
>
> Then, if you speak, you must not show your face;
>
> Or if you show your face, you must not speak. (1.4.10-13)

Isabella dons the habit in an effort to literally conceal her sexual impulses. However, these impulses, expressed in the form of unconscious seductiveness, sometimes elude her very best efforts at control.

Lucio retrieves Isabella from the convent and accompanies her as she pleads with Angelo to spare Claudio's life. Isabella, one of Shakespeare's most articulate and verbally skilled women, argues forcefully and passionately. This is the eloquent language of a woman with agency:

> . . . Well, believe this:
>
> No ceremony that to great ones longs,
>
> Not the king's crown, nor the deputed sword,
>
> The marshal's truncheon, not the judge's robe
>
> Become them with one half so good a grace
>
> As mercy does.
>
> If he had been as you, and you as he,
>
> You would have slipp'd like him, but he like you
>
> Would not have been so stern. (2.2.58-66)

She continues:

> . . . authority, though it err like others,
>
> Hath yet a kind of medicine in itself
>
> That skins the vice o'th'top. Go to your bosom,
>
> Knock there, and ask your heart what it doth know
>
> That's like my brother's fault. If it confess
>
> A natural guiltiness, such as is his,
>
> Let it not sound a thought on your tongue
>
> Against my brother's life. (2.2.135-142)

Angelo, in an aside to the audience, says "She speaks, and 'tis such sense / That my sense breeds with it" (2.2.142-3), and then dismisses Isabella. As he turns away, she requests "Gentle my lord, turn back" (2.2.144) and then adds, "Hark how I'll bribe you" (2.2.146). Angelo, startled, asks "How? Bribe me?" (2.2.147). Isabella responds, "Ay, with such gifts that heaven shall share with you" (2.2.149); she then describes these gifts as prayers from fasting maids.

Isabella's Seductiveness

Isabella displays her unconscious seductiveness as she attempts to persuade Angelo. She includes references to Angelo's body: his heart (2.2.53); his lips (2.2.78); and, in the passage quoted above, his bosom, heart, and tongue. She shifts her focus from an abstract plea for mercy to a personal inquiry about Angelo's own experience of sexual impulses at that moment, implying that he, like her brother, is a man who is acquainted with lust. Angelo's aside responds to the alluring power of Isabella's voice, as well as to his awareness of growing desire for her. Then, of course, he hears her parting "Hark how I'll bribe you" as a prelude to a sexual offer.

Lucio repeatedly interrupts the dialogue between Angelo and Isabella with asides to Isabella. Lucio's exhortations, cheering her on, resemble a kind of sexual "sportscasting," calling the "plays." At first he tells her, twice, "You are too cold" (2.2.45, 2.2.56), which echoes his earlier description of Angelo as "a man whose blood is very snow-broth" (1.4.57). Later, he cheers, "Ay, touch him; there's the vein" (2.2.70), and finally, "O, to him, wench. He will relent. He's coming. I perceive't" (2.2.125-6). Lucio's commentary, with its sexual overtones, illuminates the impulses hidden by Angelo's punitive puritanism and Isabella's insistence upon chastity. Albeit comically, he intimates that they are a "match" for each other, intellectually, verbally, and sexually.

Indeed, Angelo's snow-broth blood rapidly melts. After Isabella departs, he describes in a candid soliloquy the sudden intense desire he feels for her—"What's this? What's this? Is this her fault or mine?" (2.2.163)—and goes on to ask:

> Shall we desire to raze the sanctuary
>
> And pitch our evils there? O fie, fie, fie!
>
> What dost thou, or what art thou, Angelo?
>
> Dost thou desire her foully for those things
>
> That make her good? . . . What, do I love her,
>
> That I desire to hear her speak again?
>
> And feast upon her eyes? What is't I dream on?
>
> O cunning enemy, that to catch a saint,
>
> With saints dost bait thy hook! Most dangerous
>
> Is that temptation that doth goad us on
>
> To sin in loving virtue. Never could the strumpet
>
> With all her double vigour, art, and nature
>
> Once stir my temper: but this virtuous maid
>
> Subdues me quite. Ever till now

> When men were fond, I smil'd, and wonder'd how.
>
> (2.2.171-187)

Certainly "What's this? What's this?" can be played comically to signal Angelo's cognizance of his erection; he experiences lust and is aware of his experience. "This" could also refer to Angelo's sense that the defenses he has erected to contain and repress his sexual impulses have broken down. Angelo struggles with his lust, both compelling and repugnant to him, in soliloquys in act 2, scene 2 and act 2, scene 4; he concludes "Blood, thou art blood" (2.4.15). "This" could also, however, be an indication that Angelo is smitten with feelings of love for Isabella as well as lust and that his state of being has shifted in multiple complex ways, all new to him.

Isabella, in contrast, maintains a defensive unawareness of her sexual feelings for Angelo throughout the play. Lucio's commentary in their first meeting underlines the mutuality of physical attraction and the sense that Angelo and Isabella are a "match" in spite of a discrepancy in self-awareness.

Isabella appears alone for her second meeting with Angelo. When he asks, "How now, fair maid?" she responds "I am come to know your pleasure" (2.4.31-2). Here, the word "pleasure" rather than the more common and neutral "will" arguably reveals again the unconscious intent to seduce. (Later, in a meeting with the Duke, disguised as a friar, Isabella asks "What is your will?" [3.1.152].) Angelo proposes that the life of Isabella's brother can be saved if she has sex with Angelo, but Isabella does not initially understand the nature of his proposition. When she does, she exclaims:

> That is, were I under the terms of death,
>
> Th' impression of keen whips I'd wear as rubies,
>
> And strip myself to death as to a bed
>
> That longing have been sick for, ere I'd yield
>
> My body up to shame.
>
> (2.4.100-105)

Isabella offers Angelo a vivid vision of her body, stripped naked, whipped, and bearing welts as if they were rubies. This vision is certainly consistent with religious preoccupations and practices of her time. It is also, however, a highly provocative, seductive, sexual, sadomasochistic image.

Returning to Angelo's question, "Is this her fault or mine?", what appears to be a comic question involving perplexed projection may in fact suggest a complex mode of interaction in sexual relationships. In their first meeting, when Isabella suggests to Angelo "Go to your bosom / Knock there, and ask your heart what it doth know that's like my brother's fault" (2.2.137-9), it is as though Angelo, examining his heart, discovers that Isabella has planted his desire for her there. Possibly Isabella is unconsciously aware of his desire as she directs Angelo; she is certainly unaware of her own desire or seductiveness. The mutual sense of desire in this couple, conscious in one person and unconscious in the other, cascades back and forth between them, setting up resonant vibrations that increase in intensity and seem to arise from the other. Arousal, conscious or unconscious, diminishes the boundaries between the players and confuses the location of desire.

When they meet for the second time, Isabella senses and resonates, unaware, with Angelo's masculine desire to possess her. Her responsive sexual excitement provokes in her, again unconsciously, considerable shame and guilt. She conjures and presents to him an image of herself being beaten as punishment for this excitement. Angelo's awareness of and resonance with Isabella's submission further inflames his desire for her and intensifies his experience of lust. Is this her fault or his? In this instance, Isabella's seductiveness complicates the question, although earlier Angelo had concluded that the "fault" is his:

> The tempter or the tempted, who sins most, ha?
>
> Not she, nor doth she tempt; but it is I
>
> That, lying by the violet in the sun,
>
> Do as the carrion does, not as the flower,

> Corrupt with virtuous season. (2.2.164-168)

Faced with a young, virginal novice wearing the garb of a sister, Angelo perceives her as an innocent flower and himself as rotting flesh. He does not persist in blaming her for his lust, and in this and the subsequent soliloquy, he wrestles with the assumption of his own responsibility for his desire. These soliloquys illustrate that in his reflections he acquires self-knowledge.

Angelo understands, in spite of her seductiveness, that Isabella is not experiencing or expressing conscious desire for him. This exchange occurs in their second meeting:

> Angelo: Plainly conceive I love you.
>
> Isabella: My brother did love Juliet,
>
> And you tell me he shall die for't.
>
> Angelo: He shall not, Isabel, if you give me love. (2.4.140-144)

Isabella responds to Angelo's declaration of love with an angry threat to expose him for his hypocrisy. Angelo, no less angry, retaliates that no one will believe her and adds "And now I give my sensual race the rein. / Fit thy consent to my sharp appetite" (2.4.159-160).

Angelo and Misogyny

To elucidate Angelo's behavior, a brief consideration of the psychological origins of misogyny, arising from differences in male and female psychosexual development, will be useful here. Nancy Chodorow's classic text *The Reproduction of Mothering* and the work of Robert Stoller on gender identity formation provide some of the foundation for this discussion. Although traditional gender roles have recently been increasingly redefined, for the most part, infants and young children are still cared for by mothers and women, and this will be the assumption here.

The infant's first experience of emotional intimacy and merger creates asymmetry and subsequent difference in the development of men and women. For the baby girl, developing a sense of self requires separation from the mother, but becoming a feminine self does not require a complete break with the earliest identification with the mother. The baby boy, however, needs to separate from the mother and disavow his identification with her in order to establish a sense of masculine self. Stoller describes masculinity in males as "an achievement" (*Presentations* 18), which, in most cultures, entails a crucial break in one's earliest connection and at a very tender age.

The efforts of males to define themselves as "not-female" and to ensure this critical separation can include a rejection of intimacy and tenderness and a contempt for and devaluation of women. The perception that women are malevolent can be a consequence of the psychological defense of splitting, where one image is that of the idealized "good" mother and the other is the powerful but evil "bad" mother. The young child relates to these images as though they are two distinct figures. Later, for adolescent and adult males, the experience of lust and sexual arousal, with accompanying erections, reinforces a sense of masculinity and power.

Stoller describes "symbiosis anxiety" in men as a constant fear of a regressive psychological merger with the mother. This anxiety can be activated by loving unions with women, which may trigger a return to feelings of infantile helplessness and neediness.

Hatred of women and the angry insistence that one is "not female" aid in defense against this fear of merger. Patriarchal cultures organize around multiple misogynist assumptions, including contempt for women and a belief that female sexuality provokes, and should be blamed for, male lust. To the extent that the experience of lust evokes either an awareness of male need or male aggression, either feeling can be disavowed by the projective claim that the impulse originated in the female. It is her fault. With these misogynist attitudes in mind, let us return to Angelo.

When Angelo says, "Plainly conceive I love you," is he truly experiencing love or merely trying to put a more attractive and seductive gloss on his lust? I perceive Angelo as a man who is experiencing love as well as lust in his initial encounter with Isabella. He says, in his first soliloquy:

> What, do I love her
>
> That I desire to hear her speak again
>
> And feast upon her eyes? . . . (2.2.214-216)

> . . . this virtuous maid subdues me quite. Ever till now
>
> When men were fond, I smiled and wondered how.
>
> (2.2.222-224)

The phrase "subdues me quite" is telling. In the conventional language of romantic love, Angelo feels conquered by his desire for Isabella, but "subdues me quite," when read aloud, resembles "subdues me quiet." He wonders at his wish to hear her voice and "feast upon her eyes." This is a yearning specific to loving feelings and responses, rather than mere carnal lust. It is reminiscent of the earliest responses of an infant who is quieted and soothed by the reassuring voice, nourishing mutual gaze, and breast of a mother. "Feast upon her eyes," a wonderful condensation, incorporates the simultaneous experiences of a loving, admiring gaze, and nursing. The infant feeds at the breast, experiences a sense of both satiety and merger with the mother, and falls asleep. This loving, mirroring, soothing good mother is split off from the aggressive, controlling, sexual bad mother.

As Angelo is flooded with both love and lust for Isabella, he responds to simultaneous aspects of the imagined split mother; his own sexuality and aggression are integrated in loving desire. It is important to recall that the infant, who is helpless and small, perceives both the mother and her voice as powerful and big. Angelo's disappointment that his first experience of adult love is not mirrored or reciprocated by Isabella generates intense feelings of infantile helplessness, narcissistic injury, and rage. When Isabella fails to respond to him, the soothing, loving mother disappears; in rejecting Angelo, she now evokes responses to the split-off bad mother, castrating and powerful. He is determined to subdue her, to physically possess her body, and to quiet the powerful and seductive voice that inspired love.

Isabella's revulsion at her sexuality emerges in the second dialogue with Angelo. When he says to her that "women are frail, too" (2.4.123), she replies:

> Ay, as the glasses where they view themselves,
>
> Which are as easy broke as they make forms.
>
> Women?—Help, heaven! Men their creation mar
>
> In profiting by them. Nay, call us ten times frail. . . .
>
> (2.4.124-127)

In her anxiety, Isabella initially distances herself from women, identifying women as "they" before she switches to "us." She refers to women's vanity in the metaphor of "glasses" and then shifts to an image of the mirrors breaking as they create likenesses. Women can be "broken" as they make babies—they can die in childbirth. When she adds "men their creation mar in profiting by" women, Isabella reveals fear and disgust at women's participation in conception and birth. The fantasy that men would be better off reproducing on their own without women to "mar" creation removes women, and herself, from this sordid process.

Isabella's Fantasies

Isabella reveals the Oedipal nature of her unconscious sexual organization most dramatically in her only interaction with Claudio, following the second audience with Angelo. She has come to discuss Angelo's proposition that if she has sex with him, he will spare Claudio's life. Initially, however, Claudio is unaware of Angelo's offer, and says:

>   . . . If I must die,
> I will encounter darkness as a bride
> And hug it in my arms.   (3.1.82-84)

Isabella replies:

> There spake my brother: there my father's grave
> Did utter forth a voice. . . .   (3.1.85-86)

At first Isabella assumes that Claudio will die to preserve her chastity; he reminds her of idealized beloved father, speaking from the grave to protect her.

But when Isabella finally clarifies Angelo's offer, Claudio urges:

> Sweet sister, let me live.
> What sin you do to save a brother's life,
> Nature dispenses with the deed so far
> That it becomes a virtue.   (3.1.131-134)

Isabella's reaction is vitriolic:

> O, you beast!
> O faithless coward! O dishonest wretch!
> Wilt thou be made a man out of my vice?
> Is't not a kind of incest, to take life
> From thine own sister's shame? What should I think?
> Heaven shield my mother play'd my father fair:
> For such a warped slip of wilderness
> Ne'er issued from his blood. Take my defiance,

> Die, perish! Might but my bending down
>
> Reprieve thee from thy fate, it should proceed.
>
> I'll pray a thousand prayers for thy death;
>
> No word to save thee.   (3.1.135-146)

After Claudio asks her to have sex with Angelo, her odd vision of this as incest suggests that she perceives Claudio as identifying her with her mother. Isabella clearly devalues her mother and abhors her mother's sexuality.

Isabella exposes a fantasy that the beastly Claudio must have been conceived in an affair between their wanton mother and someone other than "her" father. In her intense rage, she sees Claudio, not herself, as their mother's child: I am not like my mother; you are a dishonest wretch like my mother. Perhaps Isabella's vision extends to a view of herself as her father's solo creation in which he did not "profit by" her mother. Isabella's assessment of Claudio switches instantly from seeing him as a brother she identifies gratefully with an idealized father to seeing him as someone whom she likens to a devalued mother. Isabella has mobilized the defense of splitting and revealed her Oedipal dynamics in this process. The pressure to yield her virginity, coming first from Angelo and then from Claudio, creates intense panic in Isabella. She remains eloquent, but the cogency and logic of her words deteriorate in response to her anxiety and rage.

The siblings' conversation is interrupted by the eavesdropping Duke, in his friar's disguise. It is at this moment that the Duke's interventions and manipulations become central to the action of the play. He explains to Isabella that he will arrange a "bed trick" in which Angelo, thinking he is with Isabella, will have sex with Mariana, the fiancée he had rejected. The Duke reassures her that the benefit of this scheme outweighs its deceit. Isabella, upon magically finding salvation in this "good father" (3.1.238), declares that "the image of it gives me content already, and I trust it will grow to a most prosperous perfection" (3.1.260-261). She believes she has been rescued. The growth will prosper in Mariana's belly, not hers.

This "good father" falsely takes "confession" from Juliet and Claudio. He absolves Isabella and Mariana of the deceptions of the bed trick with his "religious" authority. Later, still disguised, he instructs Isabella to approach the Duke and accuse Angelo of seducing her with a false promise not to execute her brother. She follows the "father's" instructions, experiencing great humiliation as she perjures herself in front of a crowd. Isabella is blindsided when the Duke then publicly accuses her of madness and has her arrested and sent to prison for slandering Angelo. This is only the first of his several malevolent manipulations. Eventually, the Duke reveals the "bed trick," subjecting Mariana as well to public shaming, and orders Angelo to marry her. Finally, the Duke orders that Angelo be put to death for his supposed execution of Claudio. Isabella kneels, joining Mariana, and pleads for Angelo's life:

> . . . I partly think
>
> A due sincerity govern'd his deeds
>
> Till he did look on me. Since it is so,
>
> Let him not die. My brother had but justice,
>
> In that he did the thing for which he died:
>
> For Angelo,
>
> His act did not o'ertake his bad intent,
>
> And must be buried but as an intent
>
> That perish'd by the way. Thoughts are no subjects;
>
> Intents, but merely thoughts. (5.1.443-452)

At the play's ending, in a stunning reversal, the Duke produces Claudio, unharmed, pardons Angelo, and twice proposes to Isabella. The last words of the play belong to the Duke:

> . . . Dear Isabel,
>
> I have a motion much imports your good;
>
> Whereto if you'll a willing ear incline,
>
> What's mine is yours, and what is yours is mine.
>
> So bring us to our palace, where we'll show
>
> What's yet behind that's meet you all should know.
>
> (5.1.531-536)

Measure for Measure concerns itself with the regulation of lust detached from affection. The three major characters employ combinations of strategies to contain sexual impulses. The Duke, Angelo, and Isabella all use repression and denial. Isabella seeks to augment her internal defenses by joining a convent. Angelo attempts to restrain lust through violent punishment of others. His dehumanization of sexuality and the harshness of his retaliatory aggression—literally, chopping off men's heads—suggest projection with pornographic castration. The Duke employs social engineering to constrict passion and restore social order: this includes spying, deception, and the ultimate weapon, marriage.

Isabella does not assent to either of the Duke's proposals. She says nothing. The words she speaks, kneeling, on Angelo's behalf, are her last words in the play. Compared to her brilliant pleas for mercy in act 2, this last speech is pallid and terse. This heroine who begins with a powerful and persuasive voice, with agency so striking in her verbal eloquence, is reduced to silence—in the Duke's words, to "a willing ear."

The meaning of her silence is not clarified in either the text or stage directions. Is she consenting to, or refusing, the Duke's proposal? Recall the Sister's injunction: "if you speak, you must not show your face; / Or if you show your face, you must not speak" (1.4.12-13). As men gaze at her, is Isabella choosing to withhold her voice, assuming the restraint on speech imposed by the convent? The sight of the silenced Isabella presents a condensation of multiple narratives collapsed into a single, mute image. She has been propositioned by Angelo, who fell in love with her and was able to acknowledge his love and desire, but responded to her rejection with the wrath of a man scorned. She has been repeatedly manipulated and humiliated by the Duke, who is chillingly like a puppeteer pulling the strings of his subjects; he exploits others to achieve his own ends.

Early in the play, the Duke disabuses Friar Thomas of the notion that he is seeking a disguise to pursue sexual interests: "Believe not that the dribbling dart of love / Can pierce a complete bosom" (1.3.2-3). Referring to Cupid's weapon as a "dribbling dart" implies that the arrow is ineffectual; at an unconscious level it may hint at his own impotence. Later, the Duke explicitly exposes his belief that women are responsible for male desire; when the pregnant Juliet freely admits that her sin with Claudio was "mutually committed" (2.3.27), he tells her "Then was your sin of a heavier kind than his" (2.3.28).

When this sterile, cold patriarch proposes marriage to Isabella, one senses that he relishes this further assertion of his male hierarchical power. By possessing Isabella, he intends to acquire what Angelo has desired and to block Isabella's planned escape from the social order into the convent. The "bed trick," presumably designed to "rescue" Isabella, also conveniently traps Angelo, who loves Isabella, into a marriage with Mariana.

Isabella's Oedipal conflicts, and the shame, guilt, and masochism that are consequences of those issues, combine with repression and denial to prevent her from ever recognizing her sexual feelings. Had Isabella expressed her desire to Angelo—"If you love me, marry me"—we could imagine a different ending. Instead, she leaves her encounters with Angelo aroused, angered, and anxious. When Claudio pressures Isabella to yield her chastity to Angelo, however, the lucidity of her arguments deteriorates. But it is, finally, the misogynist cruelties of the patriarchal Duke, the alleged "good father," that subdue Isabella and quell her eloquent voice.

Acknowledgments

I am deeply grateful for the keen eye and insightful and eloquent assistance of Edwina Cruise with many drafts of this paper. I am also indebted to Amrita Basu, Jack Cameron, Barry Farber, Richard C. Friedman, L. Brown Kennedy, Naomi Miller, and Suzanne Slater for their much appreciated ideas, critiques, and support.

Note

1. Previous psychoanalytic readings of this play include the articles by Desai, Paris, Skura, and Williamson.

Works Cited

Adelman, Janet. *Suffocating Mothers*. Routledge, 1992.

Breuer, Josef, and Sigmund Freud. *Studies on Hysteria*. Translated by James Strachey, Basic Books, 1957.

Chodorow, Nancy. *The Reproduction of Mothering*. U of California P, 1978.

Desai, Rupin W. "Freudian Undertones in the Isabella-Angelo Relationship in *Measure for Measure*." *Psychoanalytic Review*, vol. 64, 1977, pp. 487-94.

McWilliams, Nancy. *Psychoanalytic Diagnosis*. Guilford, 2011.

Paris, Bernard J. "The Inner Conflicts of *Measure for Measure*: A Psychological Approach." *The Centennial Review*, vol. 25, no. 3, 1981, pp. 266-276.

Shakespeare, William. *Measure for Measure*. Bloomsbury Arden Shakespeare, 2015.

Skura, Meredith. "New Interpretations for Interpretation in *Measure for Measure*." *Boundary 2: A Journal of Postmodern Literature and Culture*, vol. 7, no. 2, 1979, pp. 39-60.

Stoller, Robert. *Perversion: The Erotic Form of Hatred*. Karnac, 1975.

———. *Presentations of Gender*. Yale UP, 1985.

Williamson, Marilyn L. "Oedipal Fantasies in *Measure for Measure*." *Michigan Academician*, vol. 9, 1976, pp.173-84.

Trauma in Shakespeare's *Macbeth*

Robert C. Evans

The topic of trauma, which has been very important in recent discussions of literature, has received surprisingly little attention in discussions of Shakespeare in general and *Macbeth* in particular.[1] Commentary on the relevance of "trauma theory" to literary texts has been so pervasive since the early 1990s that the relative lack of apparent interest in trauma and the writings of Shakespeare is puzzling. The purpose of this essay, then, is to survey contemporary thinking about trauma and to use some of that thinking to explore issues of trauma in one of Shakespeare's most important tragedies. I will begin by surveying various references to traumatic (or potentially traumatic) events in the first parts of the play and then move to a more focused discussion of trauma in the work's final act.

The *potential* for trauma—which we can briefly define as severe, even debilitating, psychological wounding—appears almost immediately in *Macbeth* and grows in intensity as the play proceeds.[2] The startling presence of the witches in Act 1, scene 1 is unsettling but not traumatic: nothing they say or do at this point is deeply disturbing. Duncan's reference to a "bloody man"—a man literally covered in blood—in 1.2.1 is the text's first clear reference (both in language and in costuming) to potential trauma. Duncan's words seem deeply ironic in retrospect: eventually he himself will be the play's truly "bloody man" (and so, too, will the beheaded Macbeth in the tragedy's final scene). At this point, however, no one (including the captain to whom Duncan's words refer) seems traumatized by the combat that has just been taking place. This early scene does emphasize plenty of bloodshed: Macbeth is said to have fought his enemies "with bloody execution" (1.2.18—another bit of irony, given what Macbeth will later do to Duncan and what will eventually happen to Macbeth himself). Macbeth is even described as having "unseamed" (or sliced) an enemy soldier "from the nave to th'chaps [or "chops"]. In other words, he has nearly cut a man in half, either from the navel or genitals right up to his jaws. His gruesome violence here foreshadows much that will come later in the play (including Macbeth's own beheading), but no one seems traumatized by either the vicious act or the startling description. Macbeth has simply been doing his duty. He and his comrade Banquo have both been fighting (according to the reporting captain) as if "they meant to bathe in reeking wounds" (1.2.39). Once more, language early in the play foreshadows the later slaughter of both Duncan and (with superb irony) even Banquo and Macbeth themselves.

When we first actually *see* Macbeth and Banquo, however, neither of them seems traumatized by the gruesome violence they have simultaneously witnessed, performed, and been threatened with. Macbeth, it is true, is apparently startled and fearful when confronted by the witches (1.3.49), and even Banquo worries that he and Macbeth, having seen the witches, may be going insane (1.3.82-3). Soon, however, Macbeth is being congratulated by Ross precisely for failing to be traumatized by the killings he has committed on the battlefield: Ross reports that King Duncan (again with irony the king can never suspect at this point) admires Macbeth for being "Nothing afeard of what thyself didst make, / Strange images of death" (1.3.94-95). If there is trauma in these opening scenes, it is mostly trauma that results from *imagined* or *potential* wounds, not wounds that have yet occurred. Thus Banquo worries that the witches may be "instruments" of Satan (1.3.122-25). And Macbeth feels similar worries and shows the first physical and mental suggestions of trauma when he contemplates what it may take for him to fulfill the witches' prophecy and become king; he wonders about the mental suggestion

> Whose horrid image doth unfix my hair
>
> And make my seated heart knock at my ribs
>
> Against the use of nature[.] Present fears
>
> Are less than horrible imaginings. (1.3.134-37)

Psychological trauma has now truly begun to enter the play, and part of what now traumatizes Macbeth is not the realization of the killings he has committed on the battlefield (since those can be viewed as dutiful and heroic) but of the evil and treason he may in the future commit to achieve his own ambitions. He has begun to fear himself; he has begun to dread his own "black and deep desires" (1.4.51).

Enter Lady Macbeth

The first appearance of Macbeth's wife also involves yet another of the play's rich ironies. The fear *she* first expresses is ironically the fear that Macbeth may be too kind to win power by killing the king (1.5.14-16). Paradoxically, she fears that Macbeth will be incapacitated by his own fear (1.5.22). She worries that if he cannot control his facial expressions, his fear will be perceptible (1.5.69-70). Increasingly, in this section of the play, Macbeth seems traumatized by the fear of fear itself. He worries that if he kills Duncan he may suffer punishment or a similar fate (1.7.7-12). He fears he will endure "deep damnation" and opprobrium if he kills the king (1.7.16-28). He is, in a sense, becoming traumatized (wounded) himself before he has inflicted any actual wound on Duncan. Three times in a mere ten lines (1.7.35-45), Lady Macbeth mocks her husband's fearfulness. He now, then, must also fear the prospect of feeling like (and appearing to be) an emasculated "coward" both in his wife's eyes and in his "own esteem" (1.7.43). He fears failure (1.7.59), fears his wife's apparent fearlessness (1.7.72-74), and fears the murder even as he agrees to commit it (1.7.80).

If Macbeth is, at this point, not yet traumatized (incapacitated by fear), he has certainly begun to suffer what might, in modern parlance, be termed "panic attacks." He even begins to hallucinate, as when he imagines he sees a dagger floating in the air (2.1.33-34). He feels "fear" that the very stones he walks on will "prate of [his] whereabouts" (2.1.57-58). After he actually commits the murders of Duncan and Duncan's two guards, he cannot stop thinking about the horror of his deeds (2.2.29-77). Indeed, it is in the immediate aftermath of the murders that Macbeth begins to exhibit many classic symptoms of a traumatized person. (For a detailed list, see Ringel and Brandell 1-12). These include a sense of paralysis. Macbeth recounts, for instance, how, when he "had most need of blessing," the word "'Amen' / Stuck in [his] throat" (2.2.35-36). Displaying two other classic symptoms of trauma as outlined by Ringel and Brandell, Macbeth has begun to relive the event and to dwell on it: he cannot get it out of his mind. Speaking more prophetically than she realizes, Lady Macbeth tries to calm her husband by saying that "These deeds must not be thought / After these ways; so, it will make us mad" (2.2.36-37). (Of course, by the end of the play, she will, ironically, be even more traumatized than Macbeth himself.)

Meanwhile, Macbeth begins to show again a susceptibility to suggestions and illusions—another standard trait of traumatized persons, according to Ringel and Brandell: "Methought I heard a voice cry "Sleep no more! / Macbeth does murder sleep" (2.2.-38-39). His language, like that of many traumatized individuals, soon becomes obsessively repetitive: "Still it cried 'Sleep no more!' to all the house. / 'Glamis hath murdered sleep, and therefore Cawdor / Shall sleep no more. Macbeth shall sleep no more'" (2.2.44-46). It is as if Macbeth is presently in a hypnotic state and has begun to experience dissociative thinking. He is behaving, in the words of Ringel and Brandell, "as if the original traumatic situation were still in existence" (3). Partly he is so traumatized because he committed the murders alone; no one else can be blamed. Trauma theorists have long noted that men in battle (like Macbeth at the beginning of the play) are less likely to be traumatized if they feel as if they are acting as part of a strong, close-knit unit with strong leaders. Feeling part of such a unit can help prevent or at least mitigate the sense of "overwhelming terror" of fighting, killing, and facing the possibility of death (Ringel and Brandell 3).

Lady Macbeth grows increasingly frustrated (but perhaps also alarmed herself?) by Macbeth's apparent hallucinations about hearing voices:

> Who was it that thus cried? Why, worthy thane,
>
> You do unbend your noble strength to think
>
> So brainsickly of things. Go get some water
>
> And wash this filthy witness from your hand. (2.2.47-50)

The irony of her words will, of course, become fully apparent by the end of the play, when she becomes completely obsessed with washing her own hands—an obsession that signals her own descent into traumatized madness (5.1.23-27). When she orders Macbeth to rub blood all over the king's dead guards (to make them appear to be the king's killers), Macbeth displays more standard symptoms of a traumatized person, including avoidance and revulsion: "I'll go no more. / I am afraid to think what I have done. / Look on 't again I dare not" (2.2.53-55). Unfortunately, Lady Macbeth proves to be anything but an effective therapist. She belittles and mocks Macbeth (2.2.55); she tells him not to be emotional when being emotional is all he feels he *can* be at the moment (2.2.37-38); and she tells him to stop fearfully obsessing about the past (2.2.33), when, in fact, fearfully obsessing about the past is one of the clearest signs of trauma. She tries to shame him by telling him he is behaving like a child (2.2.57-58); she briefly leaves him alone with his terrifying memories (2.2.62-66); and she tries to shame him twice more (2.2.67-68, 71-72).

Act 2, scene 2 is thus the first scene that depicts trauma in the fullest, deepest, most diverse senses of the term. Near the end of the scene, when Macbeth hears someone knocking, he behaves in ways that perfectly illustrate the conduct of a traumatized person:

> Whence is that knocking?
>
> How is 't with me when every noise appalls me?
>
> What hands are here! Ha, they pluck out mine eyes.
>
> Will all great Neptune's ocean wash this blood
>
> Clean from my hand? No, this my hand will rather

> The multitudinous seas incarnadine,
>
> Making the green one red. (2.2.60-66)

Here Macbeth displays such standard traumatic symptoms as "hyperarousal," "hypervigilance," "anxiety," and "dysphoria" (Ringel and Brandell 6). But throughout this scene, he exhibits numerous other manifestations of trauma in the fullest clinical senses. These include "[r]ecurrent and intrusive distressing recollections"; [a]cting or feeling as if [the traumatic] events [are] recurring"; demonstrating "[i]ntense psychological distress to clues" (such as the knocking); displaying "[p]hysiological reactivity to clues"; avoidance of such things as "thoughts," "feelings," and "reminders" associated with the traumatic event; a "[r]estricted range of affect" or feelings; and, finally, "[h]pervigiliance" and an "[e]xaggerated startle response" (as in his response to the knocking). (On all these points, see Bisson, Box 1.) Later in the play, especially at its end, Macbeth will exhibit even further symptoms, but by the end of act 2, scene 2, he already seems clearly and multiply traumatized.

Trauma in Macbeth and Others

As the play develops, Macbeth continues to display signs of trauma, but various other characters will eventually seem traumatized in numerous ways as well. Moreover, as the play proceeds, Macbeth tries to cope with his own trauma through multiple methods. Thus he says in passing that the "labor we delight in physics pain" (2.3.42). In other words, doing work and fulfilling obligations is one way to distract ourselves from painful thoughts. He also tries, again, to practice avoidance: when Lennox, over the course of six terrifying lines, reports hearing "strange screams of death, / And prophesying, with accents terrible, / Of dire combustion and confused events . . ." (2.3.48-50), Macbeth responds quickly and curtly (with almost comic understatement) by minimizing events: "'Twas a rough night" (2.3.53). Macbeth is so terrified by what he knows he has done that he dares not respond more fully. Instead, it is now Macduff, who has just discovered the butchered bodies of the king and his guards, who now seems openly traumatized: "O horror, horror, horror, / Tongue nor heart cannot conceive nor name thee" (2.3.56-57). For much of the rest of this scene, it is Macduff who will articulate the trauma that others (including, secretly, Macbeth) inwardly feel. Thus, members of the audience know the double meaning of Macbeth's words when he publicly says, "Had I but died an hour before this chance [i.e., the king's murder], / I had lived a blessèd time" (2.3.84-85). The more Macduff proclaims his own intense pain at Duncan's murder, the more traumatized Macbeth must feel and the more he must dissemble his own guilty knowledge of the facts.

Macbeth now begins to say and do what he knows he is *supposed* to say and do (2.3.90-92). He starts to play a role, but he also starts, partly and deceptively, to confess. He admits that he killed Duncan's guards (2.3.99-100), claiming that he impulsively punished them for allegedly killing the king, but as he describes the murder scene he inevitably relives the murderous event (2.3.101-11). He simultaneously deceives and reveals; he both lies and tells the truth. Like many traumatized persons (especially those who also know themselves guilty of causing trauma, like the American soldiers in Vietnam at the aptly named "My Lai Massacre," with its bizarrely appropriate name), Macbeth feels doubly traumatized: he is burdened both by the original deed and also by the need to lie about it. The more he lies, the more he cripples his conscience. The more he deceives, the deeper the trauma embeds itself in his mind. He now uses (and corrupts) his reason to concoct untruths he knows to be untruths. Ironically, feeling genuinely traumatized, he also now feels the need to *pretend* that he felt traumatized when he killed the king's guards: "Who can be wise, amazed, temp'rate, and furious, / Loyal, and neutral, in a moment? No man. / Th' expedition of my violent love / Outrun the pauser, reason" (2.3.101-04). The psychological complexities implied by these words are astonishing. Macbeth uses a calculating, deceitful rationality to claim that he was irrational when he impulsively killed men whom he had actually killed in an act compounded of both reason *and* passion. Paradoxically, the more Macbeth uses his reason to disguise his crimes, the deeper he descends into true irrationality.

By the time we reach act 3 of the play, Macbeth has begun, more and more, to use corrupted reason to cope with his own trauma. He now increasingly performs the roles of the typical villain and tyrant, partly because he has *become* those roles and partly because only by acting in these ways can he preserve his power and make sense of his existence. If he had continued to allow his sense of trauma to dominate his mental and emotional life, he would either have gone insane or would have been recognized, and executed, as a traitor and king-killer. Instead, he must now embrace being a tyrant and act accordingly. Such action often involves inflicting trauma on others. Thus he secretly plots the killing of his friend Banquo by consulting with two characters designated, in the script, simply as the "Murderers" (3.1.76). Rather than killing again himself, Macbeth this time will hire professionals. He does this partly to avoid detection (3.1.119-22), but perhaps he also does it partly to avoid another bout of trauma. Killing his king was horrific enough; directly killing his friend and his friend's son might, potentially, be even worse. And so Macbeth hires contract killers.

The play occasionally reminds us, however, that Macbeth himself is still somewhat traumatized, and it is in fact his continuing attacks of conscience that make him a nobler, more genuinely tragic character than, say, Richard III or Iago. His ongoing battle with trauma implies that he is not a simple, total villain. Thus, not long after meeting with the murderers, he converses with his wife, who once more rebukes him for seeming depressed:

> How now, my lord, why do you keep alone,
>
> Of sorriest fancies your companions making,
>
> Using those thoughts which should indeed have died
>
> With them they think on? Things without all remedy
>
> Should be without regard. What's done is done. (3.2.8-12)

Paradoxically, the more Lady Macbeth accuses her husband of being irrationally obsessed with what "is done," the easier it is to feel some residual respect for him. But Macbeth's reply to his wife, which suggests he is more concerned about being *punished* for killing the king than about the actual killing itself (3.2.13-15), diminishes any lingering sympathy we may feel for him. Increasingly, Macbeth seems traumatized not by what he has done but by the consequences he may suffer for having done it. He speaks of "the affliction of these terrible dreams / That shake us nightly" and mentions what it is like to feel "the torture of the mind" and "to lie / In restless ecstasy." He even envies the dead Duncan, who is now at peace (3.2.18-22). Speeches like this are intriguingly ambiguous: if Macbeth is still feeling traumatized for having killed the king, we can feel at least *some* sympathy for him. But if he is suffering because he fears being found out and punished, any sympathy vanishes. Whatever the causes of his trauma (whether he recalls the literal wounds he himself inflicted or fears the real wounds he himself may suffer), he is clearly traumatized.

The middle of the play is full of moments when we cannot be sure (at first) precisely why Macbeth feels traumatized. Thus, at one point he exclaims, "O, full of scorpions is my mind, dear wife!" (3.2.36). We might at first assume he is feeling some lingering pangs of conscience, but instead he quickly makes it clear that he feels tormented not by Duncan's death but by the continuing life of Banquo and his son (3.2.37). But Banquo and his son, Fleance, themselves are soon traumatized: Banquo is wounded both physically and psychologically and quickly dies, while Fleance is wounded psychologically but manages to flee (3.3.19-21). Macbeth, hearing that Fleance has escaped, now feels traumatized anew: "Then comes my fit again. . . . now I am cabined, cribbed, confined, bound in / To saucy doubts and fears" (3.4.20-25). Macbeth's trauma, however, results less from the killing of his friend than from the fact that his friend's son (a potential rival) survives. By this point, and indeed until the play's end, Macbeth is traumatized less by guilt than by fear. Guilt does, however, seem to play a major role in one of the play's most famous scenes: the one in which Banquo's ghost appears.

Seeing the ghost for the first time, Macbeth at first seems somewhat paranoid, as when he asks his guests, "Which of you have done this?" (3.4.49). Then he seems to feel guilty; speaking to the ghost, he declares, "Thou canst not say I did it. Never shake / Thy gory locks at me" (3.4.50-51). Lady Macbeth, trying to calm the situation, tells the guests that Macbeth's "fit is momentary; upon a thought / He will again be well" (3.4.55-56). Speaking to Macbeth himself, she again tries to shame him: "Are you a man?" (3.4.58). Macbeth replies, "Ay, and a bold one, that dare look on that / Which might appall the devil" (3.4.59-60). His wife calls the ghost a figment of Macbeth's fearful imagination and again tries to shame him (3.4.60-68). Meanwhile, readers (and/or witnesses of a) performance cannot be sure precisely *what* to think: is the ghost in fact "real"? Are we meant to see it, too? Or is it in fact "merely" imaginary? If it *is* meant to seem real, then readers and audiences can rightfully feel somewhat traumatized themselves: the play may imply that death is not final, that the undead can return to terrify not only Macbeth but (potentially) anyone else as well, including ourselves. Macbeth, the experienced soldier and battlefield killing machine, thinks back fondly to simpler days of military slaughter: in those days, "when the brains were out, the man would die, / And there an end. But now they rise again / With twenty mortal murders on their crowns / And push us from our stools" (3.4.79-82).

In trying to cope with this new trauma (a trauma far worse than anything he has faced so far), Macbeth reacts in various ways and tries a number of different strategies for dealing with the ghost. After his initial shock, he expresses distrustful anger at others (3.4.49), confronts the ghost (3.4.49), denies the ghost's presence (3.4.50-51), calls for confirmation of its presence (3.4.69), challenges the ghost (3.4.69-70), insists to his wife that his vision was accurate (3.4.74), tries to regain composure and explain away his fright to his guests (3.4.85-87), and expresses a combination of extreme fear, profound avoidance, and desperate defiance (3.4.93-107). Later, after the ghost seems to disappear, Macbeth tries frantically to process the whole event (3.4.110-26). He exhibits just about as many standard responses to trauma as one can imagine (see

Ringel and Brandell 1-12 and also Bisson). So, too, do his wife and guests. Her reactions include distress, embarrassment, anger, and desperate attempts to regain control of Macbeth and of the whole situation. The guests are mostly mystified and frightened by Macbeth's own anger and fear. It is as if Shakespeare intended to run the whole gamut of Macbeth's possible traumatic reactions and of others' responses to his trauma.

In one of the most intriguing—and terrifying—scenes in the entire play, Lady Macduff converses with Ross, one of her husband's thanes. She wants to know why her husband has fled Scotland. Ironically, in language that sounds much like Lady Macbeth's attacks on Macbeth, Lady Macduff attacks her own husband: "His flight was madness. When our actions do not, / Our fears do make us traitors" (4.2.3-4). In other words, she, like Lady Macbeth, accuses her own husband of insanity and terror; she thinks he has been traumatized for some reason she cannot understand. Ross tries to defend Macduff: "You know not / Whether it was his wisdom or his fear" (4.2.4-5). But Lady Macduff is not persuaded; she once again accuses of her husband of being so irrationally terrified that he has abandoned his wife and children: "All is the fear, and nothing is the love, / As little is the wisdom, where the flight / So runs against all reason" (4.2.12-14). Attempting to defend Macduff, Ross describes a feeling of massive, widespread social trauma, widely felt by nearly everyone (4.2.18-22). This social trauma, engendered by Macbeth, even affects readers and playgoers, especially when they read and/or behold the wanton slaughter of the young son of Lady Macduff and her husband (4.2.80-82). The trauma in this play, which originally began with the murder of an innocent king, now descends to the murder of an innocent child. It is as if Shakespeare wants to remind us that children are very often the defenseless, traumatized victims of willful, evil adults.

As if to create one more variation on the theme of trauma in this play, Shakespeare later describes Macduff's reaction to the news that his entire household—"Wife, children, servants, all / That could be found" (4.3.213-14)—have been slaughtered at Macbeth's behest:

> All my pretty ones?
>
> Did you say "all"? O hell-kite! All?
>
> What, all my pretty chickens and their dam
>
> At one fell swoop? . . .
>
>   Did heaven look on
>
> And would not take their part? *Sinful Macduff,*
>
> *They were all struck for thee!* Naught that I am,
>
> *Not for their own demerits, but for mine,*
>
> *Fell slaughter on their souls.* Heaven rest them now.
>
>   (4.3.218-30; italics added)

    Macduff's traumatized reaction to the deaths of all his loved ones is perfectly understandable. But the words I have italicized show us, I think, the first example of survivor's guilt in the play. Such guilt is a very common reaction to trauma and is, of course, a form of trauma itself (see, for instance, Janoff-Bulman 132). Macduff feels responsible for the deaths of his wife, children, and servants. If Macbeth has felt guilty for actually committing and ordering murders, Macduff feels guilty for being unable to prevent them. But Macduff soon begins to cope effectively with the trauma he feels. He now plots vengeance on Macbeth and redemption for Scotland (4.3.235-38).

Act 5: Trauma Abounding

Act 5 of *Macbeth* is the most consistently traumatic section of the play. Earlier acts had presented intermittent traumas (Macbeth's reaction to killing Duncan; Macbeth's reaction to Banquo's ghost; the traumatic killing of young Macduff; Macduff's own traumatized reaction to the deaths of his son, wife, and servants). But it is in act 5 that the full impact of trauma is felt not only by Macbeth but also by his wife. Ironically, their roles in this act are now reversed:

whereas earlier she had mocked his trauma and tried to reason him out of it, now it is she who is completely traumatized and beyond the reach of reason (on this point, see Nesselhauf). All the fundamental assumptions on which she had earlier built her mental and emotional world have now collapsed (a standard definition of the causes and effects of trauma; see, for instance, Janoff-Bulman 5). She is now sleepwalking (5.1.3-7), saying things (as she sleepwalks) that her servant refuses to repeat (5.1.12-16), and feeling constantly in need of light (even when sleeping) to protect her from the dark (5.1.19-20). She washes her hands continually and thinks she sees a spot of blood remaining on them (5.1.23-27). She speaks aloud (when sleeping) as if she is talking to Macbeth; she repeats her earlier mockery of him but now acknowledges the horror of Duncan's murdered body (5.1.30-34).

In other words, Lady Macbeth (like many traumatized persons) hallucinates, engages in repetitive behavior, relives traumatic events, has lost her sense of self-worth, and has lost any fundamental assumption that she can control events and preserve her psychic world. She no longer feels invulnerable and can no longer make sense of negative events by assimilating them to a solid psychological framework. She feels threatened at a deep psychological level, as if her very survival is at stake. She knows that Macbeth's survival is also threatened, and she has begun to suffer what Ronnie Janoff-Bulman (author of one of the most-praised studies of trauma) calls a "massive disintegration" of her "symbolic world" (60). Her mind is now "pervaded by thoughts and images representing malevolence, meaninglessness, and self-abasement" (Janoff-Bulman 63). She is hyper-aroused and hypersensitive; she feels humiliated and powerless; she feels quite literally "sullied and tarnished" (Janoff-Bulman 80); and in her mind, "recurrent, intrusive thoughts and images . . . alternate with periods of denial and emotional numbing" (Janoff-Bulman 108). In all these ways and many others, she exhibits many of the standard symptoms of a person consumed by trauma. (On all the points just mentioned see, for instance, Janoff-Bulman 5, 10, 13-14, 19, 53, 55-59, 65, 67, 78.) Ironically, it is now Lady Macbeth who feels traumatically paralyzed. Macbeth, at least, still feels reasons to hope that all is not yet lost. He now copes more effectively with trauma than she does. It comes as no surprise when we later learn that she has (apparently) killed herself (5.5.16). Suicide, of course, is an option often chosen by traumatized persons, and if this is the choice she has made then she will (according to common beliefs of Shakespeare's time) spend the rest of eternity in hell, traumatized forever.

Like his wife, Macbeth, after some initial optimism, is eventually overtaken by trauma as act 5 proceeds. Like her, too, he displays many of the classic symptoms of someone who has been (and is being) traumatized. His enemies think he's "mad" (5.2.13) and burdened by guilt and/or fear of revenge (5.2.16-17). He is (and feels) increasingly isolated (5.2.19-20). Sometimes he is in denial; sometimes he is desperately defiant (5.3.1-3, 10). The great traitor ironically feels betrayed (5.3.8). He is easily agitated, cannot control his temper (5.3.11-12, 14-15), is angered by others' apparent fear (5.3.16-17), and threatens his own followers (5.3.16). He is, in short, in a slow process of psychic collapse. He feels hopeless and "sick at heart" and thinks he has "lived long enough" (5.3.19, 22). He displays many of the same symptoms already mentioned in connection with his wife, including isolation, shame, self-contempt, and contempt from others (5.3.22-28). Indeed, the Doctor's diagnosis of Lady Macbeth—"she is troubled with thick-coming fancies, / That keep her from her rest" (5.3.39-40)—recalls Macbeth's own condition, especially earlier in the play. Likewise, Macbeth's response to the doctor (as Nesselhauf notes) applies equally as well to his own present situation as to his wife's:

> Canst thou not minister to a mind diseased,
>
> Pluck from the memory a rooted sorrow,
>
> Raze out the written troubles of the brain,
>
> And with some sweet oblivious antidote
>
> Cleanse the stuffed bosom of that perilous stuff
>
> Which weighs upon the heart? (5.3.41-46)

Both Macbeths, having traumatized so many others, are now at this point themselves thoroughly traumatized. Or at least this seems true of the wife. Macbeth, feeling incapable of following the doctor's advice to "minister to himself" (5.3.47), chooses defiant denial and prepares for battle (5.3.49) but then self-pityingly confesses his sense of growing isolation (5.3.50). Later, after hearing of his wife's death, he lapses into a kind of deep depression, a melancholy sense that life is utterly meaningless (5.5.18-27). This is by far one of the most common symptoms of a person who feels traumatized (see, for instance, Janoff-Bulman 63, 78, 123, 149). By the end of 5.5, he feels almost utterly hopeless; his only choice is defiance: "Blow wind, come wrack, / At least we'll die with harness on our back" (5.5.51-51). He has no alternative but to commit a kind of psychic suicide, although he steadfastly rejects the real thing (5.8.1-2). Pathetically, just before he is killed, Macbeth admits his guilt, telling Macduff, on the battlefield, "get thee back, my soul is too much charged / With blood of thine already" (5.8.5-6). By now, of course, it is far too late for such an admission to do any good, either to Macduff or to Macbeth. Any hope that Macbeth might be on the brink of a dramatic pre-death confession, conversion, and repentance, however, is dashed by his quickly ensuing boastful claim, "I bear a charmèd life" (5.8.12). But, in fact, he doesn't, and within a few lines, he is dead.

Fittingly, the last time we see Macbeth, we see only his bloody, severed head, perhaps on a pole, or perhaps held by the hair (as in the famous illustration by John Gilbert). "Behold," Macduff declares, "where stands / Th'usurper's cursed head" (5.9.21-22). Finally Macduff has won some small (inevitably inadequate) revenge for all his suffering. How appropriate it seems that Macbeth, who both experienced and caused so much trauma in this play, should finally himself be reduced to a traumatic image. Surely the bloody head was intended both to satisfy and to frighten the play's audience. The now "dead butcher" (5.9.36) has himself been butchered. As our ears listen to the final speeches of Macduff and Malcolm, our eyes, surely, are glued on Macbeth's gruesome head. If his head was hacked off while he was still alive, he has suffered one of the most traumatic deaths imaginable. If his head was hacked off after he died, then he has still suffered an especially gruesome and degrading fate. In either case, the literal presence of his severed head (where all his traumatized thinking once took place) is one of the most memorably traumatizing images with which this pervasively traumatic, traumatizing play could possibly have ended.

Macbeth beheaded. Illustration by John Gilbert. From The Works of Shakespeare, *edited by Howard Staunton, illustrations by John Gilbert. Vol. 3, George Routledge & Co., 1858—60, p. 516.*

Notes

1. For the fullest collection of essays on Shakespeare and trauma, see Brooks et al. For general comments, see the introduction to the book by Starks-Estes. The books by Anderson, Cahill, and Silverstone contain no references to *Macbeth*. The only extended discussion of *Macbeth* in terms of trauma seems to be the brief article (in German) by Nesselhauf. Van der Kolk mentions *Macbeth* a few times in passing but never discusses the play at length.
2. For various relevant discussions of trauma, see especially Ringel and Brandell; Janoff-Bulman; Bisson; Charles and O'Louhglin; Follette and Naugle; and O'Laughlin.

Works Cited

Alexander, Jeffrey. *Trauma: A Social Theory*. Polity, 2012.

Anderson, Thomas Page. *Performing Early Modern Trauma from Shakespeare to Milton*. Ashgate, 2006.

Bisson Jonathan I. "In-Depth Review: Post Traumatic Stress Disorder." *Occupational Medicine*, vol. 57, 2007, pp. 399-403. occmed.oxfordjournals.org/content/57/6/399.full/. Accessed 25 Jan. 2017.

Brooks, Douglas A., Matthew Biberman, and Julia Reinhard Lupton, editors. "Shakespeare After 9/11: How a Social Trauma Reshapes Interpretation [Special Issue]." *Shakespeare Yearbook*, vol. 20, 2011, pp. 1-289.

Cahill, Patricia A. *Unto the Breach: Martial Formations, Historical Trauma, and the Early Modern Stage*. Oxford UP, 2009.

Charles, Marilyn, and Michael O'Loughlin. "Fragments of Trauma: An Introduction." *Fragments of Trauma and the Social Production of Suffering: Trauma, History, and Memory*, edited by Marilyn Charles and Michael O'Loughlin, Rowman and Littlefield, 2015, pp. 3-24.

Follette, William C., and Amy E. Naugle. "Functional Analytic Clinical Assessment in Trauma Treatment." *Cognitive-Behavioral Therapies for Trauma*, edited by Victoria M. Follette and Josef I. Ruzek, 2nd ed., Guilford, 2006, pp. 17-33.

Gilbert, John. Illustration of Macbeth Beheaded. *The Works of Shakespeare*, edited by Howard Staunton; illustrations by John Gilbert. Vol. 3, George Routledge & Co., 1858-60, p. 516.

Janoff-Bulman, Ronnie. *Shattered Assumptions: Toward a New Psychology of Trauma*. Free Press, 1992.

Nesselhauf, Jonas. "'In restless ecstasy': Traumaerfahrungen in Shakespeares Werken am Beispiel von 'Macbeth.'" *Literaturkritik.de*, vol. 4, April 2014, n.p.

literaturkritik.de/public/rezension.php?rez_id=19131&ausgabe=201404/. Accessed 25 Jan. 2017.

O'Loughlin, Michael. "Introduction: The Ethics of Remembering and the Consequences of Forgetting." *The Ethics of Remember and the Consequences of Forgetting*, edited by Michael O'Laughlin and Claude Barbre, Rowan and Littlefield, 2015, pp. 1-33.

Ringel, Shoshana, and Jerrold R. Brandell. *Trauma: Contemporary Directions in Therapy, Practice, and Research*. SAGE, 2012.

Shakespeare, William. *Macbeth*, edited by A. R. Braunmuller, Cambridge UP, 1997.

Silverstone, Catherine. *Shakespeare, Trauma and Contemporary Performance*. Routledge, 2011.

Stark-Estes, Lisa S. *Violence, Trauma, and Virtus in Shakespeare's Roman Poems and Plays: Transforming Ovid*. Palgrave Macmillan, 2014.

van der Kolk, Bessell. *The Body Keeps the Score: Brain, Mind, and Body in the Healing of Trauma*. Viking, 2014.

John Donne, Neuroscience, and the Experience of Empathy

David Strong

In a number of John Donne's romantic poems in his *Songs and Sonnets* collection, the speaker reciprocates the same actions, behaviors, and sensations as his beloved. This reciprocity not only prompts him to experience feelings akin to hers, but also helps establish the surety of their romantic bond. To grasp the full literary and biological significance of this kind of romantic behavior, this article employs, as an interpretive tool, some recent advances in neuroscience. For example, the discovery of mirror neurons—neural networks that are activated both in the performance of particular motor actions and in the observation of others performing such actions—helps account for the process of imitating another's acts, both in regular behavior as well as in Donne's poems. Understanding the mirror neuron system and how it cultivates a mutual intimacy helps explain how Donne's male speakers relate so passionately to their female beloveds.

Cognitive scientists have discovered that some neurons activate when persons or animals observe certain actions (such as laughing or crying) or when they perceive a direct representation of such actions. These neurons then duplicate the neural stimulation produced by that action so that the observer experiences the same kinds of affective sensations as the person who experienced them originally. When I see another person laugh, my brain replicates, to some degree, the experience of laughing and the feelings associated with that experience. Although such responses should not be interpreted as equivalent to precisely sharing or even understanding another's emotions, they do provide empirical proof of another's feelings and help observers discern and appreciate the observed person's condition. An informed study of the neural systems that cause replication suggests the psychological accuracy of Donne's portrayal of romantic love. In such poems as "The Ecstasy" and "A Valediction Forbidding Mourning," he depicts the complex interplay between the feelings and the flesh, the mind and the body, the spiritual and the physical. He shows how imitative reciprocity can intensify mutual devotion.[1]

The Mirror Neuron System

Recent neuroanatomical evidence shows that the process of matching another person's demeanor is rooted in the mirror neuron system (Gallese, "Action Recognition"). This system, discovered first in macaque monkeys in 1992, stimulates imitation of another creature's motor actions and mental states (Watson & Greenberg 126; Rizzolatti & Fabbri-Destro). Located in the premotor cortex of the human brain as well as in the superior temporal cortex, insula, and amygdala, these neurons help one person viscerally experience another person's thoughts and feelings (Iacoboni, "Within"). An illustration may help clarify how this system works:

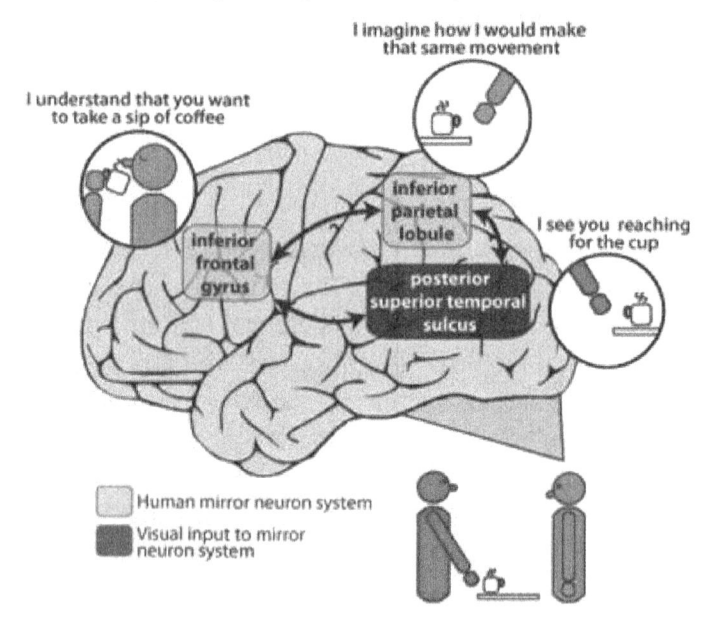

Although mirroring is mostly unconscious, studies show that both imitating and being imitated increase mutual liking and that more empathic individuals tend to imitate other people to a much greater degree than do less empathic individuals (Chartrand &

Bargh). Various studies have emphasized the specific role mirror neurons play in adapting and shaping a person's emotions to produce an internal understanding of another's feelings (Schulte-Rüther). This kind of unconscious imitation thus serves as a basic component of empathy. People who share the same thoughts and feelings also share the same unconscious neural experiences.

Whereas conscious, calculated words and actions can be informative as well as manipulative, the non-conscious, automatic responses of the mirror neuron system provide a stable base to help define one person's identity in relation to another person's identity. In other words, the processes of the neural system cannot be faked or insincere: the brain responds automatically.

Significantly, Donne's verse privileges these ways of knowing: ways of knowing that remain uncorrupted by calculation or self-interest. By simulating the beloved's movements, the speaker in Donne's romantic poems confirms their mutual desire and implies a distinct sense of individuality founded upon the self being both subject and object. The romantic couple's emergent mutual identity draws from the physical cues they exchange. By imitating each other's behavior, they literally come to share in a mutual self—a self deeply rooted in the neural systems of their brains.

Donne consistently portrays imitation as cultivating a passionate intimacy. A close familiarity prompts each lover to copy the other's movements. The couple's love may flourish on a transcendent level, but it must "to body first repair" (Donne, "Ecstasy" lines 59-60). After all, it is in the body where the simultaneous encoding of sensory input and the activation of similar physical expression occurs. The brain's neural matching mechanism provides an intense, if subconscious, awareness of the beloved. The emotional relationship becomes deeply embedded in each partner's brain.

"A Valediction Forbidding Mourning"
The assumption that one person can gain insight into another's emotional state through observation of physical phenomena informs Donne's famous poem titled "A Valediction Forbidding Mourning."[2] In this poem, the speaker and his beloved ideally

share a deep understanding of each other's intentions, as attested to by the ways they imitate each other's actions (and even each other's non-actions). For instance, at one point the speaker, who must go on an extended journey away from his beloved, urges her to accept their separation quietly, without overtly displaying intense emotion: ". . . let us melt, and make no noise / No tear-floods, nor sigh tempests-move" (lines 5-6). Wanting to preserve the sanctity of their bond, the speaker does not want others to misconstrue their relationship. If they displayed intense public emotion when separating, they would cheapen their love. It would be cheapened not only in their own eyes and understanding, but also in the eyes and understanding of others. By imitating each other's quiet acceptance of the necessary, unpreventable separation, both lovers will share similar neural responses, similar emotions, and a similar sense of their relationship's special elevation. By unconsciously simulating each other's thoughts and feelings, they will achieve, at a very deep level of the brain, a sense of their distinct mutual intimacy. The very subtlety of this shared neural connection will prevent the "laity" (common, spiritually unelevated persons; line 8) from misinterpreting the nature of their relationship. The lovers will feel a connection far more profound than can easily be observed or comprehended by others.

This muted expression of sublime happiness may fail to awaken the curiosity of others, and in fact, it is *intended* to go unnoticed by others. But the deep, if quiet connection between the lovers will allow the couple to immerse themselves in each other's beings. Physically they will be separate, but spiritually and emotionally—that is, in the deepest neural senses—they will be united. By copying each other's behavior, they will achieve an understanding that surpasses merely rational comprehension. While their knowledge of each other inevitably draws on the senses, it will not rely upon them exclusively. Instead, the lovers' shared empathy (an empathy both generated and sustained by similar neural events in each person's brain) will affirm their mutual mental, emotional, and spiritual devotion and free them from merely physical dependence on one another. Because their love will be grounded in similar neural experiences, they will "Care less, eyes, lips or hands to miss" while the male speaker is off on his distant journey (line 20). Their relationship will involve shared experiences that occur *inside their* brains; therefore, their bond can withstand any mere bodily separation. No matter how far they may be from one another physically, they will be experiencing the same mental, emotional, and spiritual cognitions. In other words, they will share the same basic mindset (the same basic neural experiences) even if they do not share exactly the same location. The certitude generated by their neural reciprocity will prevent personal insecurities from undermining the relationship. Their stimulus-linked acts will create an inter-animated space where their affective and cognitive modes of knowing will complement one another.

At one point late in the poem, Donne famously compares the lovers' relationship to a geometric compass to illustrate the integral role that simulation plays in their relationship. An illustration can help clarify the speaker's imagery and argument:

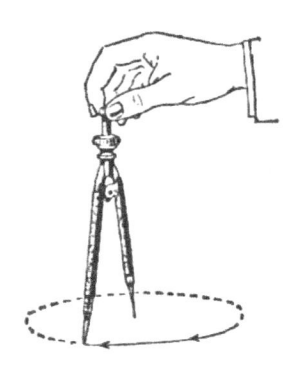

If (the speaker says) their souls are (in a certain sense) two souls,

> . . . they are two so

As stiff twin compasses are two;

Thy soul, the fixed foot, makes no show

To move, but doth, if the other do.

> And though it [i.e., the fixed foot] in the center sit,
>> Yet when the other far doth roam,
> It leans and hearkens after it,
>> And grows erect, as that comes home.
>
> Such wilt thou be to me, who must,
>> Like th' other foot, obliquely run;
> Thy firmness makes my circle just,
>> And makes me end where I begun. (lines 26-36)

    The compass, consisting of two identical pointed branches joined at the top by a pivot, highlights the semblance between the lovers and the ways a strong connection informs their bond even when they are separated by great distances. Just as the compass's branches stay exactly aligned with each other as they chart a geometric shape, so the two lovers remain aligned and connected emotionally, cognitively, and spiritually (i.e., through similar neural events) even when they are physically and geographically distant. Wherever the wandering speaker may go geographically, his stay-at-home beloved remains connected to him at the deepest mental levels. She resembles the fixed foot of the compass while he resembles that foot that actually moves: "Such wilt thou be to me, who must, / Like the other foot, obliquely run" (lines 33-4). By sharing the same thoughts, feelings, and desires, they grasp each other's point of view and remain "inter-assured of the mind" about each other's commitment to the relationship (line 19). Although Donne may not specifically have intended the word "mind" here to refer to the brain, interpreting the word as referring to the brain fits nicely with the argument offered in this essay.

    The pivot joining the two branches of the compass symbolizes how the speaker can readily determine where one self ends and another self begins. When the speaker says that his beloved's "firmness makes my circle just, / And makes me end where I begun," he implies that he maintains a continuous awareness of her presence in relation to his (lines 35-6). He thinks about her constantly, and his thinking helps create and sustain their emotional and spiritual bond. Her mental, spiritual, and emotional "firmness" deeply affects his very person and helps control his own thoughts and feelings and (therefore) his own behavior. The empathic neural connections they share, despite their physical separation, link them far more deeply than if they were merely, literally touching. No matter how far he travels, his resolute conviction draws from and returns to hers. This cycle of reciprocity generates, as Gallese et al. state, a specific phenomenal state of "intentional attunement" that constitutes a fundamental biological basis for one creature to understand another other creature's mind.

Nevertheless, this mutual understanding depends upon maintaining a sense of distinction. One cannot know another person until one has a sense of one's own identity. Knowing whose actions and emotions belong to whom ensures that each person's individuality remains intact. Such knowledge both preserves their distinct senses of self and ensures that their bond remains intact when they are separated. The speaker and the beloved in Donne's poem are not identical, just as the two feet of the compass are not identical. Instead, they are at once very similar and inseparably bound together.

As the speaker and his beloved spiritually track each other's movements with pinpoint accuracy, their gestures (whether physical or emotional) indicate their shared capacity to participate in each other's feelings and ideas. From any point on the circle, the speaker can look towards his beloved and intuit that her desires align with his. By sharing in the same experience, each perceives the other both as a distinct being and also as someone with whom each has a substantial relationship. These shared mental experiences rely upon brains that process and act upon shared information and shared neural connections.

"The Ecstasy"

Such connections also play an important role in "The Ecstasy" which begins as follows:

> Where, like a pillow on a bed
> 	A pregnant bank swell'd up to rest
> The violet's reclining head,
> 	Sat we two, one another's best.
> Our hands were firmly cemented
> 	With a fast balm, which thence did spring;
> Our eye-beams twisted, and did thread
> 	Our eyes upon one double string . . . . (lines 1-8)

Here, the speaker engages in a series of acts that trigger the beloved's neural pathways to model her actions upon his. In this poem, as in "A Valediction," a close familiarity between the couple exists, and the pronouns in the opening stanza emphasize this closeness by referring to them as "we two" and by claiming that they are "one another's best" (line 4). Each person completes the other, so that neither loses sight of what he or she contributes to the relationship. When the speaker looks into his beloved's eyes, he feels their close emotional and mental connection: "Our eye-beams twisted, and did thread/ Our eyes upon one double string" (lines 7-8). Each partner must acknowledge the other in order to make their experience mutual. This intertwining illustrates how the experience that neurologists call "affective matching" facilitates communication and, in the process, produces a state of being in one person that aligns itself with the other's sense of self. As opposed to passively staring, the kind of ocular twisting Donne describes indicates a genuinely active engagement: each person uses simulated responses to discern the other person's intentions. Each person becomes both a subject and an object (a perceiver and someone perceived). Synchrony allows the poem's speaker to experience the beloved as another "I," so that their bond is informed, not constrained, by physical expression.

The understanding implied and propagated by this intentional gaze has led some scholars, such as Catherine Gimelli Martin, to view the lovers' connection here as evidence of a rapturous, transcendent, almost "out of body" experience. However, the intense affection that permeates the bodies of Donne's lovers keeps this moment tied to this world. The "pictures on our eyes" remain fixed as each partner strives to immerse himself and herself in the other's feelings (line 11). They share an internal awareness discovered through shared sight.

To appreciate the source of this love, they must retain their individuality. As the conjoining of their "hands" and "eyes" brings them closer together, the collective pronoun the speaker uses—"*our* hands" and "*our* eyes" (emphasis added)—signifies the necessary and distinct contribution each person makes in deepening the relationship. A clear self/other differentiation comes to the fore when the focus shifts from the body to a heightened emotional state; here, the speaker specifically identifies "her and me." He says, "Our souls, . . . to advance their state/ Were gone out, hung 'twixt her and me" (lines 15-16). The word "souls" signifies not simply a spiritual dimension to their relationship but also a profound empathetic connection. The intensity of their physical exchange incites a perspective that enables the lovers the freedom to ponder their mutual devotion—*especially* its mutuality. While an individual's self may be invested in and imagine how it relates to another person's self, the speaker in Donne's poem must nonetheless distinguish his consciousness from hers. If not, he would suffer from an egocentric bias, erroneously believing that she feels and thinks in exactly the same way he does. If such complete duplication and integration were to occur, then his sense of self would be lost. The boundaries of empathy are not overly porous; instead, they are rigid enough to allow each partner to maintain his or her own integrity. Thus the emotional transference conveyed through simulated acts does not cause either person to forsake his own her own identity.

The bodies of Donne's couple abet both this connection and this distinction by lying still, "like sepulchral statues" (line 18):

> Our souls (which to advance their state
>
> Were gone out) hung 'twixt her and me.
>
> And whilst our souls negotiate there,
>
> We like sepulchral statues lay;
>
> All day, the same our postures were,
>
> And we said nothing, all the day. (lines 15-20)

Words prove unnecessary. Instead, shared sensory-motor knowledge helps the couple gain a greater sense of themselves as independent beings who desire to strengthen the relationship. Their empathetic connection "makes both one, each this, and that" (line 36). The self exists simultaneously on its own *and* in relation to the other; the shared moment exists precisely because of their singularity. Somehow, they remain separate but are also deeply united:

> But as all several souls contain
>
> Mixture of things, they know not what,
>
> Love these mix'd souls doth mix again
>
> And makes both one, each this and that. (lines 33-36)

Since their simulated stillness primarily operates as a non-conscious process, each partner can deliberate upon the underlying significance of their congruent feelings. Their shared experience of stillness fosters an appreciation in each person of the other person's perspective, encouraging them to consider the source of their commitment.

> This ecstasy doth unperplex,
>
> We said, and tell us what we love;
>
> We see by this it was not sex,
>
> We see we saw not what did move . . . . (lines 29-32)

The inviolable link between perception and action enables them to see what before they "saw not." They realize that the origins of their love lie not in the body (not in mere sexual impulse), but that their spiritual connection is rooted in physical experience. By directing his mental energies toward her, the speaker ignites neurons in his brain that also fire in hers. This shared firing sparks a fully realized empathy that allows them to comprehend that what individuates them—a longing for the other—also brings them together. Their ecstasy finds meaning neither in language nor body alone, but via the knowledge produced by the neurophysiologic response system. Mirroring the other's stillness incites an awareness of the desires affecting each of them. Their familiarity with one another ensures that the simulated response conveys the proper emotional valence and accurately represents the other's psychological state. This shared understanding removes any doubt about the authenticity of their commitment.

Donne's emphasis upon both affective (emotional) and cognitive (intellectual) elements as the basis of any substantive relationship reappears in a letter to his friend Sir Henry Goodyer. In that letter, Donne writes that "we consist of three parts, a Soul, and Body, and Minde: which I call those thoughts and affections and passions, which neither soul nor body hath alone, but have been begotten by their communication" ("To Sir H.G." 70). As before, the word "soul" can signify either a spiritual entity or an empathetic resonance that promotes an active exchange of knowledge. Brian Cummings avers that the phrase "soul's language" suggests a discourse of ardor (line 22). "The emotions," Cummings says, "constitute our means of communication, they 'interinanimate' us, or make us, we might say, using a word Donne would have loved and might easily have invented, 'intersubjective'" (71). This interlinking between body, thought, and feeling causes an acute awareness of the other's selfhood and appears repeatedly throughout "The Ecstasy." Verbs such as "twisted," "intergraft," and "negotiate" describe a behavioral reciprocity that culminates in an intense emotional experience (lines 7, 9, 17). Each partner's behavior activates the partner's mental representation or re-experiencing of the thoughts and feelings that produced that behavior. The couple's shared behavior increases their intangible intimacy:

> When love with one another so
>
>   Interinanimates two souls,
>
> That abler soul, which thence doth flow,
>
>   Defects of loneliness controls.
>
>
> We then, who are this new soul, know
>
>   Of what we are compos'd and made,
>
> For th' atomies of which we grow
>
>   Are souls, whom no change can invade. (lines 41-48)

The "new soul" that results from the union of their separate souls is stronger ("abler") than either of their separate souls alone. The thoughts and feelings they share (and the mutual empathy they have attained) are by definition strong by their union than they could possibly have been if they had remained separate. The bond between them strengthens them both; each draws strength from the empathy they now share—an empathy anchored in the neural mirroring that has occurred in their brains.

    Their desire, like the single violet that reproduces not through seeds but though an extensive root system, redoubles the strength of their affective matching. This effect of desire creates multiple conduits that allow them to share each other's state of being. Since mirror neurons do not fire indiscriminately but are limited to goal-directed actions, their firing verifies an interdependence linking one creature to another. It is this interdependence that prompts an emotional cognition (which combines feeling and thought). By participating in his beloved's emotions and other mental states while maintaining his own identity, the speaker shows that he cares about her for her own sake. Rather than trying to control or dominate her mind, feelings, and soul, he empathizes with them.

By simulating one another's thoughts, feelings, and behaviors, this couple distinguish themselves from all others. But they also realize that they cannot exist purely or only on some lofty spiritual plane. Instead,

> . . . pure lovers' souls [must] descend
>
> T'affections, and to faculties,
>
> Which sense may reach and apprehend,
>
> Else a great prince in prison lies. (lines 65-8)

The body's neural matching mechanism enables them to reach a higher plane, where each shares in the other's emotional understanding. Even in moments of pure rapture, however, the body remains integral in providing insight into and surety of this empathetic experience. Empathy springs partly from the body's experiences, which reveal the beloved to be not just another individual, but one who seeks the same end as the speaker. The links between them are neurally realized, refine their identity, and affirm the purity of their desire.

In both of the poems discussed in this essay, the beloved's presence is the focus and animating center of the speaker's perspective. Even though the conditions surrounding the couples differ in each poem, both works explore the physiological effects of the beloved's affection upon the speaker. Using knowledge of the mirror neuron system as an interpretive tool can help us plumb the depths of the couples' commitments. The shared intimacy shared by the couples in these poems activates the same neural substrates in both the speaker and the woman to whom, or about whom, he speaks. Both the lover and the beloved share the same internal neural experiences. Through a process of affective matching, the speaker decenters himself from a self-oriented state to an other-oriented one. From this position, he cultivates an emotional interpersonal cognition and, in the process, forges a profound empathetic link. The kind of thoughts, feelings, and behavior Donne depicts resemble those described in the recent neuroscientific literature. That literature helps explain some of what is going on in Donne's love poems, just as his poems help illustrate recent scientific discoveries about the origins of empathy in the human brain.

Notes

1. For another view of Donne from a cognitive perspective, see the book by Winkelman, which incorporates a number of his previous writings on the subject.
2. All citations from *Songs and Sonnets* from *John Donne's Poetry*, edited by Donald R. Dickson, 2007, New York: Norton.

Works Cited

Byatt, A.S. "Feeling Thought: Donne and the Embodied Mind." *The Cambridge Companion to John Donne*, edited by Achsah Guibbory, Cambridge UP, 2006, pp. 247-58.

Carr, L., et al. "Neural Mechanisms of Empathy in Humans: A Relay from Neural Systems for Imitation to Limbic Areas." *Proceedings of the National Academy of Sciences of the United States of America*, vol. 100, 2003, pp. 5497-5502.

Chartrand, T. & J. Bargh. "The Chameleon Effect: The Perception-Behavior Link to Social Interaction." *Journal of Personality and Social Psychology*, vol. 76, 1999, pp. 893-910.

Cummings, Brian. "Donne's Passions: Emotion, Agency and Language." *Passions and Subjectivity in Early Modern Culture*, edited by B. Cummings & F. Sierhuis, Ashgate, 2013, pp. 51-74.

De Waal, F. B. M. "Putting the Altruism Back Into Altruism: The Evolution of Empathy." *Annual Review of Psychology*, vol. 59, 2007, pp. 279-300.

Decety, J. & P. Jackson. "The Functional Architecture of Human Empathy." *Behavioral and Cognitive Neuroscience Review*, vol. 3, 2004, pp. 71-100.

Donne, John. "The Ecstasy." *John Donne's Poetry*, edited by Donald Dickson, Norton, 2007, pp. 98-100.

———. "A Nocturnal Upon St. Lucy's Day, Being the Shortest Day." *John Donne's Poetry*, edited by Donald Dickson, Norton, 2007, pp. 115-17.

———. *A Sermon Preached at Pauls Cross to the Lords of the Council, and other Honorable Persons*, 24. Mart. 1616, *John Donne Sermons*, 1 Nov. 2016, http://cdm15999.contentdm.oclc.org/cdm/ref/collection/JohnDonne/id/170/.

———. *A Sermon Preached at the Spittle, Upon Easter-Munday*, 1622. *John Donne Sermons*, 1 Nov. 2016. http://contentdm.lib.byu.edu/cdm/compoundobject/collection/JohnDonne/id/3171/rec/1/.

———. "To Sir H.G." *Letters to severall persons of honour*. Printed by J. Flesher for Richard Marriot, 1651.

———. "A Valediction Forbidding Mourning." *John Donne's Poetry*, edited by Donald Dickson, Norton, 2007, pp. 71-72.

Gallese, V. "The 'Shared Manifold' Hypothesis: From Mirror Neurons to Empathy." *Journal of Consciousness Studies*, vol. 8, 2001, pp. 33-50.

———, et al. "Action Recognition in the Premotor Cortex," *Brain*, 1996, vol. 199, pp. 593-609.

Gazzola, V., L. Aziz-Zadeh, and C. Keysers. "Empathy and the Somatotopic Auditory Mirror System in Humans." *Current Biology*, vol. 16, 2006, pp. 1824-1829.

Greteman, Blaine. "'All this seed pearl': John Donne and Bodily Presence." *College Literature*, vol. 37, 2010, pp. 26-42.

Habinek, Lianne. "Untying the 'Subtle Knot': Anatomical Metaphor and the Case of the rete mirabile." *Configurations*, vol. 20, 2012, pp. 239-77.

Iacoboni, M. "Within Each Other: Neural Mechanisms for Empathy in the Primate Brain." *Empathy: Philosophical and Psychological Perspectives*, edited by A. Coplan and P. Goldie, Oxford UP, 2011, pp. 45-57.

———, et al. "Grasping the Intentions of Others with One's Own Mirror Neuron System." *PLoS Biology*, vol. 3, 2005, pp. 529-539.

Lipps, T. "Das Wissen von Fremden Ichen." *Psychologische Untersuchungen*, vol. 1, 1907, pp. 694-722.

Martin, Catherine Gimelli. "The Erotology of Donne's 'Extasie' and the Secret History of Voluptuous Rationalism." *Studies in English Literature 1500–1900*, vol. 44, 2004, pp. 129-47.

Powrie, Sarah. "Transposing World Harmony: Donne's Creation Poetics in the Context of a Medieval Tradition." *Studies in Philology*, vol. 107, 2010, pp. 212-235.

Puttenham, George. *The Arte of English Poesie*. 1589.

Rankin, K., et al. "Structural Anatomy of Empathy in Neurodegenerative Disease." *Brain*, vol. 29, 2006, pp. 2945-2956.

Rizzolatti, G., and M. Fabbri-Destro. "Mirror Neurons: From Discovery to Autism." *Experimental Brain Research*, vol. 200, 2010, pp. 223-237.

Schulte-Rüther, M. "Mirror Neuron and Theory of Mind Mechanisms Involved in Face-to-Face Interactions: A Functional Magnetic Resonance Imaging Approach to Empathy." *Journal of Cognitive Neuroscience*, vol. 19, 2007, pp. 1354-1372.

Selleck, Nancy. *The Interpersonal Idiom in Shakespeare, Donne, and Early Modern Culture*. Palgrave, 2008.

Shamay-Tsoory, S., et al. "Two Systems for Empathy: A Double Dissociation between Emotional and Cognitive Empathy in Inferior Frontal Gyrus versus Ventromedial Prefrontal Lesions." *Brain*, vol. 132, 2009, pp. 617-627.

Sugg, Richard. *Murder after Death: Literature and Anatomy in Early Modern England*, Cornell UP, 2007.

Targoff, Ramie. *John Donne, Body and Soul*. U of Chicago P, 2008.

Van Baaren, R., et al. "Being Imitated: Consequences of Nonconsciously Showing Empathy." *The Social Neuroscience of Empathy*, edited by J. Decety and W. Ickes, MIT P, 2009, pp. 31-42.

Watson, J. & I. Greenberg, L. "Empathic Resonance: A Neuroscience Perspective." *The Social Neuroscience of Empathy*, edited by J. Decety and W. Ickes, MIT P, 2009, pp. 125-38.

Winkelman, Michael A. *A Cognitive Approach to John Donne's Songs and Sonnets*. Palgrave Macmillan, 2013.

Zimmer, Mary E. "'In Whom Love Wrought New Alcimie'": The Inversion of Christian Spiritual Resurrection in John Donne's 'A Nocturnall upon S. Lucie's Day.'" *Christianity and Literature*, vol. 51, 2002, pp. 553-567.

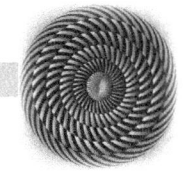

Poe's Ideal of Love and the Broken World: Crowd Psychology in Some Tales and Poems

Jeffrey Folks

Edgar Allan Poe's idealized conception of marriage in "Ligeia," "Eleonora," and other tales and poems can be viewed as understandable responses to the precarious and damaged conditions of Poe's existence. By applying the principles of Elias Canetti's psychology of crowds, it is possible to understand the role that fantasies of ideal love, male gallantry, and withdrawal from the world play in Poe's imagination. Although Poe is often viewed as an author whose aesthetic is dominated almost exclusively by a tendency toward the macabre, his habitual response to the losses he suffered tended to involve fantasies of ideal, if improbably happy resolutions. By idealizing the female object of his affections and adhering to the code of male gallantry, Poe attempted to maintain the undamaged and uncorrupted world of his imagination in the face of the devastating incursions of the actual world. In terms of Canetti's theory, however, Poe's marriage group of tales do something more important yet: they bring actual understanding to bear on the dynamics of social oppression and individual response. By doing so, they offer up a meaningful and real resolution to the macabre situations that Poe so often confronted.

As Canetti explains in his landmark study, *Crowds and Power*, the individual's relationship to various sorts of crowds, both real and imagined, plays a central role in human psychology. All human beings define their existence in relationship to crowds consisting of other human beings, other living and dead creatures, objects, and ideas. Participation in crowd behavior can be both productive (allowing for what Canetti termed "release") and oppressive (resulting in responses ranging from flight to paranoia). In many cases, response to crowds can take the form of a sense of persecution, subjection, and even terror. The mounting sense of harm that one collects over a lifetime, which Canetti referred to as "the burden of stings," can create an unbearable impediment that must be addressed either by passing the stings along to others, by escaping via physical or mental flight, or by applying understanding and thus amelioration to the process of subjection. An intricate part of this process is "the command," an element of control that runs through nearly all aspects of human relationships and which Canetti regards as "the most dangerous single element in the social life of mankind" (333). A familiar response to such perceived harm is the creation of the role of "the survivor," the figure who triumphs over the world by surviving all others.

Poe's Personal Psychology

Perhaps no other writer in American literature understood the psychology of crowds as clearly as did Edgar Allan Poe. I would argue that the intensity of Poe's idealized conception of love originated in psychological burdens he accumulated as a result of a repeated experience of exclusion and loss. Just before he turned three, Poe lost his beloved mother Eliza, whose image he carried with him for the rest of his life. After being taken in but never adopted by the Allan family, Poe was eventually cut off entirely from support, despite the great wealth of John Allan. From his earliest days, perhaps in response to his frosty relationship with his male guardian, Poe had shaped his identity around his relationship to an idealized woman, whether it be his mother, his co-guardian Frances Allan (who died in 1829, when Poe was eleven), his maternal surrogate Jane Stanard, his teenage fiancée Elmira Royster, or his wife Virginia (and following Virginia's death, Mrs. Nancy Richmond and Sarah Helen Whitman). All of these women had abandoned him, either by way of death or by breaking off the relationship, and the paradigm of lost love was so much a part of Poe's psyche that it entered into much of what he wrote.

From January 1842, when she fell ill, to January 1847, when she died, Poe witnessed the gradual demise of his wife Virginia within the close space of their Fordham cottage and under unimaginable conditions of poverty, hunger, and cold, terminating a period of five years that Poe referred to as "the horrible never-ending oscillation between hope and despair" (1368). Virginia's death was followed by a desolate year of illness and lassitude on Poe's part. In the remaining year and a half of his life, Poe produced the long metaphysical treatise *Eureka*, his important critical essay "The Poetic Principle," and such poems as "Annabel Lee" and "The Bells." During this period of recovery, he also lobbied in support of his project of founding a superior literary magazine, to be called "The Stylus," and he became engaged to his childhood sweetheart, Elmira Royster Shelton. However, it can hardly be said that during this period Poe's psychological condition stabilized.

In 1846, months before her death, Poe wrote to Virginia that she was his "greatest and only stimulus now, to battle with this uncongenial, unsatisfactory, and ungrateful life" (1367). That conception of romantic love as a sanctuary against hostile crowds, of the sort that Canetti classified among others as baiting crowds, prohibition crowds, lamenting packs, war packs, and crowds of the dead, is a common feature in Poe's writing and in the romantic imagination in general. One point to be made, which Poe himself stressed in response to his critics, is that the gothic extremes of his aesthetic were not the result of mental instability, alcoholism, or some other personal attribute: they were a familiar and indeed rational response to the seemingly unbearable conditions of existence. Poe's dependence on a conception of idealized love was hardly anomalous in his day, or for that matter is it in our own. It represents a universal response to the uncertainties and fears associated with the condition of the individual in society and with the condition of mortality itself. Poe's aspirations toward the ideal are grounded in his desperate attempt to survive amid a broken world of loss and betrayal.

While it would be possible to examine any of Poe's tales in terms of Canetti's theory of crowds, a study of several of his so-called marriage group will reveal several key elements of Poe's psychological response. In his representation of romantic relationships, Poe presents the reader with couples whose very existence is threatened by the force of crowds and who respond to this pressure with a determination to survive, often by means of the application of superior intellect, artistic power, or will. By creating an undying and rarified bond between the lovers, grounded in absolute fidelity and chastity, Poe suggests the possibility of a sanctuary from the oppressive realm of the command.

"Ligeia"

In "Ligeia," a story that recounts the first-person narrator's ethereal relationship with the exquisite and otherworldly figure of Ligeia, all of the elements of Canetti's crowd theory are clearly present. At the beginning of the tale, Poe's narrator lives within a carefully constructed sanctuary in a remote castle on the Rhine, a secluded and protective existence that, by its complete withdrawal from others, attests the destructive force of society's oppression. The narrator's identification with Ligeia is practically absolute, so much so that he lives within a childlike condition of pupil in relation to Ligeia's abounding knowledge and force of personality. In this regard, Canetti's theory of the burden of childhood commands is quite pertinent. "It is a miracle," writes Canetti, "that [children] ever survive the pressure and do not collapse under the burden of the commands laid on them. . ." (306). To the degree that one is harmed, however, one responds with exceptional efforts. "What spurs men on to achievement is the deep urge to be rid of the commands once laid on them" (Canetti 306). By this reckoning, both Ligeia and the narrator must have suffered enormously from the cruelty of parents and teachers, as did Poe himself if we accept the evidence presented by Kenneth Silverman.[1] In response to this suffering at the hands of a pack of assailants, Ligeia and her lover, and Poe himself as their creator, seem to have entered into a defensive bond based on a very particular conception of marriage.

Every command contains within it the threat of punishment, the greatest of which, Canetti writes, "is the original penalty, which is death" (308). All forms of interrogation and command rest upon the implicit threat of punishment, and they elicit "the anxiety of command" (Canetti 309). A familiar response to the burden of command is the act of transformation—an action that is crucial to the relationship of Ligeia and the narrator and to the revival of Ligeia after death.[2] The "most elementary thing" about transformation, Canetti states, "is that *one body is equated with another*" (340). It is precisely this close identification or merging with the beloved that is involved in the relationship of the narrator and Ligeia and that explains the narrator's seemingly odd behavior following the loss of his beloved. After Ligeia suffers illness and death, the narrator flees Germany and soon enters an engagement with Lady Rowena Trevanion. Unlike the idealized relationship with Ligeia, the narrator's marriage to Rowena is characterized by the all-too-earthly emotions of frustration and anger. Clearly, Rowena does not possess the transcendent qualities of mind and spirit necessary to protect the narrator from society's stings—or from his own sense of inadequacy—but she does possess one virtue: a vital physical frame that can be employed for the revivification of Ligeia.

Throughout the tale, the narrator's affiliation—and presumably Poe's as well—is with Ligeia and not with Rowena. Hutchisson speculates, as have others, that Poe and Virginia never consummated their nuptials or, if so, "it did not happen for the first two years of their marriage" (55). As several commentators have suggested, Poe's selection of the thirteen-year-old Virginia as his wife may have involved the calculation that their nuptials could not be consummated, at least initially, and that their marriage would therefore, as he viewed it, remain uncorrupted by physical desire. Whatever the truth of his conjugal relationship, it is quite certain that in his fiction, Poe subjugates the role of sexuality in marriage to the spiritual, emotional, and intellectual qualities that are identified with Ligeia. Hutchisson is certainly correct in asserting that "Poe's male and female characters seem to exist on nonsexual planes—like mother and child, or sister and brother" (118). According to the first-hand account of Frances Sargent Osgood, a close friend of both Poe and Virginia, Poe's domestic persona was precisely of this sort: "[p]layful, affectionate, witty, alternately docile and wayward as a petted child" and invariably kind and courteous toward "his young, gentle and idolized wife" (qtd. in Hutchisson 56). The figure of Rowena, though "at all times feeble" (Poe 272), is offensive simply because she can never match the transcendent qualities associated with Ligeia. She is, in fact, a mere cipher in terms of the qualities that Poe so desperately required. Indeed, the fact that Rowena falls ill soon after her marriage during her stay in the grotesquely ornamented bridal chamber that the narrator has so carefully prepared for her suggests that the narrator plays a role in bringing about her sudden illness and death. Rowena's death makes possible the return of Ligeia, but what can be said of the relationship of the narrator to his beloved?

Despite the suggestion that Ligeia can never be known—that her mind is ineffable, her body ethereal and virginal, and her past unknown—much can be deduced from what Poe tells us. The emphasis on the antiquity of Ligeia's family is particularly important, for what takes place in the final sections of the story is, in effect, the transmigration of souls as three drops of ruby liquid pass the spirit of Ligeia into the still living body of Rowena. From Poe's perspective, the contemplation of this process afforded a unique opportunity to escape the oppressive force of mortality that was so apparent in his own history. The early death of his mother, brother, first love, and wife, and his abandonment by his father, guardian family, fiancée, and various close friends could be magically reversed by way of a powerful short story in which, as Poe asserts in the tale's epigraph by Joseph Glanvill, "Man doth not yield him to the angels, nor unto death utterly, save only through the weakness of his feeble will." That act of defiance and the psychological necessity for it are what Poe records in "Ligeia."

The mysterious person of Ligeia herself, with the suggestion of a timeless lineage stretching back to ancient Greek and Near East civilizations, embodies this mode of survival. Her beauty is exquisite but irregular and strange at the same time—interestingly, an irregularity very much present in the photographic images of Poe himself but not in those of Virginia or the other women to whom he had been devoted. The most striking feature of Ligeia, again suggested by the surviving images of Poe himself (and of his mother Eliza), are the remarkably large, dark eyes, with their "strangeness" of expression, accompanied by "slightly irregular" brows (Poe 264). The narrator identifies the indefinable expression of Ligeia's eyes with objects in the material world, "in the contemplation of a moth, a butterfly, a chrysalis, a stream of running water," "in the ocean; in the falling of a meteor," "in the glances of unusually aged people" and in "one or two stars of heaven," especially in one star of the sixth magnitude located "near the large star in Lyra" (265). Ligeia's, Poe's, and Eliza's dark orbs are repeated everywhere in creation, confirming the author's belief, expounded at great length in his last book *Eureka*, in the sentience, mutability, and immortality of all aspects of creation.

Significantly, the most remarkable quality of Ligeia, even more pronounced than her beauty or her astounding learning, is her "*intensity* in thought, action, or speech" (Poe 265). Ligeia's "passion" and "fierce energy" are connected with her mastery of "all the wide areas of moral, physical, and mathematical science" (266). She becomes the narrator's guide to the metaphysical world, and his memories of her are associated with the study, not the bedroom, which, in contrast to the elaborate description of Rowena's bridal chamber, is never mentioned. As Kenneth Silverman writes, "One reason the narrator finds the loss [of Ligeia] irremediable is that although an adult, he depends on Ligeia as if he were a child" (139). Silverman, who stresses the psychology of mourning and remembrance throughout his biography, fails to examine the nature of this dependence in "Ligeia," but it is clearly a central element of the story. I would suggest that it is not so much Ligeia's protection in and of itself but the idealized relationship, albeit not of equals but of teacher and pupil, that is most important. In Poe's mind, the ideal marriage of narrator and Ligeia, like that of himself and Virginia, assured safety, solace, and refuge within a world of suffering and pain. That conception, I would add, is hardly an anomalous one: as Canetti shows, it is a fundamental human response to a world that is always filled with burdens, stings, and threats.

Like all beloved figures in Poe's writing, Ligeia falls ill, and the couple's habitual isolation from all others suggests their foreknowledge of this eventuality, yet more so than most, Ligeia possesses the capacity to resist and overcome death. As she nears death, she expresses "the overflowing of a heart whose more than passionate devotion amounted to idolatry" (Poe 267). After intense resistance and following her last words, the passage from Joseph Glanvill ("Man doth not yield him to the angels, nor until death utterly, save only through the weakness of his feeble will"), Ligeia passes away. The narrator flees the castle by the Rhine where they had lived, suggesting not merely his grief but an inability to survive the burden of command that he had eluded in the company of Ligeia, and travels to a remote region of England where, now an opium addict, he purchases a decayed abbey in which he prepares a ghastly bridal chamber for Rowena, a bride that he has all but purchased "for gold" from her "haughty family" (270).

The bridal chamber is important, not because of the gothic frisson that it summons up but because of the association of devastation with the figure of Rowena, an earthly female who possesses none of the transcendent qualities of Ligeia and who, in fact, is notable only for the role her body plays in Ligeia's act of self-reincarnation. The bleak deathliness of the abbey's bridal chamber, pentagonal in shape and adorned with a single, immense window "of leaden hue" and a golden censer hanging from a golden chain, with the bridal couch of ebony "with a pall-like canopy above" (Poe 271), attests the narrator's unconscious wish for or complicity in the death of his second wife. In the seven angles of the chamber stands "a gigantic sarcophagus of black granite," and the walls are covered with a tapestry of golden cloth covered with black, changeable arabesque figures creating a "phantasmagoric effect" (271). Ornamenting the tapestry are figures that create the effect "of ghastly forms which belong to the superstition of the Norman, or arise in the guilty slumbers of the monk" (271). The bridal couch itself was "of an Indian model, and low, and sculptured of solid ebony, with a pall-like canopy above" (271). No bride ever received such an unwelcoming reception as Rowena, for the reason that her qualities of body and mind are the opposite of the chaste and high-minded ideal that the narrator requires to secure his escape from the burden of command. If anything, what marriage to Rowena promises is what Canetti terms "the domestication of command," a deathly and very much earthly condition of "voluntary captivity"

(307-8), which involves an acceptance of subjection in return for security of the sort involved in the relationship of mother and child.

Rowena lives with the narrator for two months following their marriage, with Rowena constantly dreading "the fierce moodiness of [his] temper" (Poe 272), until Rowena falls prey to a nervous illness triggered by sounds in her chamber and movements among the tapestries. Terrified by these ominous signs, Rowena becomes faint, and when the narrator brings her a goblet of wine, a ghostly presence near him drops "three or four drops of a brilliant and ruby colored fluid" into the wine (Poe 273). On the third night subsequent to this event, Rowena dies, and her body, wrapped in the customary winding sheet, is prepared for burial. As he sits through the night by the side of the corpse, the narrator observes another presence in the room, a presence associated in his mind with the memory of Ligeia. At this time, the corpse begins its gradual process of revivification, with sounds and movement of a living creature stirring within the shroud. Rowena's corpse alternates between life and death, as if the soul of Ligeia that has been deposited within is struggling to reanimate the body it has borrowed. This process is accompanied, and perhaps stimulated, by the narrator, whose visions of his first wife seem to coincide with, if not trigger, the animation that he observes in the corpse. In the end, Ligeia appears before him, triumphant over death. Ligeia and the narrator are reunited, and the tale can be said to have ended triumphantly (for all except Rowena), restoring the intense unity of narrator and Ligeia that serves as protection against the assaults of the physical world.

It is important to understand just what Poe has embodied in this tale, as well as what he has not. First of all, despite its supernatural motifs of ghostly presences and body snatching, "Ligeia" is not, in essentials, a tale of horror or of the macabre. It is a realistic encoding of the most familiar and formative experience of Poe's life—that of the early loss of a soulmate and the lasting grief that this event generates. More vividly than any of his other stories or poems, "Ligeia" uncovers the author's intense desire for a lasting love and his grief, and an element of guilt, in the survivorship of this loss. His imagining of the perfection and chastity of his relationship is intimately related to his fear of its loss and his intense desire for its survival. Love itself, as Poe tells us in this and other tales, is a relationship that holds magical power essential to his own survival. In other words, in Poe's mind, the degree of purity and perfection that he ascribes to the beloved is a crucial element in the preservation of his own life. The reduction of the ideal love to the terms of a worldly and corrupt imagination triggers the death of the beloved and the potential insanity of the author. Survival can only be assured by the couple's determination to remain chaste.

Largely unspoken in Poe's tales is the reality that this chastity is eventually violated. While critics have not pointed to this dynamic in "Ligeia," the illness of Ligeia follows immediately upon the narrator's losing sight of the ideal, "the goal of a wisdom too divinely precious not to be forbidden" (Poe 266). The narrator's "expectations" of being admitted into this primary sphere of metaphysical knowledge are disappointed, presumably because he is in fact human and not divine, and the realization of this weakness, evidence of the corruptibility of the narrator and of all human beings, precipitates the illness of his wife. What the narrator seeks is not just absolute knowledge but transcendence of his mortality, the assurance of his survival in a world of corruption and death. With the death of Ligeia, it appears that this security has been denied him, but by means of the combined will of Ligeia and himself, the ideal knowledge and security are restored. This resolution enacts what Hutchisson views as the central theme of Poe's entire oeuvre: "how to die and yet live, how to reunite with lost loved ones in an otherworld beyond the material one" (195). Thus, "Ligeia" can be viewed as a psychological allegory of the most essential of human fears—the fear of death and the desire, as Poe puts it, "for life—*but for life*" (268). It is what Canetti would categorize as the story of "the survivor," with all its amoral and ruthless features of denial, deflection of "stings," and determination to outlive others. As Brian M. Barbour has noted, Poe's tales display his "insight into the will-to-dominate of the autonomous individual and its destructive consequences" (48). Far more than a gothic tale of vampirism, "Ligeia" is, again in Canetti's terms, a highly familiar record of one human being's fears and griefs and of his predictable response to these. The fact that in real life his faith was repeatedly disappointed is irrelevant: in Poe's imagination, death could be overcome and survival assured if the purity of love and the separation from the world could be maintained.

"Ligeia" is Poe's most important romantic tale, a story that eerily prefigures the brevity and anguish of his marriage to Virginia. Like Poe's other major stories and poems on the same theme, "Ligeia" is the tale of an ideal love, chaste and ethereal, but one that is doomed by some unknown malevolent force in the universe—a force that could otherwise be viewed quite simply as the human condition. As in the other tales, the lovers struggle against this demon force and are successful in overcoming the condition of death that separates them. Significantly, all of Poe's major romantic tales and poems conclude with a triumph of the lovers' will over the adversity that faces them. Given the failure of so many of Poe's actual human relationships, these triumphant conclusions may be seen as fantasies of happiness or as expressions of faith in the redemptive potential of love. What they are *not* is the macabre imaginings of ghostly, and at times malevolent, apparitions or, worse yet, the pathetic imaginings of an unbalanced mind. In light of the circumstances under which Poe and his contemporaries lived, with average life expectancies of less than forty and the ubiquitous presence of pestilence and want, Poe's idealization of love and his fantasy of its deathless ties is entirely reasonable. "Ligeia" and similar tales are not expressions of psychological aberrations but understandable attempts to combat and defy the devastation of everyday life.[3]

"Eleanora"

A fundamental tension exists within all of Poe's marriage tales between the mundane limitations of the lovers and their aspirations toward an ideal plane of existence, with the intrusive force of sexuality lurking in the background of all of these stories. No other tale so perfectly resolves the dilemma posed by the earthliness of desire and Poe's need to idealize it as does "Eleonora." In the tale, as in life, the narrator marries his first cousin, with whom he had "always dwelled," as did Poe and Virginia from the time she was eight. In the story, Poe fantasizes an ideal landscape, the "Valley of the Many-Colored Grass," an isolated but verdant and fruitful paradise in which he and Eleonora live alone. The guileless Eleonora, "a maiden artless and innocent as the brief life she had led among the flowers" of the valley (Poe 470), is described as having an unworldly brightness in her eyes and the loveliness "of the Seraphim" in her expression (470). Having lived in the valley chastely together for many years, the narrator and Eleonora, then twenty and fifteen respectively, enter into a "delirious bliss" (470), Poe's shorthand, presumably, for a sexual relationship.

Eventually, as if in response to the consummation of their love, Eleonora sees "the finger of Death . . . upon her bosom" (Poe 471), and she becomes obsessed with the topic of death. The sequence of events suggests that the lovers' transgression of chastity brings about Eleonora's illness and death, though this connection is never explicitly stated. Poe does affirm that his mistress, like that of countless subjects of romantic poems and tales before, was too perfect to survive in this world: "[L]ike the ephemeron, she had been made perfect in loveliness only to die" (471), and as in other tales and poems, Poe's narrator implies that supernatural forces envy the perfection of his chaste love and are involved in Eleonora's death. Still, death holds no terror for Eleonora except that she fears her beloved will flee the sheltered valley and discover another love in the outside world, unprotected by the idealization of love. Significantly, Eleonora's fears are not an expression of jealousy but concern for the welfare of her husband, since in the outside world and in the company of a less ethereal mate, he will place himself at risk. The narrator swears that he will never remarry, and Eleonora dies peacefully, vowing to watch over him in spirit.

For years the narrator remains in the valley, but the beauty of the place withers away even as he continues to be visited by the spirit of Eleonora. With a void in his heart, he leaves the valley, enters the world, and meets the "ethereal Ermengarde," in whose "memorial eyes" he encounters not only his new love but also the eyes of Eleonora. Having married a second time, he nonetheless escapes the curse of his vow to Eleonora, who in a visitation exclaims that "the Spirit of Love reigneth and ruleth, and, in taking to thy passionate heart her who is Ermengarde, thou art absolved, for reasons which shall be made known to thee in Heaven, of thy vows unto Eleonora" (Poe 473).

The significance of this ending cannot be overestimated. Despite the devastating particulars of Poe's life, the general impression of his marriage group was that of an observer who wished to bring understanding and healing to what he had witnessed and experienced. The salvation offered in "Eleonora" is, of course, entirely magical and irrational, but on the level of Canetti's crowd theory it is completely logical. Under extreme pressure following his wife's death and after a period of devastating grief, the protagonist is "pardoned" and allowed to continue living, albeit in the company of a less perfect soulmate and within a more worldly, realistic environment. This passage confirms the fact that, in spite of the devastation he had endured, Poe could envision happiness within the world of society. In fact, this was the tendency of his thinking in "Landor's Cottage" and "Hop-Frog," late and important tales in Poe's canon that might be said to convey his final word on the issue of the cycle of victimization in society.

Poe and Crowd Psychology

In "Ligeia" and his other romantic tales, Poe is enacting what Canetti, with a precise clinical meaning to the term, meant by the term "survivor." To say that Poe wrote obsessively about paranoia and survival, in Canetti's special sense of these terms, should not be taken to suggest psychological abnormality. Indeed, Canetti believed that his model of crowd behavior, including the behavior of individuals in reaction to the crowd, was endemic. Every person within society feels himself or herself to be wounded by the stings inflicted by others, and in return, every person resorts to defense mechanisms such as flight, dominance, or passing the sting along to others. Thus, an endless and mounting cycle of aggression and response, involving not just a few "pathological" cases but all human beings, is established, and this cycle can only be ameliorated by knowledge that reveals to all the condition that they share.

From this perspective, Poe's writing should be considered an artistic rendering of a universal condition of victimization that Poe was among the first to diagnose. One of Poe's late contemporaries, Gustave Le Bon (1841–1931), author of *The Crowd: A Study of the Popular Mind* (1895), produced the first important scientific analysis of crowd behavior, upon which Canetti drew and which he expanded. It would be interesting to know whether Le Bon borrowed ideas from Poe, a writer more highly esteemed in France than in the United States. In his case, Canetti's crowd theory was deeply influenced by what the author observed during the rise of fascism in Europe during the twenties and thirties and by the Götterdämmerung that it produced in the 1940s. It was during this period that Canetti composed his seminal work, *Crowds and Power* (1960), and it is remarkable that, given the seemingly placid decades during which Poe lived, he could have anticipated so many elements in Canetti's work. In reality, the first half of the nineteenth century in America was hardly placid: it was an era of epidemics, poverty, widespread alcoholism and drug addiction, and social disruption. There was more than enough in Poe's life to supply matter for a theory of hostile crowds and survival responses.

In sum, Poe was among the first authors to explore what Elias Canetti would later analyze in his theories of crowd behavior. Poe's marriage tales, dominated by the author's intense desire for idealized love, are allegories as well of the cycle of aggression and flight that he observed in society. However horrific the experience portrayed in "Ligeia," "Eleonora," and other tales and poems, in all of which the idealized mate dies and the male is left grieving, the resolution of these tales suggests healing and amelioration, not a continuance of the cycle of violence. The softening of outlook that one observes in Poe's marriage group confirms that Poe had worked through the puzzle that Canetti posed in *Crowds and Power*: how to end the cycle of violence and restore an order based on acceptance and love.

Reading Poe's short stories with the aid of Canetti's crowd theory reveals that, beneath the veneer of horror and grotesque, there exists a universal humanity in Poe's writing. Poe's fears were neither outlandish nor excessive: they reflect the commonplace burdens and responses of all mankind. The desperate hope that Poe's narrator in "Ligeia" expresses, recounting the lady's struggles "for life—*but* for life," echo the elemental hopes of all human beings. Poe's stories should be read not as gothic entertainments but as deep insights into the psychological burdens of social existence and of the human response to these burdens. By bringing understanding to these psychological responses, Poe advances a sense of common humanity and thereby furthers the potential for compassion and forbearance in human affairs.

Notes

1. Poe's relationship with John Allan and with his teachers in England and America demonstrate that the accumulation of "stings" began early in the author's life. Poe relationship with Allan, at first amicable, grew distant as Poe's rebellious proclivities and his artistic ambitions began to surface. Again and again, Allan accused his ward of ingratitude, as when he wrote that Poe "possesses not a Spark of affection for us, not a particle of gratitude for all my care and kindness toward him" (qtd. in Ackroyd 27). As Peter Ackroyd relates, "Poe told a friend, in later years, that his school days in England had been 'sad, lonely and unhappy'" (20). At Richmond Academy after the family's return to America, it appeared to others that Poe "harboured a grudge against the world" (Ackroyd 23).

2. Another response is to remain absolutely rigid, as in the behavior of soldiers under command. Interestingly, Poe evinced a strong affinity for the military, achieving the highest non-commissioned rank, that of Sergeant Major, before enrolling in West Point. Poe's peculiar physical manner, often described as "formal" and "restrained" (Silverman 263), also suggests an individual suffering from the burden of command. Poe's taste for the formal may also underlie his fascination with the arabesque, a form of design that Jacob Berman has explored in connection with "Ligeia" and other works by Poe. Noting that Poe's use of the form "resists easy categorization" (135), Berman goes on to suggest that in Poe's writing, "the arabesque destabilizes the sanctity of home with its degenerate potential, its proximity to the grotesque, primitive, and monstrous" (137). This is certainly the case with its use in the description of Rowena's bridal chamber, where it functions

as a visual trope to convey the destructive force under which Poe's ideal of marriage operated.

3. In this sense Poe's tales may be said to have an important "moral" content—something that critics from Louis D. Rubin to James M. Hutchisson have not detected in his work. Certainly, one must question Rubin's blanket pronouncement that in Poe "no moral sense is satisfied" (136), as also his statement that for Poe's characters "[n]o escape into nature is ever possible" (137). Hutchisson presents considerable evidence of the restorative influence of nature in Poe's life, as when Poe moved his family to a rural farmhouse on the Brennan farm five miles outside of New York City. Here Poe took long walks, stopping "for quiet contemplation of nature" and seeking an escape from the pressures of city living (Hutchisson 156-57). "Landor's Cottage," a story written after Virginia's death as a tribute to "Annie" (Mrs. Nancy Richmond), suggests just such an escape. Part of Rubin's difficulty in assessing Poe's moral imagination has to do with a mistaken conception of southern "community" and of Poe as "a sensibility that was not merely disinherited but violently dissociated from its culture and community" (155). Rubin seems to assume that one automatically "belongs" to the community of one's birth and to the culture of one's region. The other side of the coin is overwhelming evidence that Poe sought to remove himself from the provincial culture of the South and to align his art with a more universal intellectual community that was not geographical but abstract in nature. A striking example of this is Poe's immediate attraction to the Jesuit faculty of St. John's College in New York despite his own lack of religious affiliation. As Hutchisson shows, Poe visited St. John's (later Fordham University) "quite frequently," and "befriended Father Edward Doucet" and others on the staff (194). As it was throughout his life, Poe responded to men whom he judged to be "gentlemen" (194) and who shared his interests in art and intellectual inquiry.

Works Cited

Ackroyd, Peter. *Poe: A Life Cut Short*. Doubleday, 2008.

Barbour, Brian M. "Poe and Tradition." *Southern Literary Journal*, vol. 10, no. 2, pp. 1978, 46-54.

Berman, Jacob Rama. "Domestic Terror and Poe's Arabesque Interior." *English Studies in Canada*, vol. 31, no.1, 2005, pp. 128-150.

Canetti, Elias. *Crowds and Power*. Translated by Carol Stewart, Farrar Straus Giroux, 1984.

Hutchisson, James M. *Poe*. UP of Mississippi, 2005.

Poe, Edgar Allan. *Poetry and Tales*, edited by Patrick F. Quinn, Library of America, 1984.

Rubin, Louis D. *The Edge of the Swamp: A Study in the Literature and Society of the Old South.* Louisiana State UP, 1989.

Silverman, Kenneth. *Edgar A. Poe: Mournful and Never-ending Remembrance.* Harper Perennial, 1992.

Death and Freud in the Poetry of Edna St. Vincent Millay

Jenna Lewis

One of the most frequent themes of Edna St. Vincent Millay's poetry is death, a theme that appears in numerous poems, including "The Suicide," "Moriturus," "The Little Ghost," "The Shroud," "Elegy Before Death," "The Curse," "Burial," "Dirge Without Music," "Conscientious Objector," "What's this of death, from you who never will die," "The Poet and His Book," "The Death of Autumn," "Mortal Flesh, Is Not Your Place in the Ground?" and many more. In many of Millay's death poems, her speakers are either dealing with the actual dead or *are* the dead. This back-from-the-dead type of narrative, which is quite consistent within Millay's works, begs to be explored more closely. In particular, the possible impact of Freudian psychology on Millay's attitudes toward death deserves much greater attention than it has previously received.

Two *poetic* traditions most likely helped shape these poems by Millay. First, the Victorian tradition of mortuary poetry—popularized by poets like Lydia Huntley Sigourney and Julia A. Moore—portrayed the dead in romantic, and oftentimes overly dramatic, terms. Moore, who was so bad a poet that Mark Twain satirized her works in *Huckleberry Finn*, exemplifies how the ritual of death in Victorian literature was often maudlin and oversentimental. Take, for instance, this excerpt from Moore's poem "Hiram Helsel" (1876):

> Just before little Hiram died—
>
> His uncle and aunt were there—
>
> He kissed them both—bid them farewell,
>
> They left him with a prayer.
>
> Now he is gone, Oh! Let him rest;
>
> His soul has found a haven,

> For grief and woe ne'er enters there,
>
> In that place called heaven. (lines 25-32)

The unsophisticated rhyme scheme, the common meter, and the even less sophisticated subject matter, in which Hiram becomes sick due to being struck by lightning, are almost comical. While it is unfair to use Moore as a prime model for Victorian mortuary poets, death was often portrayed in literature in very dramatic ways. Margarete Holubetz explains:

> Due to the ritual dramatization of death prevailing at the time, most nineteenth-century deathbed scenes seem intolerably melodramatic to the modern reader. Death in the Victorian novel is generally conceived as a spectacle. The hour of death is often presented as a grand scene of farewell and judgment, and many nineteenth-century protagonists meet death as decorously and with as seemly sentiments as any Jacobean hero. . . . This theatrical grandeur in the face of death . . . strikes us as shallow and incongruous in the context of domestic realism. However, if the reader today objects to the presumed artificiality of the fictional death-bed scenes, he has to bear in mind that these descriptions were, in fact, fairly accurate sketches of the behavior at the time they were written. . . . We tend to forget that the ritual celebration of death—so radically different from our customs—was the ideal to which people on their deathbeds aspired. (16)

While poets like Sigourney and Moore exemplify the type of mortuary poets writing during the Victorian era, other renegade Victorian poets examined death with a keener eye and saw a darker side to dying. Emily Dickinson, for instance, was also a mortuary poet writing during the Victorian era. However, Dickinson:

> reacted selectively to the popular gospel of consolation. Sometimes she accepted its formulas without question; sometimes she subverted them through exaggeration, burlesque, and distortion; sometimes she used them only as pretexts for outright skepticism and satire. In doing so Dickinson was continuing a process of transformation that had long appropriated classical means for romantic ends. (St. Armand 44)

Dickinson's poems are far less celebratory and perhaps more analytic than writings by the typical mortuary poets. "I felt a Funeral in the Brain" (1861) and "I Heard a Fly Buzz When I Died" (1862) both contain speakers who imagine their deaths. But rather than imagining a glorious passing into a spiritual world, the poems seem to portray a type of failed transcendence. For instance, in "I Heard a Fly Buzz When I Died," a fly, "With Blue – uncertain – stumbling Buzz" (line 13) disturbs the process of passing into another world, as the speaker explains that she "could not see to see – " (line 16). Dickinson is oftentimes skeptical about life after death, and it is precisely this type of skepticism that allowed future poets, such as Millay, to consider death and the process of dying differently.

The Impact of Edgar Lee Masters

While Millay would have been familiar with the Victorian tradition of mortuary poetry, she would have also been influenced by Edgar Lee Master's *Spoon River Anthology* (1915), which was a huge success just as Millay was beginning her career. This collection of over 200 "dead speaker" poems might be argued to offer a sort of anti-Victorian rejoinder to the old Victorian tradition. It influenced everything from Sherwood Anderson's *Winesburg, Ohio* and Ernest Hemingway's *In Our Time* to William Faulkner's *Go Down, Moses*. In "Voice of America," John Hollander describes just how much of an impact this famous anthology of fictional rural epitaphs has had on American literature:

> *Spoon River Anthology* is one of those remarkable, seemingly sui generis American books...which seem[s] to mark milestones in the long, strange course of our country's effort to understand itself. It creates a fictional community through the short dramatic monologues spoken by its deceased inhabitants, rather than by overt description. . . . The volume appeared for the first time in 1915 [and]. . . . [i]t was an immediate success, praised extravagantly and also condemned for its skeptical energy, its erotic specificity, its reforming naysaying coupled with romantic transcendent yearnings, [and] its unfamiliar structure and mode of verse. (47)

Masters' interpretations of the dead are much less sentimental than those found in most Victorian mortuary poetry. "Sam Hookey" is perhaps one of the more comical epitaphs that turn the serious matter of dying into a hilarious one:

> I ran away from home with the circus,
>
> Having fallen in love with Mademoiselle Estralada,
>
> The lion tamer.
>
> One time, having starved the lions
>
> For more than a day,
>
> I entered the cage and began to beat Brutus
>
> And Leo and Gypsy.
>
> Whereupon Brutus sprang upon me,
>
> And killed me.
>
> On entering these regions
>
> I met a shadow who cursed me,
>
> And said it served me right. . . .
>
> It was Robespierre! (lines 1-13)

Millay would have been influenced by Masters' visions of what the dead might be thinking. She shared with Masters a similar "skeptical energy" concerning the afterlife. This can be seen in her poem "Mortal Flesh, Is Not Your Place in the Ground?" (1939), in which the speaker urges "Mortal flesh" to "Learn to love blackness while there is yet time, blackness / Unpatterned, blackness without horizons" (lines 7-8). Rather than admiring the scenery of "the trees in autumn" (line 9), the speaker thinks it is better to "Learn to love roots instead, that soon above your head shall be as branches" (lines 17-18). Poets like Dickinson and Masters were able to break away from the traditional notions of death and reimagine death on their own terms, and so they paved the way for a new generation of mortuary poets.

The Impact of Freud

Millay—like Dickinson and Masters—contributes to this "evolving genre of dead speaker poems" (Jamison 191) by offering far less mystical views about death than those generated by typical mortuary poets. However, Millay's access to new developments in psychology provided a chance to explore more deeply her culture's internalized beliefs about dying and the dead. Dickinson, who died in 1886, would not have been familiar with the psychoanalytic works of Sigmund Freud, who enjoyed most of his public reception during the early twentieth century. This unfamiliarity with Freud would also, of course, be true of other renegade poets of the Victorian era, such as Edgar Allan Poe, who also dabbled in poems about the dead long before Freud wrote about the subjects of death and dying. But because Millay was writing during the height of Freud's popularity, her poems about the afterlife seem to reflect this new Freudian context.

Despite Freud's great fame in the early twentieth century, current Millay scholars have failed to find any correlations between him and Millay. Yale Kramer, in his essay "Freud and the Culture Wars," explains that "nineteen hundred and nine, when Freud was 53, marked a turning point in the vicissitudes of his professional life, the beginning of worldwide fame and of the spread of popular Freudianism—and it all began in Worcester, Massachusetts," where Freud delivered a famous set of talks (38). Kramer goes on to explain that "[m]ost of the American academic world of psychology and psychiatry came to hear Freud's ideas, and he didn't disappoint. In five brilliant introductory lectures, he dashed off a reprise of his theories on dreams, the sexual life of children, and the neuroses. Even William James, who was no admirer, was reportedly impressed" (38). It is hard to tell just how much of an impact Freud made on Millay, especially because no references to him appear in Nancy Milford's biography, nor does his name appear in *Letters of Edna St. Vincent Millay*. Moreover, most scholarly work done on Millay fails even to mention Freud. However, Kramer does briefly claim that Millay was, in fact, influenced by Freud:

> [T]he most powerful disseminating force [for Freudian ideas] during the years before and after the Great War was the cadre of writer-intellectuals who became patient-advocates of psychoanalysis and Freudianism. They wrote for the *New York Times*, the *New Republic*, and *Vanity Fair*, and their social center was the Liberal Club in Greenwich Village. They wanted to practice free love and to escape from the morality of the past—and they found their intellectual justification in Freud. Walter Lippmann writing for the *New Republic*, Eugene O'Neill, Edna St. Vincent Millay, Sherwood Anderson, Van Wyck Brooks writing for the *Masses* and the *Little Review*—rebels, all, against Puritan morals—became spokesmen for a Freudianism that went beyond Freud. For them psychoanalysis meant sexual fulfillment and miraculous personal transformation; and, furthermore, it was easy, almost effortless. All you needed was a good imagination, good verbal abilities, and a good education. It was made for them. They consulted analysts like Smith Ely Jelliffe and A. A. Brill for short periods of time and wrote about their experiences. Max Eastman told his readers in *Everybody's Magazine*, "We have but to name these nervous diseases with their true name, it seems, and they dissolve like the charms in a fairy story." (40)

It is highly probable that Millay was naming "these nervous diseases with their true name" (Kramer 40) in many of her poems about the afterlife.

Nancy Milford explains in her biography that Millay was an alcoholic, addicted to morphine, and had suicidal tendencies. Furthermore, her bizarre death, in which she drank a bottle of wine, toppled down the stairs, and broke her neck, raises serious questions about whether or not her demise was accidental. In this essay, I propose that Millay's poetry about the afterlife engages with Freud's theories about the so-called "pleasure principle" and "death drive." Although it is difficult to determine whether the origin of Millay's engagement with Freudian thinking was coincidental or resulted from her actual reading of Freud, there is an obvious correlation that begs to be explored.

Drawing from Max Eastman's idea that writers from Millay's era "name these nervous diseases with their true names" in order for them to "dissolve like the charms in a fairy story," I argue that Millay's poems about the afterlives possibly function as a coping strategy for dealing with the pain of desiring what cannot be had. For instance, Millay makes clear in many of these "afterlife poems" that although she desires immortality, to live forever is obviously impossible. Take, for instance, her poem "Moriturus" (1928; *Collected Poems* 199-207):

> If I could have
>
>   Two things in one:
>
> The peace of the grave,
>
>   And the light of the sun;
>
> My hands across
>
>   My thin breast-bone,
>
> But aware of the moss
>
>   Invading the stone,
>
> ....
>
> If I might be
>
> Insensate matter
>
> With sensate me
>
> Sitting within,

  Harking and prying,

I might begin

  To dicker with dying.

....

Death, however,

  Is a spongy wall,

Is a sticky river,

  Is nothing at all.

Summon the weeper,

  Wail and sing:

Call him Reaper,

  Angel, King;

Call him Evil

  Drunk to the lees,

Monster, Devil,—

  He is less than these.

Call him Thief,

  The Maggot in the Cheese,

The Canker in the Leaf,—

  He is less than these.

Dusk without sound,
   Where the spirit by pain
Uncoiled, is wound
   To spring again;

The mind enmeshed
   Laid straight in repose,
And the body refreshed
   By feeding the rose,—

These are but visions;
   These would be
The grave's derisions,
   Could the grave see . . .
. . . What thing is little?—
   The aphis hid
In a house of spittle?
   The hinge of the lid

Of the spider's eye
   At the spider's birth?
"Greater am I
   By the earth's girth

Than Mighty Death!"

   All creatures cry

That can summon breath;—

   And speak no lie.

For He is nothing;

   He is less

Than Echo answering

   "Nothingness!"—

Less than the heat

   Of the furthest star

To the ripening wheat;

   Less by far,

When all the lipping

   Is said and sung,

Than the sweat dripping

   From a dog's tongue.

(lines 1-8, 22-28, 37-64, 81-104)

    The speaker here clearly does not adopt a mystical vision of the afterlife, though she does wish that her soul would live on after her death. In this sense, Millay's thinking reflects problems that also arise in psychoanalytic thought about death. For instance, in his article "How to Look Death in the Eyes: Freud and Bataille," Liran Razinsky explains that "Death's place in psychoanalysis is very problematic. Beginning with Freud, death can be variously said to have been repressed, reduced, pathologized, or forgotten altogether" (63). One might argue that "Moriturus" adopts the strategies of reducing and repressing death rather than pathologizing it or forgetting it altogether. For Millay's speaker, death "Is a spongy wall, / Is a sticky river, / Is nothing at all" (lines 38-40); death is less than "The Maggot in the Cheese / The Canker in the Leaf" and ". . . the sweat dripping / From a dog's tongue" (lines 103-04). "Moriturus," which is one of Millay's lengthier poems, ends with the speaker concluding that she will put up a hard fight with the personified Death:

> With all my might
>
> > My door shall be barred.
>
> I shall put up a fight,
>
> > I shall take it hard.
>
> With his hand on my mouth
>
> > He shall drag me forth,
>
> Shrieking to the south
>
> > And clutching at the north. (lines 141-48)

Rather than facing death, or even embracing it in the way that many Victorian mortuary poets did, the speaker here hides from it, fights it, and "take[s] it hard" (line 144). To her, death is something abnormal and incomprehensible. She admits, after all, that if death were more than nothingness, if she could have both "The peace of the grave, / And the light of the sun" (lines 3-4), then she ". . . might begin / To dicker with dying" (lines 27-28). Writing about death was most likely Millay's way of naming the nervous diseases of anxiety and fear so that they might "dissolve like the charms in a fairy story" (Kramer 40).

Two other poems by Millay share a similar tone with "Moriturus." Each of these poems seems to function as a coping strategy: because Millay does not want to die, she becomes obsessed with death. Through writing about dying, Millay is able to maintain a sense of control and pleasure. In his classic text *Beyond the Pleasure Principle*, Freud explains:

> In the theory of psychoanalysis we have no hesitation in assuming that the course taken by mental events is automatically regulated by the pleasure principle. We believe, that is to say, that the course of those events is invariably set in motion by an unpleasurable tension, and that it takes a direction such that its final outcome coincides with a lowering of that tension—that is an avoidance of unpleasure or a production of pleasure. (3)

Millay, however, seems to cope with her pain by making her pain pleasurable. The future confrontation with death, unlike the nostalgic longing for the past, is a realistic concern, and by controlling that concern by writing poetry about it, Millay tries to triumph over death's undesirability. Although a longing desire for the past can never be fulfilled, Millay manages (or at least tries to manage) to escape the undesirability of the future. This kind of reversal of expectations surrounding death is expressed, for instance, in her poem titled "Burial" (1921; *Collected Poems* 98):

> Mine is a body that should die at sea!
>
> And have for a grave, instead of a grave
>
> Six feet deep and the length of me,
>
> All the water that is under the wave!
>
>
>
> And terrible fishes to seize my flesh,
>
> Such as a living man might fear,
>
> And eat me while I am firm and fresh,—

> Not wait till I've been dead for a year! (lines 1-8)

The speaker triumphantly opens the poem with a bold declaration, and the tone remains victorious throughout. The rhythm is emphatic and propulsive, and although the image of razor-teethed fish ripping apart a body's flesh suggests the body's vulnerability, the speaker nonetheless celebrates a sense of self-achievement.

By turning a painful experience into something pleasurable, Millay responds to death in a way best explained by Freud. Freud claims that inhibition of the pleasure principle—which is "proper to the primary method of working on the part of the mental apparatus" (7)—is "a familiar regularity" (7). This is because "from the point of view of self-preservation of the organism among the difficulties of the external world, [the pleasure principle] is from the very outset inefficient and very dangerous" (7). The healthy way to combat the pleasure principle is to apply the method of the reality principle, which "demands and carries into effect the postponement of satisfaction, the abandonment of a number of possibilities of gaining satisfaction and the temporary toleration of unpleasure as a long and indirect road to pleasure" (7). However, "the replacement of the pleasure principle by the reality principle can only be made responsible for a small number, and by no means the most intense, of unpleasurable experiences" (7). We can examine this alternative (and far more dangerous) method of replacement by taking a closer look at "Burial."

In "Burial," Millay seems to suggest that manipulating her own psyche through mind control is powerful enough to: (a) weaken feelings of suffering due to unobtainable desires for pleasure and (b) create pleasurable feelings due to obtainable desires for pain. In other words, the speaker attempts to avoid the fear of dying by picturing her body's decomposition process as satisfactory: rather than imagine worms slowly eating away at her flesh, she'd rather be consumed by "terrible fishes . . . / Such as a living man might fear" (lines 5-6). Since unpleasure is inevitable, she converts it to pleasure.

By rejecting a conventional burial, the speaker can minimize the fear of dying and maximize the pleasure of pain. Freud explains that this sort of release of "unpleasure":

> is to be found in the conflicts and dissensions that take place in the mental apparatus while the ego is passing through its development into more highly composite organizations. Almost all the energy with which the apparatus is filled arises from its innate instinctual impulses. But these are not allowed to reach the same phases of development. In the course of things it happens again and again that individual instincts or parts of instincts turn out to be incompatible in their aims or demands with the remaining ones, which are able to combine into the inclusive unity of the ego. (8)

In other words, Freud believed (according to Ulrike May) that "beyond":

> the pleasure principle there was a compulsion to repeat that was independent of pleasure, an urge to return to an earlier state, even if this state was predominantly unpleasurable. . . . He saw this urge as being stronger than the wish for pleasure, and it seemed to have a biological analogue; that is, ontogenetic development tends to repeat stages of phylogenetic development—and beyond that, stages in the development of life itself. In Freud's view, life developed out of the lifeless, the anorganic, and thus one could, if one wanted, think [of] the urge to return to an earlier state, applied to the extreme . . . [as] a return to lifelessness, the anorganic state. (May 210-11)

Through repression, these unevolved instincts that are dangerous to one's survival often find roundabout paths "to a direct or substitutive satisfaction" (Freud 8). We see in "Burial" a conflict between the will to live versus the will to die, a conflict that is also present in "Moriturus." The speaker attempts to immortalize herself, but she does so by fantasizing a paradoxically terrifying yet exultant burial. The complete submergence of the body under water, in which she desires to ". . . have for a grave, instead of a grave /. . . All the water that is under the wave" (lines 2-4), also signifies a form of repression: the speaker is attempting to drown these less-developed impulses, but they reemerge as substitutive satisfaction. In his article "Between the Quills: Schopenhauer and Freud on Sadism and Masochism," Robert Grimwade explains that when "projected inwardly," this impulse to die "is masochist." Throughout Millay's poetry, masochism emerges as an eagerness to die—an eagerness related to Freud's idea of "the death drive."

Millay and the Freudian "Death Drive"

Millay's obsession with (and treatment of) death seems to reflect Freud's theories about the death drive. Jon Mills explains that while "contemporary psychoanalytic theorists tend to view the death drive as fanciful noise, an artifact of imagination" (373), and while Freud himself "largely believed that his ideas on the death drive were left to further investigation" (Mills 373), evidence about it has appeared and continues to reappear within literary and historical settings. Although no consensus exists concerning the real existence of such a drive, Mills' views strike me as persuasive:

> Freud's thesis on the death drive is one of the most original theories in the history of ideas . . . [and] potentially provides a viable explanation to the conundrums that beset the problems of human civilization, subjective suffering, collective aggressivity, and self-destructiveness. . . . Freud accounts for an internally derived motivation, impulse, or activity that is impelled toward a determinate teleology of destruction that may be directed toward self and others, the details of which are multifaceted and contingent upon the unique contexts that influence psychic structure and unconsciously mediated behavior. . . . Freud was committed [to the idea] that the mind seeks 'a return to an earlier state,' a notion that is verifiable through clinical observation. Despite the psyche's inherently evolutionary nature, death becomes the fulcrum of psychic progression and decay. (Mills 373)

Millay's reoccurring theme of death symbolizes "the compulsion to repeat" negative actions. By imagining herself as dead, or imagining others as dead, Millay performs a self-destructiveness that is arguably rooted in the instinctual desire to return to a state of quiescence.

"The Suicide" (1917; *Collected Poems*, 25-31)—which was written three years before *Beyond the Pleasure Principle*—is an earlier poem by Millay that shows signs of the death drive. This poem begins with the speaker contemplating suicide: "Curse thee, Life, I will live with thee no more!" (line 1). After she goes on to lament the cruelties and hardships of life, she explains that "Thus I to Life, and ceased; but through my brain / My thought ran still, until I spake again" (lines 15-16). At this instance, we see how Millay enters into a modern psychoanalytic discourse: the impulsive self-destructive thoughts reside in her brain, or psyche, and tempt her to go through with the suicide, but the speaker seems to detach herself from this impulse by using her words to distract her from her thoughts, thus delaying her suicidal plans. One might argue that this self-distraction occurs because the speaker, saddened by her lack of pleasure, is also subconsciously aware that she should postpone pleasure and temporarily endure pain for the sake of survival. The speaker seems to be influenced by her ego's instinct of self-preservation, and for a few moments, there remains the chance that her pleasure principle will be replaced with what Freud calls the reality principle (5). Soon, however, the speaker communicates in a way that seems relevant to Freud's theories about a desire to return to an earlier state:

> Ah, life, I would have been a pleasant thing
>
> To have about the house when I was grown
>
> If thou hadst left my little joys alone!
>
> I asked of thee no favour save this one:
>
> That thou wouldst leave me playing in the sun!
>
> And this thou didst deny, calling my name
>
> Insistently, until I rose and came.
>
> I saw the sun no more.... (lines 28-35)

Here we see a typical kind of psychological change: as a child grows into an adult, life becomes more complex. The law of evolution requires us to adapt, in many ways, to harder terms of survival. Eventually, the speaker comes upon a strange door that marks the entrance into the unknown:

> But turning, straightway, [I] sought a certain door
>
> In the rear wall. Heavy it was, and low
>
> And dark,—a way by which none e'er would go
>
> That other exit had, and never knock
>
> Was heard thereat,—bearing a curious lock
>
> Some chance had shown me fashioned faultily,
>
> Whereof Life held content the useless key,
>
> And great coarse hinges, thick and rough with rust,
>
> Whose sudden voice across a silence must,
>
> I knew, be harsh and horrible to hear,—
>
> A strange door, ugly like a dwarf.—So near
>
> I came I felt upon my feet the chill
>
> Of acid wind creeping across the sill. (lines 58-70)

This door is yet another example of Millay's vision of the afterlife. The imagery she uses to describe it correlates with Freud's ideas not only of life developing from nothingness but also of a human's impulse to return to this state of nothingness. However, the ending of the poem, in which the speaker finds that God does exist, conflicts with this Freudian idea and could be seen as a way for the speaker to confront dismal beliefs about the death drive. For instance, although the speaker longs for continued pleasure, she will not receive this until she goes to Heaven:

> "Child," my father's voice replied,
>
> "All things thy fancy hath desired of me
>
> Thou hast received. I have prepared for thee
>
> Within my house a spacious chamber, where
>
> Are delicate things to handle and to wear,
>
> And all these things are thine. Dost thou love song?
>
> My minstrels shall attend thee all day long.
>
> Or sigh for flowers? My fairest gardens stand
>
> Open as fields to thee on every hand.
>
> And all thy days this word shall hold the same:
>
> No pleasure shalt thou lack that thou shalt name. (lines 127-36)

Here, Millay seems to imply the reality principle's secret weapon: finding pleasure in serving God. By busying one's self with do-good tasks, one is able to focus on helping others and forget self-suffering. However, when the speaker finally has access to infinite pleasure, she becomes bored and begs God for a task, to which He responds: "'But as for tasks—' he smiled, and shook his head; / 'Thou hadst thy task, and laidst it by,' he said" (lines 137-38).

Throughout her poetry, Millay often uses the metaphor of the sea (in poems such as "Night is my sister, and how deep in love" and "I shall go back again to the bleak shore" [*Collected Poems* 105-6, 593]) to evoke memories of childhood, memories of the embryonic stage in which the sea symbolizes a womb, and memories of the origin of evolution. Furthermore, Millay often uses apocalyptic settings to imagine either an innocent childhood faith in God or the prehistoric world corrupted by man. In a sense, then, the nostalgic experiences of these constructed worlds present unattainable desires, much like her poems about the afterlife. But interpreting Millay's poetry about death through a Freudian lens provides only further insight into this desire to regress. For Millay, the Freudian "death instinct" seems to have been an impulse central to much of her private thinking as well as too much of the poetry she composed.

Works Cited

Freud, Sigmund. *Beyond the Pleasure Principle*, edited by James Strachey. Norton, 1975.

Grimwade, Robert. "Between the Quills: Schopenhauer and Freud on Sadism and Masochism." *International Journal of Psychoanalysis*, vol. 92, no. 1, Feb. 2011, pp. 146-69.

Hollander, John. "Voice of America." *New Republic*, vol. 207, no. 5, 1992, 47-53.

Holubetz, Margarete. "Death-Bed Scenes in Victorian Fiction." *English Studies*, vol. 67, no.1, 1986, pp. 14-34.

Jamison, Anne Elizabeth. *Poetics en Passant: Redefining the Relationship between Victorian and Modern Poetry*. Palgrave Macmillan, 2009.

Kramer, Yale. "Freud and the Culture Wars." *Public Interest*, vol. 124, 1996, pp. 37-51.

May, Ulrike. "Freud's 'Beyond the Pleasure Principle': The End of Psychoanalysis or its New Beginning?" *International Forum of Psychoanalysis*, vol. 22, no. 4, 2013, pp. 208-216.

Milford, Nancy. *Savage Beauty: The Life of Edna St. Vincent Millay*. Random House, 2001.

Millay, Edna St. Vincent. *Collected Poems*. Harper & Row, 1956.

———. *Letters of Edna St. Vincent Millay*, edited by Allan Ross Macdougall, Harper and Brothers, 1952.

Mills, Jon. "Reflections of the Death Drive." *Psychoanalytic Psychology*, vol. 23, no. 2, 2006, p. 37382.

Razinsky, Liran. "How to Look Death in the Eyes: Freud and Bataille." *Substance: A Review of Theory and Literary Criticism*, vol. 38, no. 2, 2009, pp. 63-88.

St. Armand, Barton Levi. "Dark Parade: Dickinson, Sigourney, and the Victorian Way of Death." *Emily Dickinson and Her Culture: The Soul's Society*, Cambridge UP, 1984, pp. 39-78.

Grasping *The Great Gatsby*: **A Cognitive Approach**

Nicolas Tredell

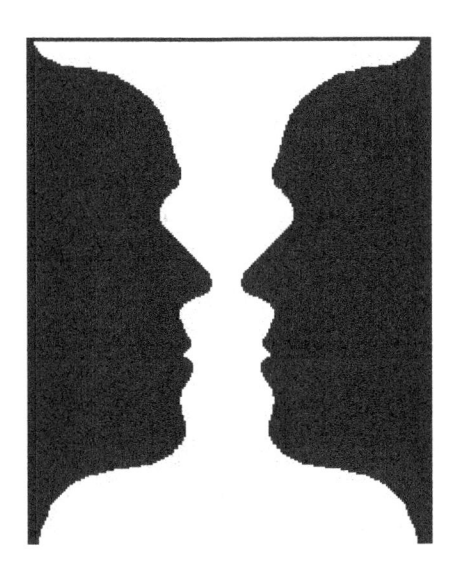

In chapter two of *The Great Gatsby*, while Tom and Myrtle make love in the bedroom of the latter's apartment, Nick Carraway sits down "discreetly in the living room" and reads a chapter of Robert Keable's novel *Simon Called Peter* (1921)—or rather, fails to read it: "either it was terrible stuff or the whiskey distorted things because it didn't make any sense to me" (Fitzgerald 26). Fitzgerald here is taking a shot at a novel he thought immoral (185-6n), and associating it with the adultery, drunkenness, and violence that take place in Myrtle's apartment; but he also dramatizes a more general situation in which the act of reading fails to take place because the crucial element—making sense—is missing. Making sense of a text entails cognition—gaining knowledge of that text and its subject matter through the senses and the understanding and in combination with the pre-existing knowledge the reader brings to bear—and if the text is fictional, it also entails a simulation of the characters, situations, and actions. This simulation is both mental and physical, drawing on and related to experience in and of the actual world. It involves sensory representations that flash or linger upon the inward eye and the other internalized senses, and the reader's body may prepare to respond to situations in fiction as if they were real, for example by tensing muscles, even though the actions that might follow in actual life would not ensue. In a cognitive perspective, there is a continuity between real-life experiences and those modelled in literary texts, though a key part of our cognition of a literary text is that it is not real. This essay aims to grasp *Gatsby* by mean of three key perspectives drawn from cognitive literary criticism: figure and ground; mental spaces; and the embodied reader.

Figure and Ground

"Figure and ground cognition," in Peter Stockwell's phrase (9), is a basic form of perception and knowledge and is best illustrated by those visual images in which the perceiver can, by an act of attention, reverse foreground and background, like the drawing that can be seen as either a vase or two profile faces opposite each other:

Gatsby provides a notable example of figure and ground cognition in its description in chapter three of how Nick, glancing back as he leaves the first Gatsby party he attends, sees Gatsby himself:

> The caterwauling horns had reached a crescendo and I turned away and cut across the lawn toward home. I glanced back once. A wafer of a moon was shining over Gatsby's house, making the night fine as before and surviving the laughter and the sound of his still glowing garden. A sudden emptiness seemed to flow now from the windows and the great doors, endowing with complete isolation the figure of the host, who stood on the porch, his hand up in a formal gesture of farewell. (Fitzgerald 46)

In this passage, elements that have been prominent earlier in the chapter—such as Gatsby's garden and house and guests, the noise of car horns, the sound of revelry by night—become the ground and background against which the figure of Gatsby stands out.

This example might suggest a static tableau, but if we trace the figure of "Gatsby" throughout the novel, it becomes clear that figure-and-ground cognition in relation to him—as to other key elements of the text—is dynamic and changing. In this respect, we can apply Stockwell's further notions of "trajector" and "landmark" (72). Gatsby, as a figure, is a "trajectory" who moves and changes, describes a trajectory, against a series of landmarks in the novel. He is what Stockwell calls an "attractor" (20) who draws the reader's attention. It should be stressed that "attractors" are not necessarily characters in a fiction but words or combinations of words that may attract the reader at any given point in a text. These may, but need not be, words that describe characters.

Gatsby is initially identified as an attractor by the appearance of his name in the novel's title. When Nick first mentions his name, in the third paragraph of the novel, he is isolated and thrust into prominence by being preceded by "Only," used as an adverb—"Only Gatsby" (Fitzgerald 5)—and then endowed with a series of attributes that enhance his power as an attractor: he has "something gorgeous about him," he possesses "some heightened sensitivity to the promises of life," enjoys "an extraordinary gift for hope," exhibits an unprecedented "romantic readiness" (6)—indeed each of these terms could serve in itself as an "attractor," and, in coalescing around "Gatsby," they boost his "attractor" status. Gatsby then, however, disappears from the text for a time; a succession of other figures emerges. These include Nick himself; West Egg; the exterior and interior of the Buchanan house; and Tom Buchanan, first seen standing "on the front porch" (9) in a way that both anticipates and contrasts with Nick's image in chapter three, quoted above, of Gatsby standing "on the porch" (46). In both cases, the preposition "on" indicates an immediate location and, in the contexts, a relationship of proprietorship between a person and his residence. The succession of figures also includes Daisy Buchanan; Jordan Baker; and the telephone, that "fifth guest" at the Buchanans with its "shrill metallic urgency" (16). We can trace here the way in which the figure can emerge from and change back into the ground or background—as the Buchanan house does—and also start to chart the recurrence in the text of certain figures introduced here—not only the characters of Tom, Daisy, and Jordan, but also, for instance, the telephone, which reappears in several places, including chapter three, when the butler says to Gatsby "Philadelphia wants you on the phone, sir" (44); chapter eight, when Nick and Jordan quarrel on the telephone; and chapter nine, when Jordan, reminding Nick of that quarrel, says, "You threw me over on the telephone" (138).

Stockwell suggests that the fundamental cognitive mechanism of perceiving and grasping figure/ground relationships is the basis of "prepositional positioning" in language—that is, of where prepositions (such as "on," "in," "by") are placed to indicate a relationship between two entities. To take an example from chapter two of *Gatsby*: in the clause the "little dog was sitting on the table" (Fitzgerald 31), the "dog" is the figure and "the table" the ground, and the preposition "on" specifies the respective position of one in relation to the other. The figure need not be animate, as another example shows, from chapter three of *Gatsby*: "Every Friday five crates of oranges and lemons arrived from a fruiterer in New York" (33). Here the crates of fruit are the figure, and the animate entity, the fruiterer, is the ground, with New York City as the background. The preposition "from" indicates the relationship between fruit and fruiterer—the latter is the provenance of the former—while the preposition "in" indicates the relationship between the fruiterer and New York City in terms of location.

In the first appearance of Myrtle Wilson in chapter two of *Gatsby*, there is a striking example of figure and ground and of the unusual use of a preposition to indicate the relationship between them. So far in that chapter, successive figures have emerged, like the Valley of Ashes, the billboard with the eyes of Dr. T. J. Eckleburg, Tom Buchanan (again), George B. Wilson's garage, Wilson himself—even though the last-named is described in largely negative terms such as "spiritless" and "anaemic" (Fitzgerald 22), he does occupy the foreground of the reader's attention when he is first introduced. But Myrtle's debut relegates all these preceding figures, for the moment, to ground and background status. At first, it has the aspect of a static, if vibrant tableau: Myrtle blocks out the light from the office door, carries "her surplus flesh sensuously," and has "an immediately perceptible vitality about her as if the nerves of her body were continually smouldering" (23). Then she smiles and moves, "walking through her husband as if he were a ghost" (23). The preposition "through" is a deviation from the norm here; "by" would be the more usual preposition. Literally, in a realistic text, it is impossible that Myrtle should walk "through" her husband (though the "ghost" simile alludes to a genre, that of the supernatural story, in which it would be possible); the preposition is to be understood metaphorically, and this linguistic and generic anomaly helps to enhance Myrtle's status, at this point, as an attractor; her successive appearances in this chapter further augment this status (an attractor is not necessarily "attractive" in the sense of being likeable) until her trajectory is crushed by Tom's brutal assault. From that point, Myrtle will emerge as a figure again only five times, and on three of these occasions, she will be dead. In chapter four, Nick briefly glimpses her "straining at the garage pump with panting vitality" (54) as Gatsby drives him into New York. In chapter seven, she dashes into the dusk and Michaelis and the driver of another car find her torn corpse. In the same chapter, Nick, Tom, Jordan, and the other onlookers in Wilson's garage see her body, which "lay on a work table by the wall" (108)—here the preposition "on" assumes a ponderous force, since it no longer denotes a relationship between a living and an inanimate object; Myrtle is now, in both senses of the term, a deadweight. Finally in chapter seven, Nick confirms to Gatsby that the accident killed her and graphically elaborates that "it ripped her open" (112), though both men refer to Myrtle by pronouns ("she," "her") rather than her proper name.

The process of moving between figure and ground, trajectory and landmark, of which we have given key examples here, is an important part of the way in which the reader of *Gatsby*, combining input from the text with the scenarios they bring to it, constructs mental spaces.

Palpable and Phantom Marriages

In cognitive linguistics, mental space theory sees producing and understanding language, whether in written or spoken form, as involving what Elena Semino calls the "construction of networks of interconnected mental spaces"—"mental spaces" being defined as "short-term cognitive representations of states of affairs" assembled from a combination of verbal input and the hearer's or reader's existing knowledge (89). In grasping a fictional text, these mental spaces can be established in terms not only of what actually happens in that text but also in terms of what does not happen but is, at key points, projected as possible, and perhaps desired by one or more of the characters.

We can see this establishment of "mental spaces" in reading *Gatsby* in relation to the actual and potential marriages that feature in the text. We might call the former "palpable marriages," in the sense that, within the fiction, they seem tangible to the reader, and the latter "phantom marriages," in the sense that they haunt the text as projections of desire and fantasy but are never actualized within it and perhaps never could be (this is open to debate). The two major actual, palpable marriages are those of Tom and Daisy Buchanan and George and Myrtle Wilson. There is also the more peripheral but still palpable marriage between Chester and Mrs. McKee (the text does not supply the latter's forename), which chapter two of the novel renders in vivid vignettes.

The phantom marriages, which one or more of the characters explicitly or implicitly desire, are those of Gatsby and Daisy, Tom and Myrtle, and Nick Carraway and Jordan Baker. One further phantom marriage, very difficult for critics to articulate or perhaps even to perceive until the later twentieth century, is between Nick and Gatsby—a relationship prefigured by the ambiguous encounter between Nick and Chester McKee at the end of chapter two that concludes with the former standing beside the bed of the latter, who is sitting up beneath the sheets in his underwear holding "a great portfolio" (Fitzgerald 32).

The reader brings to the marriages in *Gatsby*, as to the other situations in the novel, scenarios, in Gerard Steen's sense of the word: "complex conceptual structures consisting of sequences of action concepts"—"action concepts" being ideas of "which actions are to be performed in recurrent situations with a particular goal" (68). Marriage scenarios, like those of love, "are general cognitive models that may be presumed to be possessed in at least some partial form or other by most people in a particular culture" (72). If the scenario stipulates that the primary goal of marriage is that the married partners act towards each other in such a way as to attain mutual happiness, it is clear that the palpable marriages in *Gatsby* do not attain this, and in this respect, they activate in readers other scenarios, which range from concepts of actions that might be taken to try to preserve or improve a marriage to those that might be taken to end it, such as separation, divorce, or the death of one or both of the partners (as happens with Myrtle and George).

In terms of the happiness goal of marriage, Tom and Daisy fall far short. Tom is unfaithful, and many twenty-first century readers would be inclined to process him through a "predator" scenario; he preys sexually on women who are socially and economically vulnerable, like Myrtle, or the chambermaid at the Santa Barbara Hotel who is a passenger in Tom's car and suffers a broken arm when he crashes into a wagon on the Ventura Road soon after his marriage, or the "common but pretty" girl (Fitzgerald 83), as Daisy calls her, whom he pursues at the Gatsby party he and Daisy attend. In this respect, what might seem rather a desperate expedient on Nick's part when he first realizes what is happening in the Buchanan marriage—"my own instinct was to telephone immediately for the police" (16)—anticipates twenty-first-century attempts to introduce legal sanctions into marital, cohabiting, or extramarital relationships.

The marriage of Tom and Daisy is, however, a strong one, as Nick recognizes near the end of chapter seven, when he looks through the kitchen window at Tom and Daisy together and knows that this sets the seal on Gatsby's defeat. "They weren't happy [. . .] and yet they weren't unhappy either. There was an unmistakable air of natural intimacy about the picture" (Fitzgerald 113). Here the scenario in which the goal of marriage is happiness has been replaced by a deromanticized version in which its goal is the stability of the institution of marriage and, through and beyond that, of society. The "picture" is like a Dutch genre painting that affirms the security, the inviolability of the home and the marriage bond.

The eleven-year-old marriage of George and Myrtle Wilson seems to have broken down more fundamentally than that of Tom and Daisy. Initially, it activates another scenario: that of the "failed man" who cannot satisfy his wife sexually or control her behavior and who should assert himself if the marriage is to have a chance of surviving—a scenario that, in the twenty-first century, has elements of a sexist stereotype. As we have already seen, Myrtle Wilson, on her first appearance, walks "through her husband as if he were a ghost" (Fitzgerald 23). In Myrtle's apartment, when Nick asks her sister Catherine if Myrtle does not like her husband, Myrtle, overhearing, gives a "violent and obscene" answer (29). When Catherine asks her why she married him, she responds that she thought he was "a gentleman" who "knew something about breeding but he wasn't fit to lick my shoe" (30), and here, Wilson's alleged lack of breeding indicates not only what Myrtle sees as his inferior social status—not "a gentleman"—but also, implicitly, his incapacity to breed, in the sense of producing children. She denies Catherine's claim that she was "crazy about him for a while" (30) with the kind of vehemence that could seem to vindicate that claim, and if it were true, it would set up a parallel with Daisy, who, according to Jordan, was crazy about Tom for a while: on Daisy's return from her honeymoon, Jordan "thought I'd never seen a girl so mad about her husband" (61). In both marriages, there seems to have been an initial phase, literally or figuratively a "honeymoon period," which fit the scenario of a new wife being besotted with (crazy/mad about) her husband, but in both cases, this quickly vanished, in the one case, through the husband's infidelity, and in the other, through his lack of social and economic status and (it is implied) virility.

If we turn to the two major phantom marriages in *Gatsby*, those that the reader constructs in those mental spaces Elena Semino calls the "possibility" spaces (90) of narrative, the most prominent and elaborate is, of course, that of Gatsby and Daisy, and it opens up as a possible space at two successive dates: 1917, when Daisy and Gatsby met and made love in Louisville; and 1922, when, in chapter six, Gatsby tells Nick his plan that he and Daisy, after her divorce from Tom, should "go back to Louisville and be married from her house—just as if it were five years ago" (Fitzgerald 86). In a sense, of course, the phantom marriage has already been consummated in Louisville, as we learn in chapter eight: "He took what he could get, ravenously and unscrupulously—eventually he took Daisy one still October night, took her because he had no real right to touch her hand" (116). We saw earlier that Tom could correspond today to a "predator" scenario; in this instance, the same could be said of Gatsby, and, in his earlier life, though not in his post-Daisy days, he has shown a pattern of such behavior: "He knew women early and since they spoiled him he became contemptuous of them, of young virgins because they were ignorant, of the others because they were hysterical about things which in his overwhelming self-absorption he took for granted" (77). Indeed, given that Gatsby had taken Daisy "ravenously and unscrupulously," and "certainly [. . .] under false pretences" (116) in allowing her to believe that his social and economic position was similar to hers, his possession of her could be construed, in a twenty-first-century perspective, as rape. We hear nothing of Daisy's immediate response; but it creates, for Gatsby, a kind of sacramental, quasi-religious bond: "He had intended, probably, to take what he could and go—but now he found that he had committed himself to the following of a grail [. . .] He felt married to her, that was all." (116-17). The brief throwaway clause, "that was all," is an understatement that does not diminish, but deepens by contrast, the religious-quest scenario activated by "the following of a grail"; it makes Gatsby's commitment seem more profound.

If this account of Gatsby's first possession of Daisy and its consequences for him gives a greater intensity and probability to the "possibility space" of a Gatsby-Daisy marriage, the question remains: could it ever have been realized? In 1917, the social and economic barriers seemed insuperable; in 1922, the economic barrier has dissolved but Gatsby is still a parvenu, a nouveau-riche in contrast to Tom who has "old-money" status, and there remains the fact that the main source of Gatsby's wealth appears to be organized crime: bootlegging and bond fraud. In chapter seven, especially during the Plaza Hotel scene, Tom skilfully brings out Gatsby's involvement in the former by his references to the drugstores that, because they were legally allowed to sell alcohol on prescription for medicinal purposes during Prohibition, could serve as a front for peddling illicit booze.

There is also the question of whether Gatsby and Daisy's feelings for each other change after their reunion in Nick's bungalow in chapter five. There are hints, even as Gatsby takes Daisy around his house on that afternoon, that the configuration of emotions and ideals, which exalted her to the heights, is changing and shrinking, as when he points out to her the green light on her dock and Nick speculates: "Possibly it had occurred to him that the colossal significance of that light had now vanished forever [. . .]. His count of enchanted objects had diminished by one" (Fitzgerald 73). But while we know that, after their first meeting, "Daisy comes over [to Gatsby's house] quite often—in the afternoons" (88), and it seems they may have become lovers again, we learn no more. In a letter in 1925 to his friend and mentor Edmund Wilson, first published in the Wilson-edited volume of Fitzgeraldiana, *The Crack-Up* (1945), Fitzgerald himself wrote that the "worst fault" in *Gatsby* was, he thought, "a BIG FAULT: I gave no account (and had no feeling about or knowledge of) the emotional relations between Gatsby and Daisy from the time of their reunion to the catastrophe" (270). This is one of the key cognitive gaps in *Gatsby*, though it is open to question whether it is a "fault" or the kind of "underspecification," to use Terence Cave's term (2), which enriches the novel and contributes to its identity as a modernist text.

With the phantom marriage of Tom and Myrtle, the reader is on surer ground. The readers infers that there is a passionate physical relationship between them, not least from the way in which they almost immediately disappear into the bedroom to make love when they arrive at Myrtle's apartment (it is at this point that Nick tries to read *Simon Called Peter*). But the reader who brings to the novel a certain knowledge of how class division operates is also likely to think, from the outset, that marriage between Tom and Myrtle is highly unlikely because of their differing social status. This is confirmed by what we hear and see later in chapter two: from Myrtle's sister, we learn that Tom has told Myrtle that Daisy is a Catholic—a lie intended to block Myrtle's aspiration to marry Tom; and, most definitively, the brutal blow Tom inflicts when Myrtle insists on shouting Daisy's name is a physical demonstration of the fact that Daisy and Myrtle belong to different social spheres and that any attempt to transgress the barrier between those spheres will meet an emphatic and, if necessary, violent response.

This act of violence—the most extreme one portrayed directly in *Gatsby*—leads on to a further aspect of Fitzgerald's novel to which a cognitive perspective can be brought to bear: its representation of physical, somatic experience.

Gatsby's Bodies

As a premise in this section, we can recall the assertion made in the first paragraph of this essay: in reading a fictional text, the body of the reader may prepare to respond as if the situations evoked in that text were real, for example by tensing muscles, even though the actions that might follow in real life would not ensue. In other words, the reader is always an embodied reader. For all its romanticism and idealization, *Gatsby* is a very physical novel—and indeed this strengthens the intensity and credibility of its romantic and idealistic elements.

The major physical disciplines and traumas of war and sport take place offstage, but they bear strongly upon the text and become manifest in memories and bodily traces. For example, Gatsby's account of his martial experiences in chapter four—to which his medal from Montenegro gives some credence—evokes the "piles of dead" (Fitzgerald 53) in the Argonne Forest, which would activate in many readers a World War I scenario in which mass slaughter is a key element; one of those named on Gatsby's guest-list at the start of the same chapter, "young Brewer," "had his nose shot off in the war" (50), an all-too-visible disfigurement even if it had some prosthetic masking.

Where sport is concerned, Tom's days as a football star are in the past but, in Nick's view, haunt him: "I felt that Tom would drift on forever seeking a little wistfully for the dramatic turbulence of some irrecoverable football game" (Fitzgerald 9). Jordan Baker is a feminine counterpart of Tom in his now-faded football heyday in that she is a famous amateur golfer who has to watch what she drinks and go to bed at ten o'clock. In 1922, she loses in the finals of a golf tournament and is rumored to have cheated on at least one occasion (a rumor Nick seems to credit, though he has no apparent corroborative evidence and never seems to try to find out the truth of the matter directly from Jordan herself). In other words, Jordan is subject to the kind of pressures that fall upon famous athletes in the twentieth and twenty-first centuries, even though Nick shows little sensitivity to, or awareness of these. The interplay of sport and cheating is exemplified less ambiguously and on a larger scale by Gatsby's revelation to Nick, in chapter four, that Wolfshiem is "the man who fixed the World's Series back in 1919" (58). The physical disciplines of sport are compromised by definite or possible corruption.

This is incarnated in what Tom has become. In chapter two, Nick evokes the ex-footballer's physique with peculiar attention; as we observed in the first section of this essay, Tom has already emerged as a "figure" from the "ground" of his house and garden, but this description increases his density:

> Not even the effeminate swank of his riding clothes could hide the enormous power of that body—he seemed to fill those glistening boots until he strained the top lacing, and you could see a great pack of muscle shifting when his shoulder moved under his thin coat. It was a body capable of enormous leverage—a cruel body. (Fitzgerald 9)

In "Another Reading of *The Great Gatsby*" (1979), a pioneering essay that opened up the homoerotic implications of the novel for critical discussion, Keath Fraser pointed out that this quotation portrays "a body of rather more interest to Nick than the one he courts in Jordan Baker" (335) and suggested that it indicates Nick's repressed homosexuality, his fascination with muscular male corporeality. Without excluding this interpretation, the more general sense the embodied reader would have would be of the scale, force, and menace of Tom's body, conveyed by, for example, the adjectives "enormous" (used twice), "great" and "cruel," and this would produce an incipient physical reaction, a preparation for possible physical responses, not perhaps primarily of a sexual kind, to such a body, especially if its potential violence and sadism were unleashed.

The other body of which Nick is especially aware in chapter two is that of Jordan Baker. Although he first sees her lying "completely motionless" on a divan (a stasis that itself indicates a certain bodily self-discipline), she resembles, even when wholly still, a kind of acrobat, "her chin raised a little, as if she were balancing something on it which was quite likely to fall" (Fitzgerald 10). This description may likewise prompt an incipient bodily response in the embodied reader, a subdued preparation for performing a similar mime of a balancing act. Nick's description of Jordan after she stands up emphasizes her deportment before alighting on her eyes: "She was a slender, small-breasted girl with an erect carriage which she accentuated by throwing her body backward at the shoulders like a young cadet" (12). Again, the conventionally masculine implications of this description could serve as evidence of Nick's repressed same-sex preference ("I enjoyed looking at her" [12] because, the subtext might run, she resembled a young male) and perhaps contributed to Lionel's Trilling's description, back in 1945, of Jordan as "vaguely homosexual" (252); but more generally, they are likely to produce, in the embodied reader, an incipient sense of what it might be like to hold one's body like this and how it might impinge upon one to see, and be in proximity, to a body held like this. Jordan shares a certain muscularity with Tom, though in a more elegant key; when she is reading aloud from the *Saturday Evening Post* to Tom, Nick observes that "she turned a page with a flutter of slender muscles in her arms" (18). It is also worth noting that this scene is, of the three scenes of reading in the novel, the only one that suggests that actual comprehension is taking place while reading, and it shows reading as a physical, bodily act, involving the voice and the arms.

The violence Nick sees as inherent in Tom's body in chapter one is unleashed near the end of chapter two, when, as already mentioned, Tom hits Myrtle after she refuses to stop shouting Daisy's name. The blow strikes home in a short, one-sentence paragraph:

> Making a short deft movement Tom Buchanan broke her nose with his open hand. (Fitzgerald 31)

Here, Fitzgerald's lyrical, graceful prose gives way to a sentence that could fit into a hardboiled thriller of the period, a stylistic switch that helps to convey the brutality and debasement of the act: the physical strength and adroitness that made Tom a star footballer have come to this. For many twenty-first-century readers, the scene would also accord with the scenario of "violence against women," thus linking with the scenarios of Tom and Gatsby as predators and Gatsby's first possession of Daisy as a kind of rape. Part of its accordance with the "violence against women" scenario would be the way in the action sequence that follow the blow involve covering up and passing over the violence—Nick does not feel here, as he did at the Buchanan house in chapter one, an "instinct [. . .] to telephone immediately for the police" (Fitzgerald 16) and does not appear even to remonstrate with Tom (which might, admittedly, be physically dangerous for him)—we hear of only "women's voices scolding" (32). The embodied reader will also incipiently mimic, in a physical way, both the perpetration and the impact of the violence—making that short deft movement, wincing at the stunning force and pain of that blow.

As noted earlier, this is the most violent act that is directly represented in the novel. It is not lethal, although it does contribute to a fatal outcome insofar as Myrtle's return from the city "with her face bruised and her nose swollen" (Fitzgerald 122) feeds into Wilson's suspicions of his wife, which eventually lead him to imprison her in the upper room and thus help to trigger the tragedy.

None of the three major deaths in the novel—Myrtle's, Gatsby's, or Wilson's—is directly portrayed. But the novel does dwell on Myrtle's mutilated corpse with a graphic physicality absent from the descriptions of the murdered Gatsby (the evocation of the swimming pool and its laden mattress at the end of chapter eight never mentions his body directly) or the self-slain Wilson (whose corpse gets only one mention at the end of that chapter). This is Nick's account, based on the evidence of Michaelis, the café owner who was Wilson's neighbor:

> [The driver of the car heading for New York] hurried back to where Myrtle Wilson, her life violently extinguished, knelt in the road and mingled her thick, dark blood with the dust.
>
> Michaelis and this man reached her first but when they had torn open her shirtwaist still damp with perspiration they saw that her left breast was swinging loose like a flap and there was no need to listen for the heart beneath. The mouth was wide open and ripped at the corners as though she had choked a little in giving up the tremendous vitality she had stored so long. (Fitzgerald 107)

This graphic description could be seen as voyeuristic, even necrophilic. But the primary response of the embodied reader would be one of corporeal and imaginative identification—how appalling it would be to suffer such mutilation—and this response combines with other key elements of the description—for instance, the phrase "tremendous vitality" (the third time the noun is applied to Myrtle in the novel), to arouse feelings of empathy and compassion for such a thwarted life. These feelings can then be related to a wider critique—for example, of repressive social attitudes to women—but they begin in the responses of the embodied reader.

Conclusion

This essay has aimed to show we can apply three key perspectives drawn from cognitive literary criticism—figure and ground, actual and possible mental spaces, and the embodied reader—to a canonical literary text. Of course, there are many other perspectives from cognitive literary criticism we could also apply, but the ones employed seem to strengthen our grasp of a text that the great Fitzgerald scholar, editor, and biographer Matthew J. Bruccoli rightly called "inexhaustible" (12). These cognitive perspectives are not intended to exclude others—for instance, psychoanalytic approaches that would focus on repressed sexuality, feminist readings that would concentrate on representations of violence against women, gay readings that would highlight a homoerotic subtext—but they do offer a conceptual network that, without false universalization, can subtend such readings and that is drawn from the processes of cognition, involving mind, body, and senses, which operate in all human beings, in reading literature and living life.

Works Cited

Bruccoli, Matthew J. "Introduction." *New Essays on The Great Gatsby*. Cambridge UP, 1985, pp. 1-14.

Cave, Terence. *Thinking with Literature: Towards a Cognitive Criticism*. Oxford UP, 2016.

Fitzgerald, F. Scott. *The Great Gatsby*. Cambridge UP, 1991.

Fraser, Keath. "Another Reading of *The Great Gatsby*." *English Studies in Canada*, vol. 5, no. 3, Autumn 1979, pp. 330-43.

Gavins, Joanna, and Gerard Steen, editors. *Cognitive Poetics in Practice*. Routledge, 2003.

Semino, Elena. "Possible Worlds and Mental Spaces in Hemingway's 'A Very Short Story'." Gavins and Steen, pp. 83-98.

Steen, Gerard. "'Love Stories': Cognitive Scenarios in Love Poetry." Gavins and Steen, pp. 67-82.

Stockwell, Peter. *Texture: A Cognitive Aesthetics of Reading*. Edinburgh UP, 2012.

Trilling, Lionel. "F. Scott Fitzgerald." *The Liberal Imagination: Essays on Literature and Society*. Secker and Warburg, 1955, pp. 243-54.

Wilson, Edmund, editor. *The Crack-Up*. New Directions, 1993, pp. 270-71.

Hemingway's Suicides: A Psychobiographical Approach to Literature

Jeffrey Berman

"My father was a coward," Ernest Hemingway declared in a canceled passage of *Green Hills of Africa*. "He shot himself without necessity. At least I thought so. I had gone through it myself until I figured it in my head. I knew what it was to be a coward and what it was to cease being a coward. Now, truly, in actual danger I felt a clean feeling as in a shower."

Hemingway's observation, which appears in Carlos Baker's 1970 biography (809), raises many disturbing questions, especially to those who take a psychobiographical approach to literature. Why did Hemingway equate suicide with cowardice rather than with hopelessness and depression, both of which, as nearly every mental health professional then and now would suggest, are far more accurate predictors of suicide? What was it in Hemingway's life and culture that compelled him to link suicide with cowardice, or unmanliness?

There are more questions. How did Clarence Hemingway's suicide in 1928 affect his son's life? Why did Ernest believe that he had succeeded in overcoming the moral failure to which his father had succumbed? Why did Hemingway sentence so many of his fictional characters to suicide, either the unambiguous suicide we see in "Indian Camp," the first story in his 1925 collection, *In Our Time*, or the disguised suicide we see at the end of his 1940 novel, *For Whom the Bell Tolls*? Finally, and most troubling of all, why did Ernest Hemingway repeat his father's fate when he fatally shot himself in 1961 at the age of sixty-one, an act long foreshadowed in his fiction?

Hemingway was not yet ready to reveal his complicated feelings about his father's suicide in the nonfictional *Green Hills of Africa*, his 1935 travelogue of a month-long safari he and his then wife, Pauline Pfeiffer, took in East Africa two years earlier. He *was* ready to write about it, under the guise of fiction, five years later in

For Whom the Bell Tolls, his long, sprawling account of the Spanish Civil War. Fiction allowed Hemingway to reveal personal truths that he dared not express in nonfiction. Or as Picasso famously observed, "art is a lie that tells the truth."

All of Hemingway's novels are autobiographical, but what makes *For Whom the Bell Tolls* unusual is that it represents his most extended meditation on his father's suicide and its devastating impact on his own life. Hemingway offers in the novel his own psychobiographical interpretation of his father's suicide—though Hemingway's explanation, we should point out, is misleading. Robert Jordan, the novel's hero, is a University of Montana Spanish instructor who travels to Spain in the 1930s to write a book about the Spanish Civil War and then volunteers to aid the Loyalist struggle against the Fascists. Much of the novel is a discussion of the politics and military strategy of the war, but Jordan is largely apolitical, driven to Spain not primarily out of his commitment to democracy but to exorcise his private demons, which are a part of the legacy—or illegacy—of suicide.

The burden of a parent's suicide becomes evident at the beginning of the novel in a revealing exchange among Jordan; Maria, the young woman with whom he immediately falls in love; and the outspoken gypsy Pilar, Maria's surrogate mother. In dialogue charged with irony and ambiguity, Pilar and Maria declare that their fathers were Republicans, meaning that they were opposed to the Fascists; Jordan discloses that his father and grandfather were also Republicans, the latter a member of the Republican National Committee. Asked by Pilar whether his father is still active in the Republic, Jordan replies "no" and quickly tries to change the subject, despite Maria's persistent questions:

> "Can one ask how he died?"
>
> "He shot himself."
>
> "To avoid being tortured?" the woman asked.
>
> "Yes," Robert Jordan said. "To avoid being tortured.
> (Hemingway, *For Whom* 66-67)

Maria, whose father was tortured and murdered by the Fascists, assumes incorrectly that Jordan's father, facing a similar fate, was fortunate enough to have a gun to end his life. "Oh, I am very glad that your father had the good fortune to obtain a weapon," she states, to which Jordan tersely responds, "Yes. It was pretty lucky.... Should we talk about something else?" (Hemingway, *For Whom* 67). Hemingway returns to this dark event three hundred pages later, when we learn about Jordan's anger and contempt for his father who has committed suicide. Hemingway uses an interior monologue to reveal the details of the suicide, an act which, despite Jordan's statements to the contrary, continues to haunt his life.

Psychobiography

Psychobiography is the effort to understand the life of a person, usually an artist, scientist, entertainer, political leader, or religious guide, through the use of psychological and biographical theory. Psychology is a vast discipline encompassing many different theoretical approaches, including psychoanalysis, clinical psychology, cognitive psychology, social psychology, gestalt psychology, behavioral psychology, experimental psychology, narrative psychology, psychopharmacology, and neuropsychology. Psychobiography is "multimethodological and essentially theoretically anarchistic," as William Todd Schultz wryly admits in the introduction to his 2005 edited volume, *Handbook of Psychobiography* (16). The psychobiographer seeks to learn the personal, historical, and cultural factors that contribute to a person's identity and then to show the relationship between the subject's life and work. Psychoanalytically-oriented psychobiographers emphasize the importance of childhood experiences, the influence of one's parents in the shaping of personality, the role of the unconscious, and the ways in which the past shapes the present and future.

The subtitle of Alan C. Elms's 1994 book, *Uncovering Lives*, evokes the fraught relationship between two discrete but interrelated disciplines: *The Uneasy Alliance of Biography and Psychology*. Elms begins his book by citing the columnist George Will's sneering definition: "In 'psychobiography' the large deeds of great individuals are 'explained' with reference to some hitherto unsuspected sexual inclination or incapacity, which in turn is 'explained' by some slight the individual suffered at a tender age–say, 7, when his mother took away a lollipop" (4). Elms reassures us that he has never encountered an example as ludicrous as Will's Lollipop Hypothesis, but he is mindful of the strengths and weaknesses of psychobiography. Paraphrasing Henry Wadsworth Longfellow, Norman Holland, long regarded as the "Dean" of American psychoanalytic literary criticism, quipped that when psychoanalytic literary criticism is good, it is very good, but when it is bad, it is horrid. The same is true of psychobiography. As Elms points out, psychobiography's popularity, like that of other academic disciplines, ebbs and flows. "Psychological approaches to biography flowered in the 1920s and 1930s, languished for several decades, then flourished anew in the 1970s and 1980s" (3). Today psychobiography enjoys a steady interest among mental health professionals and academic scholars.

Freud's *Leonardo*

Freud, the creator of both psychoanalysis and psychobiography, had much to say about the creative process. Perhaps his most famous statement appears in his 1928 essay, "Dostoevsky and Parricide": "Before the problem of the creative artist analysis must, alas, lay down its arms" (177). Freud, however, seldom followed his own advice. His 1910 study, *Leonardo da Vinci and a Memory of His Childhood*, is generally considered the first twentieth-century psychobiography. As Peter Gay notes in his 1988 biography of Freud, "for all the brilliance of its deductions, [*Leonardo*] is a severely flawed performance. Much of the evidence Freud used to establish his portrait is inconclusive or tainted" (270). For example, Freud based his entire interpretation of Leonardo's life on an erroneous German translation of the Italian word *nibbio*, which means *kite*, not a *bird of prey*, as Freud asserted. From this mistranslation Freud concluded that Leonardo was recalling in a childhood dream or fantasy a vulture thrusting its tale into his mouth. Freud then constructed an elaborate psychobiographical interpretation of the role of the vulture in Leonardo's life, equating the bird with mother goddesses and virgin mothers. One thinks of Mark Twain's cautionary warning: "the difference between the right word and the almost right word is like the difference between lightning and the lightning bug."

Freud's study of Leonardo nevertheless remains of great interest, reminding us that biographers or psychobiographers are often "fixated" on their heroes in a special way, idealizing the biographical subject and thus distorting reality:

> In many cases they have chosen their hero as the subject of their studies because—for reasons of their personal emotional life—they have felt a special affection for him from the very first. They then devote their energies to a task of idealization, aimed at enrolling the great man among the class of their infantile models—at reviving in him, perhaps, the child's idea of his father. To gratify this wish they obliterate the individual features of their subject's physiognomy; they smooth over the traces of his life's struggles with internal and external resistances, and they tolerate in him no vestige of human weakness or imperfection. They thus present us with what is in fact a cold, strange, ideal figure, instead of a human being to whom we might feel ourselves distantly related. That they should do this is regrettable, for they thereby sacrifice truth to an illusion, and for the sake of their infantile phantasies abandon the opportunity of penetrating the most fascinating secrets of human nature. (*Leonardo* 130)

Curiously, Freud, whose psychobiographical case studies are masterfully written, among the world's great psychological literature—the only major award he received in his lifetime was the Goethe Prize for Literature in 1930—did everything he could to discourage others from writing about his own life. "That one doesn't like one's own portrait, or that one doesn't recognize oneself in it, is a general and well-known fact," he complained to Stefan Zweig in 1931, upon receiving a copy of *Mental Healers*, which contained a chapter on the psychoanalyst's life (Freud, *Letters* 402). Freud wrote an even harsher letter in 1936 to Arnold Zweig, who had expressed an interest in becoming his biographer:

> You who have so many more attractive and important things to do, who can appoint kings and survey the brutal folly of mankind from the height of a watch-tower! No, I am far too fond of you to allow such a thing to happen. Anyone turning biographer commits himself to lies, to concealment, to hypocrisy, to flattery, and even to hiding his own lack of understanding, for biographical truth is not to be had, and even if it were it couldn't be used. Truth is unobtainable; humanity does not deserve it, and incidentally, wasn't our Prince Hamlet right when he asked whether anyone would escape a whipping if he got what he deserved? (*Letters* 430)

Freud's comments reveal that it is easier to write a psychobiography than to be a psychobiographical subject. Freud's ambivalence was striking but by no means unusual. He loved uncovering the secrets of his patients and characters in history, literature, and mythography, but even though he was extraordinarily self-disclosing in his greatest book, *The Interpretation of Dreams*, he did not want to lie on the couch for others to analyze and dissect him. Freud's demand for privacy helps to explain his defensiveness when someone asked him about the symbolism of the ubiquitous cigar in his hand in all of his photographs. "Sometimes a cigar is only a cigar," he defensively remarked, unwilling to admit his addiction to nicotine that was ultimately responsible for his death. Hemingway, as we shall see, felt similar defensiveness, believing that living authors should not be the subjects of psychobiography.

Freud's comments also betray all-or-nothing thinking, or binary thinking, the mistaken belief that one can either know *all* of the truth or *none* of it. The truth usually lies somewhere in the murky middle. Psychobiography can shed much light on the elusive relationship between the biographical subject and his or her work, but complete knowledge is an impossibility. Or as William James pointed out in the conclusion of his aptly titled "A Certain Blindness in Human Beings," "neither the whole of truth, nor the whole of good, is revealed to any single observer, although each observer gains a partial superiority of insight from the peculiar position in which he stands" (149). We always need to ask ourselves what we know and do not know about a subject. Often we don't know what we don't know. Freud's favorite observation, which he quoted repeatedly throughout his life, was Hamlet's cautionary advice to Horatio: "There are more things in heaven and earth than are dreamt of in your philosophy."

Good Psychobiography

"Good" psychobiography explores the subtle interrelationships between one's life and work, illuminating the biographical subject's character and achievements. Since every interpretation reveals something about the interpreter, some psychobiographers acknowledge how their interpretations of others reveal traces of their own lives. Good psychobiography is modest, never claiming more than it has achieved, and always respectful of the biographical subject.

Elms offers many helpful suggestions for writing and judging good psychobiography. To begin with, psychobiography should avoid theoretical narrowness and reductiveness. "No one psychological theory can effectively elucidate every personality we want to understand. Therefore, psychobiography needs to incorporate as much eclectic diversity as it can find" (Elms 10). Good psychobiography should be theoretically and methodologically cautious, avoiding what Freud calls "wild analysis," the tendency toward polemical, speculative, or crude interpretation. Psychobiography should emphasize psychological health, not pathology. The artistic impulse is almost always a sign of health, not illness, an effort to understand and come to terms with inner conflict. Writing has an adaptive, reparative, integrative function that psychobiographers sometimes neglect to appreciate. Good psychobiography shuns simplicity and embraces complexity, discovering the pattern in a carpet. The more research we have in human development, personality, and social psychology, Elms suggests, the more complicated the conclusions become. "A Theory of Everything may be near enough in physics to keep a lot of physicists awake at night, but in psychology it's not even a believable dream" (11-12).

Good psychobiography, as Freud reminds us, avoids the twin temptations of idealizing and devaluing the subject. One doesn't want psychobiography to be hagiography or pathography. Good psychobiography needs to be psychologically savvy, aware of what a biographical subject simultaneously reveals and conceals. Elms's comment about "negation," or what a psychoanalyst might call denial, is particularly noteworthy. "When a biographical subject tells you who he or she is," Elms remarks, "you obviously should pay attention. But when the subject tells you who she or he *isn't*, you should pay at least as much attention, and sometimes even more" (246).

"Horrid" psychobiography spends too much time searching in vain for key biographical events, resulting in the fallacy of "originology," which Erik H. Erikson defines in *Young Man Luther* (1958) as a "habit of thinking which reduces every human situation to an analogy with an earlier one, and most of all to that earliest, simplest, and most infantile precursor which is assumed to be its 'origin'" (18). Other common errors are the pathologizing of art and the belief that the psychobiographer has uncovered the "mystery" behind the subject's life or achievements.

Psychobiography is largely a retrospective study, giving us an insight into the past that is generally not possible in the present or future. (Elms calls psychobiography a "postdictive enterprise" [187], implying prediction after the fact.) One recalls Kierkegaard's statement that we can understand our life only backward, but we must live it forward. Occasionally psychobiography is predictive, foreshadowing events that later happen.

What are the qualities necessary to be a good psychobiographer? In Elms's words, "a controlled empathy for the subject and a devotion to collecting solid biographical data" (5). The psychobiographer's empathy, Elms adds, "is often helped along if he or she has experienced similarities in life history or at least comes from a similar cultural background" (248).

Finally, we should note Dan P. McAdams's observation about the value of the psychobiographer's engagement with the biographical subject. "Psychobiographers' third-person accounts of their subjects' lives should aim to uncover, interpret, incorporate, and critique subjects' first-person narrative identities; the story the psychobiographer tells should creatively engage the story the psychobiographer thinks the subject told" (75).

Since Freud's *Leonardo*, there have been several successful psychobiographies, including Erikson's *Young Man Luther* and *Gandhi's Truth* (1969), the latter of which won both the Pulitzer Prize and the National Book Award; Maynard Solomon's *Beethoven* (1977); Gay's *Freud: A Life for Our Time*; and Kenneth S. Lynn's *Hemingway* (1987).

Returning to Hemingway

There were two traumatic events in Hemingway's life—the first occurring throughout his early childhood, the second when he was in his late twenties—which played a decisive role in shaping both his identity and his fiction. The first, as reported by Lynn, was that soon after Ernest's birth, on July 21, 1899, his mother, Grace, began to dress and raise him as a *twin of the same sex* of his one-and-a-half-year-older sister, Marcelline. The two children were dressed and *treated* alike until Ernest was six. "Besides making Marcelline and Ernest look like twins," Lynn remarks, "Grace wanted them, in Marcelline's words, 'to feel like twins by having everything alike'" (41). Hemingway later grew to despise his mother and sister, both of whom he associated with the humiliating years of his early life when he was raised and treated as a girl. Hemingway later asserted that he had always thought of Marcelline "from when I first knew her, which goes back now half a hundred years . . . as a bitch complete with handles" (97). Carl Eby has shown in painstaking detail how being raised as his sister's twin was crucial to the construction of identity and gender in both Hemingway's life and his fiction.

The second event, Clarence Hemingway's suicide, when Ernest was twenty-nine, intensified the writer's rage toward his mother. Clarence Hemingway was a physician who for years had been struggling with a mood disorder, either depression or manic-depression. He ended his life by taking his father's ancient Smith & Wesson revolver and shooting himself in the head. Ernest Hemingway always regarded his paternal grandfather as a Civil War hero, in contrast to his father, who was definitely not a hero. The son thus idealized his grandfather and devalued his father, antithetical images of masculinity he was never able to resolve. Searching for a scapegoat for his father's suicide, Ernest blamed Grace. In a 1949 letter to Charles Scribner, Hemingway accused her of destroying his father's life and perhaps trying to destroy his own as well:

> I hate her guts and she hates mine. She forced my father to suicide and, one time, later, when I ordered her to sell certain worthless properties that were eating her up with taxes, she wrote: "Never threaten me with what to do. Your father tried that once when we were first married and he lived to regret it." (Hemingway, *Selected Letters* 670)

Hemingway spoke repeatedly about his father's suicide, and he never stopped blaming his mother for the tragedy. Sometimes he implied that she might have the same destructive influence over his own life. A. E. Hotchner recalls a story in *Papa Hemingway* in which the novelist told him about receiving a Christmas package from his mother years after her husband's death. "It contained the revolver with which my father had killed himself. There was a card that said she thought I'd like to have it; I didn't know whether it was an omen or a prophecy" (116). Anyone reading this statement would be horrified by Grace Hemingway's insensitivity. The truth, however, is that her son requested the gun.

Fictional Suicides

Hemingway never stopped thinking about his father's suicide, but his fascination with the subject *preceded* Clarence's death. The Native American father inexplicably kills himself in "Indian Camp," one of the most enigmatic suicides in American literature. The next story in the collection *In Our Time*, "The Doctor and the Doctor's Wife," based largely on Hemingway's perception of his parents and their marriage, reveals a deeply depressed physician-father, Dr. Adams, who, humiliated first by a Native American who calls him a coward and then by his infantilizing wife, becomes obsessed with the shotgun he ominously holds on his knees. At the end of the story, Dr. Adams places the loaded rifle behind a dresser, a glaring violation of basic gunmanship.

Regarding suicide as a moral failure, Hemingway believed that those who attempted or succeeded in killing themselves were either cowardly, crazy, or both. In *Death in the Afternoon*, his 1932 meditation on the art of bullfighting, Hemingway writes about the spectators who gaze upon a cowardly matador. "When, lacking the technique and thereby admitting his inability to control his feet, the matador went down on both knees before the bull the crowd had no more sympathy with him than with a suicide." Hemingway's next comment, almost like an uncensored free association, is especially revealing. "For myself, not being a bullfighter, and being much interested in suicides, the problem was one of depiction and waking in the night I tried to remember what it was that seemed just out of my remembering" (Hemingway, *Death* 20).

In a veiled reference to Clarence's death, Nick Adams in the 1935 story "Fathers and Sons" reflects on his father's death years earlier: "He had died in a trap that he had helped only a little to set, and they had all betrayed him in their various ways before he died" (Hemingway, *Short Stories* 489-490). In a more obvious reference to his father, a long description of the various ways to commit suicide appears in *To Have and Have Not* (1937), including those who "used the native tradition of the Colt or Smith and Wesson" (237-238). In the posthumously published *Islands in the Stream* (1970), a character talks endlessly about killing himself and then carries out the promise, a victim of "Mechanics Depressive" (158), a mocking reference to manic depression.

The only thing that evoked more outrage in Hemingway than male suicide was female suicide, particularly unsuccessful female suicide. This becomes clear in his 1926 poem "To a Tragic Poetess," where he mocks Dorothy Parker's references to her suicide attempts in her poem "Résumé." Hemingway contrasts what he perceives to be her insincere efforts to kill herself with the more authentic successful suicides committed by desperate Spanish men whose despair he takes seriously. As I suggest in *Surviving Literary Suicide*, "'To a Tragic Poetess' is nothing less than aggression masquerading as art. The poem reflects and reinforces three dangerous myths of suicide, namely, that those who talk about suicide do not actually go through with it, that unsuccessful suicide attempts should not be taken seriously, and that those who succeed in committing suicide are somehow more heroic than those who fail" (Berman 121).

Hemingway generally has little sympathy for his fictional characters who have attempted or completed suicide, but an exception is "A Clean, Well-Lighted Place," one of his greatest and most empathic stories. An older and younger waiter discuss an old man who regularly visits their café and who recently has tried to hang himself. The older waiter's relentless questions about the failed suicide reveal that he is similarly obsessed with death. The younger waiter callously observes that the old man was in despair over "nothing," since he has plenty of money, but the word *nothing*, and its Spanish equivalent, *nada*, reveal the old man's existential and psychological crisis, the belief that there is nothing for which to live. The older waiter identifies himself with those who, like the old man, "like to stay late at the café . . . . With all those who do not want to go to bed. With all those who need a light for the night" (Hemingway, *Short Stories* 382). The narrator tells us at the end of the five-page story, a masterpiece of compression, that the reason the older waiter cannot sleep at night is because of "insomnia," but it is more than that: for so many of Hemingway's characters, much of life is a dark night of the soul.

An Anti-Suicide Pact

Hemingway could not prevent himself from thinking, talking, and writing about suicide, but he did not want another suicide in the family. Upon learning of his father's suicide, his son John recalled a promise the novelist had compelled him to make several years earlier, when John was experiencing a personal crisis. "After I left the army and was married, I was very depressed about what I was going to do, very gloomy. And Papa said, 'You must promise me never, never . . . we'll both promise each other never to shoot ourselves.' He said, 'Don't do it. It's stupid.' This was after quite a few martinis. I hadn't said anything about shooting myself, but I was obviously very depressed. He said, 'It's one thing you must promise me never to do, and I'll promise the same to you'" (Brian 262).

For Whom the Bell Tolls

Robert Jordan never made an anti-suicide pact with his father, nor does he discuss any of the reasons his father committed suicide, except to repeat and elaborate on what Hemingway decided to omit from *Green Hills of Africa*. The crucial information about the father's death appears in chapter 30 of *For Whom the Bell Tolls*, when Jordan recalls the coroner sending him after the funeral the Smith and Wesson revolver used for the suicide. "Bob, I guess you might want to keep the gun. I'm supposed to hold it, but I know your dad set a lot of store by it because his dad packed it all through the [Civil] War, besides out here when he first came out with the Cavalry, and it's still a hell of a good gun" (337). Robert Jordan's thoughts of his cowardly father immediately evoke, by contrast, his heroic grandfather, who would have been "embarrassed" by the suicide, as the grandson is. "Any one has a right to do it," Robert Jordan muses, "But it isn't a good thing to do. I understand it, but I do not approve of it. *Lache* [cowardly] was the word." He then remembers his first reactions to the suicide:

> I'll never forget how sick it made me the first time I knew he was a *cobarde*. Go on, say it in English. Coward. It's easier when you have said it and there is never any point in referring to a son of a bitch by some foreign term. He wasn't any son of a bitch, though. He was just a coward and that was the worst luck any man could have. Because if he wasn't a coward he would have stood up to that woman and not let her bully him. I wonder what I would have been like if he had married a different woman? That's something you'll never know, he thought, and grinned. Maybe the bully in her helped to supply what was missing in the other. And you. (Hemingway, *For Whom* 338-339)

Hemingway's description of the suicide is significant for several reasons. Robert Jordan claims to understand the reasons for the suicide but then qualifies himself. "But you *do* understand it? Sure, I understand it but. Yes, but. You have to be awfully occupied with yourself to do a thing like that" (Hemingway, *For Whom* 338). Similarly, Jordan claims to have forgiven his father but again qualifies himself. "He understood his father and he forgave him everything and he pitied him but he was ashamed of him" (340). Jordan blames his bullying mother for the suicide but then wonders what was missing in his father that triggered the event. He then questions, ominously, whether he is like his father. He reminds himself twice in the same paragraph not to think about his father's suicide but cannot prevent himself from doing so.

The manner in which Robert Jordan disposes of the suicide gun is also noteworthy. The day after receiving the gun, Jordan and a friend, Chub, ride on horseback to a lake purported to be eight hundred feet deep. Climbing out on a rock, he "leaned over and saw his face in the still water, and saw himself holding the gun, and then he dropped it, holding it by the muzzle, and saw it go down making bubbles until it was just as big as a watch charm in that clear water, and then it was out of sight" (Hemingway, *For Whom* 337).

Robert Jordan's image of himself in the water, transfigured by the sight of the gun, evokes the spectral figure of Narcissus, gazing upon himself in a reflecting pool. It is not Ovid's 2000-year-old myth of Narcissus and Echo that comes to mind, however, but Freud's 1914 essay, "On Narcissism: An Introduction." Freud's inquiry began a continuing exploration of the role of narcissistic injuries in personality disorders. The father's suicide in *For Whom the Bell Tolls* has resulted in the son's devastating narcissistic injury that cannot be forgotten or healed. Jordan's image of himself in the water, holding the suicide gun, links him to his dead father, an ambivalent and irresistible identification. As is usual in Hemingway's stories, a character draws attention to a conflict by refusing to talk about it. "I know why you did that with the old gun, Bob," Chub observes, to which Jordan evasively responds, "Well, then we don't have to talk about it" (Hemingway, *For Whom* 337). Jordan doesn't talk about the suicide, but he cannot stop *thinking* about it.

Jordan learns his fate early in the novel when the superstitious Pilar, endowed with the power to read the future, gazes at his palm and then, responding to his question of what she sees, says, without smiling, "Nothing" (Hemingway, *For Whom* 33). The word reminds us of the existential and psychological "nothing" that has compelled the old man's suicide attempt in "A Clean, Well-Lighted Place." We may also recall King Lear's angry response to his beloved daughter Cordelia when she refuses to tell him what he demands to hear: "Nothing will come of nothing." Much comes of nothing in Shakespeare's play and Hemingway's novel.

Robert Jordan is not the only suicidal character in *For Whom the Bell Tolls*. His predecessor, a Russian named Kashkin, described by Pilar as "the one with the bad nerves," spoke repeatedly about the necessity for suicide to avoid being captured and tortured. When Kashkin is indeed wounded, Jordan shoots him. "He was always talking of such a necessity," Pilar observes (Hemingway, *For Whom* 149). Even Maria, who had been raped by fascist soldiers, thinks about suicide. She carries in the breast pocket of her shirt a single-edged razor blade. "'I keep this always,' she explained. 'Pilar says you must make the cut here just below the ear and draw it toward you'" (170).

As *For Whom the Bell Tolls* rushes toward its climactic conclusion, after Jordan's successful dynamiting of the bridge, his left leg is shattered by enemy fire, and he makes the "heroic" decision not to escape with the rest of the guerillas but to remain behind and fight to the death. There was nothing in his military orders that prevented him from escaping with the others: his task was simply to blow the bridge when he was told to do so. The reason he remains behind, awaiting certain death from the approaching Fascists, is to prove to himself that he is not like his father:

> Oh, let them come, he said. I don't want to do that business that my father did. I will do it all right but I'd much prefer not to have to. I'm against that. Don't think about that. Don't think at all. I wish the bastards would come, he said. I wish so very much they'd come. (Hemingway, *For Whom* 469)

Jordan does not die by his own hand, thus avoiding his father's fate, but he has created a situation where his death is assured, a death that others will judge to be heroic, the opposite of his father's ending.

Hemingway's Suicide

Hemingway spent a lifetime trying to prove to himself and others that he was *not* like his father, but as his physical and psychological health sharply deteriorated during his last years, his world narrowed, and he became, as Jordan said about his father, "awfully occupied" with himself. He also lost the ability to write. Writing had always been the most important part of his life, the reason to keep on living. When asked if he had a therapist, Hemingway replied without hesitation, "Sure I have. Portable Corona number three. That's been my analyst" (Hotchner 152). Robert Jordan is himself a writer, and during his more hopeful moments, he looks forward to returning to the United States and writing about his war experiences. Like Hemingway, he regarded writing as a form of cathartic self-cleansing: "my guess is you will get rid of all that by writing about it, he said. Once you write it down it is all gone" (Hemingway, *For Whom* 165). Writing was indeed therapeutic to Hemingway; losing the ability to write was losing his most important lifeline.

Psychobiography: An Invasion of a Writer's Privacy?

Hemingway was probably the most famous novelist of the twentieth century, a larger-than-life figure whose greatest fictional character was himself. He has been the subject of countless books and articles, including Philip Young's early psychobiographical study. In his analysis of Hemingway's major characters, Young found that each suffered a disabling physical or psychological wound; Young then linked these wounds to the serious injury Hemingway received during World War I, when he was driving an ambulance and nearly killed by a mortar shell. Young implied that by writing about these wounds in his fiction, Hemingway was therapeutically working through them, much as Jordan suggests in *For Whom the Bell Tolls*.

    A doctoral student at the time, Young sent Hemingway a copy of the manuscript. The novelist was horrified. Hemingway maintained that a psychobiographical study like the one Young had written was not only an invasion of privacy but could also damage or destroy a novelist's creativity. Hemingway tried unsuccessfully to suppress the publication of Young's book by refusing to allow him to quote from the novels; the novelist later reluctantly relented, and the book was published in 1952. In the foreword to the revised 1966 edition, Young ruefully recalls the telephone calls he received on July 2, 1961, "congratulating" him for correctly predicting Hemingway's suicide.

As he notes in the foreword, Young did not "predict" the suicide; instead, he described in his 1952 book a "situation, a pattern, a process in Hemingway's life and work in which the act of suicide would not be altogether inconsistent" (3). Philip Young died in 1991, at the age of seventy-three. According to Joel Solkoff, Young "could not assuage the guilt he felt that he was responsible for the death of Hemingway. Whether he was or not is unclear to this reader, who could argue it either way." Solkoff adds that Young "ended his days severely depressed [and] unable to stop blaming himself."

Knowing and Not Knowing

Finally, we may ask what Hemingway did not know either about his father's suicide specifically or the larger problem of suicide in general. By judging suicide only in moral terms, he ruled out the genetic factors that predispose certain people, and their families, to mood disorders, a risk factor in suicide. Three generations of Hemingways suffered from severe depression or manic depression. Mood disorders, left untreated, may lead to suicide. Clarence Hemingway committed suicide, as did three of his children: Ernest, Ursula, and Leicester. Two of the novelist's sons have suffered from mental illness, and his granddaughter, Margaux Hemingway, committed suicide in 1996 at the age of forty-one. Hemingway did not know about the relationship between mood disorders and creativity, a connection the psychologist Kay Redfield Jamison explored in her groundbreaking 1993 book, *Touched with Fire: Manic-Depressive Illness and the Artistic Temperament*. A "close relationship between the artistic temperament and manic-depressive illness has many implications—for artists, medicine, and society" (7). Jamison does not write about her own family history of manic-depressive illness in *Touched with Fire*, but she does so in a later book, *An Unquiet Mind: A Memoir of Moods and Madness*, where she writes about being "manic beyond recognition," a suicide attempt that left her in a coma for several days, and her struggle against a drug, lithium, that ultimately saved her life and restored her sanity—and creativity. Had Hemingway been aware of this relationship, he might have been less harsh on both his father and himself. Like many writers of his generation, including F. Scott Fitzgerald, Hemingway feared and mistrusted psychiatry, preferring instead to medicate himself with alcohol, the liquid muse.

In the end Hemingway believed that he had run out of options. "[I]f I can't exist on my own terms," he told A. E. Hotchner, "then existence is impossible. Do you understand? That is how I've lived, and that is how I must live—or not live" (297). Mary Hemingway denied for five years that her husband had deliberately shot himself; according to biographer Jeffrey Meyers, she felt gnawing guilt that she had not hidden the key to the gun cabinet. There were several copycat suicides, as usually occurs after a celebrity takes his or her own life. Perhaps the most poignant response to Hemingway's suicide appears in John Berryman's *The Dream Songs*. Berryman, whose life also ended in suicide, evokes the haunting legacy of suicide, a problem well known by Robert Jordan:

> But to return, to return to Hemingway
>
> that cruel & gifted man.
>
> Mercy! My father; do not pull the trigger
>
> or all my life I'll suffer from your anger
>
> killing what you began. (254)

Works Cited

Baker, Carlos. *Ernest Hemingway: A Life Story*. Bantam, 1970.

Berman, Jeffrey. *Surviving Literary Suicide*. U of Massachusetts P, 1999.

Berryman, John. *The Dream Songs*. Farrar, Straus, and Giroux, 1977.

Brian, Denis. *The True Gen*. Grove Press, 1988.

Eby, Carl. *Hemingway's Fetishism: Psychoanalysis and the Mirror of Manhood*. State U of New York P, 1998.

Elms, Alan C. *Uncovering Lives: The Uneasy Alliance of Biography and Psychology*. Oxford UP, 1994.

Erikson, Erik H. *Gandhi's Truth: On the Origins of Militant Nonviolence*. Norton, 1969.

———. *Young Man Luther: A Study in Psychoanalysis and History*. Norton, 1958.

Freud, Sigmund. "Dostoevsky and Parricide." 1928. *The Standard Edition of the Complete Psychological Works of Sigmund Freud*. Translated by James Strachey. Vol. 21. Hogarth Press, 1961.

———. *Leonardo da Vinci and a Memory of His Childhood*. 1910. *The Standard Edition of the Complete Psychological Works of Sigmund Freud*. Translated by James Strachey, vol. 11, Hogarth Press, 1957.

———. *Letters of Sigmund Freud*, selected and edited by Ernst L. Freud, translated by Tania and James Stern, Basic Books, 1960.

Gay, Peter. *Freud: A Life for Our Time*. Norton, 1988.

Hemingway, Ernest. *Death in the Afternoon*. Scribner's, 1932.

———. *For Whom the Bell Tolls*. Scribner's, 1940.

———. *Green Hills of Africa*. Scribner's, 1935.

———. *In Our Time*. Scribner's, 1925.

———. *Islands in the Stream*. Scribner's, 1970.

———. *Selected Letters*, edited by Carlos Baker. Scribner's, 1981.

———. *The Short Stories of Ernest Hemingway*. Scribner's, 1966.

———. *To Have and Have Not*. Scribner's, 1937.

Hotchner, A. E. *Papa Hemingway*. Random House, 1966.

James, William. "On a Certain Blindness in Human Beings." *Talks to Teachers on Psychology: and to Students on Some of Life's Ideals*. Harvard UP, 1983, pp. 149-51.

Jamison, Kay Redfield. *Touched with Fire: Manic-Depressive Illness and the Artistic Temperament*. Free Press, 1993.

———. *An Unquiet Mind: A Memoir of Moods and Madness*. Knopf, 1995.

Lynn, Kenneth S. *Hemingway*. Fawcett, 1987.

McAdams, Dan P. "What Psychobiographers Might Learn from Personality Psychology." *Handbook of Psychobiography*, edited by William Todd Schultz, Oxford UP, 2005, pp. 64-83.

Schultz, William Todd, editor. *Handbook of Psychobiography*. Oxford UP, 2005.

Solkoff, Joel. "Lost in the Current Tragedy: Penn State is the World Center of Hemingway Scholarship." *Voices*, 13 Nov. 2011. voicesweb.org/lost-current-tragedy-penn-state-world-center-hemingway-scholarship. Accessed 16 Aug. 2016.

Solomon, Maynard. *Beethoven*. Schirmer, 1977.

Young, Philip. *Ernest Hemingway: A Reconsideration*. Pennsylvania State UP, 1966.

"Written in his face": Ambivalence and Mirroring in *Nineteen Eighty-Four*

David Willbern

In the dystopian economy of Orwell's Oceania, Big Brother invades even the pockets of the populace. State coins display his omnipotent countenance on one side, while etched on the obverse are the three paradoxical slogans of the Party: "WAR IS PEACE. FREEDOM IS SLAVERY. IGNORANCE IS STRENGTH" (4). Two sides of a coin: one a face, the other words. Handling that coin, turning it in our fingers, we can visualize both the transformation of face and language in *Nineteen Eighty-Four* and the uneasy ambivalence of change.

Faces are everywhere in the novel: on money, posters, telescreens, and people. Although placid neutrality is the mask to wear in public, in order to avoid "face-crime" (Orwell, *Nineteen Eighty-Four* 62), Winston Smith's world is physiognomically remarkable. There is the pink, sweating face of his neighbor, Parsons (56), the "bold aquiline face" of his absent wife, Katharine (66), the "duck-speaking" blank face of a man in a pub (50), the "pouched, seamed, and ruinous" face of Rutherford, the treasonous caricaturist (76), the "completely expressionless" face of Martin (168), O'Brien's Oriental servant. O'Brien's own "coarse, humorous, brutal" face (10) seems yet to offer affection and understanding to Smith, who first reads in it a brief sign of sympathy, but he is uncertain: "perhaps it was not even unorthodoxy that was written in his face, but simple intelligence" (11). Later he discovers the terror it wears in the Ministry of Love, accompanied by "gorilla-faced" guards and others with faces like "wax mask[s]" (5, 229).

The human face is the site of emotion and thought, of manifest pleasure and pain. Smiles and tears, joy and rage show themselves on its surface. It is naked to the world, the object of others' sight, of kisses and of slaps. It is the place of perception, site of the senses: eyes, nose, mouth. The face is the locus of similarity (family resemblance) and recognizable uniqueness (personal identity). It manifests youth and age, health and disease. Its smoothness figures the blankness of innocence; its wrinkles are the lines of time, the inscribed character of individual history. "At fifty," Orwell noted from his death bed, "every man has the face he deserves" (qtd. in Taylor, *Orwell* 57). The writer died in 1950, at age forty-six, one year after *Nineteen Eighty-Four* was published.[1]

Smith's childhood memories are haunted by the faces of his mother and sister, looking up at him as they sink "into the green waters" of loss (Orwell, *Nineteen Eighty-Four* 29). He remembers with lust and shame the thickly painted face of an old whore ("the whiteness of it, like a mask, and the bright red lips" [63])—a face that Julia puts on in their attic room. This is the face of desire and death, prefigured by another sight of Julia's face, "deathly white, as white as chalk" (128), when the lovers are covered with plaster dust from a rocket-borne explosion. Smith's last sight of Julia before they are taken to prison is "her face, upside-down, yellow, and contorted, with the eyes shut, and still with a smear of rouge on either cheek" (223).

Throughout the novel, faces change. Charrington's benevolent, avuncular guise becomes the terrible visage of the Thought Police; his white hair turns black, his glasses and wrinkles vanish, his whole face transmutes into the "alert, cold" gaze of tyranny (Orwell, *Nineteen Eighty-Four* 224). (The Party, O'Brien explains, is expert at plastic surgery.) The most vivid instance of the changing face is the telescreen metamorphosis of Emmanuel Goldstein's "lean, Jewish, sheeplike" face into an actual sheep (12), then into a Eurasian soldier, then into the face of Big Brother, and finally to the three slogans of Ingsoc. The Party's goal is to create a society of "three hundred million people all with the same face" (74), one constrained by conformity, distorted by hatred, or smashed by brutality. Its ritual Two-minute Hate arouses a "hideous ecstasy, a desire to kill, to torture, to smash faces in with a sledge hammer" (14). Assaults on the face express Party policy and individual anger. Smith fantasizes smashing Julia's face when he fears she is a spy, and he swears to throw acid in a child's face if so ordered by the Brotherhood (101, 172). In the Ministry of Love, he watches as a prisoner's face is beaten to a bloody pulp. As O'Brien tells Smith, "If you want a picture of the future, imagine a boot stamping on a human face—forever" (267). This is the ideology of human iconoclasm, obliterating difference by enforcing absolute conformity, a purely expressionless face. At the end, the sallow, scarred face of Julia and the bloated, coarse face of Smith confront each other under the grim smile of Big Brother in the affect-less banality of love for their leader. The effective goal of Ingsoc is the effacement of individuality.

Behind the Eyes

Since the Party seeks to abolish individual character, the only apparently safe haven for personal expression is behind the eyes, or in forbidden writing. Smith's secret diary records his hidden humanity, in terms of memory, fantasy, and rebellion. "DOWN WITH BIG BROTHER" is the repeated message, but that is only another mindless slogan (Orwell, *Nineteen Eighty-Four* 18). The politics of the diary are irrelevant to Smith. What matters is the thrill of pleasure and anxiety that he feels when he writes. In writing, he gives himself over to an autoerotics of self-expression. The "particularly beautiful" diary with "its smooth creamy paper," evokes in him "an overwhelming desire to possess it" (6). It had been, according to Charrington, "a young lady's keepsake album" (94). As Smith writes, "his pen slid voluptuously over the smooth paper."[2] This tactile intimacy of writing suggests, in Freudian terms, a regressive oral fantasy, whose pleasure in creation is inversely mirrored by Syme's aggressive appetite for destruction in preparing *The Newspeak Dictionary*. He brags to Smith, "'We're cutting language down to the bone.' He bit hungrily into his bread" (51).

Smith's regressive writing encloses his secret thoughts in the creamy margins of the female keepsake. As a nostalgic enclosure, the diary prefigures the glass paperweight within which Smith imagines being protectively encased, "fixed in a sort of eternity at the heart of the crystal" (Orwell, *Nineteen Eighty-Four* 147). The hemispherical glass, soft in color and texture "as of rainwater," enclosing "a strange, pink, convoluted object that recalled a rose or a sea anemone" (95), suggests an image of the maternal breast—also evoked by the creaminess of the diary. The pink object, Charrington adds, is coral from the Indian Ocean—an allusion to Smith's mother, sinking into the green ocean in his dream (Orwell, *née* Eric Blair, was born in India). When a Thought Policeman knocks the paperweight to the floor and shatters it, Smith sees the coral, now "a tiny crinkle of pink like a sugar rosebud from a cake . . . . How small, thought Winston, how small it always was!" (223). Nostalgia magnifies maternity, and memories can be fragile.[3]

Certainly Smith has a taste for nostalgia, bitter though it becomes. Smells of roasting coffee, chocolate, and perfume recall for him vague moments of his childhood. He suffers regularly from a "dull aching in his belly" that recalls his "clamorous hunger" as a child (Orwell, *Nineteen Eighty-Four* 162). The raw strength of mere visceral life appeals to him, indicated in his idealization of the proles and their tactile, non-thinking existence. In a critical scene, a large, singing washerwoman hanging out diapers offers an image of this idealization; she recalls and reconfigures Smith's lost mother.

The lost mother is the most crucially absent figure in the novel. Smith gets close to her through dream and reminiscence and through his free association in the creamy diary. His initial entry (4/4/84) records a news film that quickly merges into dream. Images of a machine-gunned man, or a woman holding a three year-old boy ("hiding his head between her breasts" [Orwell, *Nineteen Eighty-Four* 8]), or an explosion that throws the child's dismembered arm into the air, present a scenario in which Smith can identify with the protected child, embraced by the maternal gesture, as well as the punished child, whose grasping arm is torn off. Smith confesses to Julia, "I believed I had murdered my mother" (160). The dream itself is familiar and well-studied.[4] I will consider only its end.

After speculating that his family has been "swallowed up" in a 1950s purge, Smith dreams of his mother and sister below him, as though in a well, grave, or sinking ship, "being sucked down to death" (Orwell, *Nineteen Eighty-Four* 29). They die, he imagines, so that he might live. He then dreams of the Golden Country and the girl who throws off her clothes, thereby annihilating the Party with a simple gesture of her arm. "Winston woke up with the word 'Shakespeare' on his lips" (31). The dream is manifestly erotic; Smith might naturally be aroused by a fantasy of female nudity. In fact, he is roused out of bed to begin the "Physical Jerks," daily calisthenics directed by a woman on the telescreen (31). The confluence of erotic dreaming, arm gestures, and jerks suggests a latent masturbatory fantasy, displaced into language by the climactic phrase, "shake spear." The focus on the mouth ("'Shakespeare' on his lips") also indicates the orality of the fantasy: the gesture of the maternal arm is to pull the child to her breast.

In the confines of Miniluv, Smith encounters another maternal figure, an "enormous wreck of a woman" who enters struggling and cursing, sits on his lap, vomits copiously, then puts her arm around him and asks his name (Orwell, *Nineteen Eighty-Four* 227). As it happens, her name too is Smith; she might be his mother. Smith shows no affect, not even disgust. The woman, who may or may not be his mother (symbolically, of course, she is), simply disappears from the page. Orwell erases her completely, with no explanation (other prisoners are taken away by guards). Rather, he replaces her in Smith's emotional economy with the ambivalent tyranny of Big Brother, and the fraternal-maternal surrogate, O'Brien. "For a moment," after the electric shocks are stopped, "he clung to O'Brien like a baby, curiously comforted by the heavy arm round his shoulders" (250). Ultimately, he discovers his victorious feeling of love for Big Brother: "He gazed up at the enormous face . . . O cruel, needless misunderstanding! O stubborn, self-willed exile from the loving breast!"[5]

There are interpretations of this exile within the novel, in terms of Smith's childish theft of his starving little sister's chocolate (after which event the child dies and the mother vanishes [Orwell, *Nineteen Eighty-Four* 162-64]) and outside the novel, in speculations about Orwell, who was writing his autobiographical essay, "Such, Such Were the Joys," while working on *Nineteen Eighty-Four*. I am interested in the larger design of the novel's psychology, as the outer social world of Winston Smith mirrors his inner psychic world.[6] For instance, Smith's guilt over that past chocolate theft finds punishment in the Party's present reduction of the chocolate ration. In the primitive logic of the unconscious, if you're too greedy, Mother disappears. In Freudian terms, his superego is displaced onto the government of Oceania: Ingsoc is the structure of his paranoia. What is inside Winston Smith, in terms of guilt and the wish-fear of punishment, becomes externalized into a persecuting, torturing, and inescapable authority. The most graphic instance of this projection is the rat-mask in Room 101: it reifies the paranoid style of the novel.[7] We first discover Smith's dream of rats in the attic room. He is paralyzed with fear and imagines a moment from previous nightmares:

> He was standing in front of a wall of darkness, and on the other side of it there was something unendurable, something too dreadful to be faced. . . . With a deadly effort, like wrenching a piece out of his own brain, he could even have dragged the thing into the open. (Orwell, *Nineteen Eighty-Four* 145)

The rat-mask brings to light that dark unendurable "something" behind Smith's psychic walls (his defenses); it externalizes his worst fear.[8] This stark moment of paranoid terror turns Smith into a screaming, subhuman creature—"blind, helpless, mindless," like an infant (Orwell, *Nineteen Eighty-Four* 286). This infantile terror mirrors an earlier scene in which Smith, face to face with another animal, imagines a Keatsian moment of romantic, erotic nurturance. During the Golden Country episode of their first lovemaking, Julia and Winston are serenaded by a thrush that perches at face level, swells its breast, and "pours forth a torrent of song" (123). Smith feels "as though it were a kind of liquid stuff that poured all over him"; so engulfed by romantic love, he embraces Julia "breast to breast; her body seemed to melt into his" (124).

The mirrored opposition of rapturous bird and ravenous rat offers an emblem of the core ambivalence in the novel, between being watched over (cared for) and being over-watched (supervised, surveilled). In hopes of finding a sympathetic society, Winston Smith commits himself to the ostensibly rebellious organization,

"The Brotherhood," under O'Brien's guidance, only to find himself imprisoned, subject to O'Brien's eerily affectionate tortures. In the perverse ideology of Ingsoc, there apparently exists a fourth, occult, Party slogan: "THE BROTHERHOOD IS BIG BROTHER." The secret fraternity is also the totalitarian force. Finally it seems, on the face of it, only obvious.[9]

Paranoia and Ambivalent Mirroring

The paranoid structure of *Nineteen Eighty-Four* grounds itself in an ambivalent mirroring of the maternal face. That face is both present and absent, giving and depriving, feeding and devouring. Gazing up at an enormous face while seeking the loving breast is precisely the posture of a nursing infant. If that face is radically inconstant, the infant has no source for its own stable identification. The unstable and mutable identities of self and other in *Nineteen Eighty-Four* may thus rest on such shifting, ambivalent mirroring. The phenomenon can be considered psychoanalytically through two branches of post-Freudian theory: Kleinian and Lacanian. In the former, "the precursor of the mirror is the mother's face."[10] It is through this core expression of the infant-mother relation that identity emerges and develops. The infant learns to see and experience itself in terms of how the mother reflects it; it puts itself together in her eyes. This process of self-construction becomes more problematic in Lacanian theory, in which the child leaves the mother's arms (no longer a mere infant) and sees its image in an actual mirror.[11] In this scheme identity is built not on a relation between child and (m)other, but on a separate reflection of self, a façade. The child constructs an imaginary integrity from a distanced, alienated image of itself; it imagines a whole from reflected fragments. Lacan's picture of the Freudian ego as a fortress surrounded by hostile forces, or of the self as a fiction or mirage, generates a paranoid model of knowledge and experience ("paranoid" is Lacan's own term). In this model, Smith's dreams of dismemberment and progressive disintegration would correspond to the regressive image of *"le corps morcelé"* that precedes the illusionary unity of the mirror phase. O'Brien, the magical parent, literally pulls Smith apart. After confronting his deteriorating, skeletal face in the Miniluv mirror, Smith recovers from the nadir of reflection to realize that he no longer recalls his face at all. "It was not easy to preserve inscrutability when you did not know what your face looked like" (Orwell, *Nineteen Eighty-Four* 281). He has become an embodiment of self-alienation. Lacan's lecture on "*le stade du miroir*" was delivered in July 1949, a month after the publication of *Nineteen Eighty-Four*. The psychoanalyst's theory seems uncannily mirrored by the novelist's fiction. (One might conjecture that Donald Winnicott's comforting object-relations theory reflects the smiling face of Big Brother, while Lacan's anxious, alienated theory reveals the fierce one.)

Although Orwell was familiar with Paris and an astute cultural observer, it's unlikely that he knew of Lacan, whose public seminars did not begin until 1953. I have no evidence that Lacan read *Nineteen Eighty-Four*. Still the resemblances are intriguing. Both Lacan and Orwell were obsessed by language and the interconnections of verbal, psychological, and social structures. For both, thought existed through language. To Orwell, this was a political matter; to Lacan, it was a psychological one. Orwell's is a linguistics of consciousness and social mendacity; Lacan's is a linguistics of unconsciousness and self-deception. To examine these ideas, we can return to the theme of writing in *Nineteen Eighty-Four*.

Writing as One of the Novel's Themes

Initially there seem to be two basic modes of writing in the novel: *history*, a record of the public past (though accessible to revision), and *memory*, an apparently authentic record of private life, available through reminiscences, or through automatic writing (the recovery of the repressed). The novel posits a quarrel between social or politicized history and personal memory, privileging the authenticity of the self over the propaganda of the Party. Yet the issues are more complex. Each medium (history, memory) has a mirror opposite. Smith's job in the Ministry of Truth is to edit, rewrite, indeed fabricate historical records. (One Party project is to create a fictitious, super-heroic, soldier-patriot—one "Comrade Ogilvy"—whose brave exploits deserve recognition and honor from

Big Brother. [Orwell, *Nineteen Eighty-Four* 46-47]). Had Smith the insight to connect his own patriotic fabrications to the larger society he inhabited, he might have conjectured that none of the supremely famous political figures actually exists. There is no tyrant-savior Big Brother, no arch-enemy Emmanuel Goldstein, only crafty managers of political and rhetorical power like O'Brien, who manipulate their subjects through image and fiction and ensure loyalty through raw force.

The image of Winston Smith sitting alone in his cubicle next to his pneumatic tubes (for inter-office communication) and memory holes (for obliteration), whose occupation is basically writing (and editing and erasing), replicates an image of the author, George Orwell, journalist and novelist, embedded in his own book. Smith is not the only embedded writer. The figure of Emmanuel Goldstein, presumed author of *The Theory and Practice of Oligarchical Collectivism* (known anxiously in Oceania as *"the book"*), is not merely a satire of Trotsky: his is the voice and mind of the man who actually wrote that book-within-the-book, Orwell himself. Sections of that treatise occupy more than twenty-five pages of the novel's text. Smith's most pleasant non-sexual moment is his solitary, blissful reading of *"the book"*—whose true author reveals himself (within the fictive realm of the novel) to be . . . O'Brien, mentor and big brother to Smith. Smith wrote his diary; O'Brien wrote *"the book"*; and Orwell wrote the book that encloses both texts.

The author's use of the book-within-the-book further suggests his ambivalent identifications. That text (*"the book"*) reads like a parody of Trotskyite rhetoric *and* a serious imitation of such social analysis. It is as though Orwell wanted to make his ideological case and erase it too. More generally, his concepts of politicized discourse imply a similar ambivalence. Orwell, the author of the famous essay, "Politics and the English Language," who argues for paring the fat from language, is also the inventor of "Newspeak," which cuts it to the bone.[12] Just as Big Brother is the mirror obverse of The Brotherhood, the brutal linguistic reductions of Newspeak obversely reflect Orwell's editorial principles in that essay (written in 1946, a year before Orwell began writing *Nineteen Eighty-Four*). Orwell promoted a transparent, impersonal language ("Good prose," he asserted, "is like a window pane"), but his own writing shows how an author's face remains reflected in that pane, as in a mirror.

Another way to consider the issue is in terms of representation and censorship. At one level, censorship is political: dangerous words simply go down the memory hole, and undesirable citizens are simply vaporized. Yet censorship—as Orwell must have known—is at the core of Freudian psychology.[13] It represents an agency that oversees all human expression, even that in dreams. It lies at the origins of language, indeed it enables language, or indirect representation. As Derrida put it, in ideas that apply directly to *Nineteen Eighty-Four*, "Writing is unthinkable without repression":

> It is no accident that the metaphor of censorship should come from the area of politics concerned with the deletions, blanks, and disguises of writing. . . . The apparent externality of political censorship refers to an essential censorship which binds the writer to his own writing.
>
> We are written only as we write, by the agency within us which always and already keeps watch over perception, be it internal or external.[14]

This Freudian insight allows us to place Orwell, as author, in a more dynamic relation to his characters. Typically, critics identify Orwell with Winston Smith, helpless victim of deceit and brutality, doomed to die in a nightmare dystopia. Yet Smith is also a writer (of fabricated history and authentic experience), and *Nineteen Eighty-Four* is as much about writing as it is about anything else.

In *Nineteen Eighty-Four*, written representation struggles with censorship. Language suffers from an anxiety of repression; it seeks to express even as it seeks to suppress. The novel asserts Winston Smith's humanity even as it obscures his human connections. It proclaims individuality while it betrays relationship. In a word, *Nineteen Eighty-Four* is ambivalent. Smith's diary is his record of rebellion as well as his statement of confession. His secret confrère, O'Brien, is also his torturer; his loved one, Julia, is also the target of his aggression; "The Brotherhood," his dream of communistic revolution, is merely another face of the leader, Big Brother. Oceania is a mirror Utopia founded not on universal love but on ideologically focused hatred. This is the other side of the coin of the primary ambivalence that animates the novel. The ambivalence is so basic that its terms are elementary and alimentary: the question is what a person or a society can swallow. "They simply swallowed everything," Smith mused about his fellow citizens, "and what they swallowed did them no harm, because it left no residue behind, just as a grain of corn will pass undigested through the body of a bird" (Orwell, *Nineteen Eighty-Four* 156). Such issues emerge at the earliest moments of human development and retain a primitive power. The grounding of *Nineteen Eighty-Four* in such a primary ambivalence of love and hate directed at the face of nurturance and authority may help to explain the often-noted phenomenon of the novel's political appropriation by ideologies of left and right—regardless of the author's clear and passionate ideological declarations.[15]

The Orwell biographer and political scientist, Bernard Crick, writing about *Nineteen Eighty-Four*, asserted that any notion of "civic culture" must rely on mutual trust between citizens and government, because political legislation can be neither respected nor obeyed without it.[16] In the world of *Nineteen Eighty-Four*, mutual trust collapses into desperate individualism and self-survival. The observation is not merely political. Orwell's novel describes not just the historical occurrences of authoritarian thought in the twentieth century, but the origins of such thinking in human development. It documents the psychology of trust and the betrayal of faith or of any belief in reliable authority.[17] *Nineteen Eighty-Four* is not just a political novel or a dystopian satire. It is a novel about the origins and absence of trust.

Notes

1. In his biography of Orwell, D. J. Taylor considers the startling deterioration of Orwell's face over time (58).

2. The erotic diary entries have drawn the notice of psychologically-oriented critics. See especially Smyer.

3. For related interpretations of the glass object, see Smyer, Sperber, Lyons, and Kubal. As a nostalgic link to a broken maternal connection, the paperweight functions as a "transitional object": an object in the external world that corresponds to an inner psychic world of fantasy. See Winnicott (1-14). Winnicott terms such objects "the first possession"; typical examples are teddy bears and blankets.

4. See Smith and Smyer.

5. Smyer, relying on Freudian dream-interpretation, writes that "Room 101 is the uterus . . ., an underground chamber in the Ministry of Love" (159).

6. For speculation on Orwell's paranoia and sadomasochistic character traits, see Fiderer. See also Meyers. In his autobiographical sketch (published posthumously), Orwell wrote that he loved but distrusted his mother, and "merely disliked" his father—"a gruff-voiced elderly gentleman forever saying 'don't'" (qtd. in Taylor 19). Sperber draws several parallels between the paranoid world of the novel and Orwell's autobiographical accounts of his sadistic boarding-school experiences.

7. The number 101 is striking in several ways. As the next integer after 100, it marks a new extremity—a step beyond. Midway through the novel, as Smith fearfully foresees his eventual arrest, he thinks "how that predestined horror moved in and out of one's consciousness. There it lay, fixed in future time, preceding death as surely as 99 precedes 100" (140). This concept of sequential accumulation contrasts with other models of life, such as a series of choices or a narrative history. Erika Gottlieb, who also reads 101 as extremity, also notes that it's a mirror-number and, further, that it resembles two units facing a zero (63-84, 81).

8. See D. J. Taylor's remarks on Orwell's fearful obsession with rats (143-46).

9. A popular song that won a Grammy Award, ironically in 1984, catches the crux of the issue; it was recorded by a British group aptly named "The Police":

> Every move you make,
>
> Every step you take,
>
> I'll be watching you . . .
>
> Oh can't you see,
>
> You belong to me?
>
> Every single day
>
> Every word you say
>
> Every game you play
>
> Every night you stay

> I'll be watching you   The Police, *Synchronicity* (1983).

10. See Winnicott, 111-118.
11. See Lacan, 1-7.
12. As Thomas Pynchon notes in his Introduction to the 2003 Centenary edition of the novel, the Appendix on "The Principles of Newspeak" is actually the final section, an ironic coda: a fictitious treatise posing as historical archive (like Goldstein's *Theory and Practice*); see xxiv.
13. Paul Roazen has remarked on similarities between the ideas of Orwell and Freud, in terms of unconscious mental process, the importance of early childhood, and the social effects of sexual repression. Roazen further observes that O'Brien's torture of Smith is modeled on Freudian psychoanalysis (684-685).
14. See Derrida (226).
15. "Every line of serious work that I have written since 1936," Orwell wrote, "has been written, directly or indirectly, *against* totalitarianism and *for* democratic socialism, as I know it" (qtd. by Pynchon, Foreword, p. ix). For the custom of invoking Orwell on contrary sides of political and religious arguments, see Colls, who avers that Orwell was "both an iconoclast and a traditionalist" on a range of issues (2-3). For an assessment of *Nineteen Eighty-Four* as a critique of both communism and capitalism, see Decker.
16. See Crick, 146-159, especially 150-151.
17. Another psychoanalyst contemporary with Orwell posited the first stage of human emotional development (termed by Freud the "oral stage") in terms of "basic trust." See Erikson.

Works Cited

Colls, Robert. *George Orwell: English Rebel*. Oxford UP, 2013.

Crick, Bernard. "*Nineteen Eighty-Four*: Context and Controversy." *The Cambridge Companion to George Orwell*, edited by John Rodden, Cambridge UP, 2007, pp. 146-59.

Decker, James. "George Orwell's *1984* and Political Ideology." *Bloom's Modern Critical Views: George Orwell*, edited by Harold Bloom, Chelsea House, 2007, pp. 133-144.

Derrida, Jacques. "Freud and the Scene of Writing." *Writing and Difference*. Translated by Alan Bass, U of Chicago P, 1978, pp. 196-231.

Erikson, Erik. "Basic Trust vs. Basic Mistrust." *Childhood and Society*, Norton, 1950, pp. 247-250.

Fiderer, Gerald. "Masochism as a Literary Strategy: Orwell's Psychological Novels." *Literature and Psychology*, vol. 20, 1970, pp 3-21.

Gottlieb, Erika. *The Orwell Conundrum: A Cry of Despair or Faith in the Spirit of Man?* Carleton UP, 1992.

Kubal, David. "Freud, Orwell, and the Bourgeois Interior." *Yale Review*, vol. 6, 1978, pp. 389-403.

Lacan, Jacques. "The mirror stage as formative of the function of the I as revealed in psychoanalytic experience." *Écrits*. Translated by Alan Sheridan, Tavistock, 1977, pp. 1-7.

Lyons, John. "George Orwell's Opaque Glass in *Nineteen Eighty-Four*." *Wisconsin Studies in Contemporary Literature*, vol. 2, 1961, pp. 39-46.

Meyers, Jeffrey. "Orwell's Painful Childhood." *Ariel*, vol. 3, 1972, pp. 54-61.

Orwell, George. [*Nineteen Eighty-Four*] *1984: A Novel*. Signet, 1977.

———. *Such, Such Were the Joys*. Penguin, 2014.

Pynchon, Thomas. "Foreword." *Nineteen Eighty-Four*, by George Orwell. Plume, 1983, pp. vii-xxvi.

Roazen, Paul. "Orwell, Freud, and *Nineteen Eighty-Four*." *Virginia Quarterly Review*, vol. 5 1978, pp. 675-695.

Smith, Marcus. "'The Wall of Blackness': A Psychological Approach to *Nineteen Eighty-Four*." *Modern Fiction Studies*, vol. 14, 1968, pp. 423-433

Smyer, Richard. *Primal Dream and Primal Crime: Orwell's Development as a Psychological Novelist*. U of Missouri P, 1979, pp. 136-159.

Sperber, Murray. "'Gazing into the Glass Paperweight': The Structure and Psychology of Orwell's *Nineteen Eighty-Four*." *Modern Fiction Studies*, vol. 2, 1980, pp. 213-226.

Taylor, D. J. *Orwell: The Life*. Henry Holt, 2003.

Winnicott, D. W. "Mirror-Role of Mother and Family in Child Development." *Playing and Reality*, Tavistock, 1971, pp. 111-118.

"One Destroyed Being": A Post-Jungian Appraisal of Darth Vader

Steve Gronert Ellerhoff

Thirty-four years after Darth Vader's big screen debut, a boy dressed as him in a television commercial sold the Volkswagen Passat. In 2016, his Totenkopf helmet is a Kraft Macaroni and Cheese noodle. Vader's helmet, carved from limestone, even adorns the Washington National Cathedral in Washington, DC, perched high under a gable on the center pinnacle of a west tower. In the 1980s, a children's contest to design gargoyles for the cathedral resulted in a drawing of the screen villain being chosen: an American grotesque for America's cathedral. That his image should accent as a grotesque the National Cathedral, which yokes the US's ideological separation of church and state, is appropriate in the context of another sort of grotesque. Sherwood Anderson, opening his classic short story cycle *Winesburg, Ohio* (1921), puts forth "quite an elaborate theory" (6): "The moment one of the people took one of the truths to himself, called it his truth, and tried to live his life by it, he became a grotesque and the truth he embraced became a falsehood" (7). By this measure, the truth embraced by Vader is the dark side of the Force, that unquenchable drive to power that has rendered him, in the eyes of his former Jedi master who maimed him, "more machine now than man, twisted and evil" (*Return of the Jedi*). He is also one who discovers the folly of succumbing to the dark side's seduction, so that he becomes conscious of having "embraced . . . a falsehood."

How does a character so identified with evil step beyond his status as a character in a story and become a car salesman, a food item, and a decorative accent on a cathedral? His image, as recognizable as Elvis, Marilyn, and Mickey, is known by those who have never seen a *Star Wars* film, so that Darth Vader may be the most iconic father in cinema of the late twentieth century. Which fathers in film have commanded such presence in the popular imagination? Gregory Peck's Atticus Finch in *To Kill a*

Mockingbird (1962) comes to mind, although the contrast between the characters of benevolence and darkness could not be greater.

Star Wars has long been lauded as one of the great myths of our time. When it comes to exploring the psychology of mythology, analytical psychology, founded in the early twentieth century by Swiss psychiatrist Carl Jung (1875–1961), incorporates engagement with myths in its methods toward wholeness. Jung found from similarities in imagery the world over a common source of dream and fantasy that he termed the collective unconscious, the universally human repository of myth that always finds expression in local costume and decoration. He claimed the archetypes identifiable within stories were as present in so-called modern life as they were in the lives of our ancestors: "The most we can do is to *dream the myth onwards* and give it a modern dress" (Jung, *Collected Works* 9i: 271 [hereafter *CW*]). This emphasis on a constructive use of myth, toward a present psychological well-being, is a hallmark of Jungian therapy and has appealed to intellectuals and artists alike.

American mythologist Joseph Campbell (1904–1987) discovered in Jung's ideas a means of comparing the world's mythologies across time and cultures, building a body of work that celebrates the diversity of human beings' common tropes and themes. Given Campbell's theoretical debt to Jung, religion scholar Ritske Rensma argues that he "should be seen as post-Jungian" (200). One of his admirers in the 1970s was filmmaker George Lucas, who took from his books a means of focusing the greatest story he would tell: "Here is a lifetime of scholarship, a life of work that is distilled down to a few books that I can read in a few months that enable me to move forward with what I am trying to do and give me focus to my work. . . . It's possible that if I had not run across him I would still be writing *Star Wars* today" (Campbell, *Hero's Journey* 186-187). In kind, Campbell surmised that "*Star Wars* is a valid mythological perspective" ("The Message of the Myth"). For these reasons, a post-Jungian approach presents itself as an appropriate means by which we can read *Star Wars* and, for the purposes of this essay, Darth Vader in particular. But what is a post-Jungian approach, and what can we expect to gain from it?

Analyst Greg Singh bemoans the presence in the Jungian critical landscape of readings that incorrectly present archetypes as cookie cutter shapes without any accompanying analysis. He even invokes a character from *Star Wars* to make his point: "Obi Wan Kenobi is like the Wise Old Man archetype. Perhaps, but so what if he is? What are we to do with this information?" (Singh 16). A post-Jungian approach rejects lay critics' reductive tendency of classifying-by-archetype, promoting instead constructive archetypal readings built upon "a critical understanding of the source material, [and] the historic, cultural and sociopolitical implications of production and consumption contexts" (127). Singh urges a comprehensive scope of analysis when it comes to film—and let us include literature—because in exploring and unpacking archetypal inflections of stories and characters we stand to gain so much: namely how they grow from and instruct our understandings of life.

Darth Vader is a fine character to contemplate in this way because while we can recognize his metaphorical nature in terms of Jung's concept of the shadow, in his redemption, he defies the sort of glib, easy reading we wish to avoid. Jung conceived of the shadow as "a moral problem that challenges the whole ego-personality, for no one can become conscious of the shadow without considerable moral effort. To become conscious of it involves recognizing the dark aspects of the personality as present and real" (*CW* 9ii: 14). The idea that we all have a dark side is hardly unique to the psychologies of the early twentieth century but their perspectives on it are. Jung praised Sigmund Freud for inadvertently "awaken[ing] in many people an admiration for all this filth" (*Modern Man* 241), finding practicality in acknowledging that "the repellant things belong to the psyche" (*Modern Man* 244). But identifying the shadow does not confront and integrate it into one's being. In seeking the difficult feat of integration, Jung reminds us that "the essential thing is not the shadow, but the body which casts it" (*Modern Man* 47). Vader is a profound metaphor for this problem when we consider his body.

A head and torso, both rigged to the gills with technology, are what is left of Vader's body. His arms and legs are mechanical, as we know from *Revenge of the Sith* (2005) when Kenobi severs his legs and remaining arm in their first traumatic lightsaber duel.[1] His face, that best-known feature of the human form, is sealed behind an obsidian mask evocative of a skull. His helmet, which we momentarily see removed in his isolation chamber in *The Empire Strikes Back*, hides purple scars disfiguring the back of his hairless head. A box of lights and buttons on his chest, suggesting the breastplate of judgment worn by the High Priest of the Israelites in the *Book of Exodus*, presumably has something to do with regulating his cybernetic systems and physical health; there is nowhere he goes that the loud bellows of his respirator do not accompany him, telling us with each breath he takes (or is each breath forced into him?) that he is deeply damaged. Vader's most obvious paradox is that he possesses all the power to kill at the lift of a glove while bearing all the vulnerability of one kept alive on life support.

In Vader, Campbell saw one of the prime metaphors of the modern era:

> The problem is the machine—and the state is a machine. Is the machine going to crush humanity or serve humanity? And humanity comes not from the machine but from the heart. I think it was in *Return of the Jedi* when Skywalker unmasks his father, the father had been playing one of these machine roles, a state role. He *was* the uniform, you know? And the removal of that mask was an undeveloped man there, was kind of a worm. By being executive of a system, one is not developing one's humanity. I think that George Lucas really did a beautiful thing there. ("The Message of the Myth")

Vader does not wear a uniform; he lives it. Without his uniform, he will die. As such, the black, foreboding costume is worth considering in terms of the elements that combined to create and obscure the character living within it.

Vader as Gestalt

While drafting *Empire*, Lucas jotted down what he claimed had been the origin of the character's name:

Dark Invader – Dark Water

Death Water – Death Invader (Rinzler, *Making of ESB* 12)

As J. W. Rinzler points out, Dark and Death combined into Darth and Vader emerged from Invader via the two syllables of Water. Lucas's excavation of the name to the originating word association reveals in him a tendency to trust images and names that emerge from the unconscious. "That's just another one of those things that came out of thin air," he explains. "It sort of appeared in my head one day. . . . The early name was actually *Dark Water*" (Rinzler, *Making of SW* 172). There is no mention of Vader being just as close to *Vater*, the German word for father;[2] this need not surprise us because the character was not conceived of as being a parent until the second film was being produced. That aspect of the character, however, was nevertheless present all along in an unconscious way.

> **And hey, Darth Vader in that black and evil mask
> Did he scare you as much as he scared me?**
> (Bill Murray singing to the Star Wars theme, Saturday Night Live)

Through early drafts of the script, the name Darth Vader held fast. Others changed: Luke Starkiller became Luke Skywalker, for instance. It was not until the fourth draft that Lucas worked out Vader's past. "The backstory is about Ben and Luke's father and Vader, when they are young Jedi Knights," Lucas recalled. "Vader kills Luke's father, then Ben and Vader have a confrontation . . . and Ben almost kills Vader. As a matter of fact, he falls into a volcanic pit and gets fried and is one destroyed being. That's why he has to wear the suit with a mask. . . . It's like a walking iron lung" (Rinzler, *Making of SW* 111). That part of the story, told thirty years later in *Revenge of the Sith* (2005), would change when Vader and Anakin Skywalker became the same character. In his original incarnation, in *Star Wars*, Vader was not so biographically complex.

When it comes to his look, concept artist Ralph McQuarrie proved pivotal. While parallels to samurai helmets and masks have been popularly noted, McQuarrie remembered Lucas's requests as being varied. He initially wanted "a very tall, dark fluttering figure" with "the look of Arab costumes, all tied up in silk and rags" and "a big hat, like a fisherman's hat, a big long metal thing that came down" (Rinzler, *Making of SW* 34). In the mask, McQuarrie went for a "dog-like, vicious look, with little slots . . . like teeth" (Windham 5). The gothic, Orientalist, and animalistic elements should not surprise us, being modes wrapped up with othering, the prevailing technique in depicting villainy and monstrosity. However, the description of a fisherman's hat is peculiar. Vader would eventually be a fisher of sorts, luring his son toward the dark side, but at this early stage of his development, there were only inklings. In Western myth, the most significant angler is the Fisher King of the Grail romance. That figure, who presides over protecting the Grail, "has been very seriously wounded, and as a result of the wound, the land is laid waste. The central problem of the Grail romance is to heal the Fisher King" (Campbell, *Romance of the Grail* 25-26). This, too, is Vader's trajectory. While such a connection may strike us as far-fetched, Lucas, Campbell, Jung, and others courting the unconscious often honor coincidence by discovering meaning in it. McQuarrie, adding his own hunches to Lucas's, painted a visage whose spacesuit, initially a practicality for surviving in space, "became a part of [the] character" (Rinzler, *Making of SW* 34).

John Mollo, who won an Oscar for costume design on *Star Wars*, was tasked with creating Vader in leather, fabrics, and fiberglass. He first approximated the outfit with items found in the costume department at Elstree Studios in England, using "a black motorcycle suit, a Nazi helmet, a gas mask, and a monk's cloak we found in the Middle Ages department" (Rinzler, *Making of SW* 112). Lucas approved and rejected items until he liked what he saw. Mollo sculpted and cast the mask and helmet based on McQuarrie's artwork. "To me," Mollo says, "it looks like a Nazi helmet and pieces of trench armor that they wore in World War I" (Rinzler, *Making of SW* 130). This perspective draws Vader's look out of recent history—times of profound global trauma—and militarizes the character. For the American and British people putting Vader together in the middle 1970s, the uniforms and armor of Germany in both World Wars were stock images of the enemy. These styles still carry power; in *The Force Awakens* (2015), Vader's grandson, Kylo Ren, sports a shortened helmet even more reminiscent of those worn by the Germans during World War II.

Given the chance to play Darth Vader or Chewbacca the Wookiee, David Prowse picked Vader because, as he puts it, "people remember villains longer than heroes" (Rinzler, *Making of SW* 174). He did not know his face and voice would be stricken—or that his attraction to playing the baddie would swallow him up in the character's image. For all that, Carrie Fisher, who plays Princess Leia, admits that on set "it was hard to be afraid of Darth Vader. They called him 'Darth Farmer,' because David Prowse had this thick Welsh accent,[3] and he couldn't remember his lines" (Rinzler, *Making of SW* 186). Fisher brings up a legitimate point because despite his anger and ruthlessness, there is oftentimes something over-the-top about Vader. Lawrence Kasdan, who co-wrote the screenplays for *Empire*, *Jedi*, and *The Force Awakens*, has said *Star Wars* is "basically goofy" (Rottenberg)—and it is. In reading *Star Wars*, there is no need for us to ignore its fun, campy spirit; one of the saga's most charming aspects is its ability to address serious life dynamics while it sprints with a gentle silliness common to family films. There is something twistedly funny in Vader's habit of killing various admirals who work under him. He is a caricature of the cutthroat executive, literally terminating underlings left and right. Vader's lightsaber duels, it deserves to be noted, were played by someone else entirely—English fencer Bob Anderson—though Prowse posed for publicity shots suggestive of rehearsing fight scenes he never shot.

One of the most eloquent perspectives on Vader comes from the lifelong stutterer who voiced him. Unsatisfied with Prowse's voice, Lucas hired Broadway actor James Earl Jones for a day's work to dub over his lines. "Vader is a man who never learned the beauties and subtleties of human expression," Jones says (Rinzler, *Making of SW* 264). Some have criticized the choice of Jones for the part because he is an African American in a film otherwise seemingly devoid of African Americans. The anxiety here is one of black men, long underrepresented in film, being portrayed as evil men. For his part, Jones has claimed, "I'm simply special effects" (American Film Institute, "James Earl Jones on Being the Voice of Darth Vader"), even turning down a credit when the film was first released. The character's racial aspects—and anxiety about them—cannot be ignored, but by now it should be obvious that Vader is a multicultural precipitation of diverse elements that add up to someone bigger than run-of-the-mill film villains. When it came to *Empire*, Jones recalls, Lucas told him, "'We don't know what we did right so let's just try what we did.' Naturally I wanted to make Darth Vader more interesting, more subtle, you know, more psychologically oriented . . . and he said, 'No, no. . . . You got to keep his voice on a very narrow band of inflection.' 'Cause he ain't human, really'" (American Film Institute, "James Earl Jones on Playing Darth Vader").

Jones's voice, once recorded, underwent what sound designer Ben Burtt calls "worldizing," by which he rerecorded it in places of varying acoustics in order to find a sound quality audiences would believe came from behind the mask:

> "I remember many hours of playing back Darth Vader's voice in offices, hallways, and bathrooms, in order to get just the right acoustic quality. . . . These sessions invariably had to be done late at night when no one was around to make noise, the buzz of fluorescent lights could be switched off, and the phones wouldn't ring. It was spooky to be all alone, mic in hand, recording Vader's voice booming from the end of a darkened hallway." (Rinzler, *Sounds of Star Wars* 57)

And so Vader is an entity of the night and the dark, a voice haunting the workplace after everyone has gone home, a product of the dark side of corporate culture. Another post-production detail is Vader's breathing, by which sound designer Ben Burtt "placed a tiny microphone inside the regulator of a scuba breathing apparatus [and] just breathed in and out a number of different ways" (Rinzler, *Sounds of Star Wars* 57). There is also the music that accompanies him, scored and conducted by impresario John

Williams, who explains that "Vader's theme is a lot of bassoons and muted trombones and low things, since he is the bad side of the Force" (Rinzler, *Making of SW* 268). Williams and Burtt were awarded Oscars for their work on *Star Wars*.

All of these elements, which are creative decisions intuitively made, inform the gestalt that is Darth Vader when he appears on screen. He is a Dark Water Invader, an underwater breather, a dog wraith in Arab silks and rags, a fisher, a biker, a monk, and Nazi commandant in World War I trench gear, a mechanized man on life-support. The color of his lightsaber blade, of course, is red—like anger, like heat, like blood. There are also the personal associations each of us confront when encountering Vader's image. My friend, artist Kevin Storrar, mentions in conversation that the mask looks like something Swiss painter H. R. Giger might do had he redesigned Tutankhamen's sarcophagus mask. What is the sum that is greater than these parts? A character who is instantly recognizable as the embodiment of evil.

Vader as Evil

Analyst Murray Stein interprets Jung's stance on evil as being that it is "most primarily a category of conscious thought": "Jung did not want to see evil as an independent, self-standing and inherent part of nature, psychological, physical or metaphysical. This would lead to dualism. Evil is not quite, or not always, archetypal for Jung" (Jung, *Jung on Evil* 7). *Star Wars*, with its light and dark sides of the Force, appears to perpetuate dualism—but actually it criticizes human tendencies toward binary thought. In *Jedi*, Vader and son both transcend the good and evil that has split their galaxy for the duration of the series.[4] The danger with adhering chivalrously to notions of good and evil is, of course, that good guys are unconscious of their inherent evil and bad guys are always convinced they are the good guys. Jung insisted that people have a responsibility to meditate seriously upon evil, "for good and evil are ultimately nothing but ideal extensions and abstractions of doing. . . . In the last resort there is no good that cannot produce evil and no evil that cannot produce good" (*CW* 12: 36). The figure *Star Wars* uses to make this point is Vader.

Irvin Kershner, who directed *Empire*, interpreted Vader's motivation to be control: "Vader wants to bring order to the universe—*his* order, *his* universe" (Rinzler, *Making of ESB* 344). He is a man constantly committing terrible acts with the conviction that he does them for the greater good, failing over and over to face the destruction the dark side has brought to whole planets and even his own body. It would be easy to write Vader off as evil and never give him a second thought. Developmental psychopathologist Simon Baron-Cohen warns against this temptation, for "when we hold up the concept of evil to examine it, it is no explanation at all" (6). So what options exist for understanding those who so blatantly commit evil? James Dawes asks, "After such cruelty—cruelty that not only shocks our consciences but also destabilizes our understanding of the world—is apology possible?" (xiii). *Star Wars* does not broach apology but, with the arc of Darth Vader, does declare that atonement is possible. Vader's redemption manifests from a constellation of inner strife that, due to the films' typical distance from the characters' thoughts, we can only guess at—regret, empathy for his son's suffering, desire for redemption—and it arrives in a violent act of self-sacrifice: throwing the Emperor down a Death Star core shaft to his death.

An unsettling question when it comes to Vader is whether or not he needed to do bad in order to achieve what he does in the end by destroying himself and Emperor Palpatine. Jung would remind us that the ends-justifying-the-means does not wipe clean the fact that sin is or has been committed:

> A man who knows what he is doing when he commits evil may have a chance of being blessed, but in the meantime he is in hell. For the evil you do, even when you do it knowingly, is still evil and works accordingly. Yet if you had not taken this step, if you had not trodden this path, perhaps it would have been a psychic regression, a retrograde step in your inner development, a piece of infantile cowardice. Whoever thinks that by "knowing what you do" you guard against sin or save yourself from sin is wrong; on the contrary, you have steeped yourself in sin. (*CW*

10: 868)

Vader, steeped in black, finds his blessing when he finally acts not to dominate but to save his son. Vader's enthrallment with the dark side has made him a victim of what Baron-Cohen calls "empathy erosion," a conditioning by which "people are solely focused on the pursuit of their own interests" (9). He links this to the objectification of others; in Vader, we find a character who, with his cybernetic life-support system, is objectified in his own body. We can ask, too, if Anakin Skywalker's childhood in slavery, by which he and his mother were the property of Gardulla the Hutt and then junk dealer Watto, left him vulnerable to objectification by Palpatine later in his life.

Dawes's paradox of evil urges that "We must and must not demonize [perpetrators, because] othering the evil leads to eviling the other" (34). At the same time, "The hatred that evil calls out in us can . . . be 'energizing' to our sense of moral purpose" (35). Baron-Cohen takes this to be a moral imperative, in that "no one—however evil we paint them to be—should be treated as 100 percent bad or as beyond responding to a humane approach. . . . It is the only way we can establish that we are showing empathy to the perpetrator, not just repeating the crime of turning the perpetrator into an object and thus dehumanizing them" (182-183). In *Jedi*, what Vader receives from Luke's compassion is an opportunity to be something other than evil. And he takes that opportunity.

Does Vader overcome his evil? Though he returns at the end as a ghost alongside his former masters Obi-Wan and Yoda, he dies in order to get there. Vader does not simply shed the acts he has committed and live out a happy life in the light—doing the right thing kills him. Jung would probably find this ending psychologically sound, as he was skeptical of claims that evil can be overcome:

> People speak sometimes of "overcoming" evil. But have we the power to overcome it? It should be remembered, first, that "good" and "evil" are only our judgment in a given situation, or, to put it differently, that certain "principles" have taken possession of our judgment. Secondly, it is often impossible

to speak of overcoming evil, because at such times we are in a "closed" situation, in an aporia, where whatever we choose is not good. The important thing is to be aware that we are then in a numinous situation, surrounded on all sides by God, who can bring about either the one or the other and often does. (*CW* 10: 883)

Substitute the Force for God, and we arrive at Vader's dilemma when faced with choosing his master or his son. It is an unenviable position, but one he has brought upon himself for behaving as horrendously as he has. During the filming of *Jedi*, producer Howard Kazanjian took issue with Vader's resurrection as a fatherly ghost:

> I'd started thinking about it and I said to George, "Why? This guy—he's like Hitler. He's killed. He's done all of these terrible things and now we're saying he's equal with Yoda and Obi-Wan, as if he's gone to heaven or whatever." And George pointed at me, he was real close, and he says, "Isn't that what your religion is all about?" And, boy, that was like being slapped on the side of the face, because, yes, it is what my religion is all about, and obviously his, but I hadn't thought it through. (Rinzler, *Making of RotJ* 169)

Talking recently with my friend Sara Snyder about Vader and what happens to him, she told me, "I kind of have a soft spot for Darth." As well we all should. Some of the beauty of *Star Wars* comes through Vader's humanity deepening and then erupting as a result of his being one thing in particular: a father.

Vader as Father

Darth Vader became a father in early 1978. The first film was a huge success, still playing in cinemas across the country, and *Empire* already existed as a first draft. For that job, Lucas hired Leigh Brackett, pioneering author of space opera and co-adapter of *The Big Sleep* (1946) with Jules Furthman and William Faulkner. She died soon after finishing draft one, setting Lucas to pen the second draft himself. It was here that he first wrote out, in pencil, a scene in which Vader revealed that he is Luke's father. It was not included when Bunny Alsup typed it up for others to see; Lucas kept the twist on handwritten sheets no one else saw. "The issue of Luke's father I kept pretty quiet for a long, long time," Lucas recalls. "I didn't tell anyone, not even Kersh[ner]. I just couldn't risk it getting out" (Rinzler, *Making of ESB* 45). Even Prowse, unwittingly found guilty of plot leaks to the press, was kept in the dark while filming, given the line, "*Obi-Wan* killed your father," instead of the true one, "I am your father" (Rinzler, *Making of ESB* 216).

Up until the climax of *Empire*, the first two *Star Wars* films seem chiefly to be a frontier fantasy set across the vast expanses of an imaginary galaxy far, far away. The adventure appears to be a projection of outward modes of life, of triumph in the far reaches of outer space. But when Vader reveals to Luke that he, of all the men in that galaxy, is the young man's father, in one shocking moment, *Star Wars* collapses from galactic adventure down to a commonly intimate scale of human experience. The audience is no longer dealing with a mere flight of Saturday matinee fancy but a tragic story about a broken family. Every one of us has a father, whether he is present, absent, or deceased. Kids, for whom Lucas made these films, are especially conscious of their parents and what kinds of people they believe them to be. Fearing the impact of the reveal on small children, Lucas says, "I spoke to a number of psychologists who basically said that most kids, if it's too intense, will simply deny that Vader is Luke's father. But I was also concerned about leaving kids hanging" (Rinzler, *Making of ESB* 339, 344).

Archetypal psychologist James Hillman, who studied under Jung and later started a post-Jungian movement re-visioning psychology, deemed certain widespread notions about parents to be unhealthy: "If any fantasy holds our contemporary civilization in an unyielding grip, it is that we are our parents' children and that the primary instrument of our fate is the behavior of your mother and father" (*Soul's Code* 63). This ideology, which he calls the parental fallacy, reduces each of us to being "a mere effect" of our parents' causes (77). *Star Wars* rejects the parental fallacy outright: Luke, though he imagines himself to be Anakin Skywalker's son, is truly his own person and capable of resisting the dark side that seduced his father. It tells its audience that their sins need not be those of their parents, that they are not doomed to the same fate as those who brought them about. Religion scholar Robert Ellwood agrees, noting that *Star Wars* is "about deep-level psychic identities—above all, one's own" (129).

One of Luke Skywalker's most haunted moments in the saga occurs in *Jedi* when he asks his twin sister Leia if she remembers her mother: "I have no memory of my mother," he confesses, "I never knew her." Vader is so bad that he all but renders unconscious Luke's curiosity about his mother. He has dominated Luke's identity in terms of who the boy came from, first with adoration for the man he thought was a navigator on a spice freighter and then sublime horror when learning his father is the second most evil man in the galaxy. There is pain and guilt in Mark Hamill's portrayal of Luke when making this request of his sister, as if he is ashamed for not wondering about their mother earlier. But Vader is just that domineering, overtaking—or trying to overtake—anything and anybody who will not pay him tribute. We know from *Revenge of the Sith* that, in Vader's final moments with Padmé, heavily pregnant with Luke and Leia, he chokes her unconscious because she does not accept the dark direction he has chosen—and it appears she has brought Obi-Wan to confront him on the same grounds. Following his besting by Kenobi, he is put back together again and sealed into the iconic suit, awakening on the slab like Frankenstein's monster and asking for his bride. Vader reacts with anguish when Emperor Palpatine informs him, "It seems, in your anger, you killed her." He is doomed to living a hell of his own making.

Many terrible men are fathers; many children have fathers who do terrible things. Luke's empathy for his terrible father opens the door for Vader's saving grace. There was much discussion during the making of *Jedi* about who the audience should find behind the mask when Luke removes it. "It's always daring to take off the mask, whether it's the Phantom of the Opera's or Dr. Doom's," says Hamill, "because people's imaginations are far more comprehensive, so there's always a chance that you will disappoint them" (Rinzler, *Making of RotJ* 163). Lucas, in a July 1981 story conference with

Kasdan, Kazanjian, and director Richard Marquand, pushed for Vader-as-Dad:

> It has to be a real father. It's got to be like your father, when the mask comes off, otherwise it doesn't work. The whole point is he might have been able to live without all that stuff, but he would have been a weak pile of nothing. Now that he was on the dark side, he wanted to be greedy, he wanted to have all this. He relied on the machine. The whole machine thing becomes a partial metaphor for the dark side of the Force, which is: Machines have no feelings. (Rinzler, *Making of RotJ* 76)

Seventy-seven-year-old English stage actor Sebastian Shaw was hired to play the face behind the mask, what Campbell deemed "an undeveloped man . . . kind of a worm" ("Message of the Myth"). "When that dreadful mask was taken off," Shaw recalled of filming, "Mark nearly took my ears with it" (Rinzler, *Making of RotJ* 163). Vader's powder white, hairless, and scarred egghead—with tufted eyebrows removed from editions of *Jedi* released after 2005—presents a broken, aged man trapped for too long within a dehumanizing role, toeing the party line at the cost of his own integrity and well-being.

"It is often tragic," Jung wrote, "to see how blatantly a man bungles his own life and the lives of others yet remains totally incapable of seeing how much the whole tragedy originates in himself, and how he continually feeds it and keeps it going" (*CW* 9ii: 18). Vader's triumph in the end is that he *does* recognize his responsibility as the source of the Skywalker family tragedy. Once that is conscious, he is driven to act in such a way that he sacrifices what is left of his life to try and atone for the far-reaching harm he has wrought. There is hope for the worst of us—and the worst *in* us—as Darth Vader illustrates. "The reason these images and stories have been reiterated so often through the ages is we've found that life works out better that way," Kasdan says, "that we have within us the dark side and the light, good and evil, the devil and the angel. We're all full of conflict about which way to go. None of us fully live in the light or the dark" (Rinzler, *Making of ESB* 344). Not even Darth Vader, Dark Lord of the Sith.

Notes

1. Anakin Skywalker loses his other arm in *Attack of the Clones* (2002) when Sith Lord Count Dooku cuts it off in a duel.
2. In Dutch, *father* is *vader*.
3. Prowse is actually English, having grown up in Bristol, and has a West Country accent.
4. For more on this, please see my essay "Luke Skywalker's Individuation."

Works Cited

American Film Institute. "James Earl Jones on Being the Voice of Darth Vader." *YouTube*, 9 July 2009, www.youtube.com/watch?v=RAJgnUix2kI/.

———. "James Earl Jones on Playing Darth Vader." *YouTube*, 9 July 2009, www.youtube.com/watch?v=d0uPzrx0n90/.

Anderson, Sherwood. *Winesburg, Ohio*. Norton, 1996.

Baron-Cohen, Simon. *The Science of Evil*. Basic Books, 2011.

Campbell, Joseph. *The Hero's Journey*. New World Library, 2003.

———. *Romance of the Grail*, edited by Evans Lansing Smith, New World Library, 2015.

Dawes, James. *Evil Men*. Harvard UP, 2013.

Ellerhoff, Steve Gronert. "Luke Skywalker's Individuation." *Jung Journal: Psyche and Culture*, vol. 9, no.3, Summer 2015, pp. 44-54.

Ellwood, Robert. *The Politics of Myth*. State U of New York, 1999.

Hillman, James. *The Soul's Code*. Bantam, 1996.

John, David, editor. *Star Wars: The Power of Myth*. Dorling Kindersley, 1999.

Jung, Carl Gustav. *Collected Works of C. G. Jung*. Translated by R. F. C. Hull, vol. 9, part i, Princeton UP, 1968.

———. *Collected Works of C. G. Jung*. Translated by R. F. C. Hull, vol. 9, part ii, Princeton UP, 1968.

———. *Collected Works of C. G. Jung*. Translated by R. F. C. Hull, vol. 10, Princeton UP, 1970.

———. *Collected Works of C. G. Jung*. Translated by. R. F. C. Hull, vol. 12, Princeton UP, 1968.

———. *Jung on Evil*. Princeton UP, 1995.

———. *Modern Man in Search of a Soul*. Translated by W. S. Dell and Cary F. Baynes. Harcourt, Brace and Company, 1933.

"The Message of the Myth." *Joseph Campbell and the Power of Myth*. PBS, 22 June 1988. [Transcript: http://billmoyers.com/content/ep-2-joseph-campbell-and-the-power-of-myth-the-message-of-the-myth/].

Rensma, Ritske. *The Innateness of Myth*. Continuum, 2009.

Rinzler, J. W. *The Making of Return of the Jedi*. Aurum, 2013.

———. *The Making of Star Wars*. Ballantine Books, 2007.

———. *The Making of The Empire Strikes Back*. Aurum, 2010.

———. *The Sounds of Star Wars*. Chronicle Books, 2010.

Rottenberg, Josh. "Q&A: Star Wars Screenwriter Lawrence Kasdan on the past, present and future of 'Star Wars.'" *LA Times*, 3 Dec. 2015. www.latimes.com/entertainment/herocomplex/la-ca-hc-star-wars-lawrence-kasdan-20151206-story.html/.

Saturday Night Live. NBC. Season 3, Episode 10, 28 Jan. 1978, www.nbc.com/saturday-night-live/season-3/episode/10-robert-klein-with-bonnie-raitt-65516/.

Singh, Greg. *Film After Jung: Post-Jungian Approaches to Film Theory*. Routledge, 2009.

Star Wars, Episode I: The Phantom Menace. Directed by George Lucas, 20th Century Fox/Lucasfilm, 1999.

Star Wars, Episode II: Attack of the Clones. Directed by George Lucas, 20th Century Fox/Lucasfilm, 2002.

Star Wars, Episode III: Revenge of the Sith. Directed by George Lucas, 20th Century Fox/Lucasfilm, 2005.

Star Wars, Episode IV: A New Hope. Directed by George Lucas, 20th Century Fox/Lucasfilm, 1977.

Star Wars, Episode V: The Empire Strikes Back. Directed by Irvin Kershner, 20th Century Fox/Lucasfilm, 1980.

Star Wars, Episode VI: Return of the Jedi. Directed by Richard Marquand, 20th Century Fox/Lucasfilm, 1983. Film.

Star Wars, Episode VII: The Force Awakens. Directed by J. J. Abrams, Disney/Lucasfilm, 2015.

Windham, Ryder, and Peter Vilmur. *Star Wars: The Complete Darth Vader*. becker&mayer! Books, 2009.

The Hero's Quest in the *Harry Potter* Books and Films

Christine Gerhold Zahorchak

One main theme running through the *Harry Potter* books and films is the hero's journey, an archetypal quest that Joseph Campbell broke down into three parts: departure, initiation, and return. These parts may be broken down even further. The hero's adventure begins with either something missing, for which the hero searches, or with the hero sensing that something is lacking in his or her normal experiences. The hero can recognize this lack, or a herald can come and announce it. While some heroes choose to undertake the journey, some initially refuse the call and consequently tend to suffer. Once the hero accepts the quest, he or she receives supernatural assistance. The hero then crosses into a new, unfamiliar world. Sometimes this new world brings transformative rebirth. Departure ends, and initiation begins.

During the initiation stage, the hero now faces challenging trials, again receiving aid from a supernatural helper. Parts of these trials often involve a person of the opposite sex. A male hero may be confronted with a temptress who wants to distract him from the journey. The hero must confront this challenge and continue journeying. The male hero also often makes amends with a tyrant father figure in order to know himself better. Finally, for the male hero, the ultimate trial involves marriage to a queen-like or mother figure. He thus masters life and achieves a sense of wholeness. Later, the hero will undergo a change, sometimes suffering a complete disintegration or offering a voluntary sacrifice. Often, a superior hero results: the hero may have new abilities or a larger point of view. The hero then receives the ultimate boon, which may be a physical treasure or a new awareness. Whether the boon is tangible or not, the hero knows that his or her home society, or "kingdom," will be able to benefit from it when the hero returns.

The hero sometimes resists returning to the ordinary world after experiencing the extraordinary. Sometimes his or her new acquaintances want the hero to stay, especially if the hero is taking back an acquired object. This outcome may require the hero to flee, or be assisted with outside help to return home. The hero then crosses back into the normal, "real" world. Even though the hero returns home, he or she is fundamentally changed. The hero is now able to perceive both human and divine worlds. The fruits of the journey are then shared with society. This, then, is the hero's journey in its most basic structure, of leaving innocent and returning with a boon, which forever changes the hero and the hero's environment for the better (Campbell).

Carol S. Pearson considers Campbell's "hero's journey" a metaphor for everyday journeys. "Few of us literally slay dragons or even villains. The swords we use are less often literal weapons and more often money, status, image, power, influence, and highly developed communication skills. But the patterns remain the same" (Pearson 31). Everyday heroes need not only come from myth and fairy tales, as there are real life heroes as well. A hero can found something, be it a new age, new government, new religion, or a new art form. To do so, the hero must leave the old and quest for the new.

Pearson stresses the importance of the everyday journey: every individual has a unique journey to take, however small and insignificant it may seem. Each person seeks to discover a real identity or ideal self. The hero's journey involves saying "yes" to one's self, thus becoming more fully alive and effective. Being alive involves suffering, and life's everyday quests involve pitfalls. However, the rewards for journeying are great. "Everything seems to fall into place" as individuals are able to see the "beauty, intelligence and goodness" in themselves without worrying about having to prove anything to anyone (Pearson 5). But the hero's journey is not another self-improvement project, nor is it meant to mean reaching some ideal perfection. It is about "finding and honoring what is really true about you" (5).

When individuals refuse their journeys, not only do they themselves tend to suffer, but collective suffering results as well. Someone may be materially fortunate but still feel unfulfilled and empty inside because he or she has not taken his or her own unique journey. Life can seem to lack meaning and purpose. Anyone who has worked with a self-destructive coworker will understand how one person can depress other people as well. Society can also suffer from individuals who attempt to numb their emptiness with drugs and alcohol. "This is why the myth of the hero is so important in the contemporary world. It is a timeless myth that links us to people of all times and places. It is about fearlessly leaping off the edge of the known to confront the unknown . . ." (Pearson 2).

While the hero's journey has been described as a linear path, the hero's journey is not linear, as it appears in fairy tales whose characters live "happily ever after." Rather in life, the journey is cyclical: when one journey or turmoil has ended, another begins (Pearson). This cyclical journey is similar to Erik Erikson's theory of human development in which the individual comes to face a particular trial, which must be surpassed, only to face another crisis to surpass as well (see Cole and Cole). The journeys never end so long as the person has life.

Harry Potter: Archetypal Themes
As previously mentioned, while the hero's journey has been described as a linear path, it can also be seen as cyclical, much like a spiral, with each subsequent journey deepening the experience. Both ideas seem present in J. K. Rowling's *Harry Potter* novels and the subsequent film adaptations.

Each Harry Potter book and film follows Harry's life's journey for a year. In Harry's first story, *Philosopher's/Sorcerer's Stone*, Harry journeys from ignorance into the wizarding world. He confronts the evil Voldemort and is ultimately changed as a result. In Harry's second year, he again experiences a self-contained journey and again must face Voldemort. Harry thus achieves a deeper realization of who he is and what he is capable of overcoming.

But even within each book/movie-as-journey, micro-journeys occur. In Harry's first year, for example, Harry must acclimate to Hogwarts, the wizard boarding school where he will spend the next seven years. There he meets new people, makes friends and enemies, and learns about the Philosopher's/Sorcerer's Stone and Voldemort's interest in it. Each new challenge is a self-contained journey that also follows the departure, initiation, and return framework.

Finally, the last level of the hero's journey to look at is the journey as a whole; from the beginning all the way to Harry's final year in the book and films *The Deathly Hallows*. In Harry's first year, Harry is introduced as a ten-year-old boy. He begins a journey, not knowing that he has a series of travels ahead of him, until a herald tells Harry that he is a wizard. Harry leaves his boyhood home to enter a world of wizarding. He receives various boons (including his own magic wand, spell books, and an owl) to help prepare him for life at Hogwarts. Harry's initiation continues. At Hogwarts, he joins one of four "Houses" (Gryffindor, Hufflepuff, Ravenclaw, and Slytherin). Other House members are considered each student's family as students attend class and share dormitory and common rooms. Each House emphasizes its own qualities in its students. Ravenclaw students value wisdom and intelligence. Hufflepuffs value friendship and loyalty. Slytherins value power and influence at the price of loyalty to others. Gryffindor House, where Harry is placed, prizes bravery.

During this beginning phase, Harry also learns about the Dark Lord Voldemort, a powerful wizard who terrorized the wizard community, killing all who opposed him, thus gaining immense power. No wizard could stop Voldemort, and the wizarding community feared him, until one day when Voldemort came to the house of a one-year-old Harry Potter and his parents. Voldemort killed Harry's parents and tried to kill Harry by cursing him. But the magical curse rebounded onto Voldemort, robbing him of his body and powers. Though Voldemort disappeared, people believe he is still alive, powerless but still malevolent. The threat of Voldemort looms over all, especially Harry, who is the cause of his downfall in the first place. Voldemort is thus the main villain, a perpetually looming dark force in Harry's life, though lying dormant in the background like a shadow. This concludes the overall departure phase and leads Harry into the initiation part of the journey that extends for the remaining books up until his final confrontation with Voldemort in the end.

For the next few years (as the following books and films show), Harry experiences trials that fully challenge him. This includes finding his place among his peers, learning the magic taught in school, dealing with nasty rumors, and dating girls, to name a few. Every time he is challenged, his awareness increases, and so do his skills and self-knowledge. He also confronts different forms of Voldemort but is, each time, able to escape, usually with help from supernatural or miraculous protectors. Harry thus progresses from being a well-protected child to being a young adult who is eventually left to take care of himself.

In the final book and movie, Voldemort has emerged from the shadows, having reclaimed his body and powers, and is terrorizing the wizarding world. A seventeen-year-old Harry must now face Voldemort. In true heroic fashion, Harry even sacrifices himself to defeat Voldemort. But this sacrifice, or destruction of the ego, does not kill Harry. When he returns to face Voldemort for the final time, he has the ability to kill Voldemort once and for all. This outcome restores peace both to the wizarding world and to Harry's life. The micro-journeys taken in the years in between have prepared Harry to complete his journey of facing and vanquishing Voldemort. Harry completes the overall macro journey and brings peace to his "kingdom."

The Shadow

Because Harry is the main character in the series, the shadow is represented by everything that contrasts with him, particularly Voldemort and all he represents. Their contrast includes the archetypal qualities that make up Harry and Voldemort, as well as the personal qualities of Harry and Voldemort themselves. In addition, Harry and Voldemort are linked because Voldemort murdered Harry's mother and father and because Harry, as a baby, miraculously damaged Voldemort. This becomes even more important later, when Harry begins to struggle meaningfully against Voldemort.

Gryffindor and Slytherin are the two Hogwarts Houses that Harry and Voldemort, respectively, belong to. Gryffindor most clearly represents the Warrior archetype; its members are heroic, courageous, and most interested in personal integrity. Slytherin represents those who are most cunning, dominant, and self-concerned. There is also an element of the shadow Warrior in Slytherin, as Slytherins are interested in power, but only so they can control and rule over others.

According to Jungian thinking, the parts that make up the shadow were once part of the conscious self, the ego. They were rejected, subdued, and put into unconsciousness where they remain primitive and unrefined, but remain nonetheless (von Franz). Harry is no exception: he shares traits with Slytherins, though he denies those traits. This is first discovered when Harry first arrives at Hogwarts and is being sorted into his House.

Each first-year student puts on an enchanted wizard's hat, called the Sorting Hat, which determines which House is best suited for that student. The Hat finds Harry difficult to place. Harry has "plenty of courage, [...] not a bad mind," as well as talent and a desire to prove himself, which the Hat calls "interesting" (Rowling, *Philosopher's* 90). This desire resembles Slytherin traits of wanting to be the best, but at any cost. Harry does not want to be put in Slytherin, having heard all about the bad wizards, including Voldemort, who were Slytherins. The Hat replies "Are you sure? You could be great, you know, it's all here in your head, and Slytherin will help you on the way to greatness, no doubt about that" (Rowling, *Philosopher's* 91). But Harry sticks to his choice, and the Hat places him in Gryffindor.

Thus, while Harry wants to prove himself and be great, he is unwilling to achieve his goals by any means, like a typical Slytherin. Harry was told earlier that Voldemort did "great things—terrible, yes, but great" (Rowling, *Philosopher's* 65). Harry wants greatness, but not in any terrible, or shadow way, like Voldemort. Harry rejects Slytherin House, finding it more important to sacrifice power than to be linked with that House's dark wizards.

In Gryffindor House, Harry pushes aside the fact that the Sorting Hat thought he could have been great in Slytherin. At first, he denies any connection to Slytherin, much like an Innocent. However, just as the shadow bursts forth if not acknowledged, Harry discovers how close he is to Slytherin, especially during his second year. As a Parselmouth, Harry can talk to and understand snakes. This rare gift is linked to Slytherin's founder, Salazar Slytherin. Harry begins to fear that he should be in Slytherin and that the only reason he is not is because he asked the Sorting Hat not to place him there. Harry eventually asks the Sorting Hat if it had put Harry in the correct House. The Hat replies as earlier, saying that Harry would have done well in Slytherin. Harry dreads that he and Salazar Slytherin might even be related. But Harry dreads even more his similarities to Voldemort.

"The hero," says Jung, "has much in common with the dragon he fights—or rather, he takes over some of its qualities" (*Symbols* 367). Harry somewhat resembles Voldemort. Both Harry and Tom Riddle, the boy who grew up to become Voldemort, are half-bloods (one parent had wizard heritage; the other had Muggle, or non-magic, heritage). Both boys were orphaned and raised by Muggles, and both are Parselmouths. They share black hair and a slim build.

The theme of Harry's connection to Voldemort continues into his fourth and fifth years, where Harry starts to feel Voldemort's moods and begins having dreams that show him what Voldemort is doing, but it is as if Harry is doing the actions himself. This makes Harry feel dirty and contaminated, as he sees Voldemort attacking, even killing people, as if he himself were doing it.

Though Harry is repulsed by this connection, even denying its possibility, he eventually recognizes it and begins to use it for his own purposes. This is similar to the analytic process in therapy of becoming aware of one's shadow, the parts of one's self that are unwanted and pushed down into the psyche. It can be a painful process to come face to face with the shadow. Jung described the shadow as "a tight passage, a narrow door, whose painful constriction no one is spared who goes down a deep well. But one must learn to know oneself in order to know who one is" (Jung, *Archetype* 22).

By going deep into the psyche to meet the shadow (what has been hidden), the true Self, or fully realized person, can emerge. Harry's acknowledgment of his connections to Voldemort resembles the process of meeting the shadow and becoming a whole person.

Voldemort, as Harry's shadow, represents all Harry opposes, although they are still connected. Thus, every time Harry meets with Voldemort, he understands more about himself by confronting this shadow figure. Almost every time Harry encounters Voldemort, it is underground or a place in darkness. In Campbell's terms, the hero goes below the depths of consciousness in order to face the shadow lurking in the underworld, or the unconscious. Every time Harry returns from this dark place, he experiences not just a return from a journey, but a return with a complete sense of Self, having integrated the ego with the unconscious shadow.

Much archetypal symbolism surrounds Voldemort and Slytherin. First, the animal associated with Slytherin is a snake. Jung states that "according to Philo, the snake is the most spiritual of all creatures; it is of a fiery nature, and its swiftness is terrible. It has a long life and sloughs off old age with its skin" (*Symbols* 374). Voldemort is indeed swift and terrible. Because the snake dwells beneath the earth, it is associated with the unconscious that dwells below consciousness. The ancient and mysterious religion Orphism, said to be the founded by Orpheus, who ventured into the underworld of Hades to find his wife Euridyce, has the Uroborus as its symbol. The Uroboros is a snake that forms a circle by taking its own tail in its mouth (Hollis 94). This symbol resembles the one Voldemort claimed for himself, which is called the Dark Mark—a skull with a snake protruding from its mouth. It was conjured above every house where Voldemort's followers, Death Eaters, killed anyone. Whereas the Uroboros suggests a cycle of death and life, as the snake eats itself and forms a circle, the Dark Mark snake escapes the mouth of the skull, a symbol of death. This can be interpreted as the snake fleeing death, just as Voldemort refuses to die. Even when Voldemort was defeated by baby Harry, he was not killed. He lost his powers and his body, but he remained tethered to life by magical objects known as Horcruxes. Instead of shedding his skin as a snake would, Voldemort sheds parts of his soul that he then places in an object, making him immortal.

In addition, those in the wizarding world will not speak Voldemort's name out loud, instead calling him "You-Know-Who." People who do say Voldemort's name are considered exceptionally brave, like Dumbledore. Similarly, people typically skirt around the language of death as it makes them uncomfortable, just as people in Harry's world will not use Voldemort's name, which is associated with death. Each time Harry faces Voldemort, he faces his own potential death, though Voldemort himself refuses to ever die.

Other symbolism includes the part of the brain that lies deep within the cortex, called the "reptilian brain." This part of the brain is considered more primitive, separate from the "mammalian brain" that makes up the brain's outer cortex. The reptilian part is more concerned with basic survival, similarly to how Slytherins will save their own skin from harm at the expense of loyalty to friends so that they will survive, with Voldemort being the ultimate symbol of cheating death in order to survive.

Not only does Harry confront Voldemort, the representation of all that Harry opposes, but Harry also has confrontations, and eventual reconciliations, with two others from Slytherin House. These are Draco Malfoy, a classmate of Harry's, and Professor Serverus Snape. While these rivalries are not as intense as the one Harry has with Voldemort, they nonetheless affect Harry's development and understanding of who he is.

Almost immediately after meeting him, Harry does not like Malfoy. Malfoy is the same age as Harry and goes through a transformation through adolescence similar to Harry's. Malfoy makes friends, though these "friendships" are based less in loyalty than to being connected to people who have influence or power and subordinates who will follow his every command, such as his classmates Crabbe and Goyle. Malfoy actually tries to "befriend" Harry when he finds out who he is, as Harry is famous in the wizarding world. Malfoy also believes in wizards who have "pure blood," meaning that they come from families who have no Muggle lineage. Wizards like Malfoy are prejudiced against wizards who are half-blood or who are even Muggle-born, like Harry's mother. They consider non-Pureblooded wizards to be trash. Indeed, Salazar Slytherin did not want to allow non-Pureblooded wizards into Hogwarts to learn magic. The pejorative term for Muggle-born wizards is "Mudblood," meaning they have dirty blood. This is considered an offensive curse word. Slytherins, including Malfoy's family, celebrated Voldemort, who killed non-pure blooded wizards with extreme prejudice. This type of racial purity offends Harry, and it is another example of how he stands in opposition to Slytherins.

As same-age peers, Harry and Malfoy engage in different types of rivalries. They are rivals when they play Quidditch, a wizard's sport that requires flying on brooms. Malfoy taunts Harry's manliness, and throughout the books, both Malfoy and Harry mock each other's family and friends. They also have physical and magical fights. In addition, every time a character like Dumbledore raises his glass to efforts to stop Voldemort and his supporters, Malfoy remains still. Regardless, Malfoy goes on his own journey to find his true Self through the Harry Potter series. The reader can see how he begins in innocence and ignorance, believing the prejudices of his parents, and how he eventually grows to realize how his actions affect the world, as well as what he is and is not willing to do for Voldemort.

Snape is another character with shadow qualities, more so than Draco, but not as much as Voldemort himself. From the moment Snape meets Harry, he seems intent on embarrassing Harry, punishing him, and making Harry believe he is not special. Snape is usually seen showing favoritism to Malfoy, at the cost of fairness to Harry. In the first book, Harry believes that Snape is working directly with Voldemort to help him rise to power again with the help of the Philosopher's Stone. Though Snape does not support Harry in school, Dumbledore tells Harry that Snape was protecting Harry the whole time and that Snape is not an agent of Voldemort. While Snape is clearly unfair to Harry and his friends, being outright rude sometimes, Dumbledore has no question about Snape's position against Voldemort. Harry doubts this, as he sees how horrible Snape can be. However, as Harry grows through adolescence, the characters of both Malfoy and Snape become more complex. This is similar to the same complexities that accompany the journey through adolescence.

Harry's Journey through Adolescence

This author sees the seven books and films as an overall journey through adolescence—a journey split into two main parts. The first four books and films represent Harry as prepubescent. Themes and ideas generally on hand during this part of childhood are present and shown in the ways both Harry and his world are described. The later three books, and four films, represent Harry as postpubescent, with themes and complexities that complement this tumultuous stage in life.

Harry's childhood challenges include issues of trust, security, self-control, and exploration as he tries to fit into his environment (Erikson; Pearson). People who are "good" and people who are "bad" are clearly delineated. Everyone sorted into Slytherin House is bad, including Malfoy; Snape; and, of course, Voldemort. Everyone who cares for Harry is good, including Dumbledore, Harry's friends Ron Weasley and Hermione Granger, Ron's mother, and Harry's deceased parents. These people are all also sorted into Gryffindor House. Harry's godfather Sirius goes from being an all-bad character, accused of betraying Harry's parents, to an all-good character who never betrayed the Potters and who cares for Harry like a parent, though he must remain on the run from the law. For almost all of the first four books and movies, there is little to no grey area where these characters are considered.

After those first four years though, there starts to be character complexity that was not present before. "Bad" characters are shown to have good parts to them, and "good" characters are shown to have human flaws. This shift is similar to a child's growth from childhood (when the world seems black and white, and when one's parents seem infallible) to a world of unprotected grays inhabited both by loved ones and by hated enemies. As Harry ages, the objective truth he thought he understood is shaken, and he realizes how subjective things like the truth can be. This change is congruent with the realizations that occur during the initiation of the hero's journey and how the hero is fundamentally changed as a result of the journey (Campbell).

Erikson identified this transition in his fifth stage of human development as "identity versus role confusion," which occurs in adolescence: "In puberty and adolescence all sameness and continuities relied on earlier are more or less questioned again" (261). This statement helps explain not only the complexity going on outside of Harry, but also the changes going on within him. Harry's personality is maturing with age and he is able to let in new experiences, even if he is not able to organize or make sense of them all at once.

The Parental Figures in Harry's Life

Many adult characters in Harry's life have archetypal significance to Harry's development from child to young adult. A significant number of them represent meaningful parental figures.

The first adults who are given parental status over Harry are his maternal aunt and uncle, Mr. and Mrs. Dursley. After Harry's parents die, baby Harry is deposited at the Dursleys' doorstep. While Mr. and Mrs. Dursley accept Harry into their home, they do not show him parental love and affection. Unlike Harry's mother, Harry's aunt is not magical, and both she and her husband are ashamed of Harry and his magical lineage and abilities. Therefore, they do their best to press what they see as anything shameful out of him, discouraging Harry from asking questions and expecting him to amount to nothing. The first adults who give Harry their parental love are Ron's parents, especially Mrs. Weasley. The Weasley parents send care presents to Harry during Christmas and Easter, and Harry also spends time at the Weasleys' home. While Harry appreciates the care and affection shown by Mrs. Weasley, he does not feel the strong sense of parental closeness he wishes he had. Harry's first "parent" in this regard is his parents' longtime friend, and Harry's godfather, Sirius Black.

In Harry's third year, Sirius is first mistaken as the person who betrayed the Potters to Voldemort, a betrayal that resulted in their death. However, Sirius was framed for this crime and never really betrayed Harry's parents. The reason Sirius differs from Mrs. Weasley is that Sirius offers Harry something he never had before: first-hand knowledge about what his parents were like, as Sirius was their best friend and Harry's godfather. After Harry becomes reacquainted with Sirius, there are times when he wishes that he had a "parent" to talk to. However, he realizes that he has Sirius, even if Sirius must continue to run from the law. Sirius fills a parental void that the other characters cannot fill because of his connection to Harry's parents. Harry sees Sirius through the eyes of a child who can see no wrong in his parent, and this perception remains unchallenged until Harry is older.

Dumbledore also falls into this category of parental figure who apparently can do no wrong. Whenever Dumbledore appears, miracles happen, and Harry feels a sense of protection and goodness. In the second book and movie, he calls Dumbledore the greatest wizard in the world. In serving as a grandfatherly figure, Dumbledore plays a larger role in Harry's life as the Wise Old Man.

The Wise Old Man
Dumbledore, the wise old magician and head of Hogwarts, is the Sage, or Wise Old Man, in Harry's story. To again quote Jung, the Wise Old Man shows "knowledge, reflection, insight, wisdom, cleverness, and intuition on the one hand, and on the other, moral qualities such as goodwill and readiness to help" (*Archetype* 222). Dumbledore perfectly displays all these traits. He is a leader and shows several times how he is in charge.

Dumbledore also resembles the archetype of the mother protector: when Dumbledore is nearby, Harry feels safe and protected. Time after time, Harry knows that he can turn to Dumbledore for protection from evil. In the first book and film, while playing Quidditch, Harry is attacked by an unknown magic spell he assumes is cast by Snape. The attack almost causes Harry to fall off of his broom fifty feet in the air. At the next Quidditch game, Harry is sure he will face a similar attack, only to see Dumbledore in the stands: "Harry could have laughed out loud with relief. He was safe. There was simply no way that Snape would dare to try and hurt him if Dumbledore was watching" (Rowling, *Philosopher's* [*Sorcerer's*] 163).

Dumbledore also makes odd remarks. Commenting on the scar Harry has on his forehead from his encounter with Voldemort, Dumbledore says scars can be useful and reports that he has one above his left knee. When McGonagall, a professor at Hogwarts, calls Dumbledore a noble wizard, Dumbledore responds that he has not blushed so much since he was complimented on his earmuffs. Finally, at the beginning of term feast, in front of the whole school, he announces that he would like to say a few words. They are "Nitwit! Blubber! Oddment! Tweak!" (Rowling, *Philosopher's* [*Sorcerer's*] 92). He then sits down. These remarks are almost juvenile; they show the sort of silliness a child would exhibit. Indeed, these childish comments show that Dumbledore not only represents the Wise Old Man, but also the opposite archetype of the child. In this way, Dumbledore represents a fully individuated Self. He has integrated the wisdom of age with the childlike joy found in the Fool archetype. He resembles Yoda in *Star Wars*, who is introduced as a childish imp but who is also a wise 800-year-old Jedi (see Galipeau).

Dumbledore consistently acts as the figure who helps Harry along his journey. In the second book and film, Dumbledore vicariously offers Harry help when he faces the remnants of a sixteen-year-old Voldemort in the Chamber of Secrets, by having his pet phoenix, Fawkes, bring the sword of Gryffindor to aid Harry. In fairy tales, the Wise Old Man makes ready use of animals, especially birds (see von Franz). Dumbledore also suggests how Harry can save his newly found godfather, Sirius, from a fate worse than death in the third book and movie. Both of Harry's fourth and fifth years end with him in Dumbledore's office and Dumbledore offering guidance after great trauma. In all of these times, Dumbledore never takes the journey for Harry, nor does he remove the obstacle that is in front of Harry. But he does provide Harry with help (both magical boons and words of advice), which is consistent with the Wise Old Man archetype.

Harry is able to come to terms with his connection to Slytherin with the help of Dumbledore. In this way, Dumbledore is very much the Magician, as he names for Harry the feared similarities he has to Voldemort. In so doing, he changes how Harry understands his connection to Voldemort. Voldemort would prize Harry's resourcefulness, determination, and also occasional disregard for the rules. Yet the Sorting Hat placed Harry in Gryffindor because Harry asked it to. This shows Dumbledore why Harry is so different from Voldemort. Dumbledore echoes what many psychologists would say: that there are parts of one's self that are wild and unwanted. However, people have a choice, based on what they value, about how they want to behave and live their lives (see Bach and Moran).

Finally, Dumbledore also demonstrates a key element of the Sage: Dumbledore does not try to change circumstances beyond his control. In the sixth book and movie, when Dumbledore is cursed with only a year left to live, he does not run from the fact that he will die or try to change it. He merely looks at this fact objectively and decides how his remaining time should be spent. Harry does not learn about this development until the final book and film. In these many faces and archetypes, Dumbledore demonstrates the integrated and individuated Self, something that Harry and all people strive for.

Peers in Harry's Life

There are several peers who accompany Harry on his journey. Most important are Harry's two good friends, Ron Weasley and Hermione Granger. The two befriend Harry in his first year and are never far from Harry and his adventures. They are both secondary heroes, which means that they go through a parallel journey along with Harry, who is the primary hero. It is a common occurrence for the hero to be surrounded by two others. According to the Babylonian view, gods are grouped into triads. Christ on the cross is joined by two thieves. The Mithraic bull-sacrifice is flanked by two dadophors (Jung, *Symbols* 200). In *Star Wars*, Luke has Han Solo and the Princesses Leia as his companions. And *Buffy the Vampire Slayer's*

Buffy has her friends Xander and Willow by her side. The journeys of both Ron and Hermione could easily be analyzed. However, because space is limited, only a brief overview of their roles will now be offered.

Hermione is introduced to Harry as a bossy know-it-all and teacher's pet. Harry and Ron do not think well of her because she is so bossy and because she is clearly the smartest in their class, which causes some feelings of jealousy. Eventually, Hermione becomes more flexible, even lying to the teachers so that Ron and Harry will not get into trouble, and they all become friends. Hermione learns how to use her intelligence and cleverness to aid Harry through his various trials. She also keeps Ron and Harry on track with their studies as she continues to excel in school. She is not the prettiest nor the most social of girls. Regardless, Hermione remains the voice of reason for Harry, as well as the brains of most of his operations, unless Harry and Ron venture too far outside of school rules for Hermione to feel comfortable complying with their behavior. Harry describes his relationship to Hermione as like a relationship with a sister. Hermione's relationship with Ron, on the other hand, is more complicated. Regardless, Hermione's journey through the series is one of continuously gaining knowledge and remaining a model student, but also receiving needed humility and learning how to balance friendship with following the rules.

Ron's relationship with Harry is more straightforward. He and Harry are "best mates." Growing up in the shadow of five older brothers, Ron wishes that he were able to be successful at things like sports, though he suffers from a lack of confidence. This trait varies depending on how old he is, whether he is jealous of the attention Harry receives in his fourth year, or if he is unsure of his ability to play Quidditch in his fifth. Ron even outright abandons Harry and Hermione during their seventh year, angry at Harry and also jealous because he believes Hermione would rather be with Harry than with him. But when he returns, it becomes evident how important Ron's friendship and support are to Harry's mental health and stability. Ron's maturity and growth through the series is clear to see as he becomes more confident in himself. He is even finally able to be with Hermione romantically.

A character named Neville is interesting as a *potential* hero. Neville is in Gryffindor House, though he feels not brave or very useful. Neville is not particularly good at magic or sports, nor is he socially popular. He seems unremarkable, with one exception: Neville, like Harry, has suffered tragedy at the hands of Voldemort's forces. His parents were tortured into madness. Neville's orphaning at the hands of one of Voldemort's Death Eaters makes for an interesting parallel to Harry, who lost his parents because of Voldemort directly. The reader also learns that Neville could have been in Harry's position, poised to face Voldemort in a battle of equals. This is not to be. Instead, Neville goes through his own journey, parallel to Harry's and sometimes intersecting. Neville remains in the background of Harry's journey, but his own growth and development make him an interesting figure.

The Trickster

Four characters in *Harry Potter* possess a chaotic energy, yet also a sense of wisdom and childlike innocence, that typifies the trickster archetype. Peeves the poltergeist symbolizes a character who does things purely for joy, especially if doing so involves pandemonium. Peeves represents the trickster archetype in its purest form. Peeves is not really evil, though he has no regard for rules or regulations and appears to enjoy creating mayhem.

Two other trickster figures include the Weasley twins, George and Fred. They enjoy breaking the rules at Hogwarts for their own enjoyment and the enjoyment of those around them. They act distinctly childlike, while Hermione, who is two years younger than they are, continuously berates them for their rule-breaking and trick-playing behaviors. However, the twins find a way to harness their joke-playing mentality and incorporate their chaotic trickster sides and funnel it into positive energy. This is most clearly seen in their entrepreneurial spirit when they leave Hogwarts in order to make and sell magical tricks out of their joke shop, in which they are quite successful. This demonstrates how a child's acting-out behavior can be transformed into positive and pro-social behavior.

The final trickster in the series is Luna Lovegood, another peer of Harry's. Luna is not introduced until Harry's fifth year, but she clearly stands out among her peers for being odd. Luna does not play tricks in the same way that Peeves and the Weasley twins do. Rather, she is a Fool in her odd manner and dress. In addition, Luna will, to quote Harry in the sixth book, speak "uncomfortable truths" (Rowling, *Half-Blood Prince* 311). This foolishness gives her the same ability that the court jester had, and that is to speak to the king, or Harry in this instance, in ways that no one else could. This is particularly noticed at the end of the fifth book and film, when Sirius has died, and Harry will only speak to Luna about it.

Archetypes in the *Harry Potter* Books and Films

As even this relatively brief essay indicates, potentials for Jungian analyses of the Harry Potter books and films abound. In the novels by J. K. Rowling, as well as in the movies those novels inspired, Jungian archetypes are present practically everywhere. Their presence helps explain the enormous popularity of all these works. After all, Jung argued that the archetypes reflect psychological structures deeply buried in the human mind. Archetypes, he believed, affect the ways we think and feel, not only when we respond to books and films but in the ways we live our day-to-day lives.

Works Cited

Bach, Patricia A., and Daniel J. Moran. *ACT in Practice: Case Conceptualization in Acceptance and Commitment Therapy*. New Harbinger, 2008.

Campbell, Joseph. *The Hero with a Thousand Faces*. 1949. 3rd ed., New World Library, 2008.

Cole, Michael, and Sheila Cole. *The Development of Children*. 4th ed., Worth, 2001.

Erikson, Erik. *Childhood and Society*. Norton, 1963.

Galipeau, Steven A. *The Journey of Luke Skywalker: An Analysis of Modern Myth and Symbol*. Open Court, 2001.

Harry Potter and the Chamber of Secrets. Directed by Chris Columbus, Warner Brothers, 2002.

Harry Potter and the Deathly Hallows—Part 1. Directed by David Yates, Warner Brothers, 2010.

Harry Potter and the Deathly Hallows—Part 2. Directed by David Yates, Warner Brothers, 2011.

Harry Potter and the Goblet of Fire. Directed by Mike Newell, Warner Brothers, 2005.

Harry Potter and the Half-Blood Prince. Directed by David Yates, Warner Brothers, 2009.

Harry Potter and the Order of the Phoenix. Directed by David Yates, Warner Brothers, 2007.

Harry Potter and the Philosopher's [*Sorcerer's* in US version] *Stone*. Directed by Chris Columbus, Warner Bothers, 2001.

Harry Potter and the Prisoner of Azkaban. Directed by Alfonso Cuarón, Warner Brothers, 2004.

Hollis, James. *Tracking the Gods: The Place of Myth in Modern Life*. Inner City Books, 1995.

Jung, C. G. *Collected Works of C. G. Jung, Volume 9: The Archetypes and the Collective Unconscious*. 2nd ed. Princeton University Press, 1990.

———. *Archetype and Symbol*, edited by A. M. Rutkevich, Renaissance, 1991.

———. *Collected Works of C.G. Jung, Volume 5: Symbols of Transformation*. 2nd ed., Princeton UP, 1956.

Pearson, Carol S. *Awakening the Heroes Within: Twelve Archetypes to Help Us Find Ourselves and Transform Our World*. Harper Collins, 1991.

Rowling, J. K. *Harry Potter and the Chamber of Secrets*. Bloomsbury, 1998.

———. *Harry Potter and the Deathly Hallows*. Bloomsbury, 2007.

———. *Harry Potter and the Goblet of Fire*. Bloomsbury, 2000.

———. *Harry Potter and the Half-Blood Prince*. Bloomsbury, 2005.

———. *Harry Potter and the Order of the Phoenix*. Bloomsbury, 2003.

———. *Harry Potter and the Philosopher's* [*Sorcerer's* in US edition] *Stone*. Bloomsbury, 1997.

———. *Harry Potter and the Prisoner of Azkaban*. Bloomsbury, 1999.

von Franz, Marie-Louise. *Shadow and Evil in Fairy Tales*. Revised ed., Shambhala, 1995.

Driving Each Other Crazy: Existential Psychology in Hanif Kureishi's *The Buddha of Suburbia*

Susie Thomas

Hanif Kureishi's *The Buddha of Suburbia* (1990) is one of the most acclaimed novels of recent years. Winner of the prestigious Whitbread Award for best first novel, Kureishi's book has also been widely translated and has been dramatized by the BBC. Although the book can easily lend itself to Freudian interpretations, in the present essay, I plan to study it from the point of view of existential psychology and postcolonial theory. Postcolonial ideas inevitably imply ideas about human minds and human relationships and the close link between the ways people think and feel (on the one hand) and their relations with powerful oppressors (on the other).

The *Buddha of Suburbia* begins with the sudden breakdown of the teenage narrator's family. As Karim says, "Life goes on tediously, nothing happens for months, and then one day everything, and I mean everything, goes fucking wild and berserk" (Kureishi, *Buddha* 91). His Indian father, Haroon, has lost faith in England and his marriage, while his mother, Margaret, is trying and failing not to grumble: their "confusion and pain" is virtually tangible, and Karim panics that they are going to stab each other (50). His Uncle Ted is soon collapsing like a "dying giraffe," and Ted's wife Jean is falling down the stairs drunk. Karim's oldest friend Jamila, and her parents from Bombay, are initially "like an alternative family . . . less intense and warmer" (52). But this refuge soon turns into another battle zone as Jamila is torn between protecting her mother, Princess Jeeta, from her father's violence and resisting Anwar's attempt to force her into marriage with a man she has never met. The family of Karim's best friend, Charlie, has broken up before the novel even starts: the father is in a therapy center "where they allow it all to happen" (11) and the mother, Eva Kay, is recovering from cancer and ready to make a new life with Karim's father, Haroon. Karim thinks Eva is the "only sane grown-up" he knows but he's torn because she is "buggering up our entire family" (63). As the steely cage of family certainty collapses around him, Karim tries to make sense of what has gone wrong and who he wants to become.

The obvious psychological approach to take to *The Buddha of Suburbia* would be Freudian; or, possibly, since Kureishi is cutting edge, Lacanian. Few contemporary novelists have had such an enduring, deep, and open engagement with psychoanalysis as Kureishi. As he tells us in *My Ear at His Heart* (a memoir about his literary rivalry with his father), he first heard about the Oedipus complex when he was fourteen (87). At that time, he was getting on badly with his mother (and failing at math) so he was sent to stay with his uncle, Achoo, a psychologist who ran a school for autistic children in Somerset. The teenage Kureishi was profoundly shocked when his uncle told him he wanted to have sex with his mother and kill his father. He recalls that nothing about Freud made any sense to him at the time, but he was struck by Achoo's belief in the value of listening to the disturbed children in his care: "He said their seemingly 'mad' attitudes made sense" (87). After his father's death in 1991, feeling lost, angry, and defeated, Kureishi went into analysis: "I realised I couldn't see all of myself, read my own dreams, understand my own desire" (174). At the age of fifty-four he published *Something to Tell You* in which, as Geoff Boucher has convincingly argued, the psychoanalyst is a cultural hero.

A conventionally Freudian approach may not, however, be the most useful in relation to *The Buddha*: for a start, Karim does not want to sleep with his mother, not even in his wildest dreams; he wants to get as far away from her as possible in case her "weakness and unhappiness infect" him (Kureishi, *Buddha* 104). Moreover, although Karim definitely wants to kill his father, he is also in love with him, particularly during the first part of the novel, when he is besotted by Daddio. There is an odd moment in *My Ear at His Heart* when Kureishi recalls again what his uncle had told him, but this time, he wonders if he had got it wrong: "I wanted to have sex with my mother and kill my father—or was it the other way round?" (151). In Kureishi's novel *Intimacy*, about the break-up of the narrator's family, this reverse Oedipal thinking is even more pronounced. Jay describes his mother as "a lump of living death" (Kureishi, *Intimacy* 45) and writes with longing of his father: "He loved kissing me. We kept one another company for years. He, more than anyone, was the person I wanted to marry" (42).

Given that Freudian theory does not yield the most faithful or fruitful interpretation of *The Buddha*, I would like to read Kureishi's novel in the light of the work of two figures (R. D. Laing and Frantz Fanon) with considerable clinical experience who were familiar with psychoanalysis but more strongly influenced by the existentialist philosophy and psychology of Jean-Paul Sartre, which emphasized the human capacity for self-creation rather than determination by unconscious and libidinal forces. I will explore how Laing acts as a guide to the madness of the family in *The Buddha* and how Fanon maps the escape route by which Karim, the protagonist, frees himself from the colonial Oedipal complex that he inherits from his father.

Sanity, Madness and the Family

In a series of ground-breaking books in the 1960s, R. D. Laing rejected psychiatric definitions of schizophrenia as a disease and drew on existential philosophy and psychology, especially that of Jean-Paul Sartre, in order to enter into the world of the sufferer. In *The Divided Self* (1960), Laing argues that since the self develops in relation to others, it is necessary to acknowledge the truth of an individual's experience in her or his quest for what Laing calls "ontological security," a firm sense of being; without this, the sufferer cannot develop an authentic sense of self or find a place in the world (39-61). Laing also drew on Donald Winnicott's concept of the "false self": the attempt to conform to the world in order to construct a defense of the self, which comes to leave the sufferer feeling divorced from reality and dead inside (*Divided Self* 94-105). Like Kureishi's uncle Achoo, Laing believed that the symptoms of madness are not unintelligible but, on the contrary, make sense if they are interpreted in relation to what he termed the "family nexus" (*Sanity* 21). In order to demonstrate this idea, Laing, and his fellow psychiatrist A. Esterson, conducted interviews with the family members of eleven patients who had been hospitalized as schizophrenics; the resulting case studies were collected in *Sanity, Madness and the Family* (1964). Although Laing regarded Freud as "a hero" (*Divided Self* 25), he believed that the central issue in a person's development was not sexuality but being-in-the-world: as each member of the family speaks, it becomes clear that the child is the victim of contradictory and disturbing communications. Laing went on to argue in *The Politics of Experience* (1967) that so-called insanity is often a legitimate response to a sane society: "Madness need not be all breakdown. It may also be break-through. It is potentially liberation and renewal as well as enslavement and existential death" (110).

If Laing were to interview the members of the Amir family it would become apparent that Karim suffers from maddening communications. His father boasts proudly that his son will be "a leading doctor in London. . . . Medicine is in our whole family" (Kureishi, *Buddha* 7), but he has absolutely no idea of Karim's life in school, where he is called Shitface and Curryface by the teachers, while kids try to brand his arm with a red-hot lump of metal and piss on his shoes: "and all my Dad thought about was me becoming a doctor. What world was he living in?" (63). It is impossible for Karim to speak about the racism that dominates his daily life outside the home as that racism is not a reality that his parents are willing to recognize. When Karim fails his exams, his father is furious: "his contempt is like a typhoon," a reaction that leaves Karim feeling lower than he'd ever felt before: "Why did it have to bother him so much? It was as if he saw us as having one life between us. I was the second half, an extension of him, and instead of complementing him I'd thrown shit all over him" (110). But for Laing, Karim's failure might be understood as a form of affirmation: a refusal to construct a false self to please his father.

While Haroon stands out "like a budgerigar . . . vibrant, irreverent and laughing" (Kureishi, *Buddha* 84), Karim's mother is the voice of conformity and defeatism, worrying what the neighbors will think and trying to keep the family indoors, as if that will make them safe. When Karim goes out, she pleads with him: "Don't show us up, Karim" (7). She doesn't have great expectations of her son, but neither can she help him to discover who he wants to become: to follow his mother would be to join her in "the shadow-corners of the world" (105).

The family tensions multiply as Haroon begins an affair to which Karim is a witness. Again, Karim is placed in an impossible position: as Dad and Eva embrace in the car he squirms in the back seat "like a good son, pretending not to exist" (Kureishi, *Buddha* 38). He is not only torn between loyalty to his father and to his mother but racked by the false veneer of normality: "Our whole family was in tatters and no one was talking about it" (55). It is the silence as much as the situation which drives him crazy: "all the time, like pipes dripping, weakening and preparing to burst in the attic, around the house hearts were slowly breaking while nothing was being said" (87). It is a relief when the truth is finally acknowledged, even though it leads to the break-up of the family. Guiltily, Karim opts to move in with Haroon and Eva in London, while his mother takes to her bed in the suburbs: "Her mind had turned to glass, and all life slid from its sheer aspect" (104). When he goes back to stay with his mother, he suffers the same sense of suffocation: "Almost every night I had nightmares and sweats. It was sleeping under that childhood roof which did it" (145).

> *In London psychologists were saying you had to live your own life in your own way and not according to your family, or you'd go mad.*
> (Kureishi, Buddha 62)

Although there is an incestuous frisson in Karim's relationship with his "new mummy" (Kureishi, *Buddha* 206), sexuality is less significant than the positive sense of being-in-the world that Eva encourages. Karim certainly enjoys having Eva read him a bedtime story, knowing that his father is waiting impatiently for her in the master bedroom, but what really changes his life is the vitality and confidence that she showers on him: "ecstasy flew from her face like the sun from a mirror" (86). She lends him books, engages in serious discussions about art and music, and fosters his desire to become an actor: "Eva was unfolding the world for me. It was through her that I became interested in life" (87).

When Haroon begins his guru gigs, Karim wonders whether his father is a charlatan. The first test is Uncle Ted, who suffers variously from living what he feels to be "an untrue life" (Kureishi, *Buddha* 265), from an unhappy marriage, and from the daily grind of trying to keep his business from going bankrupt. Haroon counsels him to "follow your feelings. . . . Do what pleases you—whatever it is. Let the house fall down. Drift" (49). As Ted sobs and sinks to the bottom of the stairs, Haroon claims to have "released him" (50). The next time Karim sees Ted, he is "transformed" (103): after a long period of idleness, trips to the pub, and meditation classes, he has discovered a new direction: "Ted had lost his life in order to find it. So Ted was Dad's triumph; he really was someone Dad had freed" (101).

When Jamila, at her wits' end, seeks advice from Haroon, he spells out his philosophy after a brief nap: "I believe happiness is only possible if you follow your feeling, your intuition, your real desires. Only unhappiness is gained by acting in accordance with duty, or obligation, or guilt, or the desire to please others" (Kureishi, *Buddha* 76). Although Jamila is predictably unimpressed and apparently marries an Indian man named Changez out of duty, in order to protect her mother, she does act on Haroon's advice: she is the only character who manages to square the circle of desire and duty, aware that she "is part of the world, of others, not separate from them" (76), without being martyred on the family cross. As Jamila tells Karim: "Families aren't sacred" (55).

Haroon also helps Charlie, Eva's wayward son, who rarely sees his own father. Karim notes jealously that "he spent hours with my father, to whom he told the truth. Together they divined for Charlie's talent. Dad drew him maps to the unconscious". Karim is relieved to see that the effort is to no avail as Charlie's songs are "still shit" (Kureishi, *Buddha* 120). At the end of the novel, Haroon has given up his meaningless job in order to teach and think and listen, as he explains to Karim: "Our minds are richer and wider than we ever imagine! I will point these obvious things out to young people who have lost themselves" (226). As a stream of weepy kids appears at Haroon's West Kensington flat, Karim realizes that his father is not just a suburban eccentric: "it was clear now that he would never lack employment while the city was full of lonely, unhappy, unconfident people who required guidance, support and pity" (279). The Buddha of suburbia finds a new role in London as a therapist.

The Ideas of R. D. Laing

In *The Politics of Experience*, Laing maintained that "the relevance of Freud to our time is largely his insight and, to a very considerable extent, his *demonstration* that the *ordinary* person is a shrivelled, desiccated fragment of what a person can be" (22). Laing's Freudianism was as unorthodox as Haroon's Buddhism; the Buddha, after all, taught the renunciation of desire as the path to peace, not following your feelings. But *The Buddha of Suburbia* provides an almost textbook illustration of Laing's theories about madness and the family: not only the crippling dualities of what he called "the false-self system" but the possibility of a breakdown leading to a breakthrough into a more fulfilled life. It is not only Ted who is released but Margaret who discovers a new vitality once she is freed from the family cage.

Laing's belief that parental love can be a form of violence is most relevant to Karim's Uncle Anwar. Anwar tries to force his daughter Jamila into a marriage with a man she has never met; he thinks his efforts to make her feel guilty have succeeded when she marries Changez, but Changez can never provide Anwar with an heir because Jamila isn't having any of it. Karim is too busy with "his depression and everything" to notice what is going on (Kureishi, *Buddha* 136) but "Anwar-saab has become insanely mad" (136), as Changez points out before he ends up whacking his father-in-law with a dildo. This scene certainly invites a Freudian interpretation, but again what seems most important about the Anwar fiasco is not sexuality but the father's inability to allow his daughter to be herself. As pigs' heads fly through the shop window and racist youths attack Anwar on the street, it is understandable that he should return "internally to India" and try to resist the English by asserting authority over his family (64), but the attempt backfires badly as Jeeta and Jamila rebel against him by withholding their love. Anwar dies an exile's death, "mumbling about Bombay . . . and calling for his mother" (212). After the funeral, Karim has a Laingian epiphany:

> They hadn't even started to be grown-ups together. There was this piece of heaven, this little girl he'd carried around the shop on his shoulders; and then one day she was gone, replaced by a foreigner, an uncooperative woman he didn't know how to speak to. Being so confused, so weak, so in love, he chose strength and drove her away from himself. (Kureishi, *Buddha* 214)

Laing never got around to writing the book's section on sanity and the family; perhaps he shared Tolstoy's view that all happy families are happy in the same way. When *Sanity, Madness and the Family* was first published, it was criticized for not including a control group: without a case study of a sane family, Laing and Esterson's findings were not considered to be properly scientific. Normal families must have been a dime a dozen, but a sane one would have been decidedly different and hard to find. Perhaps the happiest family in *The Buddha* is the "family of friends" that Jamila creates in the radical commune in Peckham (Kureishi, *Buddha* 231). After her father's death, Jamila decides that she has been living too conservatively; she could easily ditch Changez at this point, but, to Karim's relief, she takes him with her: "It was only with these two that I felt part of a family. The three of us were bound together by ties stronger than personality, and stronger than the liking or disliking of each other" (214). She sets up home with her girlfriend, the father of her child, and others who want to "overthrow, not those presently in power, but the whole principle of power-over" (218), with Changez looking after the communal baby. But only Leila Kollantai's memoir would tell us whether this is a sane family or evidence for the prosecution.

Mother Country, Native Son: The Ideas of Frantz Fanon

> And we pursued English roses as we pursued England; by possessing these prizes, this kindness and beauty, we stared defiantly into the eye of the Empire and all its self-regard ... We became part of England and yet proudly stood outside it. But to be truly free we had to free ourselves of all bitterness and resentment, too. How was this possible when bitterness and resentment were generated afresh every day? (Kureishi, *Buddha* 227)

Just as Laing acts as a guide to the madness of the family in *The Buddha*, Frantz Fanon's *Black Skin, White Masks* (1952) maps the escape route by which Karim frees himself from what Fanon called the colonial Oedipal complex. In Freud's account of the superego in *The Ego and the Id* (1923) he wrote: "[The superego's] relation to the ego is not exhausted by the precept you ought to be like this (like your father). It also comprises the prohibition you may not be like this (like your father)—that is, you may not do all that he does; some things are his prerogative" (Freud 16-17) In line with such thinking, the British Empire maintained its hold by employing the rhetoric of the Mother Country, who loves you and is waiting to welcome you home. But behind this rhetoric stood the figure of John Bull (the British equivalent of Uncle Sam), who symbolized the source of the law, with the political and military power to crush transgressors. The colonized male then is engaged in an Oedipal conflict: he ought to be a mimic Englishman, but he may not enjoy white women.

There are two possible objections to the use of Fanon in this context. One potential objection is that Fanon's writing emerges from a French rather than an English colonial context; a second possible complaint is that Karim is not from the colonies but "an Englishman born and bred" (Kureishi, *Buddha* 3). Nonetheless, there are enough points of similarity between French and English colonies—in particular, as we shall see, there is the same original trauma—to make Fanon relevant to *The Buddha*; moreover, the paradigm that Fanon outlines persists in postcolonial England.

According to Fanon, there is no Oedipus complex in the West Indies. Although this claim has been widely disputed, Fanon insists: "Like it or not, the Oedipus complex is far from coming into being among Negroes" (151-2). As David Macey points out, Fanon rejected the cornerstone of psychoanalysis—the universality of the Oedipus obsession—in order to construct a scenario in which it is the relationship with the white colonizers, "and not the actual parent-child relationship, that is crucial" (197). Fanon rejects the incestuous fantasies linked to the Oedipus complex and appeals to an earlier Freudian account of neurosis stemming from real trauma. Fanon stresses the fact that the black experience is social and political as much as personal and that the universalist model of psychoanalysis ignores ethnic difference.

Fanon begins with a version of the master-slave model of colonialism:

> As long as the black man is among his own, he will have no occasion, except in minor internal conflicts, to experience his being through others. There is of course the moment of 'being for others,' of which Hegel speaks, but every ontology is made unattainable in a colonized and civilized society. (109)

According to Fanon, "Ontology [the branch of philosophy that studies the nature of existence] does not permit us to understand the being of the black man. For not only must the black man be black; he must be black in relation to the white man" (110). Fanon locates the traumatic "nigger moment" on a cold day in the streets of Lyons when he is pointed out and shamed: "'Look, A Negro!'" Fanon continues: "On that day, completely dislocated, unable to be abroad with the other, the white man, who unmercifully imprisoned me, I took myself far off from my own presence, far indeed, and made myself an object" (112). But this splitting and self-hatred is not in fact the result of an encounter with a white man but is the result of an encounter with a mother and child. At first Fanon is amused, but as the child cries out, "Mummy I'm frightened," laughter becomes impossible, and he is overcome with nausea. The model of colonialism here is the parent-child, specifically the native son and the mother country, and not the master-slave.

As bell hooks has suggested, Fanon's great insight is to show how seductive the mother country-native son relationship is—how much harder it is to break out of than the master-slave narrative because the mother-son relationship involves desire and longing as well as hatred (182). In *Black Skin, White Masks*, the three stages of colonial, postcolonial, and genuine liberation are conceived as three relationships: first, the abject, self-hating relation of the colonized to the colonizer, which makes the colonized male desire white women: "By loving me she proves that I am worthy of white love. I am loved like a white man" (Fanon 63). Second, the defiant, violent refusal to be the slave, which leads to the desire to conquer white women. Here Fanon refers to "the satisfaction of being the master of a European woman; and a certain tang of proud revenge enters into this" (69). These are the responses of what Fanon refers to as "alienated psyches" (81). Third, the way out of the colonial Oedipal nightmare, by refusing determinism and insisting on freedom as absolute and self-founding: "Superiority? Inferiority? Why not the quite simple attempt to touch the other, to feel the other, to explain the other to myself? Was my freedom not given to me then in order to build the world of the *You*?" (231-32). While this last idea may sound overly optimistic, Fanon believed in what he called "authentic love" (202) and that he had found it with a white Frenchwoman. Biographers and exponents of Fanon seem reluctant to discuss his marriage to Josie Fanon—there is an almost total silence on the subject—as if they are embarrassed by it, or as if it made him a hypocrite. But Fanon argues in *Black Skin, White Masks* that there is no necessary connection between the neurotic desire for a white woman and the fact of being black: "some individuals make every effort to fit into pre-established categories .... We can do something about it" (80). He argues for the possibility of "a healthy encounter between black and white" (80). This kind of encounter allows for a possibility of the third stage, of liberation, in which relations between the man of color and the white woman are no longer overdetermined by the colonial legacy. This is what

Fanon, in a beautiful phrase, calls "the honourable road that leads to the heart" (53).

In *The Buddha*, Fanon's first two stages of assimilation and rejection—"I am loved like a white man / I am accepted" and "Fuck /conquer the white woman as revenge"—coexist to varying degrees in Karim's relationships with Helen and even Charlie. Karim is not conventionally in love with Charlie but wants to be him: "I coveted his talents, face, style. I wanted to wake up with them all transferred to me" (Kureishi, *Buddha* 15). This is more than simple envy of the popular boy; it is part of Karim's unacknowledged loathing of his Pakistani self. But although his love for Charlie is hardly generous, Karim is not the powerful one in the relationship. When Charlie comes in Karim's hand, Karim is ecstatic: "it was, I swear, one of the pre-eminent moments of my earlyish life. There was dancing in my streets. My flags flew, my trumpets blew!" (17). But Charlie avoids Karim's lips when Karim tries to kiss him. Karim does not see what the reader is allowed to see: that he has been used and Charlie doesn't give a damn.

Later erotic encounters take a similarly exploitative turn. When Karim turns up at Helen's house, he is refused entry by her father (Hairy Back): "'We're with Enoch. If you put one of your black 'ands near my daughter I'll smash it with a 'ammer!'" (Kureishi, *Buddha* 40). Instead of describing Karim's anger and hurt, Kureishi turns the episode into a comic set piece as the family's Great Dane pursues him down the path: "The dog was in love with me—quick movements against my arse told me so" (39-40). It is only much later, and very briefly, that Karim allows himself to feel "nauseous with anger and humiliation—none of the things I'd felt at the time" (101). Helen and "dog-cock" become inextricably connected (68), so that Karim can only conceive of sex with Helen as "a delicious moment of revenge" (78).

The cycle of bitterness and humiliation continues when Karim meets Eleanor. She represents a supremely confident upper-class Englishness, of the kind Karim has only read about in children's stories—"Enid Blyton, and Bunter and Jennings" (Kureishi, *Buddha* 174). Next to her, Karim feels himself to be a boy. It is significant that Karim first meets Eleanor in the theatre: both have been chosen by Pyke, the director, to appear in an improvised play for which the actors research characters from their own backgrounds. Pike tells them: "Concentrate on the way you think your position in society has been fixed" (169). Eleanor's character "was an upper-class English woman in her sixties who'd grown up in the Indian Raj, someone who believed herself to be part of Britain's greatness but was declining with it" (179). Initially, Karim has difficulty finding his role—for different reasons first Charlie (too white) and then Uncle Anwar (too Muslim) are vetoed—but he ends up basing his character on Changez. Eleanor plays her part "brilliantly," but Karim steals the show in his role as a hapless immigrant fresh from a small Indian town: "It was me the audience warmed to. They laughed at my jokes, which concerned the sexual ambition and humiliation of an Indian in England" (220). On and off stage, Karim's position is indeed fixed by the afterlife of colonialism.

Karim hardly needs to make the leap of invention into Changez's character, since he experiences more than enough sexual ambition and humiliation first hand. During the evening he spends with Eleanor, Pyke, and Marlene, Karim naively imagines himself the darling of the rich and famous: "they accepted me and invited no one else and couldn't wait to make love to me" (Kureishi, Buddha 202). It is significant that on this occasion, he recalls the night in Eva's Beckenham garden and how he went to Charlie "for comfort" after witnessing his father's infidelity (202). Here again, he's been had. As in the scene with Hairy Back, Karim at first narrates the episode as comedy—"England's most interesting and radical theatre director" was treating him with gross sexual presumption and insensitivity (203)—but later, he begins "to suspect he'd been seriously let down" and even thinks he has been, to some degree, sexually abused (219). Although Karim does not realize it at the time, Kureishi here shows the violence of the colonizer's desire being re-enacted in a London drawing room. The hierarchical power structure is evident not only in the white male's sadistic domination of the brown boy but also by the white women's in-between position. Although Pyke offers Marlene to Karim as a "very special present" (191), in fact she uses him for her pleasure. White women's complicity in Karim's erotic humiliation is evident in the way his rape is treated either as spectacle—"Marlene cheered us on"—or with indifference—"Eleanor fixed herself a drink" (219).

The erotic encounters in *The Buddha* are not only poisoned by external factors such as racism, but also by Karim's internalization of his father's colonial Oedipal complex. Karim believes that his feeling for Eleanor is love: "Love swam right into the body, into the valves, muscles and bloodstream" (Kureishi, *Buddha* 188). At the same time, Karim also feels that this love is predetermined and as if he is merely acting a part scripted by his father:

> I remembered my father saying drunkenly to the Mayor at one of Auntie Jean's parties. . . . 'We little Indians love plump white women with fleshy thighs'. Perhaps I was living out his dreams as I embraced Eleanor's flesh, as I ran the palms of my hands lightly over her whole body, then kissed her awake. . . . Here we were, a fond and passionate pair, but to reach climax I found myself wondering what creatures men were that saw rapes, massacres, tortures, eviscerations at such moments of union. I was being tormented by devils. (Kureishi, *Buddha* 207)

What are the devils that torment Karim here? Partly, the knowledge that the white woman is more powerful, that he is somehow being forced to play the role of the little Indian longing for love and acceptance. And behind that, a deeper evisceration: his awareness that his real rival is the white male, Pyke, in his role as the colonial English governor, who directs Eleanor towards Karim before taking her for himself.

Karim is not only used, abused, and manipulated by Pyke, he is ridiculed during the scene in which this kingly male reads out his earlier sexual predictions in front of the entire cast: "Karim is obviously looking for someone to fuck. . . . It will end in tears" (Kureishi, *Buddha* 244-5). As everyone in the group looks at him and laughs, Karim wonders: "Why did they hate me so much? What had I done to them? Why wasn't I harder?" (244). He lashes out at Pyke wildly and ineffectually like an angry, hurt child before passing out under the piano.

Karim is so traumatized by these events that he almost longs to crack up: "but I knew I wouldn't go mad, even if that release, that letting-go, was a freedom I desired" (Kureishi, *Buddha* 250). What saves him is the survival instinct he inherits from his immigrant father: "Dad had always felt superior to the British: this was the legacy of his Indian childhood—political anger turning into scorn and contempt. . . . You couldn't let the ex-colonialists see you on your knees, for that was where they expected you to be" (250). At the end of the novel, Karim is still engaged in the inter-related struggle to "locate" himself and to "learn what the heart is" (284). Fanon's honorable road to the heart—love between two human beings—is frustrated by both internal and external conditions, by Karim's confused scramble for identity and by a racist society still steeped in imperial attitudes.

Neither R. D. Laing nor Frantz Fanon is mentioned by name in *The Buddha* (although they are cited elsewhere in Kureishi's work), but it is clear from the quotations (given at the start of each section of this essay) what Karim has been reading and how both writers help him leave his family and find a place in the world. Although geographically distant from each other, Laing and Fanon are linked by their common ancestry in Sartre, with his emphasis on the search for an authentic self and authentic love. *The Buddha* revels in a multiplicity of identities—in change, transformation and renewal—in a way that is sometimes mistaken for postmodernism. But the novel does not dispense with the belief in an authentic self. Karim's career as an actor teaches him a "[p]aradox of paradoxes: to be someone else successfully you must be yourself! This I learned!" (Kureishi, *Buddha* 219-220).

Works Cited

Boucher, Geoff. "The Other Kureishi: A Psychoanalytical Reading of *Something to Tell You*." Fischer (2015), pp. 99-113.

Fanon, Frantz. *Black Skin, White Masks*. Translated by Charles Lam Markmann, Grove Press, 1967.

Fischer, Susan Alice, editor. *Hanif Kureishi*. Bloomsbury Academic, 2015. Contemporary Critical Perspectives.

Freud, Sigmund. *The Ego and the Id*. www.sigmundfreud.net/the-ego-and-the-id-pdf-ebook.jsp/. Accessed 24 Jan. 2017.

hooks, bell. "Dialogue." *The Fact of Blackness: Frantz Fanon and Visual Representation*, ed. Alan Read. ICA, 1996, pp. 132-43.

Kureishi, Hanif. *The Buddha of Suburbia*. Faber and Faber, 1990.

———. *Intimacy*. Faber and Faber, 1998.

———. *My Ear at His Heart: Reading My Father*. Faber and Faber, 2004.

Laing, R. D. *The Divided Self: An Existential Study in Sanity and Madness*. Penguin Modern Classics, 2010.

———. *The Politics of Experience and The Bird of Paradise*. Penguin, 1990.

———, and A. Esterson. *Sanity, Madness and the Family: Families of Schizophrenics*. Penguin, 1990.

Macey, David. *Frantz Fanon: A Life*. Granta, 2000.

RESOURCES

F. SCOTT FITZGERALD
THE GREAT GATSBY

Psychological Pluralism: A Variety of Possible Psychological Approaches to Literature and Film

Robert C. Evans

Much psychological study of literature and film during the past hundred or so years has been dominated by the psychoanalytic approaches associated with Sigmund Freud and his followers, especially (most recently) Jacques Lacan. Yet anyone familiar with recent developments in psychology (say, developments from the last fifty or sixty years) knows that Freudian approaches cover just a small portion of the spectrum of possible perspectives. The purpose of this essay, then, is to outline, very briefly, a wide variety of ways to think about psychological interpretations of literature. These ways *include* psychoanalytic approaches but are not limited simply to those views.

To try to suggest how variously a single work can be studied from numerous perspectives, I have chosen to focus on the famous poem "On My First Son" by the English Renaissance poet Ben Jonson (1572–1637):

> Farewell, thou child of my right hand, and joy;
>
> My sin was too much hope of thee, lov'd boy.
>
> Seven years thou wert lent to me, and I thee pay,
>
> Exacted by thy fate, on the just day.
>
> O, could I lose all father now! For why
>
> Will man lament the state he should envy?
>
> To have so soon 'scap'd world's and flesh's rage,
>
> And, if no other misery, yet age?
>
> Rest in soft peace, and, ask'd, say, "Here doth lie

Ben Jonson his best piece of poetry."

For whose sake henceforth all his vows be such,

As what he loves may never like too much.

In this poem, Jonson laments the death of his young son (also named Benjamin) who died unexpectedly at the age of seven. Jonson first bids farewell to his son (line 1), then censures himself for having assumed that the boy would always be his (line 2), then acknowledges that God created the boy and therefore could justly take him back at any time God thought fit (lines 3-4). Up to this point, Jonson seems to be dealing very rationally with his grief, as reasonable Christians of his time were expected to do. He puts his trust in God's wisdom. In line 5, however, his paternal emotions burst out: he wishes that he could "lose" the painful sensation of even being a father. But then, in lines 5-8, he reminds himself that his son is now in a much better state (in heaven, with God) and that by dying at an early age, the boy has escaped all the pain of growing older. In lines 9-10, Jonson expresses pride in his son, calling him the best thing he ever made (the word "poetry" comes from a Greek word for "to make"). Finally, in the last two lines, Jonson vows that in the future, he will never again take too much personal, egocentric pleasure in anything he loves.

In suggesting briefly how this poem might be examined from various psychological perspectives, I have drawn on a standard textbook in the field (by Daniel Cervone and Lawrence A. Pervin), which is abbreviated in the text as "C&P." I have used bold print to emphasize key concepts associated with each of the psychological approaches I discuss.[1]—*Robert C. Evans*

A FREUDIAN APPROACH. Sigmund Freud (1856–1939), widely recognized as the founder of psychoanalysis, argued that the human mind consists of three major components: the **id** (which "pursues pleasure and avoids pain" [C&P 83]); the **ego** (which seeks to deal successfully with reality); and the **superego** (which seeks to live up to society's moral standards and ethical expectations). These three parts of the mind strongly resemble traditional classical and Christian assumptions that humans are influenced by passions (the id), reason (the ego), and conscience (the superego) and that it is the job of the reason and conscience to control the emotional impulses of the passions. A Freudian reading of Jonson's poem might suggest that the poem shows Jonson's ego trying to accept the reality of his son's death while the superego tries to reconcile that death to a sense of morality: Jonson tries to accept the death as resulting from God's will and God's goodness. Both the ego and superego struggle to control the emotional pain rooted in the id. It is partly this struggle that gives the poem its keen sense of complicated, convincing tension. Jonson's ego (his sense of self) feels threatened by the death of his son, partly because he thinks of the son as mostly *his* creation (the boy's mother is never mentioned). To deal rationally with his son's death, Jonson must convince himself that his son is God's creation, who can be taken back whenever God chooses, and that God's intentions (as well as the boy's final fate) are good. The boy died at a young enough age that he did not have to deal with the tensions that arise during the "**genital stage**" of development (which begins at puberty), nor did he, during his young life, pose any real threat to his father because of an unresolved "**Oedipus complex**" (Freud's controversial idea that sons wish to murder their fathers and have sex with their mothers). Jonson copes with the pain of his son's death partly through "**denial**" (my son is dead, but he is not really dead), partly through "**rationalization**" (my son has died, but he is better off because he has escaped the pain of growing up), and partly through "**sublimation**" (my son is dead physically, but now he is in heaven with God). These are just a few of the ways a Freudian might approach Jonson's poem.

AN ADLERIAN APPROACH. Alfred Adler (1870–1937) was an early associate of Freud who later broke from standard psychoanalytic ideas. "Perhaps most significant in Adler's split from Freud," according to Cervone and Pervin, "was his greater emphasis on social urges and **conscious thoughts** than on instinctual sexual urges and unconscious processes" (135). Adler particularly stressed the ways people attempt to **compensate for feelings of painful inferiority**: "it is the feeling of inferiority, inadequacy, insecurity, which determines the goal of an individual's existence" (qtd. in C&P 136). All people, as children, feel inferior in one way or another; therefore everyone has to cope with such feelings. The ways a person typically copes with feelings of inferiority become "part of his or her **style of life**" (qtd. in C&P 136). People can cope with their feelings of inferiority either in healthy or unhealthy ways—for example, either through **cooperation** and positive **competition** or through a **need to dominate or control** others." An Adlerian critic might argue that Jonson's poem seeks to cope with feelings of inferiority (especially the pain of his son's death) by accepting God's judgment, embracing his culture's teachings about dealing rationally with death (rather than being paralyzed by grief), and emphasizing his creative strength by crafting a memorable poem about his son's passing.

A JUNGIAN APPROACH. Carl Jung (1875–1961) was another early follower of Freud who eventually broke away from Freudian psychoanalysis. Jung believed that Freud had over-emphasized sexual motives and impulses and that he had also overemphasized the importance of influences rooted in infancy and childhood. "Instead, Jung believed that personality development also has a forward-moving directional tendency" (C&P 138): people try to prepare for the future, including an anticipated afterlife. Perhaps the key difference between Freud and Jung, however, was Jung's emphasis on what he called the "**collective unconscious**," which is shared by human beings everywhere at all times and which is grounded in the process of evolution. "The collective unconscious contains **universal images or symbols**, known as **archetypes**" (C&P 138). Examples include the Great Mother, the Wise Old Man, the strong Hero as well as **deeply rooted desires and fears**, such as the desire for love and the fear of death. Jung also emphasized the ways "people struggle with **opposing forces** within them" (C&P 139). On the one hand (for instance), people have their own intense feelings, but on the other, they feel the need to present an acceptable image to others. Likewise, men have feminine aspects (the **anima**, associated with tenderness) and women have male aspects (the **animus**, associated with strength and self-control). According to Cervone and Pervin, "Jung emphasizes that all individuals face a fundamental personal task: **finding unity in the self**. The task is to bring into harmony, or **integrate . . . the various opposing forces of the psyche**" (C&P 139). A Jungian critic might argue (1) that Jonson's poem shows him trying to enact the archetypal role of the wise and good father; (2) that Jonson also associates that role with God; and (3) that he sees his son as an example of the archetype of the innocent, admirable child. The poem shows Jonson trying to cope with the universal fear of loss and death, partly by embracing the widespread belief in (or at least yearning for) a happy afterlife. He expresses his tender side (associated with his anima) without losing psychic toughness (associated with his animus), and he tries to integrate the variety of his thoughts and feelings by balancing emotion with reason, pain with a sense of peace, and a sense of loss with a sense of trust in God's goodness.

A HORNEYIAN APPROACH. Whereas Freud stressed the effects of the different stages of childhood biographical development (the oral stage, the anal stage, the phallic stage, and so on), Karen Horney (1885–1952) emphasized the great impact "of **cultural conditions** on neuroses" (C&P 141). She was especially interested in the ways culture shaped **gender identities**, and she also believed that "interpersonal relationships are at the core of all healthy and disturbed personality functioning" (C&P 141). She was interested in "how individuals attempt to cope with **basic anxiety**," such as childhood isolation and helplessness in "**a potentially hostile world**" (C&P 142). Neurotic people tend either (1) to **move toward** sources of anxiety (either becoming obsessed with them or accommodating them), or (2) to **move against** them (by expressing hostility), or (3) to **move away** from them in a kind of "neurotic detachment" (C&P 142). In neurotic people, "there is a **conflict among the three trends** in the effort to deal with basic anxiety" (C&P 142). A Horneyian critic might see Jonson's poem as reflecting all three basic impulses as he attempts to cope with the anxiety caused by his son's death: he tries to move away from anxiety when he expresses a desire to "lose" the feeling of being a father (line 5), and perhaps this emotion may also express a kind of anger. Ultimately, though, he seeks to accommodate himself to God's ways and to the loss of his son. He enacts his culturally prescribed role as a strong, reasonable man who nonetheless also expresses tender aspects of his personality.

AN ERIKSONIAN APPROACH. Erik Erikson (1902–94) sympathized with many aspects of Freud's theories but emphasized the social rather than the sexual aspects of personal development. He also believed that psychological development continues throughout a person's life. Finally, he believed that people are influenced not only by their memories of their pasts but by the ways they imagine their futures. Most important for Jonson's poem are the later stages of Erikson's scheme of psychological development. The fact that Jonson's son died at the age of seven means that he died during a phase that Erikson called the "**latency**" stage, which begins around age six and is the stage during which an individual develops either "a sense of industry and success or a sense of inferiority" (C&P 102). Jonson's pride in his son and Jonson's own commitment to intellectual work would have meant that his son would have had an encouraging, perhaps demanding role model, which might have meant that the son would grow up with a strong, healthy ego (or, alternatively, a strong sense of rebellion against his father's values). Of course, there is no way to know precisely *how* young Ben would have developed, but the elder Jonson, in writing about his son, displays many of the positive traits that Erikson associated with the stage of "**early adulthood**" and "**adulthood**," including strong relationships with other people, a strong commitment to work, and the ability "to lose oneself in work and relationships" (C&P 102). Jonson tries to impose a sense of "**order and meaning**" on his life and his loss, so that during his "**later years**," he can feel content with himself and his accomplishments (C&P 102). He tries to convince himself that his son, by dying so early, has escaped all the potential negative outcomes of life, such as a sense of "**inadequacy and inferiority**," a sense of failure and inauthenticity, and all the other kinds of disappointments that the process of aging can bring (C&P 102).

A ROGERIAN APPROACH. Carl R. Rogers (1902–1987) emphasized each person's "**self**" or "**self-concept**": as Cervone and Pervin put it, people are concerned both with "the self we believe we are now" and with "the self that we ideally see ourselves becoming in the future" (C&P 171). Rogers, they explain, felt that "the most fundamental personality process is a forward-looking tendency toward personality growth" that Rogers labeled "**self-actualization**" (C&P 175). People seek a sense of "**self-consistency**": "To Rogers, achieving a consistent sense of self is so important that people seek out experiences that are congruent with their existing self-perceptions" (C&P 178). Using such processes as "**distortion**," "**denial**," and "**subception**," we defend ourselves against experiences that threaten our senses of self-consistency. Subception involves blocking a threatening perception before we are even fully conscious of it (C&P 178). All people feel a "**need for positive regard**" from others, but they also need to feel a sense of "**authenticity**," as if they are not merely playing an approved social role. The relevance of all these "Rogerian" ideas to Jonson's poem are obvious. Threatened by the loss of his son, Jonson tries to enact the kind of role his culture expects: he tries to be strong and rational in the face of overwhelming emotional pain. Yet he also gives temporary vent to the depth of that pain before regaining self-control. He tries to live up to his own highest standards of what it means to be a good Christian; he accepts God's will rather than rebelling against it. He presents himself as he would like to be perceived by others and as he would like to perceive himself. He wants to grow as a person from the pain his son's death has caused him. He wants to accept his son's loss without feeling that he has sacrificed his own sense of authenticity.

A MASLOWIAN APPROACH. Abraham H. Maslow (1908–1970) "proposed that people are basically good or neutral rather than evil, with everyone possessing an impulse toward growth and the fulfillment of potentials" (C&P 207). He argued that people have basic **physiological needs** (such as the need to eat, drink, sleep, etc.). Next, they have needs for **safety**, then needs for **belongingness**, then needs for **esteem**, and finally needs for **self-actualization** (C&P 208). Psychologists like Maslow, and others influenced by him, have argued that more attention needs to be paid to "highly functioning, self-actualized individuals" (C&P 209) since by focusing on such people we can gain a better sense of real human potentials. Too often psychological theorists have paid most attention to neurotic or pathological individuals; they have overlooked "**human strengths**" and have ended up "with a distorted picture of personality that underemphasizes the positive" (C&P 209). Jonson's poem presents a bereaved father who nonetheless manages, by the end of the poem, to display great emotional, psychological, and spiritual strength. By embracing his culture's deepest spiritual values, he achieves a sense of belongingness; by responding as stoically as he does to his boy's death, he can achieve a sense of self-esteem as well as the esteem of others; and by responding and writing as he does, he engages in a sort of self-actualization that allows him to live up to his own highest ideals as a father and as a Christian.

AN ALLPORTIAN APPROACH. Gordon W. Allport (1897–1967) was one of the first and most influential of the so-called "trait theorists." Trait theory—which is still immensely influential today—suggests that there tend to be "consistent patterns [or "**traits**"] in the way individuals behave, feel, and think.... Trait terms, then, have two connotations: **consistency** and **distinctiveness**" (C&P 238). Allport "believed that traits are the basic units of personality ... and are based in the nervous system.... Traits can be defined by three properties—**frequency**, **intensity**, and **range of situations**. For example, a very submissive person would frequently be submissive over a wide range of situations" (C&P 243). Allport distinguished among cardinal traits, central traits, and secondary traits. "A **cardinal trait** . . . is so pervasive and outstanding in a person's life that virtually every act is traceable to its influence. . . . **Central traits** (e.g., honesty, kindness, assertiveness) express dispositions that cover a more limited range of situations . . . . **Secondary dispositions** are traits that are the least conspicuous, generalized, and consistent" (C&P 244). Anyone familiar with Jonson's poetry would recognize in the poem on his son a number of his most characteristic traits as a person and writer. These include a love of children, pride in being a father (both literally and symbolically), a commitment to rational behavior, and pride in being a writer, to mention just a few. The kindness and compassion that emerge in this poem can seem unusual in a writer known as one of English literature's greatest satirists, just as the vulnerability this poem discloses is not a trait that seems especially common in many of Jonson's other writings. Indeed, it is the presence of these relatively unusual traits that helps add to the complexity and effectiveness of this particular poem.

A CATTELLIAN APPROACH. Raymond B. Cattell (1905–1998) was another early "trait theorist"; he added, to earlier ideas, such concepts as "**surface traits**," "**source traits**," "**ability traits**," "**temperament traits**," and "**dynamic traits**" (C&P 249-50). Most interesting for our present purposes is Cattell's listing of **sixteen different basic "personality factors"** that most humans tend to display. These include (as summarized by Cervone and Pervin) (1) being reserved or outgoing; (2) being less intelligent or more intelligent; (3) being stable and possessing "ego strength" vs. displaying emotionality and neuroticism; (4) being humble or assertive; (5) being sober or happy-go-lucky; (6) being expedient or conscientious; (7) being shy or venturesome; (8) being tough-minded or tender-minded; (9) being trusting or suspicious; (10) being practical or imaginative; (11) being forthright or shrewd; (12) being placid or apprehensive; (13) being conservative or experimenting; (14) being group-dependent or self-sufficient; (15) being undisciplined or controlled; and (16) being relaxed or tense.

Cattell, according to Cervone and Pervin, "did not view persons as static entities who behaved the same way in all situations." Instead, they were also affected by specific "**states**" and "**roles**"—that is, by specific internal emotions or moods at any given time and by specific social expectations. The Jonson who emerges in the poem on his dead son can nevertheless be analyzed in terms of the sixteen traits enumerated above. In this poem, he seems: (1) reserved; (2) intelligent; (3) stable (although briefly emotional); (4) humble; (5) sober; (6) conscientious; (7) somewhat shy; (8) simultaneously both tough-minded and tender-minded; (9) trusting; (10) practical; (11) forthright; (12) placid; (13) conservative; (14) group-dependent in the sense that he embraces the values of his culture; (15) controlled; (16) and finally relaxed, if relaxation is ever truly possible in such situations.

AN EYSENCKIAN APPROACH. Hans J. Eysenck (1916–1997) was another early trait theorist (and also a strong critic of Freudian psychoanalysis [C&P 256]). By conducting "secondary factor analysis," he correlated and reduced Cattell's sixteen traits to a more manageable number. Calling these very basic traits "**superfactors**," he identified such very fundamental tendencies as: (1) "**introversion**" vs. "**extraversion**"; (2) **neuroticism**; and (3) **psychoticism**. For instance, neuroticism tends to be characterized by anxiety, depression, guilt feelings, low self-esteem, tension, irrationality, shyness, moodiness, and emotionality (C&P 259). Psychotic people tend to display aggressiveness, coldness, egocentricity, impersonality, impulsiveness, antisocial feelings and conduct, lack of empathy, creativity, and tough-mindedness (C&P 260). The relevance of these ideas to Jonson's poem seems clear: Jonson uses his poem to combat and overcome any neurotic and psychotic tendencies that his son's death might make him feel. He does initially feel depression, guilt, and emotionality, but by the end of the poem, he has mastered these feelings and seems to have come to a kind of peace with himself and with God's ways.

A FIVE-FACTOR APPROACH. The "five-factor model of personality" is a model very widely embraced by contemporary psychologists. As Cervone and Pervin explain, many "researchers believe that individual differences can be usefully organized in terms of five broad, bipolar dimensions . . . widely known . . . as the **Big Five**" (269). These are often abbreviated as "**OCEAN**": openness, conscientiousness, extraversion, agreeableness, and neuroticism (C&P 270). Some more recent theorists have proposed adding a sixth factor to this list: honesty (289). People who score high on tests for **openness**, for instance, tend to be curious, creative, original, imaginative, untraditional, and have broad interests, while people who score low on tests for this trait tend to be conventional, down-to-earth, unartistic, unanalytical, and have narrow interests. People who score high on tests for **conscientiousness** tend to be organized, reliable, hard-working, self-disciplined, punctual, scrupulous, neat, ambitious, and persevering, while people who score low on tests for conscientiousness tend to be aimless, unreliable, lazy, careless, lax, negligent, weak-willed, and hedonistic. People who score high on tests for **extraversion** tend to be sociable, active, talkative, person-oriented, optimistic, fun-loving, and affectionate, while people who tend to score low on tests for extraversion tend to be reserved, sober, unexuberant, aloof, task-oriented, retiring, and quiet. People who score high on tests for **agreeableness** tend to be soft-hearted, good-natured, trusting, helpful, forgiving, gullible, and straightforward, while people who score low on tests for this trait tend to be cynical, rude, suspicious, uncooperative, vengeful, ruthless, irritable, and manipulative. Finally, people who score high on tests for **neuroticism** tend to be worrying, nervous, emotional, insecure, hypochondriacal, and plagued by feelings of inadequacy, while people who tend to score low on tests for neuroticism tend to be calm, relaxed, unemotional, hardy, secure, and self-satisfied (for all these traits, see C&P 271). Cervone and Pervin discuss the strengths, potential weaknesses, and possible complexities of the "five factor" approach in great detail (271-309). The point worth remembering is that this is one approach very commonly favored by contemporary trait theorists (C&P 309). To discuss Jonson's poem in terms of all of the specific sub-traits listed above would take far more space than is available here. Suffice it to say that by the end of the poem, he has exhibited most of the positive traits associated with the OCEAN model and has worked his way through any neurotic traits he may at first have displayed.

A BEHAVIORIST APPROACH. Behaviorism is an approach to psychology associated with such major early figures as Ivan Pavlov (1849–1936), John B. Watson (1878–1958), and B. F. Skinner (1904–1990). Pavlov's idea of "**classical conditioning**" suggested that both animals and humans could be trained to respond in predictable ways to specific stimuli. For example, dogs that salivated when presented with food would learn to salivate "at the approach of the person who brought the food," or they would salivate if they simply heard a bell they associated with the presentation of food, even if no food was now actually presented to them (C&P 380-81). In another famous experiment, Watson showed a baby a white rat, with which the baby was quite comfortable, but then the experimenters began making loud noises whenever the rat was presented. The noises terrified the baby, who eventually became tremendously frightened by the rat even when the noise was no longer made. In fact, the baby came to fear not only the white rat but "other white and furry objects," such as "the white beard of a Santa Claus mask" (C&P 384). The baby had developed what Watson called a "**conditioned emotional reaction**" (C&P 384). Psychologists following such leads later argued that if reactions could be conditioned, they could also be unconditioned by using such processes as "**systematic desensitization**" or "**counter-conditioning**" (C&P 385). Skinner built on earlier behaviorist ideas, especially by stressing the importance of a "**reinforcer**," which is "something that follows a response and increases the probability of the response occurring again in the future" (C&P 394). Although the history and vocabulary of behaviorism are lengthy, the basic behaviorist assumption is that responses can be taught, learned, and uneven unlearned with the right kinds of **conditioning** and **stimuli**. A behaviorist reading of Jonson's poem might suggest, for example, that Jonson's culture, with its deep religious grounding and its strong commitment to stoicism, has helped Jonson unlearn the intense grief he might otherwise have continued to feel at his son's death. He has been conditioned by his culture through a kind of "systematic desensitization" to the fact of death. He has been conditioned to behave according to various valued social roles, such as the role of a male in control of his feelings, a reasonable person in control of his emotions, and a Christian capable of counteracting depression and despair.

A SOCIAL COGNITIVE APPROACH. Social cognitive theorists, such as Albert Bandura (1925–) and Walter Mischel (1930–) emphasize the importance of the ways people *think* and how their **thinking** is shaped by their **social environments** (C&P 450). These theorists feel that psychoanalysts "*over*emphasize unconscious forces and the influence of early childhood experience" (C&P 451). Social cognitive theorists are also "highly critical of trait theory," especially its fundamental assumption that "personality can be understood in terms of people's overall, average tendencies" (C&P 451). They think that people "are at least partly 'in control'" of their thoughts and behavior (C&P 451). These theorists emphasize such basic assumptions as "**people as active agents**"; the "**social origins of behavior**"; "**cognitive (thought) processes**"; both average and variable behavior; and "the learning of complex patterns of behavior in the absence of rewards" (C&P 451). They also emphasize the importance of **reason** and **reflection** (C&P 456). Cognitive theory "highlights **people's capacity to overcome environmental influences and animalistic emotional impulses**" as well as their ability "to gain control over the course of their lives" (C&P 456). They believe that people can develop various "**competencies**" that operate in **specific contexts**. They think that people are influenced by their "**expectancies**" and "**goals**" concerning the future (C&P 457-59). "**Perceived self-efficacy** . . . refers to people's perceptions of their own capacities for action in future situations" (C&P 460). Cognitive theorists assume that "**people's subjective impressions of themselves** have a unique causal influence on their behavior" (C&P 463). They think that people exhibit distinct "**behavioral signatures**" *in specific situations or contexts* (C&P 474). People tend to learn by observing others (so-called "**observational learning**"), especially by observing others who serve as "**models**" (C&P 476). People try to control their own thoughts, feelings, and behavior through "**self-regulation**" (C&P 480). These are just a few of the various concepts associated with social cognitive theory (for many others, see C&P 494-534). Trait theory and social cognitive theory are the two theories that "are built on the largest and most systematic sets of scientific evidence. This is surely why they long have been the two most influential frameworks in modern personality science" (C&P 530).

The relevance of these ideas to Jonson's poem is obvious. In this poem, Jonson tries to use his reason to control his emotions. He thinks of himself as a rational Christian person and tries to live up to the standards his culture has set for a mature, reasonable Christian believer. He tries to live up to the models of ideal behavior that his culture has embraced, and he tries to serve as a role model for others. Anyone familiar with the philosophy of stoicism, which was tremendously influential in classical culture and in the Christian culture of Jonson's day, will recognize the numerous similarities that exist between stoicism and social cognitive psychology. Little wonder, then, that Jonson—who was enormously attracted to stoic ideas—would write a poem that can be so easily explicated in social cognitive terms.

AN EVOLUTIONARY PSYCHOLOGICAL APPROACH. Evolutionary psychology is one of the most recent, most popular, and most controversial approaches to psychology (for a good overview see, for instance, Workman and Reader). Evolutionary psychologists tend to make a number of very basic assumptions, including these: (1) **evolution occurs**: all living things, including humans, are the products of millions of years of evolution; (2) **adaptation occurs**: all living things (including humans) must adapt to their specific environments in order to survive; (3) **genes either survive or fail to survive**: if an organism is well adapted to its environment, it will survive and pass on its genes to the next generation, but if an organism is not well adapted to its environment, it is less likely to survive and pass on its genes; (4) **predispositions are inherited**: current living organisms possess, encoded in their genes, various predispositions that helped their ancestors survive in their ancestors' environments; (5) **competition affects survival**: all living organisms must compete with other organisms, especially organisms of the same species, to survive. Organisms that compete most successfully are most likely to pass on not only their genes but also their adaptive genetic predispositions to the next generation. Although these are just a few of the most basic touchstones of evolutionary psychology, their relevance to Jonson's poem is clear. First, Jonson mourns his son's loss because his son has not survived to an old enough age to pass on his genes (including the genes he inherited from Jonson) to the next generation. Secondly, Jonson's own thoughts and feelings are the results of millions of years of evolution. These have led human beings to prize and value their children, especially male children. Male children are especially likely to be valued because they have the capacity to sire many more children in a limited amount of time than any female child could produce in the same amount of time. By controlling his emotions, Jonson shows that he is better adapted to his environment than someone, say, who would commit suicide at the loss of a child. By behaving reasonably and responsibly and by exhibiting his sincere commitment to his role as a father, Jonson displays many of the traits that would have made him an attractive mate in the first place.

Summary Comments

The approaches outlined above are just a few of the many approaches that have been most relevant to the psychological study of literature and film during the past hundred or so years. These approaches do not include the many older perspectives that existed before the founding of modern psychology in the mid-nineteenth century. Most of the great philosophers, from the time of the ancient Greeks and afterwards, speculated about psychological topics. Plato, for instance, formulated various ideas (such as the need for reason to control passion) later developed in distinctive ways by Freud. The tendency of recent literary and cultural critics to focus so intensely on the continuing relevance Freudian approaches means that many other possible psychological approaches to literature and film remain vastly underexplored.

Note

1. For lively, stimulating discussion of the ideas outlined in this chapter, I wish to thank the students in my fall 2016 course in literary criticism, particularly Mashael Alharbi, Whitney Barrett, Jordan Chapman, Marlee Damrell, Patsy Davidson, Tyler Devore, Derrick Gates, Laken Harris, Sara Headley, Kiarah Holloway, Elizabeth Huggins, Leigh Newby, Jean Kathryn Parnell, and Alysha Suchaski.

Works Cited

Cervone, Daniel, and Lawrence A. Pervin. *Personality: Theory and Research*. 10th ed., John Wiley, 2008.

Workman, Lawrence, and Will Reader. *Evolutionary Psychology: An Introduction*. 3rd ed., Cambridge UP, 2014.

Chronology

ca. 350 bce	Aristotle. *De Anima*.
ca. 350 BCE	Aristotle. *On Memory and Reminiscence*.
1637	René Descartes. *Discourse on Method*.
1649	René Descartes. *Passions of the Soul*.
1662	Baruch Spinoza. *On the Improvement of the Understanding*.
1689	John Locke. *An Essay Concerning Human Understanding*.
1705/1765	Gottfried Wilhelm Leibniz. *New Essays on Human Understanding*.
1709	George Berkeley. *An Essay Towards a New Theory of Vision*.
1710	George Berkeley. *Treatise Concerning the Principles of Human Knowledge*.
1739–1740	David Hume. *A Treatise of Human Nature*.
1748	David Hume. *An Inquiry Concerning Human Understanding*.
1749	David Hartley. *Observations on Man*.
1765	Gottfried Wilhelm von Leibniz. *New Essays on the Human Understanding*.
1782	Immanuel Kant. *Critique of Pure Reason*.
1786	Immanuel Kant. *Metaphysical Foundations of Natural Science*.
1788	Thomas Reid. *Essay on the Active Powers of the Human Mind*.
1843	John Stuart Mill. *A System of Logic*.
1855	Herbert Spencer. *Principles of Psychology*.
1859	Charles Darwin. *The Origin of the Species*.
1863	Wilhelm Max Wundt. *Lectures on Human and Animal Psychology*.
1865	Francis Galton. "Hereditary talent and character."
1871	Charles Darwin. *The Descent of Man*.
1874	Franz Brentano. *Psychology from an Empirical Standpoint*.
1874	Wilhelm Max Wundt. *Principles of Physiological Psychology*.
1880	Francis Galton. *Statistics of Mental Imagery*.
1890	William James. *The Principles of Psychology*.
1884	John Dewey. "The New Psychology."
1885	G. Stanley Hall. "The New Psychology."

1890	William James. *The Principles of Psychology*.
1894	John Dewey. "The Ego as Cause."
1896	John Dewey. "The Reflex Arc Concept in Psychology."
1898	E. L. Thorndike. *Animal Intelligence*.
1898	Edward Titchener. *The Postulates of a Structural Psychology*.
1900	Sigmund Freud. *The Interpretation of Dreams*.
1901	Sigmund Freud. "The Psychopathology of Everyday Life."
1905	Sigmund Freud. "Three Essays on the Theory of Sexuality."
1912	Max Wertheimer. *Experimental Studies of the Perception of Movement*.
1913	George H. Mead. "The Social Self."
1913	John B. Watson. "Psychology as the Behaviorist Views It."
1916	Alfred Binet. "New Methods for the Diagnosis of the Intellectual Level of Subnormals."
1916	Lewis M. Terman. *The Measurement of Intelligence*.
1917	Sigmund Freud. *Introduction to Psychoanalysis*.
1922	Kurt Koffka. "Perception: An introduction to the Gestalt-theorie."
1923	Sigmund Freud. "The Ego and the Id."
1927	Alfred Adler. *Understanding Human Nature*.
1927	Gordon W. Allport. "Concepts of Trait and Personality."
1927	Ivan P. Pavlov. *Conditioned reflexes: An investigation of the physiological activity of the cerebral cortex*.
1935	B. F. Skinner "Two Types of Conditioned Reflex and a Pseudo Type."
1936/1952	Jean Piaget. *The Origins of Intelligence in Children*.
1937	Anna Freud. "The Ego and the Mechanisms of Defense."
1937	B. F. Skinner. "Two Types of Conditioned Reflex: A Reply to Konorski and Miller."
1939	Kenneth B. Clark and Mamie K. Clark. "The Development of Consciousness of Self and the Emergence of Racial Identification in Negro Preschool Children."
1940	Kenneth B. Clark and Mamie K. Clark. "Skin Color as a Factor in Racial Identification of Negro Preschool Children."
1943	Abraham Maslow. "A Theory of Human Motivation."
1945	Karen Horney. *Our Inner Conflicts*.

1946	Viktor Frankl. *Man's Search for Meaning*.
1947	Hans Eysenck. *Dimensions of Personality*.
1947	Carl R. Rogers. "Some Observations on the Organization of Personality."
1948	B. F. Skinner. "'Superstition' in the Pigeon."
1950	B. F. Skinner. "Are Theories of Learning Necessary?"
1951	Eric Hoffer. *The True Believer: Thoughts on the Nature of Mass Movements*.
1951	Carl Rogers. "Client-centered Therapy."
1952	Hans J. Eysenck. "The Effects of Psychotherapy: An Evaluation."
1953	B. F. Skinner. *Beyond Freedom & Dignity*.
1953	B. F. Skinner. *Science and Human Behavior*.
1953	Carl Jung. *The Archetypes and the Collective Unconscious*.
1959	Wolfgang Köhler. "Gestalt Psychology Today."
1961	Albert Ellis and Robert Harper. *A Guide to Rational Living*.
1961	Carl Rogers. *On Becoming a Person*.
1962	A. Ellis. "Reason and Emotion in Psychotherapy."
1965	R. D. Laing. *The Divided Self*.
1966	Jean Piaget. *The Language and Thought of the Child*.
1969/1982	John Bowlby. *Attachment and Loss: Vol. 1. Attachment*.
1969	Viktor Frankl. *The Will to Meaning*.
1970	Abraham Maslow. *The Farther Reaches of Human Nature*.
1975	Jerry Fodor. *The Language of Thought*.
1975	Melanie Klein. *Envy and Gratitude*.
1975/1985	Jean Piaget. *The Equilibration of Cognitive Structures: The Central Problem of Intellectual Development*.
1975	E. O. Wilson. *Sociobiology: The New Synthesis*.
1976/1979	Jean Piaget. *Behaviour and Evolution*.
1979	E. O. Wilson. *On Human Nature*.
1980	Isabel Briggs Myers. *Gifts Differing: Understanding Personality Type*.
1983	Howard Gardner. *Frames of Mind: The Theory of Multiple Intelligences*.
1986	Albert Bandura. *Social Foundations of Thought and Action: A Social Cognitive Theory*.

1992	Jerome Barkow, Leda Cosmides, and John Tooby. *The Adapted Mind.*
1997	Leda Cosmides and John Tooby. *Evolutionary Psychology: A Primer.*
2002	Steven Pinker. *The Blank Slate: The Modern Denial of Human Nature.*
2004	David M. Buss. *Evolutionary Psychology: The New Science of the Mind.*
2005	Malcolm Gladwell. *Blink: The Power of Thinking Without Thinking.*

Editor's Note: Excellent resources on the historical development of psychology include the following websites:

Brewer, Charles L. "Psychology in an Historical Context: A Timeline." http://bcs.worthpublishers.com/webpub/Ektron/myershs9e/History%20of%20Psychology%20Timeline/Myers8e%20timeline.pdf

Green, Christopher D. "Classics in the History of Psychology." http://psychclassics.yorku.ca/

Online Psychology Laboratory. The History of Psychology. http://opl.apa.org/contributions/History%20of%20Psychology%20Timeline/HistoryOfPsych.htm

Pereira, Marcos Emanoel. History of Psychology. http://www.oocities.org/~emanoel/en_linha.htm#-600

Additional Works on Psychological Approaches to Literature

Austin, Michael. *Useful Fictions: Evolution, Anxiety, and the Origins of Literature.* U of Nebraska P, 2010.

Barash, David P., and Nanelle Barash. *Madame Bovary's Ovaries: A Darwinian Look at Literature.* Delacorte Press, 2005.

Berman, Jeffrey. *Narcissism and the Novel.* New York UP, 1990.

Bonaparte, Marie. *The Life and Works of Edgar Allan Poe: A Psycho-Analytic Interpretation.* Imago, 1949.

Bouson, J. B. *The Empathic Reader: A Study of the Narcissistic Character and the Drama of the Self.* U of Massachusetts P, 1989.

Boyd, Brian. *On the Origin of Stories: Evolution, Cognition, and Fiction.* Harvard UP, 2009.

———, Joseph Carroll, and Jonathan Gottschall, editors. *Evolution, Literature, and Film: A Reader.* Columbia UP, 2010.

Carroll, Joseph. *Evolution and Literary Theory.* U of Missouri P, 1995.

———. *Literary Darwinism: Evolution, Human Nature, and Literature.* Routledge, 2004.

Crane, Mary Thomas. *Shakespeare's Brain: Reading with Cognitive Theory.* Princeton UP, 2001.

Davis, Robert Con. *The Fictional Father: Lacanian Readings of the Text.* U of Massachussets P, 1981.

Dissanayake, Ellen. *Homo Aestheticus.* U of Washington P, 1995.

———. *What Is Art For?* University of Washington P, 1990.

Dutton, Denis. *The Art Instinct: Beauty, Pleasure, and Human Evolution.* Oxford UP, 2009.

Easterlin, Nancy. *A Biocultural Approach to Literary Theory and Interpretation.* Johns Hopkins UP, 2012.

Ellmann, Maud, editor. *Psychoanalytic Literary Criticism.* Longman, 1994.

Fraiberg, Louis. *Psychoanalysis and American Literary Criticism.* Wayne State UP, 1960.

Gordon, David J. *Literary Art and the Unconscious.* Louisiana State UP, 1976.

Gottschall, Jonathan. *Literature, Science, and a New Humanities.* Palgrave Macmillan, 2008.

———. *The Rape of Troy: Evolution, Violence, and the World of Homer.* Cambridge UP, 2007.

Gunn, Daniel. *Psychoanalysis and Fiction: An Exploration of Literary and Psychoanalytic Borders*. Cambridge UP, 1988.

Hoffman, Frederick J. *Freudianism and the Literary Mind*. 2nd revised ed., Louisiana State UP, 1957.

Holland, Norman N. *The Dynamics of Literary Response*. 1st ed., Oxford UP, 1968.

———. *Holland's Guide to Psychoanalytic Psychology and Literature-and-Psychology*. Oxford UP, 1990.

Knapp, Bettina L. *A Jungian Approach to Literature*. Southern Illinois UP, 1984.

Kris, E. *Psychoanalytic Explorations in Art*. International Universities P, 1952.

Lesser, Simon O. *Fiction and the Unconscious*. U of Chicago P, 1957.

Manheim, Leonard, and Eleanor Manheim. *Hidden Patterns: Studies in Psychoanalytic Literary Criticism*. MacMillan, 1966.

Mollinger, Robert N. *Psychoanalysis and Literature: An Introduction*. Nelson-Hall, 1981.

Nordlund, Marcus. *Shakespeare and the Nature of Love: Literature, Culture, Evolution*. Northwestern UP, 2007.

Reppen, Joseph, and Maurice Charney, editors. *The Psychoanalytic Study of Literature*. Analytic P, 1985.

Richardson, Alan. *British Romanticism and the Science of the Mind*. Cambridge UP, 2001.

Rudnytsky, P. L. *Transitional Objects and Potential Spaces: Literary Uses of D. W. Winnicott*. Columbia UP, 1993.

Ruitenbeck, Hendrik M. *The Literary Imagination: Psychoanalysis and the Genius of the Writer*. Quadrangle Books, 1965.

Storey, Robert. *Mimesis and the Human Animal: On the Biogenetic Foundations of Literary Representation*. Northwestern UP, 1996.

Sugg, Richard P., editor. *Jungian Literary Criticism*. Northwestern UP, 1992.

Swirski, Peter. *Literature, Analytically Speaking: Explorations in the Theory of Interpretation, Analytic Aesthetics, and Evolution*. U of Texas P, 2010.

———. *Of Literature and Knowledge: Explorations in Narrative Thought Experiments, Evolution, and Game Theory*. Routledge, 2007.

Tennenhouse, L., editor. *The Practice of Psychoanalytic Criticism*. Wayne State UP, 1976.

Tsur, Reuven. *What Makes Sound Patterns Expressive: The Poetic Mode of Speech Perception*. Duke UP, 1992.

Turner, Frederick. *Natural Classicism: Essays on Literature and Science*. Paragon House, 1985.

Turner, Mark. *Death Is the Mother of Beauty: Mind, Metaphors, and Criticism.* U of Chicago P, 1987.

———. *Reading Minds: The Study of English in the Age of Cognitive Science.* Princeton UP, 1991.

Vermeule, Blakey. *Why Do We Care about Literary Characters?* Johns Hopkins UP, 2010.

Vice, Sue, editor. *Psychoanalytic Criticism: A Reader.* Polity Press, 1996.

Williams, Linda Ruth. *Critical Desire: Psychoanalysis and the Literary Subject.* Edward Arnold, 1995.

Wright, Elizabeth. *Psychoanalytic Criticism: A Reappraisal.* Routledge, 1998.

———. *Psychoanalytic Criticism: Theory in Practice.* Methuen, 1984.

Zwaan, Rolf A. *Aspects of Literary Comprehension: A Cognitive Approach.* John Benjamins, 1993.

Bibliography

Benvenuto, Bice, and Roger Kennedy. *Works of Jacques Lacan: An Introduction.* Free Association, 1986.

Berman, Jeffrey. *Talking Cure: Literary Representations of Psychoanalysis.* New York UP, 1985.

Brown, Carolyn E. *Shakespeare and Psychoanalytic Theory.* Bloomsbury Arden Shakespeare, 2015.

Carroll, Joseph. *Reading Human Nature: Literary Darwinism in Theory and Practice.* SUNY Press, 2011.

———, Jonathan Gottschall, John Johnson, and Daniel Kruger. *Graphing Jane Austen: The Evolutionary Basis of Literary Meaning.* Palgrave, 2012.

Davis, Robert Con, editor. *Lacan and Narration: The Psychoanalytic Difference in Narrative Theory.* Johns Hopkins UP, 1984.

Bettelheim, Bruno. *The Uses of Enchantment: The Meaning and Importance of Fairy Tales.* New York: Knopf, 1976.

Charney, Maurice, and Joseph Reppen, editors. *Psychoanalytic Approaches to Literature and Film.* Fairleigh Dickinson UP, 1987.

Easthope, Antony. *The Unconscious.* Routledge, 1999.

Edelson, Marshall. *Hypothesis and Evidence in Psychoanalysis.* U of Chicago P, 1984.

Erwin, Edward. *A Final Accounting: Philosophical and Empirical Issues in Freudian Psychology.* MIT Press, 1996.

———, editor. *The Freud Encyclopedia.* Routledge, 2002.

Evans, Dylan. *An Introductory Dictionary of Lacanian Psychoanalysis.* Routledge, 1996.

Fike, Matthew A. *The One Mind: C. G. Jung and the Future of Literary Criticism.* Routledge, 2014.

Forrester, John. *Dispatches from the Freud Wars: Psychoanalysis and Its Passions.* Harvard UP, 1997.

Fox, Alistair. *Speaking Pictures: Neuropsychoanalysis and Authorship in Film and Literature.* Indiana UP, 2016.

Gottschall, Jonathan. *The Storytelling Animal: How Stories Make Us Human.* Houghton Mifflin, 2012.

———, and David Sloan Wilson, editors. *The Literary Animal: Evolution and the Nature of Narrative.* Northwestern UP, 2005.

Grünbaum, Adolf. *The Foundations of Psychoanalysis: A Philosophical Critique*. U of California P, 1984.

Hinshelwood, R. D. *A Dictionary of Kleinian Thought*. Free Association Books, 1991.

Jacobus, Mary. *The Poetics of Psychoanalysis: In the Wake of Klein*. Oxford UP, 2015.

Kaplan, Morton, and Robert Kloss. *Unspoken Motive: A Guide to Psychoanalytic Literary Criticism*. Free Press, 1973.

Lucas, F. L. *Literature and Psychology*. Cassell, 1951.

Malin, Irving, editor. *Psychoanalysis and American Fiction*. Dutton, 1965.

Moore, Burness E., and Bernard D. Fine, editors. *Psychoanalysis: The Major Concepts*. Yale UP, 1995.

Morrison, Claudia C. *Freud and the Critic: The Early Use of Depth Psychology in Literary Criticism*. U of North Carolina P, 1968.

Nagele, Rainer. *Reading After Freud*. Columbia UP, 1987.

Neu, Jerome, editor. *The Cambridge Companion to Freud*. Cambridge UP, 1994.

Parvini, Neema. *Shakespeare and Cognition: Thinking Fast and Slow Through Character*. Palgrave Macmillan, 2015.

Rabaté, Jean-Michel. *The Cambridge Introduction to Literature and Psychoanalysis*. Cambridge UP, 2014.

Robinson, Paul. *Freud and His Critics*. U of California P, 1993.

Rogers, Robert R. *Metaphor: A Psychoanalytic View*. U of California P, 1978.

Ruitenbeck, Hendrick M., editor. *Psychoanalysis and Literature*. Dutton, 1964.

Skura, Meredith Anne. *Literary Use of Psychoanalytic Process*. Yale UP, 1981.

Smith, Joseph H., and William Kerrigan, editors. *Take Chances: Derrida, Psychoanalysis, and Literature*. Johns Hopkins UP, 1984.

Tambling, Jeremy. *Literature and Psychoanalysis*. Manchester UP, 2012.

Turner, Mark. *The Literary Mind*. Oxford UP, 1996.

Zaretsky, Eli. *Secrets of the Soul: A Social and Cultural History of Psychoanalysis*. Vintage, 2004.

Zunshine, Lisa, editor. *The Oxford Handbook of Cognitive Literary Studies*. Oxford UP, 2015.

About the Editor

Robert C. Evans is I. B. Young Professor of English at Auburn University at Montgomery (AUM), where he has taught since 1982. In 1984, he received his PhD from Princeton University, where he held Weaver and Whiting fellowships as well as a university fellowship. In later years, his research was supported by fellowships from the Newberry Library, the American Council of Learned Societies, the Folger Shakespeare Library, the Mellon Foundation, the Huntington Library, the National Endowment for the Humanities, the American Philosophical Society, and the UCLA Center for Medieval and Renaissance Studies.

In 1982, he was awarded the G. E. Bentley Prize and in 1989 was selected Professor of the Year for Alabama by the Council for the Advancement and Support of Education. At AUM, he has received the Faculty Excellence Award and has been named Distinguished Research Professor, Distinguished Teaching Professor, and University Alumni Professor. Most recently, he was named Professor of the Year by the South Atlantic Association of Departments of English.

He is one of three editors of the *Ben Jonson Journal* and is a contributing editor to the John Donne *Variorum Edition*.

He is the author or editor of over thirty-five books (on such topics as Ben Jonson, Martha Moulsworth, Kate Chopin, John Donne, Frank O'Connor, Brian Friel, Ambrose Bierce, Amy Tan, Philip Larkin, early modern women writers, pluralist literary theory, literary criticism, twentieth-century American writers, American novelists, Shakespeare, and seventeenth-century English literature). He is also the author of roughly four hundred published or forthcoming essays or notes (in print and online) on a variety of topics, especially dealing with Renaissance literature, critical theory, women writers, short fiction, and literature of the nineteenth and twentieth centuries.

Contributors

James S. Baumlin is Distinguished Professor of English at Missouri State University, where he teaches English Renaissance literature, the history of rhetoric, and critical theories. He is the author of a book on John Donne and rhetoric (Missouri) and the coeditor of other books, including *Post-Jungian Criticism: Theory and Practice* (SUNY Press). His recent publications include *Theologies of Language in English Renaissance Literature: Reading Shakespeare, Donne, and Milton* (Lexington).

Tita French Baumlin is Professor Emerita at Missouri State University, where she taught Shakespeare, history of drama, Arthurian tradition, and critical theories. With colleagues James S. Baumlin and George H. Jensen, she coedited the anthology *Post-Jungian Criticism: Theory and Practice* (SUNY Press). With Sally Porterfield and Keith Polette, she coedited the collection *Perpetual Adolescence: Jungian Analyses of American Media, Literature, and Pop Culture* (SUNY Press).

Allan Chavkin is Professor of English at Texas State University. He has published many articles on twentieth-century writers. His books include *Conversations with John Gardner* (Mississippi), *English Romanticism and Modern Fiction: A Collection of Critical Essays* (AMS), *Conversations with Louise Erdrich and Michael Dorris* [with Nancy Feyl Chavkin] (Mississippi), *The Chippewa Landscape of Louise Erdrich* (Alabama), *Leslie Marmon Silko's* Ceremony: *A Casebook* (Oxford), and *Critical Insights: Saul Bellow* (Salem). He is the recipient of Texas State University's Presidential Award for Scholarship.

Nancy Feyl Chavkin is Regents' Professor of Social Work and Director of the Center for Children and Families at Texas State University. Her books include *Conversations with Louise Erdrich and Michael Dorris* [with Allan Chavkin] (Mississippi), *Families and Schools in a Pluralistic Society, The Use of Research* (SUNY), and *Family Engagement with Schools* (forthcoming 2017). She is the recipient of Texas State University's Presidential Award for Scholarship and the Minnie Stevens Piper Teaching Award for Excellence in Teaching.

Steve Gronert Ellerhoff is the author of the novel *Time's Laughingstocks*, the story collection *Tales from the Internet*, and other stories and literary criticism. He completed the creative writing MA at Lancaster University in England and the MPhil in literatures of the Americas and a PhD at Trinity College Dublin. He is the author of *Post-Jungian Psychology* and the *Short Stories of Ray Bradbury and Kurt Vonnegut: Golden Apples of the Monkey House* (Routledge) and the coeditor (with Philip Coleman) of *George Saunders: Critical Essays* (Palgrave Macmillan). He is currently writing *Mole for the Animal Series* by Reaktion Books. Find more at http://stevegronertellerhoff.net.

Dr. Jeffrey Folks has taught in Europe, America, and Japan, most recently as Professor of Letters in the Graduate School of Doshisha University (Kyoto, Japan). He has published numerous books and articles on American literature, including *Damaged Lives: Southern and Caribbean Narrative from Faulkner to Naipaul* (2005).

Jenna Lewis works as an editor at Duke University's Preston Robert Tisch Brain Tumor Center. She has both a bachelor's and a master's degree in English from Appalachian State University. Her master's thesis dealt with the poetry of Edna St. Vincent Millay.

David Strong is Associate Professor at the University of Texas at Tyler. His research has focused on medieval literature, philosophy of mind, and the interrelation between early modern poetry and cognitive neuroscience. His work has been published in such journals as *The Chaucer Review* and *Philological Quarterly*. He is author of *The Philosophy of Piers Plowman: The Ethics and Epistemology of Love* (Palgrave Macmillan, 2017).

Michelle Scalise Sugiyama received her graduate training at the Center for Evolutionary Psychology at UC Santa Barbara and currently teaches at the University of Oregon. Her work applies advances in evolution-based science to the study of art, literature, and play and is dedicated to bridging the gap between scientific and humanistic inquiry. She has published over thirty articles on storytelling in both scientific and literary journals, and she also blogs for *The Huffington Post*. Her research has been featured on CBC Radio and in the German popular science journal *Bild der Wissenschaft*.

Susie Thomas (PhD, London) studied literature at Ulster University and Royal Holloway College. She has published scholarly articles on a wide range of British writers, from Aphra Behn to Martin Amis. She is the author of a book on Willa Cather as well as of *A Reader's Guide to Essential Criticism: Hanif Kureishi* (Palgrave Macmillan, 2005), and she has also published numerous articles on Kureishi. She is Reviews Editor of *The Literary London Journal*.

Nicolas Tredell has published twenty books and over 300 essays, articles, and reviews on authors ranging from Shakespeare to Martin Amis. He taught literature, film, and cultural studies at Sussex University and is currently Consultant Editor for Palgrave Macmillan's Essential Criticism series. His recent books include *Shakespeare: The Tragedies* and a new edition of his interviews with leading literary figures, *Conversations with Critics*.

Laura B. Vogel is a practicing psychodynamic psychiatrist who earned her BA and MD degrees from the Brown University Program in Medicine. She completed her psychiatry training, as well as a fellowship, at the New York Hospital-Westchester Division in 1982. Previous publications include essays on *Antony and Cleopatra* and *As You Like It*, published in the *PsyArt* journal.

David Willbern (BA, Amherst College; PhD, UC Berkeley) is Emeritus Professor of English at SUNY Buffalo, where he served as teacher and administrator. At Buffalo, he directed the Center for the Study of Psychoanalysis and Culture as well as the Educational Technology Center. Among his essays are articles on Freud, Shakespeare, and "Scrabble" and two books: *Poetic Will: Shakespeare and the Play of Language* (Pennsylvania), and *The American Popular Novel After World War II: A Study of 25 Best Sellers, 1947–2000* (McFarland).

Christine Gerhold Zahorchak is a practicing outpatient psychologist at Pennsylvania Counseling Services in Harrisburg, Pennsylvania. She earned her undergraduate degree from Dickinson College and her PsyD at The Chicago School of Professional Psychology.

Glossary

anima
According to Jung, feminine instincts (especially when they are present in a male).

animus
According to Jung, masculine instincts (especially when they are present in a female).

anxiety
Nervousness or unease (often intense) in response to a perceived threat or danger.

archetype
Carl Jung's idea that certain common thoughts, feelings, and stories are deeply embedded in the minds of all humans. For example, Jung assumes that most humans share the same basic needs, desires, and fears. Recent theories suggest that these archetypes, or predispositions to think or feel in certain ways, are passed down genetically from generation to generation. (See "evolutionary psychology")

attachment
The idea that humans are strongly dependent on others, especially on parents (and particularly on their mothers in a child's earliest days of life). Interference with (or absence of) these attachments can create psychological difficulties that can often persist into later life.

authenticity
Being true to oneself rather than merely playing an artificial role.

behaviorism
An approach to psychology that emphasizes the ways people actually behave, especially in response to various external stimuli. Behaviorists tend to assume that human thoughts, feelings, and actions are not innate but can be conditioned. Behaviorists tend to downplay the role of inherited dispositions. For example, a child can be conditioned to fear the color red if s/he is punished every time s/he sees or reaches for something red.

catharsis
A release of emotional pressure, often by discussing one's thoughts and feelings.

cognitive psychology
The assumption that the ways we feel and react are very much affected by the ways we think (by the assumptions we make). For instance, if I assume that any failure indicates that I am a failure, I am likely to become depressed. Thus, my thoughts and assumptions help determine how I feel. In order to change my feelings, I must learn to change (by rationally disputing) any irrational thoughts and assumptions. Cognitive psychologists are also interested in the ways humans tend to perceive and think about the world, including humans' basic intellectual predispositions. For instance, they are interested in what we perceive and in how and why we perceive as we do.

collective unconscious
According to Carl Jung, this is the deeply underlying part of the mind, which all humans share, and which helps account for various instinctive ideas, desires, fears, and other feelings. The collective unconscious helps explain why almost all humans, at all times and in all places, tend to respond (according to Jung and other "archetypal" psychologists) in the same basic ways to similar stimuli.

compensation
The attempt to cope with feelings of inadequacy, inferiority, or threat by trying to appear unthreatened and/or more than adequate.

competition
The idea that each individual must compete with others for limited resources, whether those resources are material or psychological. Competition can lead to anxiety and/or to satisfaction if one competes successfully.

conditioning
The ways one's thoughts, feelings, and behavior can be shaped by outside sources and external stimuli. A concept associated with behaviorism.

conscious
The part of the mind of which we are most aware; thoughts and feelings that we know exist and can deliberately think about.

denial
The tendency to suppress, or push out of awareness, any thoughts or feelings that seem threatening or unpleasant.

ego
Freud's idea of the conscious self—the part of the self that must deal with reality (especially social reality, including the expectations of other people) as it truly exists. This is the rational, thoughtful, sensible part of the mind.

evolutionary psychology
The idea that humans share a common evolutionary past that has led, over the eons, to the selection of certain traits that promote survival and reproductive success. The assumption that certain predispositions of thought and feeling are genetically inherited and are therefore difficult to resist or change.

existentialism
The idea that each person is responsible for shaping his or her own existence through individual choices. This burden of choosing one's own meanings in an essentially meaningless universe can create anxiety or dread or can heighten one's sense of freedom and creativity.

family systems theory
An approach to psychology that assumes the family is perhaps the crucial source of an individual's relations with other people. The assumption that families function as systems and that each member of a family has a particular kind of role within the family and a particular kind of relationship with other family members. These roles and relationships help shape an individual's sense of personal identity.

gender
The idea that one's sexual identity is potentially fluid and need not have any firm connection with one's biological sex. Gender involves a rejection of the idea that there are only two firm, inflexible sexual identities (stereotypical male and stereotypical female) determined by particular sexual organs. The idea that one's sense of sexual identity can be shaped by society and is not necessarily written in stone.

id
The part of the mind, according to Freud, that is associated with the deepest human instincts, including the instinct to pursue pleasure and avoid pain. The most passionate part of the mind, which often comes into conflict with the rational ego and moralistic superego.

integration
The idea and ideal of achieving psychological balance by attaining a sense of wholeness in which competing thoughts and feelings are no longer in tension with one another.

neuropsychology
The idea that various human thoughts, emotions, and behaviors are "wired" into the brain and can be altered if the brain itself is altered in some way, whether through the use of drugs or through other kinds of medical manipulation (including surgery).

neurosis
A psychological state characterized by anxiety, fear, obsession, depression, etc.

OCEAN
A common acronym, used by "trait theorists," to designate the five "big traits" in terms of which human thoughts, feelings, and behavior can be studied and evaluated. These traits are openness, conscientiousness, extraversion, agreeableness, and neuroticism. For example, some people tend to be extraverted; others tend to be introverted; and a wide range of possible variations can exist between these two distinct poles.

Oedipus complex
Freud's controversial idea that all boys are sexually attracted to their mothers and fear being castrated by their fathers, since fathers are the boys' rivals for the mothers' affection. Similarly, girls are supposedly motivated by an "Electra complex" that makes them sexually attracted to their fathers and see their mothers as rivals for the fathers' love and attention.

personality
An individual's consistent, predictable ways of thinking, feeling, and behaving.

psychosis
A severe mental disorder in which one loses touch with reality and is unable to think rationally.

rationalization
Concocting logical explanations for emotional problems—explanations that do not really address the problems but instead try to explain them away.

repression
The tendency to try to suppress, block, or push aside unpleasant and threatening facts, thoughts, or feelings. Similar to "denial."

self
One's sense of one's own consistent, personal identity. One's own sense of self may conflict with society's definitions of the self.

self-actualitization
The process of achieving one's full individual potential as a human being. Becoming (or trying to become) one's true, "authentic" self.

superego
The third basic part of the human psyche (according to Freud); the other two are the id and the ego. If the id is the seat of emotions, passions, desires, and fears, and if the ego is the seat of reason and of efforts to deal with the world realistically, the superego is the seat of morality, conscience, lofty ideals, and ethical and social responsibility. The emotional id often comes into conflict with reason (rooted in the ego) and morality (rooted in the superego).

trauma
A kind of psychological wound so deep and so thorough that it shatters the traumatized person's most deeply held assumptions about himself, other persons, the world, and the nature of reality. Often the trauma produces profound stress and/or even a kind of emotional and psychological paralysis.

unconscious
The part of the mind of which we are not fully aware, even though it often greatly influences the way we think, feel, and behave. According to Freud, the unconscious part of the mind sometimes reveals itself (if only partially and confusingly) through dreams. The unconscious can also (according to Freud) be explored through the patient, painstaking process of psychoanalysis.

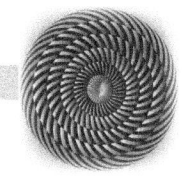

Index

abuse 9, 41
actualization 281, 282
adaptation 72, 83, 288
adolescence xiv, 40, 246, 248, 249
adulthood 76, 280
analytical psychology xx, xxvii, 222
anger 41, 84, 110, 111, 139, 189, 204, 208, 227, 229, 234, 268, 271, 280
anima xx, 279, 307
animus 279, 307
anxiety xxiii, 40, 43, 46, 47, 92, 94, 96, 106, 138, 162, 209, 216, 228, 279, 280, 284, 308, 309, 310
archetype xiii, xx, 33, 222, 223, 243, 250, 251, 252, 254, 255, 278, 279, 307
authenticity 129, 214, 281

behaviorism 286, 307
Bellow, Saul x, 37, 39, 41, 43, 45, 47, 49, 50, 51, 303
"Big Five" 285, 310
biography 52, 141, 156, 157, 187, 190, 217
body xiii, xv, xx, xxv, 16, 28, 61, 69, 87, 89, 90, 94, 113, 120, 121, 127, 129, 131, 139, 140, 142, 143, 160, 163, 164, 165, 172, 175, 181-186, 212, 217, 222, 223, 230, 231, 241, 242, 245, 270
Bowen, Murray x, 38, 50
brain xii, xxii, xxv, 28, 31, 114, 119, 120, 121, 122, 124, 129, 132, 167, 212, 246, 310
brothers 253

Campbell, Joseph xiii, 222, 236, 238
Canetti, Elias xii, 135, 148
censorship xix, 216
character xi, xvii, xviii, xxv, xxvi, 37, 38, 41, 45, 46, 48, 49, 53, 54, 79, 108, 193, 197, 200, 201, 202, 208, 209, 218, 221, 223, 224, 225-229, 231, 242, 247, 248, 254, 262, 269, 291
child xiv, xviii, xx, xxiii, 46, 57, 82, 84, 92, 96, 105, 111, 139, 141, 143, 168, 191, 208, 210, 211, 213, 242, 248, 249, 250, 251, 255, 260, 264, 266, 267, 270, 275, 279, 289, 307
cognition xiii, xvii, 131, 132, 171, 172, 173, 186
cognitive psychology ix, xiii, xxi, 29, 31, 189, 288, 308
collective unconscious xx, 33, 222, 278, 308
colonialism 266, 267, 269
complex xiv, xvii, xix, 23, 25, 32, 48, 57, 69, 89, 90, 119, 168, 177, 214, 225, 248, 258, 259, 265, 266, 270, 277, 287, 310
conditioning 231, 286
conscience 74, 107, 108, 109, 277, 311
consciousness xxiv, xxviii, 54, 56, 77, 127, 214, 218, 245
conscious thoughts 277
Crews, Frederick x, 3-19, 27, 30
criticism x, xiii, xviii, xxiii, xxv, 4, 5, 6, 11, 24, 25, 28, 30, 73, 172, 185, 186, 190, 290, 301, 304
crowd psychology xii, 135-151

313

Darth Vader xiii, 221, 222, 223, 225, 227, 228, 229, 230, 231, 232, 233, 235, 236, 237
daughter 41, 46, 75, 201, 263, 268
death xii, xiii, xxiv, 27, 37, 41, 43, 45, 48, 52, 53, 54, 58, 74, 89, 96, 97, 102, 104, 106, 109, 110, 115, 136, 137, 138, 139, 140, 141, 142, 143, 144, 145, 146, 147, 150, 152, 153, 154, 155, 156, 157, 161, 162, 163, 164, 166, 167, 168, 169, 170, 177, 192, 196, 197, 198, 199, 201, 202, 203, 208, 210, 218, 230, 245, 246, 250, 251, 258, 259, 260, 264, 276, 277, 278, 279, 280, 281, 282, 284, 287
denial 32, 85, 98, 99, 113, 114, 115, 144, 194, 277, 281, 311
depression 53, 115, 187, 195, 197, 203, 263, 284, 287, 310
desire xi, xii, xix, xx, xxi, 44, 45, 54, 55, 84, 85, 87, 88, 90, 91, 93, 99, 121, 128, 130, 131, 139, 143, 144, 145, 148, 163, 166, 167, 169, 176, 208, 209, 230, 243, 258, 261, 262, 263, 267, 269, 278, 280
development xxi, xxiii, xxvii, 16, 46, 91, 165, 193, 217, 219, 226, 230, 240, 246, 249, 252, 254, 260, 277, 278, 279, 280, 294
Dickinson, Emily 153, 170
drama xii, 303
dream xix, xxviii, 14, 44, 56, 88, 190, 193, 210, 211, 212, 217, 218, 222

ego xviii, xx, xxi, 4, 28, 30, 32, 54, 56, 165, 167, 213, 223, 242, 243, 245, 265, 272, 276, 277, 280, 283, 309, 311

emotion xvii, 32, 42, 44, 48, 122, 207, 279, 280
empathy xii, xxvii, 42, 121, 122, 127, 129, 130, 132, 185, 194, 230, 231, 234, 284
Erikson, Erik H. ix, xxi, 11, 26, 194, 240, 280
evil xxiii, 53, 56, 92, 103, 111, 221, 225, 228, 229, 230, 231, 232, 234, 235, 240, 250, 254, 282
evolutionary psychology xi, 3, 33, 34, 288, 289, 307, 309
existentialism 309
existential psychology 257, 259, 261, 263, 265, 267, 269, 271
extraversion 284, 285, 310

family x, xi, xiv, xx, xxix, 37, 38, 39, 40, 41, 42, 43, 44, 45, 47, 48, 49, 50, 51, 57, 74, 75, 77, 78, 136, 140, 142, 149, 150, 198, 204, 207, 210, 220, 227, 233, 235, 241, 247, 257, 258, 259, 260, 261, 262, 263, 264, 265, 268, 271, 272, 303, 309
family systems theory x, 37, 38, 39, 40, 41, 43, 45, 47, 49, 51
Fanon, Frantz xiv, 259, 265, 271, 272
fantasy 94, 96, 145, 176, 190, 209, 211, 218, 222, 233
father xiii, xiv, xx, 16, 40, 41, 48, 53, 57, 75, 76, 95, 96, 97, 99, 140, 169, 187, 188, 189, 191, 195, 196, 197, 198, 199, 200, 201, 202, 203, 204, 218, 221, 224, 225, 232, 233, 234, 235, 236, 238, 242, 257, 258, 259, 260, 261, 262, 263, 264, 265, 268, 269, 270, 271, 275, 276, 277, 279, 280, 282, 283, 289
fear xxiv, 53, 92, 94, 103, 109, 110, 111, 114, 144, 162, 163, 164,

165, 212, 244, 278, 279, 286, 307, 310
feelings xiii, xxiii, 19, 33, 43, 47, 89, 92, 93, 99, 106, 119, 120, 121, 122, 124, 125, 127, 128, 130, 131, 132, 164, 180, 185, 187, 235, 253, 262, 263, 278, 279, 284, 285, 287, 288, 289, 307, 308, 310, 311
female 14, 16, 47, 49, 84, 85, 91, 92, 119, 135, 139, 142, 197, 209, 211, 289, 307, 309
fiction xi, xxvii, 49, 52, 56, 57, 69, 79, 139, 172, 173, 176, 187, 195, 202, 213, 214, 215, 301
film ix, xiv, 78, 210, 221, 223, 225, 227, 228, 232, 240, 250, 251, 252, 255, 275, 289, 290, 305
Fitzgerald, F. Scott xiii, 186, 204
free association ix, xvi, xvii, 13, 30, 197, 210
Freud, Sigmund ix, x, xii, xvi, xix, xx, xxi, xxii, xxiii, xxvi, xxvii, xxviii, xxix, 3, 4, 5, 6, 7, 8, 9, 10, 11, 12, 13, 14, 15, 16, 17, 18, 19, 20, 21, 22, 23, 24, 25, 26, 27, 28, 30, 31, 32, 35, 38, 41, 50, 52, 53, 54, 55, 56, 57, 59, 61, 63, 64, 84, 100, 152, 153, 155, 156, 157, 159, 161, 163, 164, 165, 166, 167, 168, 169, 170, 190, 191, 192, 193, 195, 200, 205, 219, 220, 223, 258, 260, 263, 265, 272, 275, 276, 277, 278, 279, 280, 290, 292, 299, 300, 305, 309, 310, 311
Freudianism x, 6, 7, 9, 10, 15, 156, 157, 263, 296

genital stage 277
gestalt 22, 189, 224, 229, 292, 293
God xv, xx, xxv, 168, 169, 232, 276, 277, 278, 279, 280, 281, 284

good xxvii, 13, 15, 22, 29, 31, 46, 49, 52, 56, 59, 67, 68, 86, 88, 92, 93, 96, 97, 98, 99, 115, 157, 169, 189, 190, 192, 193, 194, 199, 229, 230, 231, 232, 235, 248, 252, 254, 261, 277, 279, 281, 282, 285, 288
grief 142, 143, 147, 153, 276, 278, 287
Grünbaum, Adolf 7, 11
guilt 5, 46, 54, 55, 84, 90, 99, 109, 112, 114, 115, 143, 203, 204, 212, 234, 262, 284

hallucination 104
Hemingway, Ernest xiii, 154, 187, 195, 205, 206
hero xiv, xx, xxv, 38, 56, 153, 188, 191, 195, 238, 239, 240, 241, 244, 245, 249, 252, 254, 258, 260
history x, xi, xiii, xvi, xx, xxvii, 19, 22, 67, 72, 76, 140, 166, 192, 194, 204, 208, 214, 216, 218, 226, 286, 303
Holland, Norman x, xviii, 15, 26, 190
horror xxiv, xxvi, 60, 61, 62, 103, 107, 113, 143, 149, 218, 234

id 30, 56, 118, 133, 272, 276, 277, 309, 311
identity xviii, xxi, xxv, xxvi, 30, 54, 91, 121, 125, 127, 131, 136, 180, 189, 195, 207, 213, 234, 239, 249, 271, 309, 311
illness 41, 137, 139, 140, 143, 144, 146, 193, 203, 204
image 30, 90, 92, 94, 96, 99, 102, 115, 136, 164, 173, 200, 210, 213, 215, 221, 227, 229, 239, 279

Index 315

imagination xii, 4, 110, 135, 137, 144, 145, 150, 157, 166, 221
individuality 121, 125, 127, 209, 216
inferiority 57, 267, 278, 280, 281, 308
insanity 53, 111, 144, 260
instinct xii, 167, 170, 177, 184, 271, 309
introversion 284

journey xiv, 122, 123, 238, 239, 240, 241, 242, 245, 247, 248, 249, 251, 252, 253, 254
Jung, Carl ix, xiii, xiv, xx, xxvii, 3, 20, 21, 22, 23, 26, 28, 31, 32, 33, 34, 38, 222, 223, 226, 229, 230, 231, 233, 235, 236, 237, 244, 245, 250, 252, 255, 256, 278, 279, 293, 299, 307, 308

Klein, Melanie xxix, 293
Kureishi, Hanif xiv, 257, 259, 261, 263, 265, 267, 269, 271, 305

Lacan, Jacques ix, x, xiii, xxi, xxvii, 3, 20, 21, 22, 23, 26, 27, 28, 29, 30, 31, 32, 34, 213, 214, 219, 220, 275, 299
Laing, R. D. xiv, 259, 263, 271, 293
language xi, xxi, xxii, xxiii, xxv, 18, 26, 28, 29, 30, 32, 38, 68, 70, 86, 93, 101, 102, 104, 111, 129, 174, 176, 207, 209, 211, 214, 215, 216, 246
linguistics 176, 214
literature ix, x, xii, xiii, xvi, xviii, xx, xxii, xxiii, xxiv, xxvi, xxvii, 3, 4, 20, 21, 22, 23, 24, 25, 27, 28, 29, 34, 58, 67, 68, 75, 101, 132, 136, 152, 153, 154, 186, 187, 191, 192, 196, 223, 275, 283, 289, 290, 301, 303, 304, 305
love xii, xx, 41, 42, 43, 44, 53, 55, 57, 75, 88, 89, 91, 92, 93, 94, 99, 107, 111, 119, 121, 122, 127, 129, 130, 132, 135, 136, 137, 140, 143, 144, 145, 146, 148, 155, 157, 169, 171, 177, 179, 180, 188, 209, 211, 212, 217, 249, 258, 263, 264, 267, 268, 269, 270, 271, 278, 283, 310
Lucas, George 222, 224, 237

madness xv, 53, 54, 55, 58, 97, 105, 111, 254, 259, 263, 265
male xii, 57, 85, 91, 92, 99, 119, 123, 135, 136, 139, 148, 183, 197, 238, 265, 267, 269, 270, 279, 287, 289, 307, 309
marriage xi, xii, 47, 72, 73, 75, 76, 98, 99, 135, 137, 138, 139, 140, 141, 142, 143, 145, 147, 148, 150, 176, 177, 178, 179, 180, 181, 196, 238, 257, 262, 263, 267
Masters, Edgar Lee 154
meaning xiii, xxi, xxiv, 25, 29, 98, 107, 129, 147, 188, 226, 240, 246, 247, 280
melancholy 52, 53, 55, 115
memory xviii, xix, xxiii, xxviii, 14, 42, 55, 114, 143, 209, 214, 215, 216, 234
men xv, xvi, 5, 74, 76, 77, 85, 86, 89, 92, 93, 94, 98, 104, 107, 138, 150, 175, 197, 228, 233, 234, 270, 279
metaphor xxii, 94, 169, 216, 223, 235, 239
Millay, Edna St. Vincent xii, 152, 153, 155, 156, 157, 159, 161, 163, 165, 167, 169, 170, 304

mirroring xiii, xxi, 93, 120, 130, 213
misogyny xi, 84, 85, 87, 89, 91, 93, 95, 97, 99
morality 56, 157, 277, 311
mother xviii, xx, xxii, xxiii, 40, 41, 42, 45, 46, 47, 48, 49, 53, 57, 92, 93, 94, 95, 96, 136, 139, 140, 143, 188, 190, 191, 195, 196, 200, 208, 210, 211, 213, 218, 231, 233, 234, 238, 242, 247, 248, 249, 250, 257, 258, 259, 260, 261, 262, 264, 266, 267, 277
myth xiii, xx, 20, 67, 79, 200, 222, 226, 236, 239, 240

narrative xix, xxiii, 67, 69, 70, 76, 79, 152, 178, 189, 194, 218, 267
neuroscience xii, xxvii, xxviii, 119, 121, 123, 125, 127, 129, 131, 132, 133, 134, 304
neurosis 28, 266
neuroticism 283, 284, 285, 310
Nineteen Eighty-Four xiii, 207, 208, 209, 210, 211, 212, 213, 214, 215, 216, 217, 219, 220
nineteenth century 148, 289
norms xi, 73, 74, 75, 78
novel x, xi, xiii, xiv, xvi, xxiii, 37, 42, 45, 48, 49, 79, 153, 171, 173, 176, 180, 181, 182, 184, 185, 187, 188, 200, 201, 207, 208, 210, 211, 212, 214, 215, 216, 217, 218, 219, 257, 258, 259, 262, 271, 304

obsession xxv, 105, 166, 218, 266, 310
oedipal xiv, xxi, 15, 16, 57, 58, 84, 94, 96, 99, 100, 258, 259, 265, 267, 270
Oedipus complex xix, 258, 266, 277, 310

opposing forces 278, 279
Orwell, George xiii, 215, 219, 220

pain xxvi, 60, 106, 107, 141, 158, 160, 163, 164, 165, 167, 184, 207, 234, 257, 276, 277, 278, 279, 281, 309
paranoia xiii, 135, 147, 212, 218
parents xx, 9, 37, 40, 75, 138, 189, 196, 233, 234, 241, 247, 248, 249, 250, 254, 257, 260, 307
parody 58, 215
pathology 18, 54, 193
perception xii, 46, 79, 85, 92, 129, 172, 196, 207, 216, 250, 281
phenomenology 23
pleasure xix, xxii, 89, 157, 163, 164, 165, 167, 168, 169, 207, 209, 269, 276, 309
Poe, Edgar Allan xi, xii, 26, 52, 53, 54, 55, 56, 57, 58, 59, 60, 61, 62, 63, 64, 135, 136, 137, 138, 139, 140, 141, 142, 143, 144, 145, 146, 147, 148, 149, 150, 151, 156, 295
poetry xii, xvii, 52, 61, 67, 68, 132, 133, 150, 152, 153, 154, 155, 157, 159, 161, 163, 165, 166, 167, 169, 170, 186, 276, 283, 304
Potter, Harry xiii, 79, 238, 239, 240, 241, 243, 245, 247, 249, 251, 253, 254, 255, 256
psyche xiii, xxvi, 30, 54, 55, 56, 136, 164, 166, 167, 223, 244, 245, 279, 311
psychoanalysis xvi, xvii, xx, 4, 5, 6, 7, 8, 9, 10, 11, 12, 13, 14, 15, 16, 17, 18, 19, 22, 26, 28, 29, 30, 31, 38, 56, 57, 157, 161, 163, 189, 190, 219, 258, 259, 266, 276, 278, 284, 311

Index 317

psychoanalytic xi, xviii, xix, xx, xxi, xxii, xxiii, xxvii, 4, 7, 8, 12, 13, 14, 16, 17, 18, 20, 23, 25, 26, 27, 28, 30, 38, 52, 56, 84, 100, 156, 161, 166, 167, 186, 190, 220, 275, 277
psychobiography 189, 190, 192, 193, 194, 202, 206
psychosis 310
psychoticism 284

quest xv, xxv, 42, 47, 49, 77, 179, 238, 239, 259

racism 260, 270
rationalization 277
readers ix, xi, xiii, xvi, xxiv, xxv, xxvi, 5, 9, 15, 25, 26, 27, 34, 58, 59, 62, 110, 111, 157, 177, 180, 181, 184
reading xii, xiii, xv, xvi, xvii, xix, xxi, xxii, xxiv, xxvii, 4, 6, 23, 24, 27, 31, 33, 38, 157, 171, 176, 181, 183, 184, 186, 196, 215, 223, 227, 271, 277, 286
reason 4, 10, 24, 29, 34, 48, 67, 68, 70, 71, 75, 85, 107, 108, 111, 113, 141, 142, 198, 201, 202, 235, 244, 250, 253, 277, 279, 287, 288, 289, 311
religion 222, 232, 239, 245
representation xiii, xix, xxii, 32, 70, 119, 130, 137, 181, 216, 246
repression 14, 54, 85, 98, 99, 165, 216, 219
response 13, 16, 17, 18, 29, 33, 45, 84, 96, 106, 114, 129, 135, 136, 137, 138, 141, 145, 146, 147, 149, 179, 181, 183, 185, 201, 204, 260, 286, 307
role xii, xiv, 37, 47, 68, 69, 76, 107, 109, 121, 123, 126, 135, 136, 139, 140, 142, 189, 191, 195, 200, 224, 235, 249, 250, 263, 269, 270, 279, 280, 281, 287, 288, 289, 307, 309
romance 226
Rowling, J. K. 240, 255, 256

sanity 204, 259, 260, 264, 272
science xvi, xvii, 6, 7, 10, 13, 19, 29, 31, 32, 34, 141, 288, 304
seduction 221
self xiv, xvi, xviii, xxiv, xxv, xxvi, 7, 8, 10, 11, 14, 23, 28, 29, 32, 37, 39, 43, 45, 49, 53, 61, 74, 79, 89, 91, 92, 113, 114, 115, 121, 124, 125, 126, 127, 128, 132, 142, 164, 166, 167, 169, 179, 183, 185, 192, 202, 209, 211, 213, 214, 217, 229, 230, 239, 240, 241, 242, 243, 244, 248, 252, 259, 260, 263, 265, 266, 267, 268, 271, 277, 279, 281, 282, 283, 284, 285, 287, 288, 309, 311
sex xi, 47, 84, 89, 94, 96, 129, 183, 195, 238, 258, 268, 277, 309
sexuality xix, xxi, 31, 46, 85, 92, 93, 94, 96, 98, 139, 145, 186, 260, 261, 263
shadow xiv, xx, xxvii, 155, 223, 241, 242, 243, 244, 245, 247, 253, 261
Shakespeare, William xi, xii, xvii, xxv, xxix, 84, 85, 86, 87, 89, 91, 93, 95, 97, 99, 100, 101, 103, 105, 107, 109, 111, 113, 114, 115, 116, 117, 118, 134, 201, 211, 295, 296, 299, 300, 301, 303, 305
short fiction xi, 52, 301
sisters 76, 86
society xii, xx, 39, 75, 137, 138, 139, 147, 148, 178, 204, 208, 212,

215, 217, 238, 239, 260, 266, 269, 271, 276, 309, 311
sons 203, 277
Star Wars xiii, 221, 222, 223, 225, 226, 227, 228, 229, 230, 232, 233, 234, 236, 237, 251, 252
stimulus 16, 123, 137
storytelling xi, 67, 68, 69, 70, 71, 72, 73, 74, 76, 78, 79, 304
sublimation 56, 277
suicide xiii, 115, 167, 187, 188, 189, 195, 196, 197, 198, 199, 200, 201, 203, 204, 289
superego 15, 212, 265, 276, 277, 309, 311
symbol xvi, xxiii, xxiv, 245, 246

temperament 7, 41, 49, 204, 283
themes 3, 19, 35, 56, 72, 73, 78, 83, 152, 214, 222, 240, 248
therapy xvi, 7, 12, 37, 222, 244, 257
thoughts xiii, xvii, xix, 19, 30, 33, 77, 97, 106, 108, 113, 120, 121, 122, 124, 125, 129, 130, 131, 132, 167, 199, 209, 230, 277, 279, 287, 288, 289, 307, 308, 310, 311
trait 11, 15, 23, 24, 29, 42, 74, 104, 218, 243, 250, 253, 280, 282, 283, 284, 285, 286, 287, 289, 309, 310
trait theory 23, 287
trauma ix, xii, xxv, xxvi, 84, 101, 102, 103, 104, 105, 106, 107, 108, 109, 110, 111, 112, 113, 114, 115, 117, 226, 251, 265, 266, 311, 319
trickster xiv, 74, 75, 79, 254, 255
trust xiii, 5, 96, 217, 219, 225, 248, 276, 279
twentieth century xxi, 7, 24, 27, 31, 56, 156, 176, 202, 217, 221, 222, 223

unconscious xviii, xix, xx, xxi, xxvi, xxvii, 16, 18, 26, 29, 30, 31, 32, 33, 45, 47, 54, 84, 86, 87, 89, 90, 94, 99, 120, 121, 142, 189, 212, 219, 222, 225, 226, 229, 234, 245, 259, 262, 277, 278, 287, 308, 311, 313, 319

victims 111
violence 45, 46, 102, 148, 171, 181, 183, 184, 186, 257, 263, 269
Voldemort 240, 241, 242, 243, 244, 245, 246, 247, 248, 249, 251, 252, 254

war 76, 137, 181, 182, 188, 202
Winnicott, Donald xviii, xxix, 26, 30, 214, 218, 219, 220, 259, 296
women xxi, 7, 46, 47, 49, 57, 74, 76, 84, 85, 86, 91, 92, 94, 99, 136, 140, 177, 179, 184, 185, 186, 265, 267, 269, 270, 279, 301
writing xii, xiii, xvi, xvii, xix, xxi, 24, 28, 52, 61, 71, 137, 141, 148, 149, 153, 156, 157, 163, 191, 193, 198, 202, 209, 211, 214, 215, 216, 217, 222, 264, 265, 280, 282, 304